Funding Feminism

JOAN MARIE JOHNSON

Funding Feminism

Monied Women, Philanthropy, and the
Women's Movement, 1870–1967

The University of North Carolina Press *Chapel Hill*

This book was published with the assistance of the Greensboro Women's Fund of the University of North Carolina Press.

Founding Contributors: Linda Arnold Carlisle, Sally Schindel Cone, Anne Faircloth, Bonnie McElveen Hunter, Linda Bullard Jennings, Janice J. Kerley (in honor of Margaret Supplee Smith), Nancy Rouzer May, and Betty Hughes Nichols.

The University of North Carolina Press has been a member of the Green Press Initiative since 2003.

Library of Congress Cataloging-in-Publication Data
Names: Johnson, Joan Marie, author.
Title: Funding feminism : monied women, philanthropy, and the women's movement, 1870–1967 / Joan Marie Johnson.
Other titles: Gender & American culture.
Description: Chapel Hill : University of North Carolina Press, [2017] | Series: Gender and American culture | Includes bibliographical references and index.
Identifiers: LCCN 2017004067| ISBN 9781469634692 (cloth : alk. paper) | ISBN 9781469634708 (ebook)
Subjects: LCSH: Feminists—Charitable contributions—United States—History. | Feminism—United States—History. | Women philanthropists—United States—History.
Classification: LCC HQ1419 .J64 2017 | DDC 305.420973—dc23
LC record available at https://lccn.loc.gov/2017004067

Jacket illustrations: Left, photograph of Gertrude Minturn Pinchot (courtesy of the George Grantham Bain Collection, Library of Congress Prints and Photographs Division, LC-DIG-ggbain-07824); right, photograph of Juliet Rublee on horseback at a woman suffrage parade (courtesy of the Harris & Ewing Collection, Library of Congress Prints and Photographs Division, LC-DIG-hec-04146).

Portions of chapters 1 and 2 were previously published in a different form as "Following the Money: Wealthy Women, Feminism, and the American Suffrage Movement," *Journal of Women's History* 27:4 (Winter 2015): 62–87. © 2015 Journal of Women's History. Reprinted with permission of Johns Hopkins University Press.

For Don, Darci, Sophie, and Elise

Contents

Illustrations

Acknowledgments

It was a pleasure to write this history of women philanthropists who funded the women's movement, and to consider ways in which these monied women used their philanthropy to give them a voice when, despite their privilege, they were perceived to be powerless due to their gender. Despite their many flaws, these women did advance equality for women in the United States, and feminist organizations now come much closer to working for equity for all, regardless of race, ethnicity, class, religion, sexuality, gender expression, and disability.

First I would like to thank the many librarians and archivists who assisted me as I worked on this book. The first archival research trip I took was to the Countway Library, Harvard University Medical School, as the recipient of a Foundation for Women in Medicine Fellowship at the Center for the History of Medicine at Countway. The library has a treasure trove of papers relating to the development of the pill and the birth control movement that complement other collections at the Library of Congress and Smith College. As have many other historians of women's experiences in the United States, I found many sources and received assistance from librarians in the Smith College Archives and the Sophia Smith Women's History Collection at Smith College, and gratefully acknowledge a grant to travel to their collections. Likewise, I was directed to a great number of sources at the Schlesinger Library, Radcliffe Institute, Harvard University. It was here that I first used a camera to take photos of materials instead of requesting photocopies, and I can no longer imagine conducting archival research without a camera. For the chapters on higher education, I traveled to several college and university archives and thus must thank the archivists at Stanford University Archives, Massachusetts Institute of Technology Archives, Scripps College Archives, and the Bancroft Library at the University of California, Berkeley. I am particularly grateful to Daniel Hartwig at Stanford, who digitized several folders of documents for me upon my return home. I traveled to Newcomb College Institute, Tulane University, where I received excellent advice from Susan Tucker and others, as well as travel funding. In addition to the Newcomb College Archives, librarians at the Tulane Law Library guided me to the bound volumes concerning the estate of Josephine Newcomb, and I read Josephine's original handwritten letters in the McConnell Family Papers in the Tulane University Archives. I also received assistance from archivists at the Historical Society of Wisconsin Archives, where the enormous McCormick–International Harvester Collection is located. Librarians at the Library of Congress make work in the manuscript room there a pleasure, and I examined the Gregory Pincus Papers in person and other collections on microfilm. Unless otherwise indicated, much of the travel and research for this book was funded by a National Endowment for the Humanities Summer Stipend, and I am grateful for that support. I finished my research with a trip to the University of Southern California, on a Wallis Annenberg Grant, to study the Armond Fields Collection. I also received last-minute assistance obtaining photographs from Alison Terana, Daniel Hartwig, Lynn Rainville, Liz Kent Leon, Nanci Young, and Chloe Raub, and I thank them for their help.

I am grateful to a myriad of colleagues for their support over the course of the research and writing of this book. In Chicago, I would like to thank colleagues in the history department at Northeastern Illinois University and the many scholars who participated in the Newberry Library Seminar on Women and Gender over the last eight years, including Darlene Clark Hine, Elizabeth Fraterrigo, Lynn Hudson, Sue Levine, Amanda Littauer, Patrick Miller, Francesca Morgan, Michelle Nickerson, Rima Lunin Schultz, and Michael Tuck, with special thanks to Chris Joe. I have enjoyed many conversations with Louise Knight over lunch in Evanston and received valuable advice. I would also like to acknowledge the tremendous work that Mary Ann Johnson, of the Chicago Women's History Center, does to promote women's history in Chicago. Carla Bittel, Kathleen Clark, Ruth Crocker, Sylvia Hoffert, Margaret Marsh, Kathleen McCarthy, Yael Merkin, Johanna Neuman, Sarah Rodriguez, and Alison Sneider all provided valuable feedback at conferences, stimulating conversation, comments on drafts, or other support. Karen Cox has been a dear friend and colleague since our first Southern Association for Women Historians (SAWH) conference in 1994. Although this book takes me beyond years of focus on southern women, colleagues from the SAWH have been friends and supporters for many years, including Kathleen Clark, Karen Cox, Shannon Frystak, Anya Jabour, Giselle Roberts, Rebecca Sharpless, Marjorie Spruill, and Melissa Walker. Special appreciation to Anya Jabour, who suggested the title, *Funding Feminism*, to me. Nancy Robertson discussed philanthropy with me when I first considered writing on this topic, and I appreciate the wealth of information she shared. My students at Northeastern Illinois University were always a source of inspiration, and I would like to especially acknowledge Marc Arenberg, Rene Delgaldo,

Nicole Grigalunas, and Marla McMackin. I appreciate the support of all my colleagues in the Office of the Provost at Northwestern University. Parts of chapters 1 and 2 appeared in the *Journal of Women's History* in an article titled "Following the Money: Wealthy Women, Feminism, and the American Suffrage Movement," and I thank editor Leigh Ann Wheeler and the anonymous reviewers for their helpful critiques.

In addition to presenting parts of this book at scholarly conferences, I spoke at several gatherings of women philanthropists and development professionals, and I appreciated the insights and questions I received there. These include the Women in Development Professions group in Chicago; the Chicago Women in Philanthropy association; and the Women Leading Philanthropy Symposium of the Women's Philanthropy Institute, Indiana University Lilly Family School of Philanthropy. The Women's Philanthropy Institute, including Andrea Pactor, has been instrumental in promoting the study of gender and philanthropy.

Working with the University of North Carolina Press has been a pleasure. Much appreciation to Mark Simpson-Vos and to others at the press who assisted with various aspects of preparing for publication, including Lucas Church, Jessica Newman, and Jamie Thaman. I am very grateful to the two anonymous readers who provided thoughtful feedback and helped me improve the manuscript in immeasurable ways.

Finally, I would like to thank friends and family who have supported me in many ways throughout the years. A special thanks goes to my book club— Susmitha Baakkoven, Priscilla Greene, Sheila McGuire, Debbie Miles, and Veena Singwi—for their many years of friendship and laughter. Thanks also to dear friends Darlene Buenzow, Barbara Cashion, Jennifer Ghate, Connie Hines, Kelly McDonnell, Jennifer O'Shaughnessy, Diane Ritchey, Karin Torain, Jackie Wilson, Julia Works, and my school and hockey carpools. Special thanks to my sister, Anne Marie Infosino, who edited the entire manuscript for me, making the subsequent submission and copyediting experience the smoothest I have ever had. My parents, Dorothy and Joseph Infosino, nurtured my passion for education and have never stopped encouraging me. My husband, Don Johnson, and my daughters, Darci, Sophie, and Elise, are the greatest source of love, laughter, and happiness in my life, and I dedicate this book to them.

Funding Feminism

Introduction

Women are learning something men have traditionally understood: money provides access.
—Karen D. Stone

Philanthropy lies at the heart of women's history.
—Kathleen D. McCarthy

Over the first six decades of the twentieth century, Katharine Dexter McCormick wrote checks totaling millions of dollars to advance political, economic, and personal freedom and independence for women. She gave her time and money to the woman suffrage movement, funded a dormitory for women at the Massachusetts Institute of Technology (MIT) to encourage women's education in science, and almost single-handedly financed the development of the birth control pill. McCormick opposed the militant tactics of some suffragists—such as picketing the White House—which were bankrolled by another woman, Alva Belmont, a southerner who stunned New York society when she divorced William K. Vanderbilt, inheritor of the Vanderbilt fortune. With her flair for the dramatic, Belmont brought crucial publicity to the woman suffrage movement and wielded power with her money, giving tens of thousands of dollars to the national suffrage associations under certain conditions—for example, that organization offices be moved; that she be given a leadership position; and, later, that the movement focus on international women's rights. Mary Garrett, another generous supporter of the suffrage movement, also understood the coercive power of philanthropy, paying the salary of the dean at Bryn Mawr College—but only if that dean was her partner, M. Carey Thomas—and orchestrating a half-million-dollar gift to Johns Hopkins University to open a medical school, with the condition that the school admit women. These monied women, and many like them, understood that their money gave them clout in society at a time when most women held little power.

Women have a long though underappreciated history of using large financial donations to make social change, in particular to support the women's rights movement. This book explores how wealthy women from the late nineteenth through the mid-twentieth centuries wielded their money to gain access for women to higher education, suffrage, and reproductive rights and to provide assistance to working-class women. This is the first comprehensive study of the significant part monied women played in the women's movement, defined as organized efforts to achieve equality and rights for women, including but not limited to woman suffrage. *Funding Feminism* shows why these white women—privileged in race and class—challenged the status of women in society and how their financial wherewithal powerfully influenced women, as they founded women's colleges, fostered coeducation, and enabled the success of the suffrage and birth control movements. It examines women's large financial contributions to the women's movement from 1870 (the death of Sophia Smith and bequest for the founding of Smith College) through 1967 (the opening of the second McCormick residence hall at MIT and death of donor Katharine McCormick).

This book argues that the trajectory of the women's movement—its priorities, strategies, and successes—was deeply affected by the donations given by monied women. Furthermore, progress for women in the form of improved access to economic and political power was made possible in large part by wealthy women. Suffrage was won only when rich women gave large contributions, including a million-dollar bequest by Mrs. Frank Leslie; some coeducational institutions welcomed women only when "coerced" into it by restricted giving; and access to birth control expanded only with money and legitimacy from society leaders. With little political power, philanthropy was perhaps the most potent tool that women had. Women philanthropists had to give money in order to bring about social change for women.[1]

Moreover, by exploring the reasons behind these women's willingness to give—their beliefs about women and equality—this book provides new insight into feminism. Although they may not have called themselves feminists, they believed in gender equality (or a lack of sex hierarchy) and in the social construction of women's condition (rather than women's condition being "predestined by God or nature").[2] They also identified with other women as a social group.[3] They saw themselves as linked to other women in their experiences and needs. They gave money to compensate for the discrimination they had experienced and to help other women access opportunities they did not have.[4] *Funding Feminism* wrestles with the feminist beliefs of these women, revisiting the development of feminism in the United States by exploring concepts of independence, equality, and sisterhood. Their own experiences of sexism, despite their race and class privilege, as well as their romantic views of economic independence undergirded their strong belief that all women needed financial independence, political equality, and the freedom to control their reproduction. Their wealth, and at times their difficulty exerting control over their money, pushed them to focus particularly on the need for women to have economic independence. Their ideas and their money shaped the women's movement.

Yet because they often tied restrictions to their giving, demanding input on tactics, strategies, and personnel, they engendered resentment in suffrage organizations and jeopardized their ability to establish cross-class coalitions. Within a movement designed to foster equality, the potential power of some women over others caused conflict. As a result, the presence of monied women, and their demands, pushed feminists to reconsider what equality meant. This book therefore explores both the possibilities and the problems of women's financial contributions.

This history of women's philanthropy in the women's movement in the late nineteenth and early twentieth centuries is essential to feminists today because while enormous progress has been made, women still face challenges to reproductive rights and are still fighting for full economic and political power. Understanding how and why women gave in the past and the tensions created over questions of wealth and power is crucial. American campaign finance law and recent court decisions provide the wealthiest Americans more power than ever to campaign for individuals and interests with their almost unlimited donations. Women will have to continue to fund women's ongoing fight for equality and political power.

The women philanthropists discussed in *Funding Feminism* embody many of the insights in Virginia Woolf's *Three Guineas.*[5] Published in 1938, it is written as an answer to a request that women support the peace movement through advocacy and financial support. In it, Woolf argues that women need to offer their financial support—their first guinea—to women's colleges so that women can be educated and hold their own point of view, distinct from that of their husbands. She proffers a second guinea to a society to help women find employment, because women are excluded from many positions and, even when hired, are paid less than men. Equal employment and pay are crucial for women, she contends, because the ability to earn their own money would free them to make independent decisions that would change society. Thus, funding women's equality in education and employment is necessary to empower women to offer their third guinea to the peace effort. Like Woolf, the women in this book recognized the connection between economic independence and the ability to make independent decisions, especially if one were married. Like Woolf, they sought to empower women through their donations to women's education and women's labor organizations, as well as to the suffrage and birth control movements. Like Woolf, they realized the ways that money could be used to bring about change in society.

AMERICAN WOMEN HAVE A long tradition of charitable work. Their aid to the poor, the sick, and others in need, from the individual lady bountiful—a rich, generous woman aiding those less well-off than herself—to women's benevolent, often church-based organizations, conformed to gender expectations for women throughout the antebellum period. Women visited the needy; provided food and fuel assistance; and raised funds for churches, temperance, and other causes. Before married women were allowed to own property, most women's charitable work was face to face. Giving was often in the form of time and goods rather than money. Women's benevolent organizations, which solicited financial donations, were often managed by a male board.[6]

In the decades after the Civil War, two new trends emerged that dramatically changed the power of women's giving. First, a new form of charity emerged. Although never completely replaced, small gifts intended to ease the suffering of those in need were now dwarfed by much larger donations from Gilded Age capitalists, who used the fortunes they amassed in a dramatically different way. This new "scientific philanthropy" called for large sums of money (particularly through establishing foundations) to bring about social change and challenge the causes of suffering, rather than simply ameliorate conditions.[7] For example, large-scale health campaigns sought to prevent disease rather than treat it, and funding for social science research supported these efforts.

Second, an organized women's rights movement, fueled in 1848 in Seneca Falls, New York, by the first women's rights conference in the world, expanded significantly. States passed married women's property acts, enabling married women to retain control over inheritances. Women's organizations grew in kind and number, with the Woman's Christian Temperance Union (WCTU), the General Federation of Women's Clubs, the National Association of Colored Women, and many others engaging women in civil society to a degree previously unseen. Through these organizations, women began to "do everything," as called for by WCTU leader Frances Willard, tackling issues from education to child labor to juvenile delinquency as well as widening opportunities for themselves in the process. Moreover, they worked directly to gain rights for women.[8]

The wealthy women featured in this book capitalized on both these developments—scientific philanthropy and a growing women's movement.

They began to give large amounts of money to change women's lives, not simply to assist poor women or improve working conditions in a local factory but rather to transform women's position in society by fighting to improve their access to higher education, better employment opportunities, political equality, and reproductive rights. Wielding power with their money, they believed that their efforts would fundamentally alter women's opportunities and that women would gain equality with men.[9] Like more commonly studied male philanthropists, they shaped their giving to reflect their values and compelling vision.[10]

Funding Feminism offers new insights into how women raised and spent money. Gifts of $1,000, $10,000, $500,000, $1 million, and more from wealthy women funded the women's movement in many ways in the late nineteenth and early twentieth centuries, including founding colleges, renting offices, paying staff, and underwriting magazines. Far from the image of a lone crusader or a morally righteous movement that was successful only due to altruistic, passionate volunteers, this book focuses on another set of personages: a network of rich women who made large financial donations. Most of these women were activists as well as philanthropists, leading organizations and speaking at public rallies, while others only wrote checks. By foregrounding this network of women, *Funding Feminism* helps explain how the women's movement mobilized. Suffragists from Susan B. Anthony to Carrie Chapman Catt understood that they could not gain the attention of the public and of lawmakers without funds for publicity, literature, and travel. Birth control advocate Margaret Sanger cultivated donors and tapped into networks among society women to raise the money she needed. Organization leaders often spent as much time fund-raising as on other duties. An infusion of resources allowed leaders to implement new tactics and strategies and to form new institutions. Examining the financial activity and spending priorities in the women's movement is critical to understanding the timing and extent of its success.

Moreover, these donations were critical because women depended more on the money contributed by other women than by men. While some men founded women's colleges, donated to the woman suffrage movement, or otherwise supported women's causes, this book shows that the women's movement owes its success to the financial backing of women. Late nineteenth-century feminists like Matilda Gage and Susan B. Anthony explicitly looked to wealthy women for financial assistance. Gage argued that women too often gave to men's colleges or other institutions that did not benefit women and should instead focus on supporting women's needs, while Anthony consistently tried to engage affluent women to contribute to suffrage.[11]

Although the women did fund more conventional causes, such as male universities, orchestras, and museums, and despite the fact that their gifts represented a small percentage of the total philanthropy of men and women in any given year during this period, this book demonstrates that their funding of the women's movement was greatly effective, radically transforming possibilities for women.

These wealthy women devoted their money (and their time) to these efforts because, while their class and race afforded them opportunities other women did not have (the women studied in this book were white), they still experienced limitations in their lives due to their gender. They resented women's lack of independence and opportunity, and they worked to change it. They came to understand how important it was for women to be able to vote, to obtain an education and a career, and to control their reproduction. Most significantly, they focused on women's financial independence—necessary, they believed, for monied women and working-class women alike. Their ideas about what feminism meant were essential to the women's movement.

Because many of these women believed that all of these rights were connected, they focused on helping women in several areas. For example, women's college founders made donations to the woman suffrage movement, and suffragists supported the American Birth Control League. Their goals were expansive: equality, not just suffrage; freedom, not just birth control; opportunity, not just education.

Historical scholarship that focuses exclusively on women's philanthropy is limited.[12] In 1990, historian Kathleen McCarthy edited *Lady Bountiful Revisited*, an important collection on women and philanthropy, which used an expansive definition of philanthropy that included women's charitable and social services—their time as well as their financial donations. *Funding Feminism*, although focused on the philanthropy of monetary contributions, is informed by McCarthy's interest in how women "wield[ed] power in societies intent upon rendering them powerless." She argues that women "most often turned to nonprofit institutions and reform associations as their primary points of access to public roles. In the process, they forged parallel power structures to those used by men."[13] Her later study of women philanthropists in the world of art, for example, found that women were most successful at creating separate institutions to legitimize decorative and modern art, rather than obtaining influence at established prestigious cultural institutions, such as the Metropolitan Museum of Art in New York. She concludes, "Indeed, the history of American philanthropy and art suggests that most women fell far short of enjoying the influence and status that their wealth and talent might have commanded, belying the contentions of classical political philosophers that power follows property. Why this lingering disparity between wealth, power, and authority?"[14]

This study of women philanthropists probes McCarthy's finding through a different lens: by exploring the ways in which women sought to expand their power in the community through donations meant to increase women's opportunities and promote equality. Even as they supported women's institutions (such as colleges) or women's organizations (such as suffrage associations), the education and political gains that women obtained from these institutions were ultimately meant to empower women within the larger society. Women used their money to exert influence in a society that did not expect it from them. At a time when they could not vote and when education, professions, and other opportunities were limited for them, philanthropy offered a unique tool. The power of the purse meant that they could use their financial resources to "realize their own will in a communal action even against the resistance of others."[15]

By wielding money to procure changes that benefited women, wealthy women had found a clever way to circumvent men's power in society. Women bribed, coerced, and forced their will through funding the organizations and institutions they believed in, the strategies they thought would be most effective, and the issues about which they felt most passionate. Women benefited in many ways: they gained publicity and financial support for labor strikes, they obtained more opportunities for higher education and professional training at both women's colleges and coeducational institutions, they attained the right to vote, and they secured access to birth control.

In addition to McCarthy's research, Kathryn Kish Sklar's article on the funding of Jane Addams's Hull House, published in *Lady Bountiful Revisited*, is a key study of women and philanthropy, drawing attention to the critical role of women in financially supporting other women's social reform work. Sklar found that after Addams nearly depleted her own inheritance of over $50,000 to support the settlement house, she relied heavily on Mary Rozet Smith, her life partner and the daughter of a wealthy paper manufacturer. Donating an average of over $4,000 annually for decades, Smith gave Addams the money she needed with no strings attached, leaving Addams free to pursue the programs she prioritized. A source of even more substantial funding was Louise deKoven Bowen, heir to a real estate fortune, who gave over half a million dollars between 1895 and 1928, often to particular projects of her own interest, such as a summer camp. She gained something in return for her donations: a platform for power as a social reformer in Chicago.[16] This book expands Sklar's insights in the dual power and purpose of women's philanthropy: its potential to fund reformers and organizations making change in society, as well as its ability to empower donors as they used their fortunes to realize their ideals.

More recently, some historians have begun to recognize the centrality of money to the success of the suffrage movement, highlighting the critical need for funding in the 1860s, as well as Harriot Stanton Blatch's efforts to recruit upper-class women in New York in the early 1900s.[17] Historians have also examined the role of wealthy allies in the labor movement, arguing that uneven financial power ultimately doomed organizations designed to bring together both working and monied women for labor activism. In the field of higher education and the history of the professions, Margaret Rossiter, in her work on women scientists, explored the "coercive" philanthropy used to open medical schools to women.[18]

In general, however, the field of women's history has been reluctant to place wealthy women and their money in the spotlight, preferring to focus instead on visionary reformers or grassroots efforts. Historians' unease with connecting women with wealth and power reflects the sources to a certain extent. For example, memoirs and histories written by participants in the woman suffrage movement marginalized the role of wealthy donors.

Furthermore, society has long dissociated women from money. In a study of businesswomen, historian Susan Yohn argues that societal belief about the nature of men and women fostered a discomfort with the idea of women as moneymakers, and that if " 'money equals power,' the unwillingness of Americans to acknowledge how much money is controlled and held by women has limited the political power women are able to exert."[19] Yohn concludes that while some businesswomen, like Mrs. Frank Leslie,[20] did give money to the suffrage movement and other women's causes, in general, "fearful of appearing to transgress gender roles, American women continued to acquire capital but did not seek to harness it to support the struggle for women's rights or to extend their power as fully as they might."[21] However, widening the lens to study women philanthropists who inherited their money from fathers or husbands rather than just businesswomen who acquired their own wealth, *Funding Feminism* argues that the money these women poured into the women's movement was substantial and extremely influential. Thus, the study of these women is essential.

Historians of capitalism note that history has long privileged the stories of the powerful: white men, especially politicians and capitalists. It has taken decades for historians to craft alternative histories and rich explorations of the marginalized: women, people of color, workers, the enslaved, and others. Some historians have recently returned to the powerful as subjects as they seek to better understand the development of the bourgeoisie as a class, exploring the social networks the wealthy created, the role of "wealth and power in a democracy," and resentment against the upper class.[22]

Given this new interest in the role of the monied class, it is not surprising that recent scholarship that examines the history of women and wealth is also growing. For example, Emily Remus and Courtney Wiersema have written about monied women, provisioning, and consumption in Chicago; Thavolia Glymph and Stephanie Jones-Rogers bring new insight into the power and economic decisions of white women who enslaved African Americans; and Marise Bachand studies the gendered mobility of elite women in the nineteenth-century urban South.[23]

By placing wealthy women front and center, this book wrestles with questions of money and power. It focuses on society's resentment and discomfort with affluent women, and the very nature of feminism itself as a nonhierarchical movement. Like many philanthropists who are motivated by a desire to show off their wealth or gain status, female philanthropists realized that their fortunes granted them leadership, status, and power. Women used philanthropy to "establish their own identities as consequential people while they redefined the scope of female involvement in civil society."[24] In the case of suffrage, when the movement became fashionable, society women wanted to be seen at public rallies rather than at discreet private parlor meetings. Philanthropy could also be self-serving for women in terms of winning political equality and reproductive rights for themselves. They derived pleasure from their gifts, from their association with other women, and sometimes from the publicity they received.[25]

This book contends, however, that their philanthropy was for the public good as well as for their own benefit.[26] Their vision for the future of all women compelled them to purposeful and influential giving.[27] These society women were not satisfied with their lives of leisure; they experienced a version of the social claim explicated by Jane Addams, which called them to serve society.[28] They gave because they believed in noblesse oblige—their moral responsibility to give back to benefit the community. More significantly, they gave because of their deep commitment to obtaining more rights and opportunities for women. Many studies of women's philanthropy argue that women have a closer connection to the causes they support financially than male philanthropists do, as will be demonstrated herein.[29]

Their commitment to women's rights led wealthy women to reconsider class and gender identity. Could they find common ground with other women despite a class divide that was growing deeper at the turn of the century due to increasingly hostile labor relations? Women have often been acknowledged for their role in maintaining class boundaries. Through conspicuous consumption and displays of leisure, their role as social arbiter has been understood to mean that women served as gatekeepers to elite society.[30]

This book argues that many women used their social status instead to aid the women's movement, by mobilizing their networks and commanding publicity. Many wanted to de-emphasize their elitism and instead create sisterhood. They thought that all women—rich or poor, with earned or inherited income—needed economic independence, as well as political equality and control over reproduction. Married female philanthropists, who were frustrated with their own lack of control over funds, romanticized working women due to their perception that working women were financially independent.

Foregrounding wealthy women's role in this movement thus forces consideration of the question, Is feminism inherently nonhierarchical and democratic? That is, is feminism not only about eliminating social hierarchy based on gender but also about challenging any form of hierarchy? Does feminism demand that organizations be collaborative rather than top down?[31] Jane Addams warned against the difficulties of overcoming the class divide if the rich did not cultivate mutual relationships with the poor.[32] While some female philanthropists gave money freely, without making demands on the movements and institutions they founded or gave to, others were determined to use their money to shape the direction of the organization or to win leadership positions for themselves.[33] Many of these women were strong willed and used to having their own way. Despite their intentions, their lives of privilege caused a cultural divide they could not bridge between them and middle- and working-class women—especially immigrant women—and they engendered resentment among the women with whom they worked.

This book therefore also examines the costs of these women's munificence. Working-class women, middle-class reformers, organization leaders, and male administrators all objected to the power that wealthy women had to dictate with their dollars. Women's calls for sisterhood were hollow if they linked their giving to their demands regarding who would hold office or where headquarters should be located. At the same time, coercion could be a successful tactic to wring benefits for women from men, most notably male university administrators resistant to coeducation. Having wealthy women appear to be an elite ruling power within the women's movement challenged American ideals of democracy and feminist goals of equality. The tension their power caused runs throughout the book.

Wealthy female donors encountered resistance from men, as well as from other women. Their political acumen and unexpectedly bold behavior enabled them to push an agenda often not favored by men. This book shows that women understood how to exercise power through financial largesse and coercion and illustrates how they reconciled such power—traditionally considered male—with their ideas about gender and women's rights. They were willing to risk the condemnation of society to promote controversial causes: the militant wing of the suffrage movement, striking laborers associated with socialism, and illegal birth control. Perhaps their extreme wealth—inheritances of tens of millions of dollars for some—emboldened them. Their fierce determination is evident from their lack of concern over the approbation of friends and family, as evidenced in divorce and legal suits with family members.

THIS BOOK IS ORGANIZED into chapters on the woman suffrage movement, the cross-class coalition with labor women, the founding of women's colleges, coeducation at universities, the birth control movement, and research into the birth control pill. It weaves the stories of many women together across several decades. Most chapters cover a span of decades in the late nineteenth and early twentieth centuries, with the opening of women's colleges and the contest over coeducation taking place primarily between 1870 and 1926; the suffrage movement's recruitment of monied women beginning in 1894 and lasting through the Nineteenth Amendment in 1920; and the birth control movement's organization peaking in the 1910s and 1920s under Margaret Sanger. Although most of the book examines the late nineteenth and early twentieth centuries, the struggle to make coeducational universities welcoming to women continued through the 1960s. The final chapter on the funding and development of the birth control pill also moves the story to the 1950s and 1960s, highlighting continuities across time as donor Katharine McCormick battled a male-dominated organization, wielding her money to continue to try to empower women. The epilogue, focused on women's funds begun in the 1970s and 1980s, asserts that despite a long tradition of powerful giving, which empowered individual donors and forced great strides in the fight against sexual oppression, women need to continue to use the power of money to challenge lingering discrimination. Spanning nearly one hundred years, this book emphasizes continuity rather than change over time, despite the advances made in women's economic, political, and social power.

It also challenges the "wave" paradigm in American women's history, which posits the suffrage movement as the first wave of the women's rights movement, and the women's liberation movement of the late 1960s and 1970s as the second wave. The wave model does capture the intense, large-scale organization of women directly agitating for women's rights through women-only women's rights associations that occurred in these two time periods. However, as historians have argued, the wave model is also problematic because it ignores the longer struggle for suffrage that began before Seneca Falls and ended after the Nineteenth Amendment passed in 1920 due to African American women's continued denial of voting rights in the South. Furthermore, it misses the continuity of women's activism, which continued in the 1920s through the 1960s in myriad forms: in women's associations like the YWCA, with men in civic organizations, in government due to the state's increased responsibility for social welfare, and in labor unions and civil rights organizations.[34] In each of these settings, while perhaps not organized solely around a women's rights platform, women injected work for women's rights into their agenda. *Funding Feminism* contributes to this long view, especially in chapters devoted to education and to the birth control movement. Suffragists Ellen Scripps and Katharine McCormick both understood that their work was not over when suffrage passed in 1920; Scripps founded Scripps College in 1926, and McCormick made donations to MIT to push the university to admit more women in the 1950s and early 1960s. Birth control supporters contributed to Margaret Sanger's organization throughout the 1920s, with McCormick remaining a dedicated supporter through the 1960s as she financed the development of the birth control pill. The fight for women's rights was continuous, as was the need for women to fund it.

Two distinctive qualities unite many of the women explored in some detail herein: their education and their single or widowed status. With limited opportunities for formal education for women throughout most of the nineteenth century, it is not surprising that most of these women did not have a college degree; what is notable is that despite the limited access, some did, with M. Carey Thomas and Elsie Clews Parsons even earning their PhDs. Others attended boarding school in France or a female seminary, while still others were either privately or self-taught, and traveled and read extensively. Furthermore, those who were denied a formal education while watching their brothers leave home for college smoldered with resentment, which fueled their desire to provide more opportunities for women.[35] Educational access for women increased dramatically after the Civil War (see chapter 4), enabling those born later in the century to take advantage of more opportunities, but whatever their options, many of the women in this book seized them.

Not surprisingly, a large percentage of these women were single or widowed, which gave them the financial independence necessary to make financial decisions. While a few husbands supported their wives' philanthropy and feminism, happily married women are in the minority in this study. A few women became active following the death of their husband, dedicating their inheritance to the cause.[36]

Many philanthropists discussed in this book supported several causes, providing insight into how suffrage, employment, education, and birth control were related and why they dominated the women's movement in the late nineteenth century and first half of the twentieth. Some women, like Dorothy Straight, Katharine McCormick, and Mary Garrett, show up in several chapters. These women's activities reveal the scope and breadth of the women's movement.

Furthermore, Straight, McCormick, Garrett, and others demonstrate the importance of social networks in contributing to their eventual success. Historians have begun to examine women's economic, intellectual, and social reform networks, which were undergirded by deep personal connections. As Carol Pal notes in her history of women intellectuals in seventeenth-century Europe, while the image of the "learned lady" is of an exceptional, solitary woman, in fact there existed an epistolary network. Similarly, the wealthy women herein were sisters, mothers and daughters, neighbors, and friends. They attended each other's weddings, corresponded for decades, and traveled through Europe together. Women developed friendships through social clubs and leisure activities within their closed elite society. The importance of women's ability to harness their social capital and use their social networks to benefit the women's movement is evident throughout the book. These connections helped enable fund-raising for women's causes. Women solicited money with the help of club membership lists as well as from friends at social events, including dances and concerts.[37]

The women philanthropists in *Funding Feminism* are white. African American and other women of color had less economic power, and although a few individual women of color, such as Madame C. J. Walker, had the ability to give thousands of dollars, most did not have the financial wherewithal. Instead, they were talented fund-raisers who raised large sums of money through enormous effort, especially to fund schools, hospitals, and other institutions, at a time when segregation closed many doors to them. African

American sororities and women's clubs were particularly important to these efforts. The parameters of this study (major gifts contributed by individuals to woman suffrage, higher education for women, birth control, and women's labor activism) are not intended to obscure the philanthropic efforts of African American women or other women of color, which also need further study.[38]

As I began the research for this book, I was surprised to learn just how many women in the late nineteenth and early twentieth centuries gave large donations—from over a thousand to over a million dollars—in life or at death to a variety of causes. There were also millions of women who gave small donations. Those small contributions and the millions of hours of service given by so many were extremely significant, and their absence from this book is not meant to discredit their importance. Rather, I chose to focus on the women who gave large amounts to specific women's causes because I came to believe that the timing and success of opening access to higher education for women, of gaining the vote, and of increasing access to birth control was dependent on the major gifts only the wealthy could give. Moreover, I saw how their feminism developed and shaped their giving, and how their ideas about economic, political, and social equality for women made real substantial change in the lives of American women. While they were not always likable subjects, they wielded power for women.

Yet this tradition of powerful giving, while empowering many of the individual donors and forcing great strides in the fight against sexual oppression, was not successful at gaining a prominent role for women in the field of philanthropy. Women today still have less income at their control than do men, and while remaining significant volunteers, there are still far fewer major female philanthropic donors than male. Foundations give a small part of their grants, less than 10 percent, to women. The creation of women's funds in the last several decades is an effort to address this inequity. The epilogue suggests ways that women's giving and the need for giving to women remain the same after a century despite enormous strides made in women's equality. The need for funding to win political and economic equality for women is still evident today.

Suffrage parades, women's dormitories, the distribution of birth control literature, the development of new methods of contraception—all of these had to be funded. Wealthy feminists shaped the direction of the women's movement with their ideas, their financial gifts, and their demands. Their money gave them a powerful voice. Women's right to vote, the birth control pill, and increased access to education were only achieved with the finances and work of women philanthropists. *Funding Feminism* tells their stories.

THE FIRST TWO CHAPTERS of *Funding Feminism* focus on fund-raising efforts within the suffrage movement, showing how the influx of major gifts allowed the movement to hire organizers, expand publicity, pay for new tactics and strategies, and win ratification of the Nineteenth Amendment in 1920. Chapter 1 examines how suffragists recruited wealthy women to the movement, who these donors were, and why they decided to give their money—and sometimes their time—to fight for political equality. This chapter argues that focusing on their feminism highlights a strand of suffragism that called for gender equality rather than emphasized maternalism, the belief that women as mothers (or potential mothers) had the right and the duty to vote in order to protect children and clean up government. Having experienced both the power of money and its limitations influenced the way women linked economic independence and political equality, which they believed were necessary whether one earned wages in a factory, was a professional with a college degree, or inherited a large fortune.

Chapter 2 demonstrates how having money at their disposal (or a lack of it) affected suffrage association officers' ability to make decisions about where and how to carry out the suffrage campaign. It also allowed for the development of new tactics and strategies alongside traditional methods. This chapter posits that gifts, including Mrs. Frank Leslie's million-dollar bequest, paid for organizers to travel to the states to campaign at the state level; initiated a publicity blitz, including newspapers and parades; and financed the "Winning Plan" that combined state-level efforts with a focus on the federal amendment, ultimately leading to passage of the Nineteenth Amendment. It offers a new way to understand the split between the two major suffrage associations by focusing on the role of money. The chapter also examines the conflict that developed when funding disproportionately came from a small number of wealthy individuals. Donors like Alva Belmont tied their gifts to demands, such as who should hold office and where headquarters should be located, causing resentment of the power of the monied in the movement.

While there are two chapters each on woman suffrage, higher education, and birth control, Chapter 3 stands alone as it examines the possibilities and problems inherent in cross-class coalitions designed to aid working-class women. I explore wealthy women's understanding of financial independence and sisterhood, themes that are crucial to the ideas of women throughout the book. The Women's Trade Union League (WTUL) largely failed to effectively develop a cross-class coalition. By studying the WTUL in comparison to Grace Dodge's working girls clubs and YWCA work, and the support of wealthy women for the 1909 Shirtwaist Strike, the chapter explores why many wealthy women sought gender equality. Their interactions with working-class women and their desire to control their own finances drove them to link financial independence with political equality. When the wealthy held the purse strings, cross-class cooperation, while potentially empowering to laboring women, was also a potent source of conflict. Working women resented the fact that the Dreier sisters dominated the funding for the WTUL and insisted on having their way, despite the sisters' deep commitment to feminism and their professed desire for cross-class coalition.

Chapters 4 and 5 focus on efforts to broaden women's access to higher education and employment. They explore the feminism of college founders, reclaiming their influence after some were marginalized by historians, and extend the concept of coercive philanthropy in coeducation from simply admitting women students to increasing their numbers through the establishment of women's residence halls, centers, and scholarships. Some women founded women's colleges that were designed to offer a rigorous academic program on par with that at the best men's colleges, such as Harvard. Chapter 4 examines four women's college founders, along with Jane Stanford, cofounder of coeducational Stanford University. They believed deeply in the abilities of women and the need to develop them through education. This chapter shows how these college founders defined women's rights and desired access to education, not only for intellectual growth but also for financial independence. Chapter 4 demonstrates the enormous influence on women's education that these women collectively had.

Chapter 5 explores what happened when women approached existing schools offering restricted gifts to benefit women. These donations either forced a school to open its doors to women or increased the number of women admitted by providing scholarships for women or erecting a women's building or a women's dormitory. Like the college founders, these donors believed that women were capable of the same intellectual achievement as men but found that many of America's best universities resisted coeducation. The women in this chapter and the gifts they gave show how money could be wielded to force changes that would benefit women, in the form of access to education and professions formerly restricted to men. Moreover, coeducation at these schools, including Johns Hopkins, MIT, and the University of California, Berkeley, was especially significant. If women were welcomed at these important institutions, they could demonstrate their intellectual and professional capabilities and equality with men.

Many feminist philanthropists believed that economic and political rights for women were incomplete without the right to control one's reproduction. America's leading birth control advocate, Margaret Sanger, was a skilled fundraiser. She carefully managed a network of society women who supported her organizations, publications, and private life. Chapter 6 takes a new approach to understanding Sanger: by moving the spotlight from Sanger to her supporters, it becomes clear that her strategic turn to wealthy women did not come at the expense of her feminism (even if she did drop her socialism), as has been argued by some historians. This chapter shows that women like Gertrude Minturn Pinchot and Juliet Barrett Rublee rallied behind Sanger, creating a Committee of 100 to defend her and promote the birth control movement. Unafraid of being arrested, their personal lives and their birth control advocacy revealed their feminism. Chapter 6 focuses on the ways that feminism undergirded rich women's donations, compelled them to take on controversial issues, and pushed them to influence Sanger and shape the movement. Furthermore, this chapter demonstrates the networks of power created by wealthy women.

While Sanger's early focus was on increasing access to and information about birth control, one of her most loyal supporters, Katharine McCormick, consistently argued for the research and development of a new method of accessible, safe, reliable contraception controlled by women themselves, at a time when diaphragms, condoms, and withdrawal were common methods of birth control. Chapter 7 posits that McCormick's feminism drove her to back development of the pill, correcting earlier historians who misunderstood her relationship with her husband. I also explain why Sanger and McCormick supported a prescription pill, which could be difficult for some women to obtain, while ostensibly trying to expand access to birth control. The chapter traces the way McCormick's scientific interest in endocrinology, which developed from her intervention in her mentally ill husband's medical care, and her feminist philosophy came together in her funding of the development of the birth control pill. At a time when Planned Parenthood was uninterested in research or concerned with developing a new contraceptive method that women could control, McCormick insisted that a pill was both possible and necessary, and she paid for its development. She then worked to ensure that women had access to the pill through its distribution at hospital clinics. McCormick single-handedly financed the expansion of reproductive rights for women through the development of the pill.

Since the late 1970s, there has been a proliferation of women's funds that pool and distribute funds from women, most often to benefit women and children. These funds have drawn attention to the growing financial power of women who are climbing the career ladder as well as inheriting wealth. This is evident in the current effort called Women Moving Millions, led by philanthropist Helen LaKelly Hunt, aimed at women giving to women through large financial donations. Today, many women's funds engage grantees in the decision-making process in order to empower disadvantaged women and, in so doing, decrease the power of the women donors. The epilogue offers some reflections on the rise of women's funds as a post–women's liberation movement phenomena, progress made in women's equality and women's philanthropy, and the need to continue to use the latter to promote the former.

Given changes in campaign finance law due to the *Citizens United* Supreme Court decision in 2010, access to political power now depends even more on access to funding than it did a century ago. Despite the growth of organizations like Emily's List, which fund-raises for female political candidates, women are outnumbered in political offices and are still fighting for issues such as reproductive freedom and equality in the workplace. Class, race, ethnicity, religion, and sexuality still cause divisions among women as well. Feminists today have much to learn from this story of women philanthropists and the women's movement. It is clear that women will have to continue to fund the ongoing fight for equality and political power for all women.

CHAPTER ONE

Following the Money

Funding Woman Suffrage

Calling it "the vital power of all movements—the wood and water of the engine," the "ammunition of war," and a "war chest," suffragists captured the importance of money in their battle to win the right to vote for women.[1] As National American Woman Suffrage Association (NAWSA) treasurer Harriet Upton urgently appealed to the 1909 convention: "The most important question before this convention is that of money."[2] Suffragists were unable to change public sentiment or to lobby legislatures without funds for travel, staff, print, or parades. The movement depended not just on the grassroots activism of millions of suffragists or the visionary leadership of association officers but also on the fortunes donated and estates left by a handful of very wealthy women.[3] At crucial moments they sustained the western state campaigns, underwrote newspapers, and paid salaries. This and the next chapter on woman suffrage argue that the movement, which by 1900 was stalled and unable to pass in any new states, emerged from the doldrums due to the infusion of money given by wealthy women, and that these donations shaped the trajectory, priorities, strategies, and ultimately the success of the movement. These women gave thousands and thousands of dollars to win the vote for women because they cared deeply about women's rights.

By recapturing the important role of wealthy women, this chapter provides new insights into feminist beliefs undergirding the suffrage cause. Some single, widowed, and divorced women had the economic means and the independence to direct their money toward the suffrage movement. Each woman embraced the campaign for her own reasons, but collectively their speeches and writings indicate common themes: the need for political equality for educated and working women honed from a desire for financial independence, and belief in the equality of the sexes.[4]

Despite their class and race privilege (all of the large donors were white), these women experienced sexism and, in particular, struggled to assert their economic independence. Therefore, most stressed the need for equality, rather than calling for the vote on maternalist grounds (that is, that mothers needed the vote to protect children and clean up government). Even when some suffragists began to use maternalism as an expedient argument in the twentieth century, the equality argument—also referred to as natural rights or justice—still persisted.[5] The ideology of monied women draws attention back to the quest for political equality and financial independence they sought in the movement.

These chapters also wrestle with the difficulties caused by wealthy women who had the ability to dominate a movement that challenged men's political dominance. When funding came from a small number of affluent women, officers and staff sometimes felt pressured to shape their agendas to please donors. Therefore, resentment shaped the stories told in memoirs and in the *History of Woman Suffrage*, written by participants in the movement, who marginalized the role of wealthy women. Historians followed suit, not focusing on rich women despite their powerful impact on the movement.[6]

Several historians have recently begun to write wealthy women back into the history of woman suffrage and to analyze the crucial role that their activism and funding played. Susan B. Anthony and Elizabeth Cady Stanton fretted over funding in the 1860s; forty years later, Anthony was still fund-raising just before her death in 1906, and Stanton's daughter Harriot Stanton Blatch set out to recruit wealthy New York women into the movement.[7] Building on these works, I focus on donors and their impact in the last fourteen years before the Nineteenth Amendment was ratified in 1920. I turn the spotlight on a group of women, including some of Blatch's recruits, who gave large amounts of money to NAWSA or the Congressional Union (CU). By following the money, I argue that woman suffrage passed when it did not only as a result of new leadership but also because of the significant influx of women's enormous donations and the officers, salaries, tactics, and strategies they underwrote. Wealthy women, through both their financial contributions and their ideas about feminism, had a significant impact on the movement.

NEW TACTICS AND STRATEGIES in the 1910s were extremely expensive. NAWSA's annual budget increased from tens of thousands to hundreds of thousands of dollars. State campaigns grew exponentially as well, with New York raising an incredible $682,500 (approximately $12.5 million in 2016) for its successful 1917 referendum campaign for the right of women to vote.[8]

With so much money needed, suffragists eventually realized that raising sizable amounts of money with only the small gifts of large numbers of women was not feasible; the movement instead came to depend on a small number of women to write large checks. A list of CU contributors shows that out of hundreds of donors, fewer than sixty gave $1,000 (approximately $20,000 in 2016) or more from its founding in 1913 through 1920. The vast majority gave between $1 and $50. Yet major supporters who gave at least $1,000 were dis-proportionately crucial to the financial success of the organization: approxi-mately sixty people represent nearly 60 percent of the CU's funding. Two women, Alva Belmont (who gave $76,502, or over $1.7 million in 2016) and Mary Burnham (who gave $38,170, or $867,500 in 2016), together contributed 20 percent of the total amount, $561,800, collected.[9] The other large contrib-utors donated in total approximately $213,000. The 1917 New York State effort was similar: only eighty-eight donors contributed more than half the money raised.[10]

Moreover, suffragists depended on other women, not men, to make large contributions. Women dominated the CU's major donor list of thirty-eight women, ten couples, and seven single men. Though suffragist Matilda Gage had said in 1880, "Who would be free must contribute towards that freedom," it was several decades before women finally began to use their financial clout to win the vote for women.[11] Men simply did not give enough money to the movement; it would take significant gifts from women to make change hap-pen for women.

Women's giving reflected changes in American philanthropy, which by 1900 was moving from "charity," to ease the suffering of those in need, to "sci-entific philanthropy," which was designed to foster large-scale social change by challenging the causes of suffering rather than ameliorating conditions.[12] Similarly, women began to give large amounts to make change for women in society, not simply to assist poor women but rather to broaden women's op-portunities and rights, including political equality. Though few women had the financial wherewithal and independence to give thousands of dollars to the suffrage movement, a small but significant group of mostly widows and single women with inherited fortunes did contribute large sums.

This chapter establishes who those donors were and why they gave. Per-haps the most striking commonality among the women discussed in detail in this and the next chapter is that only two were happily married during their time of activism and philanthropy to the movement, Mary Putnam Jacobi and Vira Whitehouse; two others, Pauline Shaw and Olivia Sage, had their husbands die in the midst of their support for woman suffrage, and their ma-jor financial contributions came when they were widows. Dorothy Straight began giving before her marriage and continued to have her husband's sup-port; the money, however, was her own inheritance. Though married, Katha-rine McCormick was independent, as her husband was mentally ill and confined in a home in another state. Others were unhappily married: Kather-ine Mackay left her husband for another man, and Helen Reid's husband was an alcoholic. Mary Garrett and Carey Thomas were a lesbian couple; Emily Howland and Mary Burnham were single; and Josephine Lowell, Louisine Havemeyer, Phoebe Hearst, Jane Stanford, Alva Belmont, and Mrs. Frank Leslie were all widows (the latter two also had previous marriages that ended in divorce). Financial independence, it will be clear, freed them to give.

Less significance can be tied to their education, as these suffragists had varied amounts. A few had college and even graduate degrees, like Carey Thomas, who had a PhD; Katharine McCormick, a biology degree from MIT; Helen Reid, a bachelor's degree from Barnard; and Mary Jacobi, an MD. Alva Belmont and Louisine Havemeyer attended boarding school in France, and Phoebe Hearst and Jane Stanford attended a local academy. Others had little to no formal education, like Mary Garrett, Pauline Shaw, Dorothy Straight, Mrs. Frank Leslie, and Katherine Mackay.

After recalling Stanton and Anthony's desperation over funding in the 1860s, the chapter charts suffrage leaders' deliberate recruitment of wealthy women into the movement, beginning in the 1890s. Stanton, Anthony, and other leaders needed money, and they purposely began to look for women who could provide the necessary funds. They also hoped that when society women opened their homes to suffrage meetings or, more significantly, participated in public rallies or parades, suffrage would become fashionable. These women could draw their friends into the movement as well as command newspaper coverage. Focusing on the strategy behind recruiting donors opens up a broader understanding of the logistics of the movement as a political campaign.

The women they recruited had strong ideas about why women needed the right to vote. The chapter's examination of the "feminism" of wealthy suffragists refocuses the spotlight on the justice strand of suffragism as they called for economic independence and equality. Wealthy women's experience with the power of money (and its limitations) helped them understand that economic independence and political equality were crucial for all women, whether working-class wage earners, educated professionals, or inheritors of large fortunes. They lamented male control over their finances, and thought economic independence would free them to live as full citizens. The ideology of equality and independence espoused by most of these affluent women marked them as feminists, even if they did not use that term. They saw the vote as a tool leading to greater opportunity in employment and civil society, and as a symbol of respect that recognized women's equal intelligence and capabilities.

As these monied women considered their own lack of power due to their gender, they began to identify more with other women. While they themselves would benefit from the right to vote, they also believed that other women would gain from political equality. Thus their concern for themselves was linked to their concern for others.[13] Philanthropy has been motivated by a desire to do good in civil society as well as by more self-centered reasons, including gaining status, displaying conspicuous consumption, and strengthening class structure. In the case of suffrage, when the movement became fashionable, society women gained cachet from their involvement, yet the most significant donors to the movement gave because they were dedicated to the cause. Many were activists as well as financial contributors, who gave much more to the campaign than their celebrity social status or their money: they gave of their time by speaking and marching, and were even willing to be arrested and defy disapproval from others to promote suffrage. They did so because they fervently wanted to change women's position in society by gaining political equality with men.

Despite their assertive, sometimes daring behavior when it came to women's rights, these white women were not willing to challenge the racial order that oppressed African Americans. Despite the long connection between abolition and women's rights in the nineteenth century, the movement, and NAWSA, had little room for African Americans, especially after white southern women became more active in the early twentieth century. Alva Belmont is a notable exception among the philanthropists funding the movement, as she met with and helped organize African American women in New York City, funding a branch of her organization in Harlem.[14]

In chapter 2, the focus moves from the donors to the donations, looking at how these new large contributions shaped the success of the movement by tracing their use. At the same time, however, some wealthy women demanded a say in how their money was spent, making it impossible to separate the money from its source. Chapter 2 therefore also contends that the largesse of the rich came with a price. By insisting on influencing where headquarters were located, who held office, and what officers should be prioritized, wealthy donors drove out long-time loyal suffragists incapable of the same munificence.

THE WOMAN SUFFRAGE MOVEMENT is usually regarded as taking off after the world's first women's rights convention, held in Seneca Falls, New York, in 1848, although both men and women had previously petitioned states for the right of women to vote.[15] At Seneca Falls, Elizabeth Cady Stanton unveiled a Declaration of Sentiments, which contested women's inequality, beginning with their lack of political power. Although Stanton, Anthony, and others worked throughout the rest of the century to gain the right to vote, by 1900 only three states—Wyoming, Colorado, and Utah—had granted women the ballot. The movement seemed stalled until a new major push invigorated it in the early twentieth century.

Success ultimately came from new leadership, including Alice Paul, the dynamic chairman of the CU; Carrie Chapman Catt, the "general" who led NAWSA; and Harriot Stanton Blatch, the leader of the Women's Political Union. Paul, Catt, Blatch, and others introduced new tactics, such as street protests and parades, and new strategies, such as returning to an emphasis on the federal amendment rather than a state-by-state campaign and engaging in political lobbying that included punishing the party in power—which had failed to pass woman suffrage—by campaigning against them.[16] Their success was possible because Paul, Catt, and Blatch all received significant funding from new wealthy donors, which allowed them to carry out their ideas. The ballot was finally won because of an infusion of cash into the movement, money that paid for these new strategies and tactics and also drew publicity to the movement.

The need for money drove the woman suffrage movement from its early days. Historian Faye Dudden contends that Stanton and Anthony, desperate for funds, made compromises over whom they associated with during the 1860s. Abolitionist Wendell Phillips was the executor for two important bequests from Francis Jackson and Charles F. Hovey. In 1858, Jackson, a wealthy real estate broker, abolitionist, and supporter of women's rights, left $10,000 to battle slavery, $2,000 for fugitive slaves, and $5,000 "to secure the passage of laws granting women, whether married or unmarried, the right to vote; to hold office; to hold, manage and devise property; and all other civil rights enjoyed by men." Hovey, a Boston dry goods merchant, gave $50,000 for antislavery and other reforms, including women's rights. He stipulated that if slavery were abolished, the women's movement would receive the remaining funds. Despite these specifications, as trustee of the funds, Phillips designated only a small amount for women's rights. Anthony was particularly bitter when Phillips continued to use the Hovey fund for black suffrage after the abolishment of slavery, causing her to posit that there would be nothing left for women. Anthony's letters reveal that she was "nearly driven to desperation" by the need for money to pay for speakers and their travel expenses, as well as the publication and dissemination of tracts. She and Stanton thus accepted an offer by George Train, the notoriously racist Democrat, to pay for a speaking tour and newspaper.[17] Dudden concludes that their descent into racist rhetoric should be understood, though not condoned, in the context of their battle with Phillips because of their need for money.

Anthony and others expended enormous amounts of time and energy soliciting money. Anthony complained that "more than half of my spiritual, intellectual and physical strength has been expended in the anxiety of getting the money to pay for the Herculean work that has been done in our movement."[18] Burned by her experience with Phillips, Anthony wanted wealthy women to prioritize giving to the movement. "One effect of our suffrage movement is that women are learning to do more for women," she said. "Hitherto when a rich woman died leaving a large legacy to some institution, it was usually one for men that derived the benefit. Women are now understanding that their own sex has the first claim."[19] Suffragist Matilda Gage also wanted women to give toward their own freedom.[20] Like Anthony, Gage lamented the fact that these women gave to other causes instead. She wrote, "Almost every daily paper heralds the fact of some large bequest . . . by rich women; but it is proverbial that they never remember the women's suffrage movement that underlies in importance all others."[21]

Suffrage fund-raiser Annie Porritt later argued that women needed to be "educated up to see that suffrage is as important as a hospital or as any other charity."[22] This is a crucial point. Wealthy women were accustomed to making charitable contributions, either through their own finances or through influencing donations made by their husbands. Women who gave to churches, hospitals, schools, and charitable organizations, such as the YWCA, demonstrated a history of generosity. Porritt wanted that munificence to turn to women's causes. Suffragists understood that they could not depend on men; it would take the financial support of women to bring about change for women.

These early bequests and the contests over them illustrate a constant conundrum in the movement: the need for money to achieve the organization and publicity necessary to obtain the right to vote, and the difficulty obtaining it in a society where women wielded little economic power. Until women obtained access to equal pay, education, and professions, and married women gained property rights, they would have little success funding a movement for political equality. Changes in married women's property laws in the second half of the nineteenth century enabled some women to control their money (usually an inheritance) while married. Widows and single women also began to inherit vast sums of money in the late Gilded Age from millionaire industrialists and financiers. A few women earned their own fortune as businesswomen. In the early 1900s, suffragists were finally able to obtain large amounts from wealthy women who now controlled their own fortunes.

By the 1890s, some suffrage leaders began to purposely recruit wealthy women to increase donations, as well as to create publicity and draw additional women into the movement. On the East Coast, Anthony turned to Dr. Mary Putnam Jacobi. When New York State held a constitutional convention that redrew voting laws in 1894, Anthony hoped Jacobi and her friends would provide the $50,000 Anthony needed to collect signatures for a petition.[23] Instead of funding Anthony's proposed door-to-door campaign, which Jacobi thought would be "useless" because "few persons would sign a petition so presented, and their names would have little influence," Jacobi decided to "arouse sufficient interest among the women who had houses and large circles of friends." She organized woman suffrage parlor meetings and held petition-signing drives at Sherry's, the fashionable confectioner in New York City.[24] Catherine Palmer Abbe, Josephine Shaw Lowell, Olivia Sage, and others—dubbed "the Sherry Committee"—helped Jacobi with the petition-signing drives.

The experiences and beliefs of Jacobi and the other members of the Sherry Committee illustrate why wealthy women began to support woman suffrage. A graduate of the Woman's Medical College of Philadelphia and the wife of Dr. Abraham Jacobi, Mary Jacobi was intensely interested in promoting women in the medical field. In 1885, she wrote an article in the *Woman's Journal* in which she explained that she had formerly opposed woman suffrage. However, after reading Plato's *Protagoras*, which argues that "the survival of states required the full participation of its citizenry," she changed her mind. Carla Bittel, her biographer, asserts that Jacobi believed suffragists would help her advance her idea that "science held the key to women's emancipation" and would promote women's ability to contribute to civil society through their scientific knowledge and health reform.[25]

Josephine Shaw Lowell came from a family of abolitionists. She was the sister of Robert Gould Shaw, a Union colonel who died while leading the all-black Fifty-Fourth Massachusetts Regiment in the Civil War, and the young widow of Charles Lowell, a Union general also killed in the war. After her husband's death, Josephine became an enormously influential reformer and philanthropist. She was one of the founders of the organized charity movement, a commissioner on the New York State Board of Charities, and founder of both the New York Consumers' League and the Woman's Municipal League.[26]

In Lowell's opinion, "if women could vote, they would have more power, and could help more directly than they can now, especially in securing the enforcement of the laws which most concern themselves." By this, she meant primarily that women could pass protective labor legislation for working women, as well as other social reform measures. Furthermore, she contended that woman suffrage would protect women from domestic violence, by granting them both the respect they deserved in society and the power as voters to expect judges to enforce punishment of male abusers. That respect would come in part from the power of their vote and their position as citizens, as well as from the "courage, self-confidence, [and] public spirit" the vote would foster. Lowell embraced the idea that women were inherently ethical and could use their voting power for the good of society. Rather than focusing on women's nature as potential mothers, as maternalist suffragists later would, she emphasized working-class women and their needs.[27] Her biographer contends that through getting to know working-class women and the conditions in which they worked, "Lowell became aware of the critical link that drew all women together in a web of responsibility and political action."[28]

The wealthiest woman of the Sherry Committee was Olivia Sage, the wife of industrialist Russell Sage. Deeply influenced by Emma Willard—women's education advocate and founder of Troy Female Seminary—Sage graduated from Troy and taught for twenty years before her marriage at age forty-one. Despite her husband's enormous fortune, his miserly ways limited her generosity during his lifetime. Her most significant philanthropic gifts came after his death in 1906, when she gave millions of dollars to various colleges and established the Russell Sage Foundation "for the improvement of social and living conditions in the United States" with $10 million.[29]

Her longtime interest in women's education brought her into the suffrage movement.[30] Sage held a parlor meeting at her home in April 1894, attracting over two hundred women. During the meeting, she complained that the governor had vetoed a bill that would have allowed for the appointment of four women to the board of trustees at Troy, her alma mater. The *New York Times* covered the meeting, and then interviewed Sage. In the interview she broadened her viewpoint concerning a lack of fairness in women's treatment by the government. Appearing in print under the headline "Views of a Millionaire's Wife," she argued that "women of means, widows and spinsters" should not have to pay taxes without the right to vote.[31]

However, newspaper coverage of Sage's views was not enough to help win the right to vote, and the indomitable fund-raiser Anthony later pointedly asked Sage for financial support. "It is very sad indeed," she wrote Sage, "that rich women do not feel the importance of helping the cause, and I want to appeal to you and to Mr. Sage to do something handsome in the way of an appropriation of money to be used in the next State campaign of 1914." After her husband died in 1906, leaving her $75 million, Sage's largest gift to NAWSA was an anonymous $20,000 to a fund in Anthony's memory.[32]

Of the Sherry Committee members, Lowell focused on working-class women, while Jacobi and Sage were particularly interested in the needs of educated and professional women. The two drew ire from some when they embraced the idea of limited suffrage, which would depend on an educational (or property) requirement. Elizabeth Cady Stanton had also espoused similar ideas, disparaging the votes of the "ignorant foreigner" while complaining that women (presumably educated and white) could not vote. These ideas, exposing their racism and class bias, marred the woman suffrage movement. Well aware of the difficulties women seeking entrance into the medical field faced, Jacobi stressed the need of educated women for political equality, as well as the benefits they would bring the polity. She argued that educated women could be political equals to men and balance out the "ignorant vote." At the same time, she argued that working-class women contributed to society and therefore deserved the right to vote.[33]

Like Jacobi, Sage offered what seemed to be contradictory arguments. Given her own education and promotion of women's higher education, it is not surprising that she contended that "woman had advanced in education, the professions, and business and she was now man's intellectual equal." She called for property qualifications for the vote, and yet in 1905 she emphasized women's solidarity despite class differences, claiming, "A rich woman is not different from a poor woman, except in the matter of money." Ruth Crocker, her biographer, contends that her suffrage ideology was flawed due to her nativism and her noblesse oblige, and that she worked on behalf of, rather than with, poor and working women. "Such benevolence," argues Crocker, "assuming responsibility over others, constitutes a kind of elite power and contracts feminism's emancipatory and democratic potential."[34]

The early effort to recruit wealthy women to the movement in New York thus demonstrates some of the benefits and pitfalls suffrage leadership faced. Wealthy women were an invaluable source for money and publicity. Their arguments in favor of woman suffrage focused on equality and fairness. They stressed women's equal capacity for engagement in politics, evident in their educational achievements and their status as taxpayers. Yet their views also forced suffragists to consider who deserved the vote and the role of classism and racism within the movement.

Around the same time that Jacobi was creating the Sherry Committee in New York, NAWSA leaders were designing a "society plan" in Colorado. In 1893, Lucy Stone and Carrie Chapman Catt tried to organize wealthy Denver clubwomen through the leadership of Ione Theresa Hanna, the first woman elected to a school board in the state. Hanna, born in New York, graduated from Oberlin College and taught before moving to Colorado with her husband, John Hanna. She was an original member of the Denver Fortnightly Club and a director representing Colorado for the Association for the Advancement of Women.[35] She brought her friends to the suffrage cause, using more "respectable" parlor meetings rather than public meetings. As the Colorado Equal Suffrage Association's Martha Pease explained, "We sent our most eloquent speakers armed with their very sweetest smiles, their most honeyed words and their best clothes" to the parlor meetings.[36]

Hanna was known for a speech she gave at the World's Columbian Exposition in 1893 on "The Ethics of Social Life," in which she complained that young women of wealth were financially dependent, shut out of careers, and waiting for life's work. She asserted that fashion and social life made life "burdensome and artificial" and left women feeling that "the unreal and unimportant" things in life "demand the most of her time." She particularly resented women's lack of access to financial knowledge. "Even if a father intend[s] to leave his daughter a handsome fortune," Hanna wrote, "he will in the majority of cases educate her to be so helpless as to be absolutely dependent upon her brothers or male relatives for business guidance and control, which is only a shade less bitter than to be dependent for one's daily necessities, rather than teach her intelligently to take care of money herself." Without access to paid employment, women felt like "pensioners on the bounty of their fathers or male relatives" and were not recognized as full human beings. Furthermore, Hanna argued that if women were to see paid employment as "discredited," they would be unable to relate to the working class.[37]

Many other wealthy suffragists found society events and leisure pursuits too limiting in scope. They also hoped that suffrage would encourage full citizenship, leading to equal opportunities in employment and financial independence. Massachusetts suffragist Blanche Ames expressed this best when she wrote, "Women must become economic equals again and cease to be parasites. . . . I know many women of wealth who are literally dying because they have nothing to do. Life means nothing to them because they have no responsibilities. . . . Women are going to use the ballot to lift themselves out of the parasitic class. . . . They are equal in importance to the human race by every law of biology."[38] Thus, rather than drawing attention to working-class women, already employed and in need of the vote to gain better labor conditions, these women saw the vote as empowering wealthy women to become financially responsible. In both cases, women's ability to care for themselves, their very independence, was at stake.

These early wealthy suffragists expressed the bitterness that drove many to embrace suffrage. Despite the privileges their wealth afforded them, they still felt excluded and restricted as women, unable to control their finances, enter professions, or hold political power (even as a school trustee). The depth of anger they felt is evident in their references to women as "parasites" or "pensioners" in their comments and speeches, and would be echoed in the words of affluent suffragists who followed in the early twentieth century. Their decision to support woman suffrage was "compensatory" in the sense that they hoped to use their donations to make changes for women that would make up for their own lack of power as women, and provide more opportunities to other women.[39]

To translate the Colorado society plan to the national level, Catt laid out a plan to recruit more wealthy women to NAWSA. She suggested that NAWSA compile lists of prominent women; that suffragists become active in the same charitable, educational, and civic organizations to which these wealthier women belonged; and that they then use these connections to recruit elite women. Though not exactly duplicitous, the plan was a sly way to develop the relationships with monied women that underlay successful fund-raising. Having been fighting for funds for decades, Anthony approved of Catt's strategy. Anthony even wanted to list names of the delegates and the alternates in the NAWSA convention program in order to advertise the prominent names becoming associated with suffrage.[40]

Despite these efforts, the society plan was slow to attract more wealthy women—or money—to the cause. Clubwomen from Denver and one of Catt's organizers from Colorado campaigned in Idaho, Montana, and Nevada. However, they found society women in small towns uninterested in their message. "As for society I have very little hope for it," concluded one worker who thought it better to recruit professional working women instead. California's unsuccessful 1896 campaign included support from some women, like Stanford University founder Jane Stanford, but it was always short of money and therefore depended heavily on volunteers rather than paid organizers.[41]

Anthony's next two important converts did not come until right before her death in 1906, when she met with M. Carey Thomas and Mary Elizabeth

Garrett in Baltimore in conjunction with the NAWSA convention being held there. Garrett's father—John W. Garrett, president of B&O Railroad—died in 1884, leaving Mary a $6 million inheritance (almost $143 million in 2016). In 1885, Garrett, Thomas, and several friends established Bryn Mawr School—a girls' preparatory school in Baltimore—and in 1894, Thomas became president of Bryn Mawr College with Garrett's financial assistance. Garrett also forced the Johns Hopkins Medical School to admit women by tying this requirement to a large donation.[42]

Anthony was eager to solicit Garrett and Thomas. "The way Baltimore is opening its arms to view us, maybe it will open its purse strings so that we should have the largest contribution of the whole series of years. . . . The money will come," she wrote a colleague.[43] Garrett and Thomas responded to Anthony's overtures, committing to raise $60,000: $12,000 annually for five years, including Garrett's own $2,500 contribution. Garrett's strategy echoed the local city committee organization of the Women's Medical School Fund she had headed a decade earlier. Garrett and Thomas designed a committee with "two [members] in each of the six principal cities of the United States—three in the East and three in the West." Committee members were charged with soliciting twenty-four women to give $500 a year for five years.[44] Through this structure, Garrett and Thomas were able to round up most of the contributors needed. Olivia Sage then anonymously donated the remaining $20,000 to complete the fund.[45] These financial contributions were crucial to Anthony's desire to strengthen NAWSA before her death and to establish a fund for salaries for officers.

In addition to their financial support, Garrett's society standing helped legitimize the movement both in Baltimore and around the nation. Garrett hosted Anthony at her home and displayed public support for the movement during the NAWSA convention. As the wealthiest woman in Baltimore, Garrett hosted receptions to which she invited Maryland's society women. Because she rarely held such social events, the receptions drew crowds and media attention. Although Garrett seldom appeared in public, she attended the convention. Newspapers eagerly described her presence, even though she refused to allow photographs of herself to be printed.[46]

Mary Garrett's conversion to suffrage came because she sought the same respect that men of means had. Her father had left her one-third of his fortune, providing her with financial independence and specifying that the money was to remain in her hands, even if she married. However, Garrett believed she had been denied the same opportunities her brothers had to obtain a college education, follow her father into the family business, or marry.

Furthermore, she fought family members and business partners who controlled the Garrett estate, ultimately suing to gain access to the books and the ability to make financial decisions.[47] Like Ione Hanna, Garrett's lack of ability to control her fortune fueled her desire for women to gain access to education, professions, and political independence.

Garrett convinced her friend M. Carey Thomas to join the suffrage movement. Thomas had been reluctant to join, due to her "elitism," until she was convinced that educated and elite women were an important part of the cause. In 1909, she claimed that suffrage was becoming fashionable to educated women and took credit for it. "I flatter myself," she wrote, "that I have made it respectable among college women."[48] Like Jacobi and Sage before her, Thomas focused on educated, professional women. After completing her undergraduate education at Cornell and gaining a PhD abroad before becoming first dean and then president of Bryn Mawr College, Thomas contended that suffrage was "an inevitable and logical consequence of the higher education of women." As a college president, she resented her lack of political power when less educated men had the vote. Educated women, she said, would demand equality, use the vote to fulfill their civic obligations, and demand the respect that suffrage bestowed.[49] Furthermore, Thomas thought wage-earning women needed the ballot to protect their interests. Working women's independence belied women's supposed dependence on men, she concluded.[50] Notably, the Garrett-Thomas fund was used in large part to pay salaries for officers, not a surprising purpose given the desire for women's professional opportunities.

Several years after Anthony's death, Harriot Stanton Blatch excelled in bringing very wealthy women to the movement in New York. She purposefully recruited society women in 1908–9 as part of her strategy to unite all women by bringing both working-class and upper-class women to the then predominantly middle-class suffrage movement. Blatch, the daughter of Elizabeth Cady Stanton, was educated at Vassar College and had worked with the British suffrage movement.[51]

Convinced that working women were crucial to the movement because of their economic independence, Blatch also came to see that a successful movement would have to be united across classes, from the wealthiest socialite to the poorest wage earner. Blatch believed that women's wage work contributed to their freedom and equality.[52] She had struggled to raise funds before recruiting wealthy women and was anxious to spend whatever was necessary to accomplish her goals. She argued, "The money lying ready for suffrage is limitless. How to tap the reservoir is the only problem."[53] Comfortable in society due to her own wealth, Blatch recruited some of New York's wealthiest and most socially elite women.[54]

Blatch's genius lay in her ability to draw new donors into a more public role, one that commanded the attention of the press. There was nothing revolutionary about a working-class woman in the streets, but a society woman on a street-corner soapbox was worth reporting in the paper.[55] As the movement began to shift from private parlor meetings to public rallies, parades, and speeches, a wealthy suffragist's presence "on display" at such public events reflected the movement's fashionable nature.[56] Thus Blatch wanted her new recruits to do more than write checks anonymously. She needed them to march in parades and give public speeches. "It was Mrs. Blatch who insisted that I could speak," wrote socialite Louisine Havemeyer, "that I must speak; and then saw to it that I did speak. I think I spoke just to please her." Louisine Havemeyer—the widow of Henry Havemeyer, who made his fortune with the American Sugar Refining Company—was a renowned art collector. After Blatch recruited her into the movement, Havemeyer decided to organize the first public exhibits of her art collection to raise money for suffrage, drawing crowds and publicity. She also created an electric torch, powered by her automobile battery and resembling the Statue of Liberty, which she marched with.[57]

CU leader Alice Paul had the same sway over Havemeyer. She demanded that Havemeyer allow herself to be arrested during the White House protests, in which an effigy of President Woodrow Wilson was lit on fire, so that she could give speeches about her experience on the "Prison Special" speaking tour. Once again, Havemeyer recalled that she initially resisted, then gave in.[58] Her speeches drew much needed media attention. In addition, she donated $20,000 to the CU.[59] Havemeyer's feminism was straightforward. Simple justice, she argued, meant that women as well as men should be able to participate in American democracy.

Recruiting wealthy socialites like Havemeyer raised the status of the movement and drove newspaper coverage. Of course, in order to draw wealthy women in, the movement had to be fashionable. To make it fashionable, wealthy women had to become part of it. Because suffrage organizations listed donors by name, as advocated by Anthony, once some socialites came on board, they used their social capital to convince friends who did not want to be left out of a now popular cause. For example, solicitations of Phoebe Hearst, wife of George Hearst and mother of William Randolph Hearst, show that the CU was eager to be able to list her name on its letterhead. "We need financial aid for this campaign," solicitor Mary Sperry admitted to Hearst, "but far more than that, we need the public utterance of women beloved and respected by all for great goodness and large helpfulness—your influence, dear Mrs. Hearst, will be of untold assistance to us, and I write this, in the hope that you will voice your favorable opinion."[60] The CU believed Hearst's name would legitimize the cause and raise its profile, attracting other women.

Another CU tactic was having the socially prominent donor and activist Alva Belmont solicit contributions "from women who had married money, but were socially insecure."[61] This meant that the suffrage movement had become fashionable enough that these women saw supporting suffrage as a way to cement their place in the social circle in which their marriage placed them.

As Ella Crossett noted in the *History of Woman Suffrage*, the movement had long suffered from not being able to recruit wealthy women. When they finally did, the press and the public became interested.[62] Newspapers began to cover suffrage events in society columns. A *New York Times* article on a street meeting, for example, reported, "It was a distinctly smart occasion from a social point of view." Noting the prominent women present, the article described their gowns and hats, and specified that they went to lunch at the tony Colony Club, a prestigious women's club, afterward.[63] Alva Belmont and other society women were experienced in garnering headline-grabbing attention for extraordinary mansions and extravagant balls. They now extended their celebrity to the woman suffrage movement. The newspapers were eager to capture the radical pronouncements of society women on woman suffrage. Novel ideas, like the torch that Havemeyer brought on parade and Belmont's decision to open her Newport, Rhode Island, mansion for tours that culminated in a suffrage rally, drew additional publicity. The press and the public showed new interest in suffrage.[64] For many suffragists, the new attention was welcome. Tired of being scorned as "manly" women, it was exciting for suffragists to be thought of as fashionable.[65]

Blatch also recruited Vira Whitehouse, wife of banker Norman de R. Whitehouse. Born in Virginia, educated at Newcomb College, and a member of the women's Heterodoxy Club of Greenwich Village, Whitehouse led the New York state suffrage campaign in 1917. She also worked for the government's Committee on Public Information during World War I, and bought and ran a leather company in the 1920s. Like many other wealthy suffragists, Whitehouse took pleasure in the activism that replaced her former focus on her social life. After the suffrage referendum defeat in 1915, she told the state convention, "We failed because we worked like amateurs; we worked for suffrage when our work did not interfere with pleasures, or when our duty to suffrage did not interfere with other duties."[66] Rather than being "hypnotized" into doubting their abilities, Whitehouse believed that women needed to assume more responsibility in fighting for suffrage.

Whitehouse linked woman suffrage to the legacies of American pioneers, revolutionaries, and Civil War soldiers, all of whom fought "for freedom, progress, and union." Women's rights, she claimed, were part of the larger American ideal, as well as part of a worldwide march toward "recognizing the new value of women."[67] Whitehouse led the incredibly successful fund-raising campaigns for the 1917 referendum, making large donations herself as well as soliciting major contributions from New York's most prominent families.[68]

Whitehouse's colleague Helen Reid, treasurer of the 1917 New York State campaign, was a Barnard graduate from Wisconsin. She worked as a personal secretary for Elisabeth Mills Reid, wife of *New York Tribune* publisher Whitelaw Reid, and married their son, Ogden Mills Reid. Ogden, an alcoholic, showed little interest in running the newspaper; however, Helen eventually became advertising director and vice president of the newspaper, then president and chairman of the board after his death. She was also dedicated to women's education, serving as chair of the Board of Trustees of Barnard College and supporting her mother-in-law's decision to turn a building she owned in Paris into a residential center for American university women (later bequeathed to Columbia University). Reid was also active in the American Birth Control League throughout the 1920s.[69] She claimed that it was in working her way through Barnard that she realized the need for women to become economically independent and contended that husbands had to expand their domestic role in housework and child care. "A woman needs suffrage for her own spiritual and intellectual development," she said.[70] Reid contributed over $13,000 to the New York campaign.[71]

Like Whitehouse, Dorothy Whitney Straight sought meaning in her activism and philanthropy. Born in 1887, her mother died when she was a young child, and her stepmother several years later. Her father died when she was seventeen, leaving her parentless. However, she inherited nearly $7 million (over $166 million in 2016). She launched and published Herbert Croly's *New Republic* with her first husband, Willard Straight, a diplomat and financier who died in 1918. Later, with her second husband, Leonard Elmhirst, whom she married in 1925, she traveled to England to create a progressive school, farm, and factory—a utopian community called Dartington.[72] When they married, Dorothy promised to love and honor but not obey him.[73]

Influenced by Thorstein Veblen, John Dewey, Jane Addams, and Lillian Wald; not content to live a life of leisure and society; and more independent than society girls with parents who limit their activities, Straight pushed the

Dorothy Whitney Straight. Courtesy of Library of Congress Prints and Photographs Division, LC-DIG-ggbain-12525.

Junior League to more progressive activism. "I soon realized that social work of a more serious nature could be undertaken by these young women. We were determined to prove ourselves capable of undertaking responsible volunteer jobs and of learning at first hand something more about the social conditions of our city," she wrote. Beginning in 1908, she dedicated extensive time to building a Junior League house for working women. When suffrage became the topic of debate in the Junior League the following year, Straight was won over, calling herself a "strong advocate and supporter." She marched in parades and even induced Willard to endorse the movement to members of the Colony Club. In 1916, she led the women's campaign for Charles Evans Hughes by donating $5,000 to him. She advocated for working simultaneously in support of World War I and woman suffrage, appearing with Catt at a patriotic suffrage meeting and heading the New York City Women's Committee for National Defense. She donated $17,000 to the New York referendum campaign and $1,250 to the CU. Guided by the sentiment "You need no priesthood but the priesthood of conscience," she also supported labor activism and progressive politics. As a woman with the wealth and independence to do what she wanted, she fought for opportunities for all women through her support of suffrage, birth control, the WTUL, the YWCA, the Junior League, and other women's organizations.[74]

Blatch's commitment to recruiting both working-class and upper-class women into the movement provides further insight into the motivation of wealthy suffragists. Many tried to espouse a sisterhood in which the common experience of sexism would trump class difference. Edith Hooker, a suffragist and birth control advocate from Maryland, explained that the "appeal for conscious sex loyalty" was meaningful for women who were discriminated against primarily because of sex—that is, not because of class, religion, or color.[75] They questioned their role as women in society, privileged in race and class but still subject to sexism.

Monied women understood the importance of economic independence no matter what their marital state. Many widows or single women in charge of a large fortune demanded the political rights they believed were necessary to sustain their independence. For others, experience with a failing marriage or divorce heightened their desire for control over their own fortune. Even those who were happily married resented the lack of power displayed when their husbands made all financial decisions.

Some of the married women solicited by suffragists had very little control over their husbands' money and no money of their own to spend. They were not given money regularly by their salary-earning husbands and had to ask for cash to spend. Husbands denied requests if they did not approve and limited some women's ability to give to women's causes, such as suffrage.[76] Olivia Sage, whose husband had restricted her ability to make major donations while he was alive, argued that a potential solution was for a cash "allowance" that wives could control, so that they would not have to be put in the position of "begging their husbands for money." However, the allowance also came under attack as a sign of "financial submissiveness" because it signaled the husbands' control, since an allowance is a gift rather than an entitlement.[77]

One woman, although living in a very large home, said she could not afford a $100 or $1,000 gift, or even $5 or $10 a month. "I don't think you understand, Mrs. Havemeyer," she apologized to Havemeyer and her fund-raising partner, Rebecca Reyher. Her husband signed the checks she wrote and did not give her a cash allowance. "If my husband doesn't approve of what I wrote in my checkbook, he either won't pay it, or I don't do it again," she continued.

"I could never give you a monthly pledge because he doesn't approve of what you are doing." Reyher explained that this woman's predicament was typical, and other wealthy women had to resort to ruses to pay their donations. For example, they could "charge a hat" on their husband's account and, instead of actually purchasing the hat, "have the shopkeeper give them the cash." Despite running the household, women were not allowed financial freedom, leaving Reyher to conclude, "My experience in trying to raise money for suffrage and equal rights taught me much about the meaning of economic independence for women."[78] Many wealthy women had learned the same lesson themselves.

With fortunes coming primarily from an inheritance, single and widowed women often had more control over spending than did married women; they also were more likely to have a profession or run a business after a death. Even so, they still struggled to assert themselves financially and gain respect for their business management, and thus they saw political equality as necessary to winning greater financial independence. Never married, Mary Garrett resented what she perceived to be her limited opportunities as the only daughter in her family and struggled to control her investments from her inheritance.

Phoebe Hearst and Jane Stanford, both suffragists and donors to women's education, experienced similar tensions as widows. Stanford explained to Anthony that her support for woman suffrage should not be surprising given her lack of power as a woman handling her dead husband's investments in a railroad company. When one of her husband's partners refused to give her railroad passes for Anthony, she had to involve her brother to get them. This she blamed on her sex and her resultant lack of power, including the right to vote.[79] Meanwhile, Anthony noted to Stanford that Hearst's management of her late husband's estate had motivated Hearst, "making her see and feel the need of woman's possessing political *power*—as well as financial freedom."[80] Hearst herself contended that women in California "have been recognized since pioneer times as physically and intellectually qualified to occupy high positions of trust and responsibility in connection with public affairs. . . . In California enterprises women have always participated not only as owners, but as directors and managers, and have certainly attained as high percentages of success in such affairs as men have." This is what led Hearst to embrace suffrage. She concluded, "The enfranchisement of women in California was the logical result of the foregoing demonstration. . . . It stands as surety to coming women that they will be free to act in public affairs and in their own business and that they will be appreciated and judged just as men are in similar under-

Mrs. Frank Leslie. Courtesy of Library of Congress Prints and Photographs Division, LC-USZ62-37933.

takings."[81] Hearst became a significant donor, contributing thousands of dollars to the CU and supporting the California suffrage movement.

The desire for financial independence and gender equality for women is a common theme among wealthy suffragists despite a variety of personal experiences and ideas. Mrs. Frank Leslie, Alva Vanderbilt Belmont, and Katharine McCormick—the effects of whose financial contributions are discussed in chapter 2—embodied a feminist ideology based in ideas of economic independence and human equality. Their ideas are crucial to this analysis of wealthy suffrage donors' ideology and feminism and thus are examined here.

Mrs. Frank Leslie donated more money than any other individual to the movement, leaving her entire estate to Carrie Catt for woman suffrage. Born in 1836 in New Orleans, Miriam Folline was known for a series of marriages, divorces, and scandalous affairs. Her first marriage to David Charles Peacock seems to have been forced on him following charges of seduction and was quietly annulled after two years. Her marriage to archeologist George Squire lasted longer but came to a strange end. After rumors that the couple had formed a love triangle with their boarder, the publisher Frank Leslie, Squire was arrested for debt and then later set up with a woman of ill repute. Being caught with the woman allowed Miriam to sue him for divorce on the basis of adultery. Her affair with Leslie already underway, she married him in 1874. Their marriage was short but apparently happy, lasting until his death in 1880. She then married William Wilde, who was an alcoholic. The marriage quickly ended in divorce.[82]

Miriam was also an astute businesswoman, writer, and editor, who fought to be taken seriously in the publishing world. When Mr. Leslie died, she changed her name to Frank Leslie, inherited his publishing business, and quickly turned the in-debt company into a profitable enterprise. She did so owing both to her editorial eye and to her business acumen—for example, consolidating publications and famously scooping other magazines with an illustration of the deathbed scene of President Garfield. Her husband apparently wanted her to take over the business at his death, specifying, "I consider no one in the country is more capable of forming correct judgment of the literary and artistic matters pertaining to the business. She has been to me a most efficient help for the last eighteen years." As he was dying, he told her, "Go to my office, sit in my place, and do my work until my debts are paid."[83]

Although she was not an activist, Leslie consistently supported the suffrage movement with small donations for well over two decades before leaving her estate to Catt. Moreover, she demonstrated through her life choices and business acumen that women were capable of economic independence. Together, Leslie's love life and business achievements reveal that she took control of her own life and her finances, despite the steady stream of men in her life—men on whom she could not rely. This independent spirit was probably the source of her dedication to woman suffrage. In fact, Leslie wrote Catt in 1910 that the cause "must be dear to every woman having children or property."[84] Leslie meant that women needed political representation as mothers to better care for children's needs or as economic producers and taxpayers. It should not be surprising that Leslie wrote that the woman of the future "must free herself from her swaddling clothes and go into the world with courage and self-reliance," traits she had already proven to have herself.[85] Leslie decided to leave her considerable fortune to Catt to use for the suffrage movement in order to provide other women a means to the independence and power she had been able to develop through the publishing business she inherited.

Like Leslie, Alva Belmont also chafed under the control of men. Born in 1853 to affluent slaveholders in Mobile, Alabama, Alva and her family moved to New York and soon began to experience financial difficulties. With the death of her mother in 1871, Alva's father was burdened with four daughters to marry off and little money to do so. Whether Alva married William K. Vanderbilt, grandson of Cornelius Vanderbilt, because she wanted wealth and status, as people claimed, or because she felt obliged to assist her family in the face of impending bankruptcy, as she stated, it is clear that she did not marry for love. Given the stigma attached to divorce in her society, she risked social condemnation when, angry at Willie's sexual indiscretion, she demanded and received a divorce.[86] In 1896, Alva married Oliver Hazard Perry Belmont. Theirs was an apparently happy marriage, which lasted until his death in 1908.

Her unhappy first marriage left her angry about the way men treated women. Belmont resented the attitude that men had toward wives whom they did not respect, leaving women "idle, useless, lonely," and humiliated by their husbands' sexual affairs. She argued that men did not protect women. Any woman who could be cheated on in a marriage and replaced by a younger woman was vulnerable. Furthermore, the oppressive conditions women factory workers endured showed that male bosses did not protect them either. If women could not depend on men, she concluded, then there should be equality between the sexes.[87] "When woman strikes off the traditional shackles of her sex," Belmont proclaimed, "she may joyously exclaim: 'The world is mine!'"[88]

Biographer Sylvia Hoffert concluded that Belmont expressed a similar need for purpose in life as Whitehouse and Ames: "Money allowed her to do anything she wanted. . . . The difference between her and her rich friends, as she saw it, was that while she cared deeply about having money, she also cared deeply about women's rights." While Belmont acknowledged that society women were not idle—in fact, the management of their social lives required skill and time—she thought that they should be putting their efforts and their money to greater purpose.[89]

Given their understanding of the power of money, women like Belmont believed that financial independence was key to women's freedom. Along with other wealthy women, Belmont developed an interest in the plight of working-class women, intertwined with her embrace of suffrage.[90] Belmont believed that despite her wealth, her shared experience of sexism and desire for financial independence increased her commonalities with the labor women in the Shirtwaist Strike of 1909 in New York.[91] Belmont explicitly tied together support for the strike and support for suffrage at a rally for strikers at the Hippodrome, sponsored by her suffrage organization, the Political Equality Association (PEA). As a suffragist, Belmont explained that working-class women needed the vote because as full citizens, they would be treated more fairly in the workplace. Supporting striking factory women in New York helped Belmont understand that as long as women were paid less than men, their work would not be as valued as men's. Conversely, the vote would grant them citizenship that they could then use to back their demands to be on "equal footing in the workplace."[92]

Belmont also advocated that women of wealth, who chafed under the rule of husbands, realize that full citizenship would allow them to reject the sexism that they experienced as well. Wealthy women and women workers were both subject to sex discrimination and needed to join forces to fight for political rights. For Belmont, her upper-class status should have meant that she would be able to "control [her] life and [her] life chances." However, as a woman, she was subject to having someone else—her husband—"determine [her] fate."[93] Her bitterness at this situation led her into the suffrage movement shortly before she began defending the women strikers against what she saw as a similar lack of power. It was clear both to factory workers and to Belmont that economic independence—whether through adequate wages or control over inheritance—was linked to political equality, and that women needed both. "Women of wealth and social power," Belmont wrote, "now believe the suffrage be a necessity for women wage-earners. . . . And having once realized that the ballot means power, these women soon decided . . . that they want this power for themselves, to protect their own interests and to enforce their own will in many directions."[94] Belmont had much in common with other wealthy women, including Ione Hanna and Mary Garrett, who, despite their enormous privilege, experienced the same difficulty exerting independence within their own families or social circle.[95]

Belmont was notable for coming to suffrage influenced by her own needs and experiences and yet expanding her vision of women's political and economic freedoms to include both working-class women and African American women.[96] Belmont was approached by three black women for her assistance organizing a suffrage organization for African American women. Belmont lent her money and her celebrity to them, just as she had to white women. Bringing Ella Crossett of the New York State Woman Suffrage Association with her, the two attended what may have been the first meeting for black suffragists in New York City on February 6, 1910, with several hundred people in attendance. Belmont linked suffrage with civil rights, asserting, "I . . . came because I know that unless this cause means freedom and equal rights to all women of every race, of every creed, rich or poor, its doctrines are worthless, and it must fail in its achievements." A reporter asked her if she "advocate[d] racial as well as political equality," to which she replied yes. Belmont met with the group a second time and paid rent for a space in Harlem for a branch of the PEA.[97] At a time when NAWSA and the other women discussed in this chapter generally ignored African Americans, Belmont's willingness to meet publicly with them and encourage their participation in the movement was remarkable. Belmont's ability to see the needs of others may have come in part from her conviction that "if you are at the top of 'fortune's wheel' you must by every law of human nature aid those not so well placed, for it is only by chance that you are there, and not because of any merit of your own."[98]

Unfortunately, her willingness to champion African American suffragists did not last, and several years later, during a visit to the South, she took the position espoused by Alice Paul—that she was not interested in fighting for racial justice, just equal rights for women. She secretly donated $10,000 to the Southern States Woman Suffrage Conference, which was organized to fight a federal woman suffrage amendment due to fears it would enfranchise black women as well as white women.[99] Thus, like other women in this book, she ultimately did not challenge racism even as she fought sexism.

Other wealthy donors focused on more abstract ideas of equality for women, based less on employment and more on intellectual equality and natural rights. Katharine Dexter McCormick was a 1904 MIT graduate and the wife of Stanley McCormick, the millionaire son from the International Harvester Company family. Shortly after their marriage, Stanley suffered a mental breakdown that resulted in his confinement in a family home in California until his death decades later. Katharine remained in Boston, where she was one of the four original "open-air" speakers, who gave outdoor speeches around the state in 1909, then considered a militant act.[100] The strong-willed and smart McCormick became auditor, treasurer, and then vice president of NAWSA.[101]

McCormick's feminist beliefs stemmed from her education at MIT, the support of her mother, and her independence while her husband was confined. McCormick was among the first women to graduate with a degree in biology from MIT, and while she was there, she had to fight to be taken seriously by professors and fellow students. Her mother, Josephine Dexter, supported her education, and after Stanley's breakdown, the two lived together in Boston and joined the woman suffrage movement. Dexter marched in the first suffrage parade in Boston, and with McCormick, she helped organize the

Katharine Dexter McCormick. Used with permission from
Bryn Mawr College Special Collections.

Bay State Suffrage Festival in 1913. At the same time she had the support of
her mother, McCormick also was free to make decisions without Stanley's
input; for example, she did not need her husband's permission to move to
New York temporarily when she took office in NAWSA. However, as one of
the guardians of Stanley's estate while he was confined, she did need the permission of the court to make donations from his estate until after his death,
when she inherited his fortune.

Like Leslie and Belmont, McCormick wanted freedom for women. She
argued that women without the vote were denied their "political freedom."
But beyond freedom, McCormick focused even more on the equality of men
and women based in their common humanity. "To all," McCormick said of
the suffrage movement, "it gives a wider horizon in the recognition of one
fact—that the broadest human aims and the highest human ideals are an inte-

gral part of the lives of women."[102] Women, she believed, should not be limited by their gender; and moreover, their capabilities were equal to those of men. McCormick also mocked anti-suffrage arguments that women were too emotional, too busy caring for children, and too concerned with being charming to want the vote by turning the arguments on their heads and applying them to men.[103]

Like Ames, Whitehouse, and Belmont, the socializing and charity work expected of society women was not enough for McCormick. She pointed out that participation in the movement offered women "cooperation of the most effective kind with others; it offers responsibility in the life of the community and the nation; it offers opportunity for the most varied and far reaching service." As ratification approached, she asked, "Who shall say we have not the brains and temper to master [the political] realm and to prove that nothing that is human is foreign to us."[104]

McCormick echoed abolitionist and teacher Emily Howland—the daughter of a wealthy farmer, banker, and merchant—who continued to speak at suffrage conventions throughout her eighties, consistently arguing that "women are human beings . . . [and] need human rights. Whatever rights or duties men have discovered to be needful for their well-being as members of the human family are equally a necessity for woman's well-being and doing."[105] Mary Jacobi, Ione Hanna, Mary Garrett, M. Carey Thomas, Vira Whitehouse, Helen Reid, Mrs. Frank Leslie, Alva Belmont, and Katharine McCormick all would have agreed with NAWSA president Catt's definition of feminism as "a world-wide revolt against all artificial barriers between women and human freedom."[106]

UNLIKE THE OTHER WOMEN in this chapter, Katherine Mackay worked to achieve suffrage for women using an increasingly popular argument that dovetailed with women's involvement in progressive reforms as "municipal housekeepers," or moral mothers cleaning up corrupt governments and ensuring that the state provided social services to protect their children. She emphasized women's maternalism rather than their political equality with men.

Mackay was one of the wealthiest and most notable New York women to work with Blatch to make suffrage acceptable among New York society women. Young and beautiful, she was the daughter of William A. and Ellen Travers Duer, both descended from distinguished families. She married IT&T founder Clarence Mackay—the enormously wealthy son of one of the men who struck it rich in the silver mines of the Comstock Lode and started the Postal Telegraph Company, later run by Clarence until he sold it to the International Telegraph & Telegram Company (now ITT). Clarence supported her suffrage work. Katherine was no stranger to activism, as she had both secured a seat on the school board in Roslyn, New York, to improve conditions in the local public schools, and succeeded in her campaign to improve the roads—efforts that raised taxes on the Mackays and other wealthy families in the area.[107]

A relative of suffragist and poet Alice Duer Miller, Katherine converted to the suffrage cause when she read the books suggested for a suffrage debate at the Colony Club.[108] An ardent suffragist, she became vice chair of the 1909 convention of the Woman Suffrage Party of Greater New York. Mackay also formed the Equal Franchise Society (EFS) with Blatch's help. As Blatch explained, Mackay wanted to enter the movement but, accustomed to leadership in society circles, was reluctant to enter an established suffrage organization under someone else's direction. Mackay's goals, according to Ellen DuBois, "were to cultivate support for suffrage among men of wealth and power, and make prosuffrage sentiment socially acceptable in the best circles."[109] Recruiting occurred at luncheons in her home, and eventually the EFS counted among its most well-known members some of New York society's most elite women: Florence Harriman, Anne Harriman Vanderbilt, and Alva Belmont.[110] Membership required that applicants be "vouched for" by current members, in addition to $2.00 annual dues, lowered from the original amount set at $5.00. (By comparison, the CU charged only $0.25.)[111]

Conservative in her approach, Mackay shunned more "militant" tactics such as parades, holding out as the only board member of her own association to refuse to participate in a 1910 parade Blatch organized. Yet Blatch was able to use funds from Mackay's organization to make beautiful banners for the parade. Although Mackay also disapproved of Blatch's desire to heighten her lobbying effort and engage in the business of politics, she paid for an office in Albany and staff to conduct a lobbying campaign in New York State. Despite her dislike for militancy, Mackay was willing to form an organization, answer mail, speak at events, write letters to the newspaper, and donate and raise money.[112]

Mackay's activism, however, was short lived. She grew increasingly uncomfortable with Blatch's growing political engagement. Maybe more significant to her exit from the movement was her personal life. She had an affair with Dr. Joseph Blake, moved to Paris with him and divorced her husband, and did not return to New York until 1930.[113] Like Mackay, there were other wealthy women who faded away quickly or never did much more than attend a luncheon or donate money; most, however, were committed to the cause until ratification. Some were even arrested for their activism.

Mackay was unusual among wealthy donors for her explicit embrace of maternalism. In the 1890s, Josephine Lowell had also emphasized women's inherent morality, but as women rather than mothers. Lowell also focused on the needs of working women and protection from domestic violence. In contrast, Mackay declared that women had a particular need for the vote as mothers, as a way to preserve their home and protect their children. She claimed that women would inject morality into government and sought the vote not for themselves but for their children's sake.[114] "The mothers of the country," she said, "who surely know and care most about the conditions that affect the education, recreation, exemption from work, correction and health of these children, should have something to say in the framing of such laws."[115]

Mackay also downplayed equality with men in favor of highlighting women's femininity. An article about her concluded that an ultrafeminine woman like Mackay could do much to bring success to the movement by demonstrating that suffragists did not want to be like men. "Many women think it would be unfeminine to vote," she said, "but it needn't be at all. When it comes to the actual casting of the ballot, I can think of a dozen ways to make it as attractive as a bridge party."[116]

Notably, this espousal of maternalism made Mackay exceptional. The other wealthy suffragists discussed here called for suffrage in order to advance women's education, economic independence, and power in society. For example, according to biographer Helen Horowitz, Carey Thomas "was not interested in women reforming society but in women attaining their rights."[117] Privileged in race and class, these women chafed against the sexism they experienced, especially their "political impotence."[118] As Ione Hanna had bitterly suggested, they did not want to be "pensioners" but sought the same political opportunities as men. Most also pushed for other rights for women, including equal pay in the workforce, access to higher education and the professions, and birth control. For many wealthy women, their own experiences with the power of money helped them understand the importance of political power and economic equality for wage-earning women. They expressed the need for a sense of purpose on the part of wealthy women who found their social lives devoid of meaning, and the understanding that economic independence was crucial for all women, whether working-class wage earners, educated professionals, or inheritors of large fortunes.

Restoring the place of wealthy suffragists in the story of the suffrage movement should therefore push historians to reassess the feminist ideology of the movement. The rise of the maternalist argument, a less threatening discourse than equality, nevertheless existed alongside continued claims for equality. Historian Aileen Kraditor's portrayal of the dominance of the maternalist argument after 1900 has been rejected by historians as exaggerated. The wide array of arguments for suffrage is evident in NAWSA publications, in the pages of the pro-suffrage *Woman's Journal*, and in the testimony suffragists offered at congressional hearings.[119]

Placing wealthy suffragists' demands for the vote, based on equality and independence, alongside those of maternalist reformers underscores the diversity of convictions among suffragists. Wealthy women's experiences with sexism, and their realization that economic independence and political equality were linked, infused their support for the movement. They continued to push for gender equality, even when it was expedient and less threatening to call for a mother's right to protect her children. Their disproportionate support for equality over maternalism suggests that resentment against wealthy donors may have arisen in part from a divide in ideology between some suffragists and the women who financed the movement.

The ideology of wealthy suffragists is also important because wealthy women garnered press coverage that other women could not always command. When women like Garrett and Belmont spoke about suffrage, newspapers eagerly quoted them. Thus, they had the ability to influence public sentiment and counter the maternalist rhetoric offered by others. Suffragists and anti-suffragists alike encountered Thomas's and Belmont's opinions in many journal and newspaper articles, with Belmont even writing a column for the *Chicago Tribune*. Howland, McCormick, Thomas, and Belmont were particularly sought-after speakers, who gave speeches at many local and national conventions, where they reached delegates and the public at evening sessions.

Purposely recruiting monied women into the suffrage movement succeeded in garnering free publicity and making the cause more popular in the early twentieth century. These women's ideas about feminism and suffrage were crucial to the debate over women's political rights. However, suffragists needed the money these women gave as much as their celebrity and speeches. NAWSA and the CU still had much work to do to push men to change laws so that women could vote. The Garrett-Thomas fund, as well as large donations from McCormick, Leslie, and Belmont, was needed to pay for old and new strategies and tactics. The money, however, caused dissension in the movement, as donors and officers struggled with the power the money wielded. Chapter 2 thus turns to the power of the purse, examining the tactics and strategies these donations financed, as well as the demands made by the donors themselves. While some donors gave anonymously or through a bequest at death, leaving power in the hands of officers, others engendered resentment when they tried to influence suffrage organization leadership and strategy, and even inserted themselves as officeholders. Their gifts forced suffragists to consider equality among women even as they fought for political power alongside men.

CHAPTER TWO

Unequal Women Working for Women's Equality

Power and Resentment in the Woman Suffrage Movement

Warren, Ohio, a small town of approximately eleven thousand, was home to the National American Woman Suffrage Association (NAWSA) headquarters in 1909. Treasurer Harriet Taylor Upton had a desk in her house, from which she corresponded and collected funds, while president Anna Howard Shaw traveled the country, making speeches and rallying supporters. Upton, who had joined NAWSA after meeting Susan B. Anthony and had served as treasurer since 1894, was accustomed to running the organization on a shoe-string budget. When New York socialite and millionaire Alva Vanderbilt Belmont joined NAWSA, she looked askance at Upton's homemade operation. NAWSA, Belmont declared, needed headquarters that could command the type of publicity necessary to start winning victories for woman suffrage once again. She offered to pay for a new headquarters, furnished and staffed with a paid press bureau, on the condition that NAWSA move to New York. Donations like Belmont's—with the benefits they provided and the resentment they engendered—are the subject of this chapter.

The financial contributions of donors like Belmont and the other monied women introduced in chapter 1 were critical to the timing and success of the woman suffrage movement. Wealthy women's increased involvement in the suffrage campaign helped draw the movement out of the doldrums after 1906 and was crucial to the victory in 1920. Attention to the significance of finances, often overlooked by historians focused on leadership and ideology, sheds new light on how the fight for the right to vote was led. It also reveals the importance of fund-raising in the split between NAWSA and the CU, which began as an affiliate of NAWSA before becoming a rival organization.

The power of the purse controlled the contours of the suffrage movement. When suffragists worked state by state, each state competed for financial assistance from the national organization. Suffragists needed funds to pay the salaries of traveling organizers, who campaigned across the states, and to print newspapers and create publicity aimed at changing public opinion. The infusion of money into the movement paid for these essentials. Donors, or the officers they funded, could direct money to the states of their choice, thus influencing which states had the necessary coffers to run successful campaigns. Wealthy contributors thus had the potential to affect the timing and success of state suffrage referendums.

Furthermore, donors shaped the tactics and strategies employed by suffrage organizations. They used their money to promote new tactics, such as parades and pickets; insist on headquarters moving closer to the powerful New York media or Congress in Washington D.C.; and champion (or axe) newspapers and other publicity tools. They financed new strategies, like NAWSA president Carrie Chapman Catt's Winning Plan, which combined lobbying for a federal amendment with continued organization in selected states, and CU president Alice Paul's militant lobbying against the political party in power.

Contributors had much say over who ran the movement. They could control who held office in the national organizations by paying salaries, tying donations to specific officeholders, and driving those who resented them or were incapable of the same bounty out of office. Anonymous or bequeathed donations similarly empowered certain officers, who would then have access to money they could spend as they liked. Catt, for example, was able to finance her Winning Plan only because of a million-dollar bequest from Mrs. Frank Leslie at her death.

NAWSA and the CU, however, paid a price for the money they received. The in-fighting among NAWSA officers increased dramatically with the influence of outsized donations by extremely wealthy suffragists in the 1910s, in part because the new donors did not give freely; they wanted the requisite power they believed their hefty contributions should command. Contributors had strong ideas about how their money should be spent and who should lead the organization, which engendered fights over who controlled the money: the donors or the organization. Due to these controversies, several NAWSA officers resigned, bitterly complaining about the power of money in the movement. The CU also experienced tension over the demands of donors. Organizations working for women's rights struggled when wealthy women had more say than other women. Their historical lack of power due to gender sensitized other women against the disproportionate influence of rich women.

Women, in particular, had to consider whether fighting against sexism implied a goal of equality across class (and race) as well as gender. The divide among wealthy, middle-class, and working-class women in the movement raised a question still under debate today, regarding whether feminism should be inherently democratic and nonhierarchical—and what happens when it is not.[1] Feminist organizations have been defined as "collectives whereby all members have equal voice in the decisions of the organization, and the organization proceeds only after consensus is reached."[2] To fulfill this ideal, women's funds today strive to include grant recipients in the decision-making process. But if wealthy donors to the suffrage movement made demands that defied consensus, did that jeopardize the effort to work for women's political equality? As one newspaper noted in 1894, attracting society women meant that "parlor meetings" could have "a degree of exclusiveness . . . that seems to be incompatible with the object to be achieved."[3]

Moreover, controversy was heightened because the infusion of money into the suffrage movement came at a moment when the country was deep in debate over "money power," as it closely followed a government investigation into J. Pierpont Morgan's banking practices. At stake was the question of how much power individuals and their private enterprises should have over the American (and global) economy, and where government oversight should begin.[4] The concern extended from men like Morgan as businessmen to their philanthropy as well, with a 1914 congressional commission investigating the power of foundations tied to industrialists.[5] The fundamental question was, according to historians Steve Fraser and Gary Gerstle, "How can a nation consecrated to freedom and equality nonetheless give rise to great hierarchies of power and wealth that undermine the very foundations of that extraordinary promise?"[6] The disproportionate power of elites, it was feared, could jeopardize democracy. In the 1910s, with industrial workers continuing decades of dissent and Theodore Roosevelt advocating trust-busting, it is perhaps not surprising that suffragists exhibited similar suspicion of wealthy women who appeared to be buying control of the movement. Furthermore, resentment was undoubtedly exacerbated by society's fundamental discomfort with women having financial clout: wealthy women were traditionally seen as consumers or benevolent charity workers but not as wielders of economic power.[7]

Historians Ellen DuBois and Sara Graham have noted the disproportionate influence of wealthy suffragists and the ways that their donations, used to organize and centralize NAWSA, had the ability to limit the organization's grassroots democratic nature. Examining Harriot Stanton Blatch's attempts to recruit both working-class and upper-class women in New York in 1908–9, DuBois concluded, "The resources upper-class women brought to suffragism— their wealth, connections to men of power, and cultural capacity to signify changing femininity—eventually gave them the wherewithal to control the movement, as against the historical initiative and numerical strength of working-class women."[8]

This chapter moves beyond DuBois's study of Blatch and Graham's treatment of NAWSA to examine the benefits and costs of the influx of money to NAWSA and the CU in the early 1900s. It demonstrates how essential these large donations were to winning the right to vote by enabling the suffrage organizations to increase publicity, pay for traveling organizers, and fund new tactics, thus shaping the state-by-state and federal strategies. Yet it also examines the costs of these donations, when monied women fostered resentment by their ability to wield the power of the purse. In particular, it focuses on the influence of Alva Belmont and Katharine McCormick, looking closely at the demands they made and the ways their money seemed to control NAWSA and the CU. Even as wealthy women made victory for suffrage possible, they also engendered resentment.

As was evident in chapter 1, monied women came to the suffrage movement with an emphasis on sisterhood, stemming from shared experiences of gender discrimination despite class privilege, and a call for all women to have economic and political independence. Yet this vision of gender equality seemed hollow when some women had more power than others. Foregrounding the problems caused by class divisions shows how difficult overcoming differences—whether class, race, ethnicity, region, religion, sexuality, or other—among women was. This story is critical to the efforts that women's organizations and foundations still make today to lessen these problems, increase inclusiveness, and share power equally among women as they fight for equal power with men.

Focusing on finances and fund-raising also offers a new approach to understanding the division between NAWSA and the CU.[9] Historians have traditionally highlighted the ideological and strategic differences between Carrie Catt and NAWSA and Alice Paul and the CU. While these were significant, the two also fought over funding. Given the importance of money to the movement, it is not surprising that NAWSA officers resented the CU's fund-raising ability and wanted to control their finances.

ONE OF THE MOST important items the new large donations paid for was salaries, which Elizabeth Cady Stanton and Susan B. Anthony had identified as the major expense (along with publicity) of the movement as early as the 1860s.[10] The money that wealthy women gave not only allowed for additional staffers but also changed who was eligible to hold office in NAWSA, opening the presidency to women who earned their own wages. Furthermore, funding for traveling organizers determined which states would have assistance from NAWSA to run effective local campaigns.

The question around officer salaries was complicated by the idealist but unrealistic idea that suffragists should volunteer their time for the cause. Quoting Wendell Phillips, Stanton claimed, "A reformer, to be conscientious, must be free from bread-winning."[11] Traditionally, suffrage associations hired paid traveling organizers but usually did not pay their officers, who were expected to cover the costs of their own correspondence and travel. Well-off officers could do so. Catt, president of NAWSA from 1900 to 1904 and 1915 to 1920, and of the International Woman Suffrage Alliance from 1905 to 1914, had money from her second husband, George Catt, a civil engineer. She did not receive a salary from either organization. Alice Paul's father owned a farm and was a banker in New Jersey. After his death, her mother sent Alice monthly checks to pay her expenses while she ran the CU.[12]

Anna Shaw, on the other hand, had to support herself, which initially kept her from being considered for the presidency of NAWSA. When Anthony wanted Shaw to replace Catt after her first term, she had to solicit funds to pay Shaw a salary.[13] Shaw's biographer, Trisha Franzen, argues that despite Anthony's backing, some leaders never fully accepted the idea of salaries for officers, and problems that Shaw later encountered in her presidency were due in part to these women's resulting distrust of the salaried president.[14] When officers were paid, controversy over their elections also increased. Southern and western women objected to the preponderance of eastern officers, who received salaries. "The fact that the money to pay these salaries," Shaw sniped, "was subscribed by eastern women does not seem to affect the objectors."[15]

Shaw herself depended heavily on easterners M. Carey Thomas and Mary Garrett. Thomas and Garrett were initially drawn into the movement by Anthony when they met in advance of bringing the NAWSA convention to Baltimore in 1906. The elderly and ill Anthony appealed to them to help NAWSA achieve financial stability. They committed to her to raise $60,000: $12,000 annually for five years, which was used in large part to pay NAWSA officer salaries, including $3,500 to Shaw and $1,000 each to the secretary and treasurer.[16]

In comparison, while the national average salary in 1910 was only $750, trade unionists could earn as much as $1,200, and professionals—such as accountants, dentists, and engineers—earned between $2,000 and $5,000 annually. Women's salaries were less: female schoolteachers, for example, averaged $55 a month.[17] Large donations therefore allowed NAWSA to pay officers and organizers generously.

Salaries for traveling organizers were another major expense. The suffrage movement from the 1880s through the early 1910s focused on winning the right to vote through the states, which depended on local and national organizers barnstorming each state to drum up publicity and lobby local politicians. Paid organizers worked full time, giving public speeches, organizing rallies, speaking to women's groups, and helping organize local suffrage associations. These organizers brought experience and the ability to draw a crowd.

Neither local chapters nor the national suffrage organizations had enough funding to pay the significant salaries required. The situation was exacerbated, according to historian Lisa Tetrault, because women could earn a living through the lyceum lecture circuit from the late 1860s through the early 1880s. Women came to expect similar lucrative payments for an appearance at a woman suffrage convention. Suffrage organizations thus had to compete with the lecture circuit when they paid for traveling speakers. Anna Shaw, for example, had made more money lecturing than NAWSA paid her.[18] As nineteenth-century feminist and suffragist Lucy Stone observed, "There would be plenty of helpers if there was plenty of money to pay." Thus, NAWSA had to raise enough funds to pay a large staff of traveling organizers.[19]

The difficulty funding state campaigns continued into the early 1900s. At the 1907 NAWSA convention, for example, officers announced that total association receipts for 1906 were $18,203 and that they had spent $18,075 on the Oregon campaign for a suffrage referendum. Even though $8,000 was raised specifically for Oregon, the expenditure on the state meant that NAWSA had well overspent its revenue and had to take money from its reserve fund. After Oregon lost the campaign, NAWSA refused a request for an additional $2,000 to try again.[20]

Anna Shaw relied heavily on one significant donor, Pauline Agassiz Shaw—who shared her last name but no family connections—to pay for traveling organizers to the states. The daughter of naturalist Louis Agassiz, Pauline had married Quincy A. Shaw, owner of the Calumet and Hecla mines, who died in 1908. She supported kindergartens, day nurseries, training schools, and civic education in addition to woman suffrage.[21] Shaw began giving to the suffrage movement through a Boston committee founded to raise funds for western state campaigns.[22] Her contributions were essential to many states. "One closely associated with her," a tribute to her asserted, "ventures the guess that Mrs. Shaw's contributions probably footed up to more than one half of all that was given by the East to the Western states."[23] Yet the self-effacing Shaw gave anonymously and without restrictions, granting power to the officers to spend her money as they liked.

Pauline Shaw's donations demonstrate one way that contributions shaped the movement: whoever controlled distribution of the money could determine which states would receive the most funding to hire traveling organizers for state campaigns. Pauline Shaw sent two checks reportedly totaling $30,000 (over $707,700 in 2016) and over 75 percent of the entire NAWSA budget in 1913 but left Anna Shaw free to spend it where she saw fit. Known as "Miss [Anna] Shaw's special fund," because Pauline Shaw wished to remain anonymous, the bounty came to Anna Shaw unexpectedly and without strings. Anna Shaw chose to pay for organizers to travel to Arizona, Kansas, Oregon, Wisconsin, Michigan, North Dakota, Montana, Ohio, and Nevada.[24]

Pauline Shaw also quietly paid the salary of organizers in Massachusetts, including Maud Wood Park. Shaw commanded organizers to take as much as she generously offered—often more than they asked for—and to keep the arrangement secret. Sending Park an additional $125 to bring her salary to $2,000 annually, Shaw reminded Park to keep the extra money "entirely between you and me."[25] Ten years later, Shaw exhorted Park, "You know I am willing to help further in the campaign fund when it comes to final needs or deficits—so don't leave anything undone that money can provide for—(*and don't tell anybody except yourself*) but don't tax yourself too much."[26] Shaw generously let the organizers spend as they needed, without directing them.

The states were so desperate for funding that even with Pauline Shaw's generous donation, NAWSA could not keep up with their demands. Finances were a problem, in part because so many states paid so little in dues to the national organization. Kentucky, for example, was the only southern state whose members sent more than $10 in dues.[27]

The results of this spending at the state level were mixed: while states like Arizona, Kansas, Oregon, Montana, and Nevada granted full suffrage in 1912 or 1914, women in states like Wisconsin and North Dakota had to wait for the Nineteenth Amendment to pass in 1920 for the right to vote. Michigan's 1912 campaign failed; according to suffragists, defeat was due to election irregularities. As for suffrage referendum defeats in other states, Catt blamed the liquor lobbyists, who thought women would vote for temperance laws, and called for greater spending to compete with them. The 1912 Ohio campaign, for example, failed when suffragists spent about $40,000 but the liquor lobby reportedly spent $630,000.[28] Decisions over which states merited financial support from NAWSA were rife with tension. Regional alliances, personalities, and the likelihood of success all played a role. Although circumstances in each state varied, Pauline Shaw's funding played a significant role in the successes in western states.

WHEREAS PAULINE SHAW'S DONATIONS were anonymous and without strings, the influx of money to the movement also came from donors who

Alva Belmont (left) and Alice Paul. Used with permission from National Woman's Party at the Belmont-Paul Women's Equality National Monument, Washington, D.C.

wanted the power they thought their donations earned them. One of the movement's largest contributors, Alva Vanderbilt Belmont, was also one of its most demanding. Her coercive giving caused the growing dissension within NAWSA to explode. After divorcing William K. Vanderbilt, she married Oliver H. P. Belmont, a marriage that lasted until his death in 1908.[29] Now a wealthy widow, she had a large inheritance and the freedom to spend it as she wished. Given her fierce resentment of women's subordinate position in society, she quickly embraced the cause.[30]

Belmont first encountered the suffrage movement in 1908 through socialite Katherine Mackay, who invited Belmont to attend a meeting held at New York's exclusive Colony Club. In 1909, following her return from London's

International Woman Suffrage Alliance meeting, where she first met Anna Shaw, Belmont accepted another invitation from Mackay to hear a lecture by NAWSA historian Ida Harper. After that, Belmont followed Harper to NAWSA meetings and eventually invited Anna Shaw to dine.[31] Shaw later said, "We staid [sic] and talked suffrage until nearly one o'clock. . . . We talked so late that I missed my train . . . but I got her for a life member of the National Association. . . . I think she will help us financially by and by."[32] Belmont's life membership dues payment was her first financial commitment to the organization.

Belmont understood the power of money and was more willing than many female philanthropists to tie demands to her gifts. Angry with the control men had over women's lives, and used to having her own way, she embraced a militant feminism and a coercive philanthropic style. She argued that women needed to cease being cowards and instead be more like the militant English suffragists. Biographer Amanda Stuart claimed, "Alva's experience of genteel poverty thus far had made her almost as 'inflamed' on the subject of money as the Commodore [Cornelius Vanderbilt]. Like him she was acutely aware of its power. She once tried to persuade Sara Bard Field to marry a rich man for the benefit of her children saying: 'You cannot help your children to advantages through sentimental romance but through money alone which has power.'"[33]

In 1909, Belmont offered to pay the rent for a new headquarters for NAWSA, but only if it moved from Warren, Ohio, to New York. She promised $7,200 for two years to cover rent for the headquarters and the national press bureau (separate offices on the same floor of 505 Fifth Avenue, alongside the New York state headquarters) as well as other expenses, including furnishing and partitioning the offices, and salaries for the press bureau.[34] Though the move to New York was strategic—Belmont knew the movement would get more newspaper coverage there than in Warren—the strings that Belmont attached to her donation caused an insurrection at NAWSA.[35]

A dramatic newspaper article in 1909 claimed that "a crisis is imminent," due in large part to the overwhelming "dominance" of Belmont. While admiring her political abilities, the article asserted that NAWSA was receiving letters from women all over the country who believed that Belmont, "whose social position and wealth, together with a close knowledge of the political field and amazing talent for making propaganda," might buy her way into office in NAWSA.[36] The article captured the problem suffragists faced: they needed Belmont's money and her talents, but they resented the power she commanded.

Because middle-class women had long dominated the movement, suffragists feared the appearance of control by the wealthy would squeeze out traditional supporters. A similar split had occurred over fifteen years earlier when NAWSA first instituted the "society plan" to recruit wealthy women. Some suffragists had rejected the plan as elitist.[37] Treasurer Upton now thought the attention to Belmont meant that middle-class women no longer felt compelled to send small contributions.[38] This was an important point. Suffragists had to consider whether the ultimate goal of obtaining the right to vote overrode the importance of bringing millions of women together in common cause.

The influx of wealthy women also threatened another new source of support: working-class women. Some suffragists now complained that in trying to appeal to society women, the movement had begun to keep out anyone designated as disreputable, including socialists. For example, in a letter to the *New York Times*, Maud Malone complained that speakers who were not liked by officers or who were affiliated with socialism were kept off the platform because "the present policy of the union is: First, 'to attract a well-dressed crowd, not the rabble.' "[39] Malone and other working-class women had a valid critique. While they continued to advocate for the vote, their role in NAWSA and the CU grew more limited as wealthy women grew more powerful.

Belmont's contributions also challenged the makeup of the leadership of the national organization. Many NAWSA officers were up in arms against Belmont. NAWSA's move to New York displaced Upton. She bitterly complained that although coverage increased under the new press bureau, NAWSA was paying five times as much in expenses, and press releases were highlighting Belmont in favor of other loyal suffragists.[40] She and other southern and western women resented the growing influence of Belmont and the New York suffragists, with Upton writing to Thomas to complain, "New York women seem to think they own the National." Thomas, however, thought that Belmont was "entitled to express her opinion, not only because she has the general interest of the cause at heart, but because she is contributing ten thousand dollars a year to it."[41]

Belmont also stipulated that Ida Harper, her first contact with NAWSA leadership, remain chair of the press bureau, threatening to lower her contribution unless Harper remained on staff. Harper admitted that if she left, "the money given would be reduced by $173.33 a month" (her salary).[42] Despite her salary being dependent on Belmont's donations, Harper reported, "Mrs. Belmont never attempts because of her financial assistance to exercise any supervision over the bureau, never dictates to it in the slightest degree, and never asks the smallest favor. . . . Her large donations are purely a freewill offering to the cause." Harper concluded, "Mrs. Belmont's contribution was most enthusiastically received by the convention," and denied newspaper reports of dissension at NAWSA.[43] When Harper finally did leave the press bureau, Belmont cut her donation. NAWSA was left with only $336.67 a month to pay the remaining workers, clipping service and telephone bills, and rent. Shaw had to ask Belmont to send the $173.33 monthly. She sent it directly to Shaw, who spent it as she saw fit.[44]

Officers also feared that Belmont's celebrity could undermine the movement, although this did not turn out to be true. Frances Squire Potter, corresponding secretary in 1909, objected to patronage, which would cause NAWSA to "lose its own and other people's respect."[45] Auditor Laura Clay feared that Belmont was not sincere about her commitment and that the publicity surrounding Belmont would result in the public's taking NAWSA less seriously. She worried "the chief impression we are making on the uninformed public is that we are a protégé of Mrs. Belmont, and the public are [sic] amused in calculating how long she will be pleased with her toy."[46]

Belmont's restricted giving was so contentious an issue among convention goers and the NAWSA board that it finally resulted in resignations. The *Daily Oklahoman* reported that Shaw "is strongly in favor of having prominent society women and women of wealth identified actively with the suffrage work." Others, however, were opposed to this policy, believing that, in the long run, the movement would "suffer more than it [would] gain by such help."[47] Treasurer Upton and VP Rachel Avery were so angry about changes made to please Belmont that they resigned from NAWSA the following year.[48]

Belmont's agreement to donate money for rent lasted only two years. In 1911, when the lease was up two months before the convention, she announced that she would no longer foot the entire bill herself, decreasing her share of the rent payment. (She offered instead to pay $1,000 toward the rent for a six-month lease.) While Clay and others were ready for NAWSA headquarters to leave New York, the state association wanted NAWSA to stay, as did Thomas in her role as president of the College Equal Suffrage League (CESL). An offer from Thomas provided an additional $1,400 to help make up the difference (in exchange for secretarial help for the CESL).[49] Having earlier demanded that Harper retain her position, Belmont now required Anna Shaw to remain president, further antagonizing Clay and others who wanted to replace Shaw, due to both her relationship with Belmont and other conflicts.[50]

The controversy grew more heated over a proposal to require the board to meet once a month at New York headquarters, a burden for southern and western officers, including Clay. Thomas suggested that NAWSA establish a fund for the officers who had to travel long distances. The suggestion caused a commotion at the convention because delegates mistakenly believed that the Garrett-Thomas fund would be used for the travel fund (a misunderstanding that Thomas cleared up only when she revealed that she was one of the anonymous donors willing to finance a separate travel fund).[51] The proposal further infuriated Clay, who sniped, "We would be unworthy suffragists to accept money with a string attached to it, and I wouldn't think so much of it, if it were the first time this kind of appropriation had been made to us," alluding to Belmont's first gift. Compromise was reached: the board was to meet every other month, and Belmont removed her condition that Shaw remain president. Belmont provided funding for an additional six months. However, discontent with Belmont's ability to dictate conditions with her dollars continued to increase.[52]

With tension over Belmont's demands at a fever pitch, NAWSA gained a new donor: Katharine McCormick. McCormick's donations lessened Belmont's impact on NAWSA, but controversy surrounded McCormick from her election to her first national office. This tension reveals more of the resentment many suffragists voiced against the powerful roles of Belmont and other rich women. It took two rounds of voting by the other NAWSA officers to confirm McCormick's nomination as first auditor in March 1912.[53] An exchange among officers reveals that NAWSA secretary Mary Ware Dennett resented McCormick's presence at the meeting where the voting took place, because McCormick should not have been invited to a board meeting until after she was elected to office. Dennett thought that by attending, McCormick made the election a formality. Although it was not Thomas who had invited her to attend, Dennett referred to "Thomas's control of 'the machine.'"[54]

Three months earlier, Mary Gray Peck—in an article on suffragists published in *Life and Labor*, the journal of the National Women's Trade Union League—also criticized Thomas's politics in NAWSA. Peck described Thomas as having "adroitness in bringing things to pass diplomatically as she wishes them to be," which Peck argued "puts her in the category of those who work for democracy in theory, while they act practically along the line of the divine right of rulers." She complained that Thomas's growing power was evident in her control over recent NAWSA elections and "the announcement of special contributions to the cause at special times."[55] Echoing these

"Mrs. Stanley McCormick and Mrs. Chas. Parker." Katharine Dexter McCormick (left) at a suffrage rally. Courtesy of Library of Congress Prints and Photographs Division, LC-DIG-ggbain-12694.

complaints, Dennett regretted that NAWSA was beholden to Thomas "for her courtesy and hospitality—and to Mrs. McCormick for her generosity." In fact, one of the main reasons Thomas had approved of McCormick was that she thought she might be willing to make a substantial donation.[56] Clearly Peck and Dennett were right. Money did provide Thomas the power to help determine NAWSA's leadership.

McCormick almost immediately became embroiled in controversy over NAWSA's desire to publish a magazine. The organization had signed a contract with Alice Blackwell—editor of the *Woman's Journal*, a decades-old suffrage magazine—in 1910. The contract made the magazine NAWSA's official organ, retained Blackwell as editor, and pledged to pay her salary. The magazine, however, had been running at an annual deficit, which NAWSA exacerbated by increasing spending in order to drive up circulation, which was still under twenty thousand in 1912, when McCormick took office.

NAWSA quickly realized that it could not afford the money-losing *Woman's Journal*. Anna Shaw admitted in despair, "We are confronted with financial disaster unless something is done at once." She thought the only solution was to fire staff and move headquarters out of New York. Noting that Thomas was unable to raise funds because she was busy caring for an ill Garrett and that Belmont had begun cutting donations and was "out of helping," Shaw concluded, "All hope of raising money is gone and we can no longer run up bills honestly which we have no prospect of paying."[57] The NAWSA board organized an unsuccessful drive for one thousand $100 donations and asked McCormick, who was now treasurer, and other officers to come up with a solution for the magazine.[58] Contemplating the $9,000 debt NAWSA had incurred due to *Woman's Journal* expenses, McCormick "reported that it seemed to her impossible for the National to carry the responsibility of an organ which it did not own and, therefore, could not control." She proposed that NAWSA drop the magazine.[59]

Discussion of the magazine at the 1912 convention caused a commotion among the delegates, many of whom sympathized with Blackwell.[60] Despite the controversy, McCormick's view won out. NAWSA and Blackwell terminated the contract and established the Literature Company, a separate stock company (with five thousand shares of stock sold at $10 each), to run the magazine. The *Woman's Journal* remained in business, still edited by Blackwell, though it was no longer NAWSA's official organ.[61]

McCormick began a series of large donations to NAWSA: $6,000 to pay off debt from the *Woman's Journal*, and $1,000 or $2,000 annual contributions thereafter, with her mother matching her contribution and doubling her impact.[62] She moved to New York to make it easier to attend NAWSA board meetings, renting an office in the city for her work as treasurer. In 1914 she proposed moving to the space used by NAWSA headquarters and the Literature Company, offering to put $600—the same amount she was spending to rent her office—toward NAWSA and the Literature Company's rent to help cut costs.[63] These were substantial contributions, and they came at a time when Alva Belmont was pulling back on hers.

As treasurer, McCormick was responsible for raising funds as well as tracking expenditures and revenue for the annual budget.[64] The lack of funding was "paralyz[ing]," according to McCormick, who worried constantly about funding.[65] She confessed that she was unwilling to hire organizers or speakers without money in hand to pay them. She was continually trying to figure out how to pay salaries of organizers in different states—who to send where for how much. She rejected the suggestion that NAWSA hire organizers and "trust to luck to raise" the money.[66]

If raising enough revenue to meet expectations was too difficult, a wealthy treasurer like McCormick could simply donate the money herself. McCormick's generosity to NAWSA, then, may have resulted from a realization that it was easier simply to give the money personally than to raise it or cut expenses. But crucially for NAWSA, if the treasurer had to supply the treasury, this severely circumscribed who could hold office. Together with questions over the propriety of paying a salary to Shaw, NAWSA thus became mired in controversy over funding and officers. Women without the fortunes of McCormick and Belmont resented the perception that women could buy their way into NAWSA leadership.

The outspoken McCormick also played a significant role in forcing the militant Alice Paul and the CU out of NAWSA. Paul had an uncompromising approach to suffrage, which included such tactics as parades and White House pickets. She prioritized lobbying for the federal amendment as well as punishing the political party in power. At the time, NAWSA officers were focused on the state-by-state approach rather than the federal amendment, as this preceded the development of Catt's Winning Plan, which combined state and federal strategies. Appointed the new chairperson of the NAWSA congressional committee to lobby for a federal amendment, Paul soon created a Congressional Union for Woman Suffrage (CU) to solicit support for the amendment from women around the country. Initially she ran both the NAWSA congressional committee and the CU, but the CU split apart from NAWSA entirely, eventually becoming the National Woman's Party.[67]

Catt, McCormick, and other NAWSA officers also disapproved of Paul's militancy and political strategy. Despite pioneering open-air speeches in Massachusetts, McCormick protested Paul's militancy. Paul was influenced by time spent in England working with militant English suffragists. In a letter to the *New York Times*, which the paper titled "On Militant Women: Treasurer of National Suffrage Body Says It Is Dumb," McCormick refused to put the weight of NAWSA behind the efforts of English suffragists.[68] She and Catt later condemned Paul's tactics, especially the White House pickets, as being too militant.

More significant than McCormick's objection to militancy was her resentment of the money Paul raised. McCormick's involvement in the conflict between the two groups highlights the role that money played, in addition to the ideological differences usually stressed. Put simply, the CU bested NAWSA at soliciting donations. Because NAWSA in 1913 favored a state-by-state strategy rather than a federal amendment, the organization focused its funds on the states, and the congressional committee had only a ten-dollar budget. Therefore Paul, appointed head of the NAWSA congressional committee in 1912, had to raise funds to pay for the more extensive activities she planned.[69] Harriot Blatch thought that NAWSA had tried "to choke [the CU] at birth" by not backing it financially, providing only an out-of-date list of Washington, D.C., members from whom to solicit money.[70] Raising money quickly was key because the CU needed rent for a larger office and funds to hold a parade (which cost approximately $14,000) the day before Woodrow Wilson's inauguration, only several months away.[71]

The CU succeeded in gaining over $12,000 in contributions in addition to ticket and literature sales, totaling over $25,000 in funding, which went into its coffers—and under its control—rather than NAWSA's.[72] This was a significant amount of money raised in a very short period of time. Paul realized the power of such a purse. She understood that the CU's ability to amass such a large amount of money could serve as leverage in talks with NAWSA officers. Rather than appearing weak, the CU could negotiate from a position of power. She noted, "If we could only raise about ten or twelve thousand . . . I think they would probably be ready to agree to anything we propose."[73]

McCormick knew how desperately needed those dollars were and how difficult it was to raise that significant a sum. McCormick did not think unlimited funds were available to solicit, and she did not want to lose NAWSA donors—or potential donors—to the CU. Paul later recalled that the problem also stemmed from their different views of how funds should be spent. According to Paul, McCormick wanted all the money raised to go to state campaigns, rather than be used on a parade in Washington to promote the national amendment.[74] Paul recalled that some officers at NAWSA supported the idea of the parade, but "they were always harping on the fact that they couldn't afford to pay anything toward it." She described McCormick as "the one who was always afraid of our sending the bills in."[75]

In her convention report as treasurer and in a statement she prepared afterward, McCormick focused on the CU's fund-raising and criticized its lack of accountability to her as NAWSA treasurer.[76] After Catt questioned why the CU had raised over $25,000 and not passed it through the national treasury, McCormick proclaimed herself "seriously embarrassed" by the lack of reporting and criticized Paul for being unwilling to make—or for not understanding what it meant to make—"financial connections" between the CU and NAWSA. Although the board of NAWSA agreed to allow Paul wide latitude in her activities so as not to squash her momentum, McCormick snippily complained that she disagreed with this approach. If the CU was raising money in the name of NAWSA, then McCormick believed the CU owed a full accounting to NAWSA—or to McCormick as NAWSA treasurer.[77]

In response, Paul accused McCormick of insinuating that the CU was guilty of financial irregularity, produced documents to show that the CU had in fact been in touch with McCormick, and called it "past reprehensible" that McCormick's only response was that she needed to check her files for the documents.[78] The battle between the two was so acerbic that McCormick at one point turned her chair around so that she would not have to face Paul.

Initially, NAWSA demanded that the CU abide by certain requirements if it were to stay part of NAWSA. The first concerned money: "That no money shall be raised by the Congressional Union in the name of the National Association without the knowledge and consent of the National Treasurer." Furthermore, the CU was not to use NAWSA stationery for fund-raising because it led to confusion. McCormick noted that NAWSA supporters were mistakenly sending money intended for NAWSA to CU headquarters.[79] The second demand was over turf: that CU organizers not enter the states without the knowledge and consent of state associations. This, too, was related to funding. Shaw was concerned enough about the CU's growing popularity that she was trying to send more NAWSA organizers into the field to combat the "falsities" she accused Paul of spreading, at a cost of $150 salary plus $150 traveling expenses monthly.[80] As treasurer, McCormick was one of four NAWSA representatives who planned to meet with Paul to discuss NAWSA's proposed requirements for the CU. Negotiations over these demands went nowhere, however, and Paul and the CU ultimately cut ties to NAWSA.[81]

While differences in ideology and personality clashes clearly played a role in driving Paul out of NAWSA, the evidence also points to a significant rift over fund-raising. As the movement began to emerge from the doldrums, gain greater publicity, and develop new tactics and strategies, the need for large donations grew more imperative. McCormick, who as treasurer was reduced to writing a check herself as she tried to turn around the deficit related to the *Woman's Journal*, resented Paul's ability to quickly and seemingly easily raise $12,000 for a parade. She and Catt demanded control over the money that Paul raised. Paul, however, well understood that the money empowered her, and she chose to leave NAWSA with her list of donors intact. With the CU on its own, McCormick assured NAWSA that it was effectively raising enough money to fund the four western states where suffrage was on the ballot, as well as continue congressional lobbying.[82]

After the break, it was simply a matter of time before Belmont withdrew from NAWSA as well. In addition to the growing financial clout of Mc-Cormick, Belmont was growing frustrated with resistance to her demands, feeling that her donations were not providing the requisite power she thought she deserved in NAWSA. In addition to wanting the organization to consider more militant tactics, which leadership refused, Belmont now wanted NAWSA to move headquarters again, this time to Washington, D.C., to be nearer to the politicians it wished to influence. Furthermore, she felt that she had been treated poorly at the conventions, given her generosity to the organization, when two of her proposed resolutions were not passed.[83]

Once assured a place on the CU executive committee, Belmont switched her allegiance from NAWSA to the CU with a $5,000 check (almost $114,000 in 2016) and a direct statement to the press in January 1914. "Inasmuch as the National Association did not see fit to agree with me [about the move to Washington, D.C.], I decided to swing my influence where I thought it would prove more effective," she bluntly stated.[84]

The CU accepted Belmont and her money with eyes wide open. They knew that her generosity came with strings attached. Board member Mary Beard told Alice Paul that she was willing to "tackle Mrs. Belmont" for money for the CU to publish its own newspaper. While acknowledging that the socially prominent Belmont "loves the limelight" and that a contribution from Belmont might have a "possible ugly string" attached to it, Beard concluded that she was a "risk worth taking." She predicted that "every swell" would attend an event planned by Belmont, admitting, "Our committee can't reach that element as she can and we need its money and support."[85] Fellow board member Crystal Benedict Eastman suggested that Belmont was "crazy about the CU. I think she's *all right* and means to give the work a big gift."[86] Eastman admitted that Belmont "says quite frankly that she won't give money unless she has some representation on the [CU] board," but concluded, "I don't think Mrs. B would want to interfere or dictate. She just doesn't like to be made a baby of—to be used just for money and not for work or advice."[87] Anne Martin, a suffragist from Nevada, encouraged Paul to meet Belmont "halfway," suggesting that Belmont "has big ideas and large purposes for suffrage work."[88]

Only Connecticut suffragist Katharine Houghton Hepburn resisted the lure of Belmont's money, recommending against "making concessions" and arguing that Belmont was "in the habit of running things absolutely," "enjoys eternally fussing about details, and would use up all your energy and then would not be satisfied."[89] Overriding Hepburn's objections, however, CU officers took the money and gave Belmont a seat on the board.

It was not always easy dealing with Belmont. Although she did not derail the CU agenda, she did annoy board members who had to keep her happy if they wanted her money. In 1900, Catt had complained about what was required to please those who had given. "There have been in our Association," she commented, "two or three women of wealth who have occasionally given to our work, and it has been said that they must be humored and petted and not antagonized before they would give. In common parlance they have been toadied because of their wealth; this has always been a humiliation and disgust to me."[90] Belmont caused similar feelings among officers who had to deal with her.

Belmont had a temper. Her wrath is evident from a three-page letter she wrote complaining that she did not get the information she wanted from a worker at CU headquarters after paying for expenses there.[91] She also "flew into a rage" over a newspaper article, leaving Caroline Reilly reporting that Belmont "said if she had to be dictated to she would do nothing. . . . She knew what was required better than anyone else, and her method must be pursued or none at all."[92] Clearly, Belmont was determined to have her way. She wanted a new headquarters in Washington, D.C., and she insisted that the CU take the top floor of a certain building while her Political Equality Association took the ground floor. Paul and Eastman explained that they did not want the top floor and that the building was too large and the rent too high, but they could not change "Mrs. Belmont's opinion in the slightest."[93] Finally, Belmont made it clear that she would withhold funding if she was made unhappy, leaving CU officers no other option than to handle her carefully. When approached by another CU officer for a small donation, Belmont became "especially" difficult. Beard had to warn CU officer Lucy Burns that no one but Burns should ask Belmont for donations.[94]

Notwithstanding the difficulties Belmont posed, the CU benefited from her fame, money, and ideas, as had NAWSA earlier. Belmont did more than garner headlines. She was extremely active in the CU. In 1914, she helped organize three events: a fund-raising ball in Washington, D.C.; a convention of social reform and society leaders at her home to raise funds and publicity; and a working conference of CU leaders to plan strategy. Her financial assistance was invaluable, as the CU treasury was down to seven dollars by June 1914.[95] Belmont's financial contributions literally kept it afloat for the first several years after she joined.

Belmont gave liberally to the CU's major strategies and new tactics. The CU decided to punish the political party in power for its lack of support for suffrage, and Belmont pledged half of the $10,000 needed for the campaign against these legislators. Officer Doris Stevens credited Belmont with pushing the CU to embrace this political strategy. Stevens noted that Belmont had already made "suffrage an election issue" in New York, and she was eager to translate that success into a national campaign.[96] Belmont also paid the rent on the new headquarters in Washington, D.C. She gave two $5,000 donations to support the controversial White House pickets, adopted in 1917 and shunned by NAWSA as militant and inappropriate during wartime. Furthermore, Belmont was responsible for the CU becoming the National Woman's Party. Paul remembered that Belmont preferred the new name: "Belmont was so pleased . . . and so full of interest that she . . . pledged . . . [a] tremendous sum of money."[97] Thus, Belmont agreed with and funded the CU's most significant strategies, enabling it to adopt new tactics, such as parades and pickets, and underwriting its political strategy of working for the federal amendment and punishing the party in power if necessary.

Paul's strategy, according to Belmont biographer Sylvia Hoffert, was to allow Belmont to work on the projects she was most interested in, such as the rally at her Newport mansion, and hope that she would not interfere with the rest of the CU agenda.[98] Belmont more than satisfied Paul's goal, for she gave at least some monetary support to the rest of Paul's plans. As long as Belmont continued to support the strategy dictated by Paul, the problems she caused were relatively minor. Because she had not been able to change NAWSA's policy or philosophy, she gave her money instead to Paul and the CU, which was aligned with her goals of a federal amendment, more militant tactics, and a political strategy of challenging the party in power.[99]

Paul was also able to handle Mary A. Burnham, the CU's second most significant donor. Burnham gave over $38,000 to the CU from 1912 to 1920 (approximately half of what Belmont gave during the same period). Although she did not seek office or attach demands to her gifts like Belmont, Burnham was difficult because she questioned some of Paul's strategies. The unmarried daughter of George Burnham, a co-owner of Baldwin Locomotive Works, she was an active member of the New Century Club—a Philadelphia women's club that focused on working women and their children—and she chaired the Good Government League. In 1912–13 she was one of four women out of twenty-two members on the city's Vice Commission, investigating prostitution. The commission was notable for refusing to condemn female prostitutes while excusing their male customers.[100] Burnham also donated to the

Women's Medical School Fund, organized by Mary Garrett to build a coeducational medical school at Johns Hopkins.

Burnham belonged to the Equal Franchise Society of Philadelphia. She lent her automobile (and a driver) to the Equal Franchise Society (EFS) for three months during its state constitutional effort. The car, called the Burnham Winner, was painted purple and yellow, suffrage colors. She also joined the effort to hang posters around the city with other prominent women—a sight unusual enough for the newspapers to cover, with well-dressed ladies using buckets of paste to hang posters on walls.[101]

The EFS championed Paul's style and strategy and shifted allegiance from NAWSA to the CU in 1914. In June of 1914 Paul wrote Burnham to explain how the CU had formed and to elucidate its side of the conflict with NAWSA. Apparently her explanations satisfied Burnham, and she began to give generously to the CU.[102]

Later, after Burnham complained about Paul's policy of working against the party in power, Paul sent someone from the CU to talk to Burnham, whom she described as "very wealthy" and therefore needing to be convinced "we were on the right track."[103] Despite dutifully giving $1,000 to support the White House pickets, Burnham grumbled, "I do not see in this activity any push for National Suffrage. I find in any discussion of these arrests and jailings that the Cause is lost sight of in general comment on 'police powers' 'free speech' etc." She thought the pickets were "a tangent" distracting the campaign and turning the focus on the suffragists rather than the cause. Panicked officers asked her to "hang on out of sheer loyalty to the cause," which she did, donating approximately $2,000 a year.[104] Dora Lewis wrote her mother, "Miss Burnham is sending a thousand and will send more later. Is she not lovely to do this when she disapproves of our demonstrations?" Lewis noted that Burnham joked that her money should not be used for "wood or oil" for their protest fires, in which they burned Woodrow Wilson's speeches. She assured Burnham that the money would be used for the legislative battles, and that they would get wood from the New York CU branch.[105] Despite disagreeing with Paul, Burnham continued to write checks.

This ability to foster loyalty among her donors was a hallmark of Paul's genius.[106] After leaving NAWSA, confident that she could raise the money she needed for her new agenda at the CU, she continued to raise significant funds. Holding on to both Belmont and Burnham, both of whom had formerly supported NAWSA, Paul drew tens of thousands of dollars to the CU. This money fueled the CU's rise as a rival organization to NAWSA and funded Paul's militant publicity tactics; the Washington, D.C., parade; and the White House pickets. Belmont's contributions also enabled Paul's political strategy: congressional lobbying for a federal amendment and campaigning against the party in power.

AFTER BELMONT LEFT NAWSA, taking her money, her ideas, as well as her imperious personality to the CU, NAWSA officers remained in disarray. Belmont's exit did not assuage those officers who resented the power of wealthy women in the organization. Tension grew among McCormick, Shaw, Dennett, and the board, which resulted in Dennett's resignation, citing the board's inability to adhere to the budget and subsequent cutting of Dennett's budget to make up funds. Dennett harshly criticized the "money influence" or the "money power" in NAWSA, echoing the language of the public's concerns over J. P. Morgan's banking monopoly. She argued that wealthy women had too much influence, causing the organization to become involved in crazy schemes. Dennett had even insinuated that Shaw was motivated by personal gain, as Shaw complained to Thomas: "[She said that] I am entirely controlled by money. That I sold the organization out to you two years ago at Philadelphia, and that this year I had sold out the association and the cause to Mrs. Stanley McCormick."[107] Dennett thought that Shaw succumbed to Thomas's and McCormick's proposals because of their financial contributions. McCormick continued to snipe at Dennett even after Dennett resigned. She tried to get Dennett to pay an outstanding $50 pledge Dennett had made to NAWSA before resigning and asked Dennett to return keys to the office and cease consulting office files without permission.[108]

Meanwhile, Upton had also complained that Shaw was controlled by money. According to Upton, because Shaw was paid a salary that came from contributions (the Garrett-Thomas fund, and additional contributions solicited by Thomas), she became less dedicated to the cause and more dedicated to her own self-aggrandizement and the donors who facilitated it. In a letter that was passed around among other officers, Upton wrote, "As long as she [Shaw] was fighting for principle, she was a powerful woman, but the money she made and which was handed to her, caused her to prostitute these principles. . . . She has grown more and more self important and degraded all the time."[109] Clearly, both the wealthy donors and the officers who received their donations were suspect.

Shaw herself grew to resent the women who were initially generous to her or NAWSA but did not remain loyal to her or the organization. In 1909, she had positively judged Belmont to be "not quite so determined to have her own way about everything" in comparison to donor Katherine Mackay. But eventually Belmont's demands and desire for public prominence made Shaw rethink her opinion of Belmont. Later, when Belmont left NAWSA for the CU, Shaw sniped, "I certainly think that the Congressional Union will pay dearly for the 'unlimited financial backing' which, I have no doubt, they can have if they will put Mrs. Belmont in the forefront and let her name stand as the great leader of the suffrage movement in this country."[110]

Shaw also changed her mind about McCormick. When McCormick first took office in NAWSA, she and her mother not only made contributions to NAWSA but also gave personal gifts to Shaw, buying her clothing to wear at a convention. Ultimately, however, McCormick began to back Catt over Shaw. McCormick first tried to engineer moving Shaw out of the NAWSA presidency for a New Yorker or Pennsylvanian and Catt into a more prominent role.[111] Finding herself increasingly unpopular for a variety of reasons, Shaw resigned. When Catt replaced Shaw as president, McCormick became vice president under Catt. After leaving office, Shaw complained that she resented McCormick and her mother's contributions, now suggesting that they did not give freely to her or the cause, but always had their own objectives in mind.[112]

McCormick helped NAWSA president Catt by championing her vision. She continued to criticize the militant tactics of the CU and embraced Catt's Winning Plan. Perhaps most significantly, she endorsed Catt's call for suffragists to support the war effort when the United States entered World War I. McCormick chaired the NAWSA War Service Department and, along with Shaw and Catt, served on the Woman's Committee of the Council of National Defense.[113] Catt and McCormick believed that women's demonstration of loyalty during wartime was a much more effective way to win Wilson's support for woman suffrage than Paul's White House pickets.

McCormick remained one of Catt's most important workers, though she no longer played as prominent a role as a donor to NAWSA. Her contributions had been supplanted by the bequest that Mrs. Frank Leslie left to Catt. When Catt became president again in 1915, it was with the public knowledge that Leslie had left her entire estate valued at over $1.7 million to Catt for woman suffrage. The scandalous Leslie, divorced and married several times, had inherited her husband's then failing publishing business and turned it around, resulting in her large estate. Leslie left Catt the money to spend on woman suffrage as she liked, with no strings attached. Legally, according to Leslie's will, Catt did not even have to spend the money on woman suffrage. After fighting off relatives and others who wanted a share of the fortune and paying attorney fees and taxes, Catt netted $977,875 ($22,224,431 in 2016), out of an original bequest of $1,737,478.[114] Catt then established the Leslie Woman Suffrage Commission to oversee the fund, wisely retaining control over the money rather than merging it into the NAWSA general budget. The size of the bequest and the fact that it had no restrictions on how it was to be spent freed Catt to pay for whatever strategy or tactics she wanted, and was indispensable to the passage and ratification of the Nineteenth Amendment.

Given the mixed record of state campaigns funded by NAWSA in the past, Catt used the Leslie bequest to abandon the state-by-state strategy, which had been so costly and difficult to implement, and focus instead on her Winning Plan. The plan directed the national organization to focus on winning the federal amendment through campaigns in selected states as well as through lobbying Congress. The selected states would give momentum to the passage and ensure ratification of the national amendment.

The plan was successful because Catt was able to centralize suffrage fundraising and spending. She had already successfully orchestrated a constitutional change requiring all local suffrage societies to become affiliates of their state division of NAWSA and to pay a percentage of their revenue to the national body.[115] After state associations submitted their plans to the national board, the dues they paid supported either the federal amendment congressional committee lobbying force in Washington, D.C., or the states determined to have a good chance at winning suffrage.[116] Some of the dues-paying organizations opposed the revenue plan. The Women's Political Union— Harriot Stanton Blatch's organization—was so successful at fund-raising that it withdrew from NAWSA rather than pay the percentage.[117] The CU, before ultimately leaving NAWSA, had realized that if it were to change from an "affiliated" society of NAWSA, which paid 5 percent of revenue, to an "auxiliary" of NAWSA, it could pay a flat $100 annual dues instead.[118]

Catt argued that with the Leslie Commission funds focused on the Winning Plan, NAWSA would no longer be obligated to step in and assist states who had pushed for a state referendum too soon or with ill-conceived plans.[119] Unsurprisingly, not everyone liked this approach. States not included in the plan were not happy.[120] Others opposed the central control Catt wielded, with Upton grousing that NAWSA chose how much to send where, and often used the money to pay for its own traveling speakers rather than giving the states money to spend as they wanted.[121]

On the other hand, the states in which suffrage was on the ballot or that were otherwise prioritized in the Winning Plan did benefit from Leslie's beneficence. Catt's home state of New York did particularly well with $25,000 in funding, as did Oklahoma, Michigan, and North Dakota, which split $20,000 among them. With the influx of money, these four states all won suffrage in 1917 and 1918. States holding senatorial races also received funding as they tried to elect pro-suffrage legislators who would vote to pass the federal amendment. In 1918, Catt authorized $10,000 to several states in this situation. Because NAWSA did not actually have the money, she had to ask the Leslie Commission to make the payment. Within its first two years, the Leslie Commission sent $60,000 to states. In addition to money, NAWSA sent directives to states to organize their efforts.[122]

The Winning Plan also required work in Washington, D.C., lobbying congressmen to pass the federal amendment. NAWSA's congressional committee, which had been limited to a ten-dollar budget before the CU turned its attention to the federal amendment, now needed funds to compete with the CU lobbyists. NAWSA and the Leslie Commission covered around $20,000 a year for congressional committee lobbying expenses. With the new influx of money from the Leslie Commission, NAWSA could now rent a house, called the Suffrage House, in Washington, D.C., for a corps of lobbyists to live and work in. The Leslie Commission immediately began paying rent and expenses for the Suffrage House.[123]

Now generously funded, both individual states and the Winning Plan strategy began to experience success. Working in more than one state at a time to win over public opinion was expensive and required strategic decisions about how much to spend where. Lobbying for a federal amendment was also expensive, necessitating a headquarters and a small committee of lobbyists in Washington. Catt could do both only because of the Leslie bequest and other large donations. Harriet Upton, who had previously lobbied Congress with Anthony, understood the importance of the bequest and the headquarters in Washington, D.C. "I sometimes wonder," she wrote after suffrage was won, "if we would still be going up to the Capital if Mrs. Leslie had not made that bequest."[124]

The Leslie bequest also provided substantially more money for publicity. Suffragists published everything from tracts to weekly newspapers to full-scale books documenting the movement, organizing its workers, and trying to convert the public to their cause. Having a mouthpiece "so we can sauce back our opponents," as Susan B. Anthony once said, was important to suffragists.[125] Without the vote, women depended on men to pass woman suffrage for them, making education essential to their ability to wield any power over legislators. When Catt received the Leslie bequest, she argued that giving direct donations to politicians who were beholden to other special interests was ineffectual. Rather, a suffrage education campaign would create the national sentiment in favor of woman suffrage that would pressure politicians to vote for it.[126]

Finally, the Leslie bequest provided the funding necessary for a massive publicity blitz. Suffrage education was the biggest expense funded by the Leslie bequest. The commission created a Bureau of Suffrage Education, with a staff of twenty-five trained publicity experts and journalists taking over the fifteenth floor of the headquarters building in New York, all paid with Leslie money. Rose Young, the director of suffrage education, created six departments. The Publicity and News Department offered five services: The news service sent daily press releases to newspapers around the country, and the photo news service sent photographs biweekly. A bulletin service created a weekly compendium of suffrage news, which suffragists around the country could use to write weekly columns. The "stunts" service helped local efforts with conventions, automobiles, parades, and other big events, and a motion picture service created propaganda films.

The Feature Department offered suffrage publicity through cartoons, stories about leading suffragists, testimonials in favor of suffrage, and "plates" (ready-to-print news). It also provided "intelligence," or statistical information and legislative updates gathered by the Research Department. A Field Press Department helped ensure that all this information reached the local presses and local organizers, who were charged with reaching out to their local papers. The Magazine Department created a new suffrage magazine, while an Editorial Correspondence Department followed through with editors and rebutted anti-suffrage editorials.[127] These services and departments underwent changes and consolidation as the bureau carried out its work, though the essence of the plan remained the same.[128]

The broad approach of the bureau reflected the influx of new publicity tactics into the movement, which began around 1908. The parlor meetings that originally drew wealthy women to the suffrage movement because of their respectable nature were soon eclipsed by a more public strategy. Public speaking symbolized this new approach, which placed suffragists on street corners, in cars, on trains, and wherever else they could gather a crowd. McCormick and the Massachusetts open-air speakers led a session at the NAWSA convention to train and inspire women around the country to take up these new tactics. Blatch and Paul both creatively used parades to showcase the diversity of support for woman suffrage. While some efforts cost little—for example, soapbox speakers who needed little more than a box to stand on—the parades required costumes, floats, and so on. Individuals like Katherine Mackay and Alva Belmont provided funding that NAWSA and the

CU needed for these new tactics, as did the Leslie bequest through funding of the stunts and motion picture services.[129]

Publishing a magazine was a more traditional publicity tool that suffragists continued to prioritize even as they developed open-air speeches, parades, and other new publicity tactics. After the failed experiment in running the *Woman's Journal*, NAWSA published a newsletter, the *National Suffrage News*, but Catt kept her eye on the *Woman's Journal*. Although she knew it kept losing money, $8,000–$20,000 annually since 1912, and circulation was under forty thousand, she still thought it crucial to have a mouthpiece for the movement.[130]

Furthermore, the CU had launched its own weekly magazine, the *Suffragist*, in November 1913. CU chairperson Alice Paul had first tried to convince Blackwell to publish the *Woman's Journal* from Washington, D.C., hoping it would include information on the CU's lobbying campaign without costing the CU anything. Blackwell was not interested, so Paul began her own weekly. Within a month, the CU claimed twelve hundred paid subscribers and enough advertising revenue to cover the magazine's cost. Ultimately, though, as the magazine grew, so did the costs—including salaries. By 1920, the CU was in a similar situation as NAWSA and had a deficit of almost $56,000.[131]

Given NAWSA's continued desire for a magazine and competition from the *Suffragist*, the Leslie Commission finally bought out Blackwell's shares in the *Woman's Journal* and merged it with the Woman Suffrage Party of Greater New York's *Woman Voter* and NAWSA's *National Suffrage News* to form the *Woman Citizen*, retaining Blackwell as a contributing editor. Total cost for the new journal was approximately $75,000 the first year, including salaries, office rent, printing, and postage. Because advertising and sales only brought in $25,000, the Leslie Commission paid the remaining $50,000 in expenses.[132] After spending approximately $400,000 on the *Woman Citizen* in twelve years, Catt finally recommended ceasing publication in 1929.[133] Paul later complained that under Blackwell, the *Woman's Journal* had been friendly to the CU (even though it did not include the lobbying information she had hoped for), but that once Catt got the Leslie donation and took over the magazine, it no longer included positive coverage of CU activities.[134] Catt thus used the magazine not only to "sauce back" male opponents of woman suffrage but also to try to quash publicity around her competitor's efforts for suffrage.

SUFFRAGISTS HAD STRUGGLED FOR years to produce a suffrage magazine and the other publicity materials necessary to create public sentiment in favor of votes for women. The million-dollar bequest from Leslie finally freed Catt to create a publicity machine unlike anything suffragists had been able to achieve for decades.[135] The money allowed suffragists to reach and influence many more people. In fact, the suffrage movement came closer to the $2–2.5 million that the Democratic and Republican parties spent on national political campaigns.[136] The publicity and NAWSA's Winning Plan were essential to the passage of the Nineteenth Amendment.

As was evident in chapter 1, because they believed in women's equality and the need for economic and political independence, monied women gave generously to the movement. The donations from and bequests left by wealthy women enabled the movement's success. Pauline Shaw, Alva Belmont, Katharine McCormick, and Mrs. Frank Leslie all provided the funding that NAWSA and the CU needed to pay salaries, support campaigns in the western states, move headquarters to New York, support a money-losing magazine, picket the White House, and conduct simultaneous state campaigns and federal lobbying. The demands of the donors, and the vision of the officers they gave to, shaped the tactics and strategies of the movement.

AS THE MOVEMENT GREW in the 1900s and 1910s, officers consciously reached out to college women and working-class women as well as monied women. Suffragists often wanted the right to vote to satisfy their own needs: reformers demanded the vote in order to pass reforms, working women to provide protections for workers, and the wealthy to enable their financial independence—or because, given their other privileges, they felt the lack of political power acutely. The common desire for political equality bound these different women together. But under the surface, their differences caused tension. Resentment of inequality pervaded the movement for equality. The demands made by donors undermined their emphasis on sisterhood even as they called for suffrage to ensure financial and political independence for all women.

Leaders in NAWSA and the CU had been desperate for money to fund the movement. Although suffrage leaders sometimes succeeded in recruiting donors either whose ideas aligned with theirs or who gave freely, they also had to accept restricted gifts that left more power in the hands of the donor. The women who wielded financial power caused dissension among suffragists when they sought the power they believed should accompany their contributions. Ideally, a movement that sought equality and independence for women would not have been beholden to a few women who could buy their way into office, decide where headquarters should be located, or otherwise tie their gifts to demands. Their role in the movement reveals the power of philan-thropy for women as well as the problems it could cause.

These problems in some ways limited their victory. Despite attaining the vote, the women's movement after 1920 seemed to splinter: black women re-mained disenfranchised, the CU sought an equal rights amendment, and labor women rejected the amendment in favor of protective legislation. Birth control was a controversial topic, and a conservative backlash to progressive era reformers dampened the activism of some. Questions of power and in-equality among women, often concerning race or sexuality, resurfaced during the women's liberation movement five decades later. Today, many women's organizations seek greater inclusivity and try to prevent uneven power through certain measures—for example, by including grantees in decision making.

Suffragists were not the only feminists to struggle with these questions in the early twentieth century. The desire for sisterhood and the emphasis on economic independence that had led many wealthy women to embrace suf-frage also drew them to support labor women. Their attempts to foster cross-class labor coalitions suffered from similar problems, as will be evident in chapter 3. Working-class women, like middle-class suffragists, would also re-sist the power of wealthy women.

CHAPTER THREE

Dictating with Dollars
Funding Equality for Working-Class Women

"I find that Mrs. Robins pays everybody's salary, all other necessary expenses, and as a consequence she has no opposition in the entire organization," wrote Pauline Newman to Rose Schneiderman in 1911.[1] Newman and Schneiderman, both factory workers who became labor activists, belonged to the Women's Trade Union League (WTUL), an organization expressly designed to bring together wealthy women, referred to as "allies," and working-class women, referred to as "girls," to fight for rights for working women, including unionization and suffrage. Newman's complaint, that WTUL president Margaret Dreier Robins dominated the group due to her financial wherewithal, echoed resentment flourishing in the suffrage movement that same year. Newman's was sharp criticism of a woman who was said to understand working-class women and who was president of an organization created to avoid just such power on the part of the affluent allies. If, despite safeguards that included requiring working women to assume half the positions of leadership, Robins could still dictate with her dollars, then the organization failed at the very thing it intended to do. Wealthy women's activism with, and on behalf of, working-class women exposes some of the deep class fissures in the women's movement for equality, as well as the keen desire of many that common feminist interests overcome the divide.

Although this is the only chapter to explore organizations focused explicitly on working-class women, monied women throughout this book espoused a sense of sisterhood across class that was critical to their engagement in the women's rights movement. Their decisions to work for the right to vote, for access to higher education, and for reproductive rights reflected their aspiration for all women to be financially independent and politically powerful, a desire they believed connected them with working-class women. Thus, when their money gave them a voice, they chose to use it to make changes for all women, working women in particular.

This chapter draws on a rich body of archival and historical studies of the WTUL and the Young Woman's Christian Association (YWCA), another organization dedicated to the needs of working women. The YWCA initially focused on working women's lives outside the workplace, cultivating religious faith and wholesome recreation, and only later embraced protective labor legislation and unionization to create better conditions on the shop floor. Historians have focused on the WTUL because it was expressly designed to unite workers and allies, looking at what happened when the WTUL set out to work *with* working women instead of *for* them. Several accounts of the association have found that the WTUL came closer than others, including the YWCA, to forming a true cross-class organization but in the end could not achieve this goal.[2]

This chapter builds on these studies by focusing on the leadership of Margaret Dreier Robins and her sister Mary Dreier in the WTUL, as well as that of Grace Hoadley Dodge in Working Girls' Societies and the YWCA. It shows how their desire for sisterhood motivated their attempts to work with working-class women, yet their financial clout sometimes marred their efforts. In her history of feminism, historian Estelle Freedman argues that feminists have had to think about whether the concept of sisterhood extended past race, ethnicity, and class. They had to consider, "Did the identity 'woman' include all women, or only those entitled to rights based on their race or class?" Is there a universal womanhood?[3] Wealthy women throughout this book wrestled with these questions, though perhaps none more so than those who chose to dedicate their money, time, and effort to the problems that working-class women faced. Differences in class, and frequently ethnicity, race, and religion as well, meant that upper-class and working-class women had profoundly different life and cultural experiences. Yet some wealthy women insisted that the bonds of womanhood united all women across class.

As the primary benefactors and leaders in their organizations, Dodge, Robins, and Dreier tried to bridge the gap between themselves and the working women they wanted to assist. Ideally, friendship would connect them. They believed that the relationship worked in both directions: Dodge, Robins, and Dreier were deeply influenced by the women they aided.[4] The three agreed in theory that working women knew best what their own needs were, that working women needed to take leadership in their organizations, and that sisterhood and cooperation should mark their organizations and make them different from those dominated by wealthy women working *for* poor women, rather than *with* them.

Moreover, that sisterhood was heightened when some allies examined their own lack of power as women, especially a lack of financial independence despite their wealth.[5] They believed that although they had not earned wages themselves, they understood the importance of financial independence for women. When Dodge declared, for example, that her inheritance was a form of "wages earned in advance," she was trying to foster a link between herself, a wealthy heiress, and the working women who earned meager hourly wages in a factory. Upper-class women sometimes so admired the independence they assumed working-class women enjoyed that they could not comprehend the responsibilities and cares of working women.

Yet despite these high ideals and the warm personal relationships they formed with working women, even a woman like Margaret Robins was accused of trying to dominate with her dollars.[6] As with the woman suffrage movement, the contradiction of the disproportionate power that a few in an organization held was especially troubling within an association explicitly formed to be democratic. This was even more so, given that the women sought more power for women in a society that excluded them in many ways.[7] Their organizations bred conflict between "the allies" and "the girls," a disquieting clash in feminist associations designed to be nonhierarchical.[8] A closer examination of both the ideals they expressed and the actual relationships they formed shows the difficulties that women of wealth encountered when they tried to work with working-class women. The power they wielded through their financial contributions limited their ability to create genuine cross-class alliances.

WEALTHY WOMEN SOUGHT TO assist the working class in several ways. Traditionally, the wealthy "lady bountiful" was expected to provide charity (food, clothing, wood for fuel, and other necessities) to the deserving poor. During the Progressive Era of the late nineteenth and early twentieth centuries, ideas about charity began to change. The organized charity movement sent "friendly visitors" to assess a family's needs (and worthiness) and then sought to coordinate the efforts of various charitable organizations to avoid duplication. Later, many reformers in this movement, as well as the foundations established by Andrew Carnegie, John D. Rockefeller, Olivia Sage, and others, moved away from charity designed to meet a family's immediate needs and toward eradicating the causes of poverty and disease, a strategy known as scientific philanthropy.[9] Despite these progressive reforms and a spirit of the day that promoted the possibility of harmony between rich and poor, the class divide only grew.[10]

As women began to move their efforts from charity to progressive reforms, they took the lead in several organizations, including woman's exchanges, the National Consumers League, the YWCA, and the WTUL. Each of these was interested not just in "the poor" but especially in the particular problems that working women—or women who needed to earn wages—faced. The woman's exchange movement, begun in the nineteenth century, was an effort to provide work for women by establishing exchange stores, where their handmade goods could be sold on consignment. The organizers originally assisted formerly wealthy women who had fallen on hard times. By doing fancy needlework at home, these women were assured privacy and avoided the factory floor. Later, the exchanges included more working-class women.[11] The Consumers League focused on wealthy women's power as consumers to advocate for workers, pledging to shop only at stores with good working conditions for saleswomen, and to buy products made in factories with good working conditions for women.[12]

The YWCA initially developed along two lines in the last four decades of the nineteenth century. In urban areas, led by the New York Ladies' Christian Association founded in 1858, groups nurtured Christian faith and provided wholesome recreation, housing, and other services to unmarried working women. These groups, centered in the Northeast, became known as the "International Board," while the "American Committee" developed in the Midwest, where local associations focused on activities for Christian college women. With Grace Dodge's mediation, the two came together in 1907 to form the national YWCA, which continued to operate in both urban areas and on college campuses.

The WTUL from the beginning had a different focus: leaders wanted working women to improve their pay and working conditions through joining labor unions, as well as through gaining the right to vote and passing protective labor legislation. Although founded in 1903 at the American Federation of Labor (AFL) convention, the WTUL had an uneasy relationship with the AFL. Working women in the early twentieth century faced enormous difficulties in the labor movement. A conservative labor leader like the AFL's Samuel Gompers explicitly admitted that he was not interested in including women in labor unions because they brought down wages for male workers, and their presence in the workplace belied the argument for a higher family wage for a male breadwinner. Even socialists like Bill Haywood did not recognize the unique needs and interests of women workers, including, for example, birth control.[13]

Despite the challenges, the initial strategy of the WTUL was to encourage women factory workers to unionize and strike if necessary. The allies in the WTUL helped walk the picket line to draw publicity to strikes; made donations to funds that paid striking women's expenses, including bail money; organized consumer boycotts; and otherwise tried to assist strikers.[14] Frustrated by strikes and unions that barely changed working conditions, by the late 1910s the WTUL shifted its emphasis to woman suffrage and protective labor legislation, including the eight-hour day and the minimum wage.

The women in the WTUL were willing to criticize the men of their social set who owned factories.[15] The growing distance between labor and capital during these decades had strengthened class identity, which made the efforts of women to break down that distance even more important.[16] Thus, women workers depended on other women for interest in their plight as well as financial support for strikes and labor organizing.

GRACE HOADLEY DODGE FERVENTLY believed that she could develop a deep and genuine friendship with working girls, through which she would help them develop their religious faith and virtue. Her strong faith drove her to find commonality with working women because she believed in the brotherhood—in this case, sisterhood—of all God's children and, in particular, in the innate virtue of women. Yet at the same time, Dodge had little interest in bettering the conditions of women in the workplace. Rather, her focus on shared religious faith and sexual morality caused her to prioritize elevating their home lives. Both the Working Girls' Societies, which she founded, and the YWCA, which she ultimately led, initially focused on faith and morality. When these groups increased their attention to labor activism, they did so without her. Dodge left the Working Girls' Societies just as its agenda was changing and died before the YWCA expanded its focus.

Dodge was born in 1856 to Sarah and William Earl Dodge Jr. Her grandfather and father headed the Huntington and Dodge (later called Phelps, Dodge, and Company) mercantile firm, trading in real estate, cotton, metal, copper, lumber, and railroads.[17] As a young woman, Grace spent years caring for her ill mother as well as serving as hostess and manager of the household; like suffragist Mary Garrett, she was not allowed to go to college (she attended Miss Porter's School while her brother went to Princeton) or join the family business as her brother did. Instead, she put her considerable business acumen to the service of several organizations. She was a skilled fund-raiser and leader, and strategically called for expansion, merger, and centralization when necessary.

Her quiet dedication, decades of volunteer work, and donations of millions of dollars to bettering the lives of working women was motivated by the example of her grandfather and father, religious men who donated generously to charity and actively supported the Young Men's Christian Association. When her father died, he left his money to his wife and his children to continue to give as he had done, "for the advancement of the cause of our blessed Redeemer and for all humane and benevolent objects."[18] Grace took her father's admonition seriously, and she made it her duty to give her money

Grace Hoadley
Dodge, circa
1890. Used with
permission from
the Grace Hoadley
Dodge Papers,
Sophia Smith
Collection, Smith
College Archives,
Smith College.

with purpose and effect. She became devoted to working women and fought
to improve their lives.

As a tall and insecure teenager, Grace Dodge was serious, religious, and
more interested in serving God than in marriage. Rather than attend debutante
parties, she asked her father if she could have luncheons with accomplished
people in order to learn from them how best to follow Jesus. Wisely, her father
introduced her to Louisa Schuyler, a wealthy New Yorker who had helped
lead the Women's Central Association of Relief (auxiliary to the United States
Sanitary Commission) during the Civil War.[19] After the War, Schuyler harnessed her organizational experience and skills to create the State Charities
Aid Association (SCAA), which called for wealthy elites, including many
women, to monitor New York's institutions for the poor and mentally ill and
render them more efficient.[20] Through her association with Schuyler, Dodge
worked on the Committee on the Elevation of the Poor in Their Homes and
the Bellevue Hospital Visiting Committee. Her biographer, Esther Katz, argues that she eventually left the SCAA because its focus on state-run charities

required its leaders to lobby for funding, while she was more interested in the personal interactions she enjoyed with individual families.[21]

These encounters with the needy led her to prioritize assistance to working "girls." In the 1870s and early 1880s, novelists, journalists, and public officials had begun to problematize and dramatize what they believed to be excessive vice among young working women.[22] In 1881, Dodge met with a group of silk workers to provide them information on topics, including self-improvement, health, dress, proper behavior, and domestic skills. Dodge quickly learned that the young women were put off by her wealth and leadership. She changed the format of the class to allow them to choose topics themselves, explaining (albeit somewhat patronizingly), "An American girl will not be patronized, meeting with her, you have to be her equal, and treat her with the tenderest consideration."[23] The class led to the formation of a Working Girls' Society, followed shortly by an organization of the first eleven societies like it, called the Association of Working Girls' Societies.[24]

By the mid-1890s, Working Girls' Societies around the country began to democratize, with new leadership composed of councils that included workers, instead of a single wealthy president like Dodge. Their agenda also began to change, away from classes on behavior and deportment toward improving industrial conditions and creating labor unions, driven by the economic depression of the early 1890s. Historian Priscilla Murolo argues that wealthy club sponsors, while sympathetic to poor working conditions, were unable or unwilling to embrace trade unionism and eventually supported industrial education instead. Unable to come to consensus on labor issues, the clubs eventually devolved into a focus on greater opportunities for recreation (especially mixed-sex dances) before the movement died out in the 1920s.

By the time things began to change in the 1890s, Dodge was transferring her energy and time to industrial education through the Kitchen Garden Association (later called the Industrial Education Association). Her original push for sisterhood and friendship was lost as the Association of Working Girls' Societies grew and changed. At the same time, her inability to allow the girls themselves to set the agenda, despite her stated intentions, is clear. When they moved in a direction at odds with Dodge's focus on purity, she shifted her time and effort to the Kitchen Garden Association, an organization better aligned with her purposes.[25]

Dodge carried her emphasis on sisterhood into her work in the YWCA in the early 1900s. In 1907, she led the effort to unite the two separately established branches of the YWCA, the International Board and the American Committee. These two groups clashed over establishing a branch in

Washington, D.C. After successfully bringing them together, she became president of the newly combined YWCA of the USA, a position from which she continued to advocate for sisterhood.[26]

Dodge differed from most of the women in this book in that she did not explicitly use language promoting women's equality or freedom but instead emphasized womanly virtue. However, she believed that working women should be treated with respect, and she spent decades trying to assist them. Furthermore, her interest in industrial education, which she thought taught domestics skills and therefore improved the home life of poor young women and girls, led her to think more deeply about women's education. She began to prioritize professionalizing women teachers (initially the industrial education teachers), helping to found Teachers College (later a part of Columbia University), where she served as treasurer and to which she donated extensively. Dodge believed that better training would lead to better jobs for women in teaching and nursing. She was also appointed to the New York Board of Education in 1886.

After this experience in public service, she refused to join her aunt Josephine (Mrs. Arthur) Dodge, a staunch anti-suffragist who presided over the National Association Opposed to Woman Suffrage. In 1894, the *New York Times* reported that Grace Dodge did not join a protest against suffrage "on the grounds that she believes it to be very essential that women should serve on the various educational boards." She and her mother attended suffrage meetings at Sherry's, and she presided over a private meeting between suffragist Mary Putnam Jacobi and anti-suffragist Mrs. James McKeever. Ultimately, Grace made a $2,500 donation to the Garrett-Thomas woman suffrage fund in 1907.[27] Dodge also donated to the Women's Medical School Fund, which Garrett organized to make Johns Hopkins's new medical school coeducational. In these ways, she supported women's higher education (including coeducation), women's professions, and woman suffrage.

Dodge believed she could help guide working girls to a life of purity and morality. Her focus on moral elevation is evident throughout her publications in the 1880s. In *A Bundle of Letters to Busy Girls on Practical Matters*, "A Private Letter to Girls," and "Practical Suggestions Relating to Moral Elevation and Preventive Work among Girls," Dodge emphasized modest behavior and sexual purity, and warned working women of the dangers of masturbation and unchaperoned interactions with men.[28] She also started a Three P's Circle (purity, perseverance, and pleasantness), which required a pledge to strive for purity and cheerfulness.[29] Dodge believed that women of any class needed to aspire to highly moral behavior. She wanted to provide the information and example she thought working-class women did not get from their own mothers because they were limited by their circumstances, including housing so small it did not allow for privacy and modesty. Thus, she believed that working-class women and wealthy women were alike in their inherent morality as women and that this would be the basis of their friendship. However, she also thought that chastity had to be taught to working-class women and that they needed to be warned of the dangers in their living conditions that could lead them astray from their natural tendency toward goodness.

Dodge's focus on moral elevation meant that she did not investigate working conditions or advocate unions. Dodge thought that working women did not focus enough on their personal lives due to too many hours spent at work (or on potentially immoral recreation). She wanted to improve their lives by improving their home lives (rather than their working lives).[30] Although she never personally shifted her tactics, she did appear more sympathetic to consideration of work life later in her life. According to Margaret Robins, in 1907 she donated $10,000 to underwrite a study of "social and wage conditions," and before she died, she arranged for the WTUL to use the YWCA training school building for its conference.[31]

Dodge believed she could cultivate relationships with individual working women. This personal interaction would allow both her and the individuals to move beyond their class differences and meet on equal terms as women. In "Sisterhood and Cooperation," a syndicated article that ran in forty newspapers, Dodge argued that women had a duty to one another. "Co-operation," she wrote, was necessary in life, and individuals depend on one another even if they have different "positions, opportunities, obligations." The only way to nurture this mutual dependence was by getting to know one another in a "loving, personal way," or "heart-to-heart."[32] Sharing would lead to a deeper knowledge and understanding. Dodge argued that "many [evils] will be remedied when women come to recognize a common sisterhood, and learn to honor and admire what is good in each other."[33] Like Jane Addams, who promoted mutual cooperation and listening to the needs of settlement-house clients, Dodge thought that she and young working women could learn from each other. Just "because my father and grandfather worked and because they have accumulated funds," she said, "am I not owing more to the busy girls than they owe to me, and as I have said to you, I want to sit at their feet and learn from them, for they can teach me so much."[34] For Dodge, feminine moral character connected all women, despite their disparate experiences and wealth.

According to her biographer, her "gender-based sense of identification with these women . . . seemed to transcend differences in class, religion or ethnicity."[35] Although Dodge did not marry, nor have children of her own, she cared for her invalid mother for years, a service that required her to spend many hours at home. She felt that this responsibility helped her understand the cares of working women, who had to contend with child care and housework (even though Dodge did not have paid employment and had servants in her home to do housework).[36] Furthermore, she claimed her lack of formal education allowed her to be close to the factory girls. "If I had been educated," she contended, "I would not have been in such close touch with them."[37] She tried to deflect attention away from herself and her wealth. Dodge declined interviews and refused to allow her photograph to appear in the newspaper.[38]

Dodge believed friendship with working girls was possible due not only to shared gender identity but also to Christian faith. A YWCA report written well before she joined perhaps best expresses ideas similar to hers about bridging the gap between wealthy and working women. "We are helping to solve the problem in social science, as to how to bridge the gulf that divides the favored from the less fortunate," the report stated. It suggests that a deeply religious understanding of human fellowship was necessary. "It is no dilettante or sentimental philanthropy that will serve the purpose," the report continued, "but that 'enthusiasm of humanity' born of the conviction of kinship and fundamental unity. In other words, we are to vitalize the teachings of our Lord, that 'we are members one of another.' "[39] Dodge believed that as children of God, rich and poor were united. Furthermore, she believed that Jesus set an example that she, a wealthy woman, should follow. "When on earth He practically met and helped those men and women who came to Him," she said. "He was not above them, but was one with them."[40]

Dodge translated her desire for unity into practical suggestions as to how to promote working women's leadership in cross-class organizations like the working girls' clubs and the YWCA. Crucial to this was her understanding that working women wanted to support themselves financially and not be thought of as charity cases. She declared that Working Girls' Society members would pay a small amount of dues, which would enable the club to be self-supporting and at least theoretically lessen the influence of donors like herself.[41] She also understood that they wanted leadership roles. When she was originally asked to serve on the YWCA board, she refused because the young working women had no governing role. "The girls of the Association were not part of it," she recalled. "They were something worked for. . . . My hope is that in our Association our active membership friends who pay a dollar a year, will possibly be considered more than the sustaining member who pays five thousand dollars." To do so, the YWCA had to take practical steps to accommodate working women. She was dismayed by the wealthy women who acknowledged that working women could not meet in the day-time yet still refused to meet in late afternoon to accommodate the workers.[42] She was disheartened to see only committee and board women as well as the secretaries at the YWCA convention in 1909. "Where are the [working] girls?" she asked.[43]

The most telling statement Dodge made regarding her sense of sister-hood with working women despite her wealth was that she was also a working girl, who simply had "wages earned for her in advance" by her father and grandfather.[44] For Dodge, a millionaire at a time when female factory workers made a few dollars a week, to make such a claim seems to show a profound lack of awareness, yet it is at the heart of her interest in the Working Girls' Societies and the YWCA. She had to try to de-emphasize her fortune in order to forge relationships with the working women she hoped to know and help. Furthermore, the expression captured her sense of duty and the dignity of work—Dodge believed she still had to work to earn her wages even if her wages were paid before the work. "He has received his advance from God, and from society," an editorial elaborating on her phrase wrote. "He will then want to do all he can for God and society."[45] "I have no right to this inheritance," she concluded, "but what shall I do with it?" Unable to go to Princeton like her brother or work at her father's firm, Dodge still sought the independence she thought meaningful work of-fered. Significantly, Dodge lived in opulent surroundings, but she used her home as an office.[46] Promoting the idea that she, too, was a working girl enabled her to move past the sexism she experienced in her own family and to take up a role where she "earned" her inheritance through her volun-tary labor.

YWCA secretary Mabel Cratty argued that Dodge demonstrated this atti-tude by assuming that everyone she worked with was capable, responsible, and trustworthy.[47] In a letter to a YWCA coworker, Dodge emphasized friendship and asked for constructive criticism of her leadership. "We are co-laborers," she asserted, despite her position as chair of the national board, and as such, they were to "freely talk things over."[48] If her coworkers ever found her tone to be condescending, they never said as much. Perhaps they were disarmed and flattered by the fact that she implicitly seemed to recognize and yet dismiss the difference of class and position between them.

DODGE BELIEVED SHE WAS entrusted with money to spend wisely for the benefit of others.[49] An early biographer, Abbie Graham, explained, "In regard to the possession of money, she had come to the conclusion that it was inevitable that wealth should accumulate in the hands of the few. The few who possessed it should use it not for themselves but should hold it in trust for all."[50] Thus, like Andrew Carnegie, she did not criticize capitalism or the accumulation of wealth. Rather, she thought the wealthy had a duty to use their money for the good of society.[51] For Dodge, this obligation meant sharing the benefits of living by moral values, such as purity, which her wealth enabled her to do. She wrote, "Has not the Master given us our larger homes and separate bedrooms, our good localities, our greater education and knowledge, all the purifying and refining influences in our lives, as a trust for the good of the many, in order that we may diffuse a higher standard of living?"[52] Dodge's understanding of a higher standard of living suggested that material benefits (including larger homes that provided more space for modesty) enabled high moral standards.

Given this view of her manners and her wealth, it was difficult to build a bridge between workers and herself. Foremost among the factors limiting their ability to relate to each other was the very thing that Dodge thought would bring them closer together: Dodge's desire for a personal relationship. Although she was only twenty-five when she started the first Working Girls' Society, her tall, commanding appearance and rich clothing made her seem like a stately matron to the teenaged workers, many of whom were immigrants. This made forging a friendship based in commonalities difficult for her. Dodge's emphasis on sexual purity in working women's social lives may also have clashed with some young women, even though many initially shared her impulse to prove their virtue to those who doubted it.

Furthermore, Dodge's singular interest in the women's personal lives, rather than their work lives, was too limiting. Positioning herself as just one of the girls, Dodge tried to connect with them based on a shared gender interest in spirituality and morality. Without an adequate understanding of their work conditions, however, she could do little to substantially change the circumstances of their lives. Later, Mary Kenney O'Sullivan, a bookbinder and labor organizer active in the WTUL, complained that she had been a member of a working girls' club, but the club focused too much on recreation and not enough on wages.[53]

It took several decades for the YWCA to begin to discuss industrial conditions. YWCA industrial secretary Florence Sims admitted that her first interest was encouraging the women's religious beliefs, then organizing entertainment and recreation. But industrial programs, she concluded, did not take root until YWCA members realized they needed to provide working women with the freedom to determine their own agenda. In the 1920s, allies in the YWCA finally became interested in organizing for higher wages, maximum hours, and other industrial conditions.[54]

Despite these shortcomings in her relationships with working women, Dodge was blessed with vision and goals, and the money to carry them out. In order to unite the two groups into a combined YWCA, she used her diplomatic skills and her own money, which paid for the expenses of the merger committee. She created a strong centralized national organization, built a new headquarters building in New York, and tried to put the national YWCA on firmer financial footing. This was necessary because the YWCA would remain united only if a strong national organization could oversee its branches.

As president, she almost single-handedly kept the new organization afloat by subsidizing the national board headquarters.[55] According to records, headquarter expenditures in 1907 were $82,000, of which she gave $48,000; in 1914, they were $240,000, of which she gave $98,000. She contributed $450,000 for a new headquarters building, and $50,000 to start an endowment fund for building expenses. In addition, she left the YWCA $500,000 plus $80,000 in her will for a year of operating expenses following her death (to make up for the funds she donated annually to operating expenses). In total, she donated over $1,719,000 to the YWCA.[56]

Dodge also wanted to bring African American women more fully into the organization. Separate branches for blacks and whites developed, with about ten black branches in 1906, although only four of these were affiliated with the new national organization. Dodge urged white women to meet to discuss what they called "the Colored Question" the following year; at this time, they did not consider inviting black women to join the meeting. Southern black branches could be administered through the national headquarters in New York rather than through unwelcoming southern state organizations. However, national meetings remained white only. Black women continued to press for expanded participation in the YWCA. Dodge made a substantial financial contribution that allowed black women to open a branch in Harlem despite opposition from white members. She then called for more discussion of race within the YWCA, leading to a conference in 1915 organized by the Sub-Committee on Colored Work, which took place after her death.[57]

Eventually the YWCA desegregated and became a leading women's group, calling for integration well before the civil rights movement of the 1950s and 1960s.

At her death, Dodge willed $500,000 to Teachers College in New York, $200,000 to the New York YWCA, and many smaller gifts of $5,000 to $25,000 to organizations and individuals.[58] Her extraordinary generosity stabilized the institutions she helped build. Dodge had the financial clout to realize her vision for a strong, centralized, and unified YWCA, and a notable college for teachers—primarily women.

Despite her ability to lead the YWCA down the paths she wanted, Dodge was careful to downplay power over the organization when she and her friends gave money. In a proposed YWCA budget for 1907–8, she explained that she would be willing to raise additional needed funds but that they would simply be listed as from an "interested friend," without revealing who the donors were. Dodge asked if the board members were willing to accept this condition. "Nothing would be so harmful for a movement like ours as to have the field at large feel that a few people were responsible for the work or the expenditures," she cautioned. "All must feel it is theirs and that in consequence they will have to share in giving as well as working."[59] This approach potentially diffused resentment from the other leaders over the role that Dodge played. How much the working girls knew about Dodge's gifts is not clear.

Ironically, despite her seemingly naive claim that she had simply been paid her wages in advance, she also had a sophisticated understanding of how her financial support could undermine the very organizations she was supporting. Her careful attention to how the gifts would be perceived shows a self-awareness that Margaret Dreier Robins, despite her more insightful dedication to working conditions, did not share when she financed the WTUL.

MARGARET AND HER YOUNGER sister Mary Dreier were wealthy leaders of the WTUL, an organization that came closer than any other during the Progressive Era to a cross-class coalition. Although historians have judged the WTUL coalition ultimately lacking, the sisters' use of the money they inherited to further the organization spoke to both their feminist ideals and their progressive vision. Margaret, Mary, and their three siblings were born to German immigrants Theodor and Dorothea Dreier in Brooklyn, New York. Theodor was a partner in an English iron firm and a member of the German Evangelical Church.

Margaret Dreier Robins. Courtesy of Library of Congress Prints and Photographs Division, LC-USZ62-113066.

The younger sister, Mary, born in 1875, met Leonora O'Reilly, a former factory worker who became a leader in the WTUL, at Asacog House, a settlement house in Brooklyn. O'Reilly brought Mary to the WTUL, where she quickly became president of the New York branch. She lived with her partner, Frances Kellor, from 1905 until Kellor's death in 1952. A lawyer and activist, Kellor focused on the difficulties immigrant working women faced, and led various state and private organizations dedicated to immigration and Americanization.[60]

Mary introduced her older sister Margaret, born in 1868, to the WTUL. Margaret already had an interest in working women and had chaired the legislative committee of the Woman's Municipal League. Soon after joining the WTUL, she met and married Raymond Robins, a preacher, lawyer, and settlement-house worker, as well as a former Alaskan miner.[61] The couple moved to Chicago, where, despite their wealth, they lived on the top floor of a tenement building. While there, Margaret continued her work with the

Mary Dreier. Courtesy of Library of Congress Prints and Photographs Division, LC-USZ62-53517.

WTUL, becoming president of the Chicago chapter and the national body in 1907. Margaret and Raymond retired to Chinsegut Hill in Florida in 1924. Used to her role as older sister, Margaret was well organized and had a commanding presence, whereas Mary was more introverted.

Correspondence between the sisters reveals their deep interest in what Mary called "the cause of Woman's freedom." Both the Dreiers worked in the WTUL and the suffrage movement to ensure that all women across classes could be free.[62] After years of activism in the WTUL, frustration with unionization ultimately led Mary to see suffrage, rather than labor unions, as the best vehicle for empowering working women. In 1916, she wrote, "The enfranchisement of all women is the paramount issue for me . . . [and] the only way to obtain it is to go after it, irrespective of all else. . . . The attitude of the labor men to the working women has changed me from being an ardent supporter of labor to a somewhat rabid supporter of women and to feel that the enfranchisement of women and especially my working class sisters is the supreme issue." Both sisters were avid suffragists, often asked to speak in favor of suffrage for working women, and they made substantial financial contributions to the movement. They both also believed in women's rights, particularly for working-class women.[63]

Robins and Dreier had very different ideas from Grace Dodge about the needs of working women. While Dodge emphasized purity and morality, Robins and Dreier called attention to women's low wages and exclusion from labor unions. They did not question women's primary responsibility for children but used it to draw attention to the plight of working women who faced discrimination in the workplace and the burden of caring for the house and children at home.[64]

The WTUL gained attention from many wealthy women during the Shirtwaist Strike of 1909 in New York City. This strike involved tens of thousands of female garment workers from various factories.[65] A group of affluent women, dubbed "the Mink Brigade," marched on the picket line with the strikers and joined the WTUL. According to Schneiderman, "They lent prestige and, more important, an aura of respectability to our demonstrations. This was most important for it helped to weaken the attempts of the unsympathetic to force the women back to work through prison sentences and physical violence."[66] After Dreier was arrested on the picket line, the police had to modify the violent treatment given to strikers due to the publicity surrounding the arrest of a wealthy woman.[67] Thus, wealthy women brought publicity and legitimacy to the labor strike, just as they were doing for the suffrage movement and would also do for the birth control movement.

Robins, Dreier, and many of the new allies made crucial donations to strikers. Ally and reformer Carola Woerishoffer donated $10,000 to the strike fund. Woerishoffer was born in 1881. Her father, an investment banker, died a year later, leaving her a million dollars. Woerishoffer attended Bryn Mawr College and then started volunteering with settlement work, factory inspection, and the WTUL.[68] In order to investigate conditions, she worked one summer in a steam laundry. She died in a car accident while checking on immigrant labor camps in 1911.[69] Because Woerishoffer understood the potential for power that her wealth provided, she tried to avoid it by giving anonymous and unrestricted gifts. One admirer, Vladimir Simkhovitch, recalled an argument they once had: "I accused her of wanting to have her own way, because she was paying for it! . . . She told me later that nothing could hurt her or insult her more than being accused of money-rule—because it was the sole and only thing in the world that she was always determined to avoid."[70] During the Shirtwaist Strike, she went to the courtroom with a check for $75,000 and declared she would pay bail for every girl for the entire strike, then gave a contribution of $10,000 to create a fund for the Strike Council, to cover all strikes of women workers.

Socialites Dorothy Whitney Straight, Alva Vanderbilt Belmont, and Anne Morgan, daughter of J. P. Morgan, also were drawn into supporting workers during the strike. Belmont loved the limelight and was gaining extensive publicity for her role in the woman suffrage movement. Between their own donations and their solicitations for strikers, Belmont and Morgan helped the WTUL raise over $5,500. Morgan was elected to the executive board of the WTUL, underwriting publicity work.[71] Belmont organized a mass rally at the Hippodrome on December 5, to which she invited suffragists to speak, and called for the rally to be "political" as well as pro-union. Morgan sponsored a tea to raise money for strikers at the Colony Club. Straight became a regular contributor, and in 1916, Robins reported that after years of smaller donations, Straight had pledged a large sum over several years. Later, Straight raised $20,000 for a building for the WTUL, including her own contribution.[72]

Despite the publicity and money, strikers resented upper-class women's attempts to control their actions or image.[73] Morgan angered strikers with her comments disparaging socialists' influence over them as well as her push for strikers to reach agreement and settle without achieving all their demands, most notably the demand for union recognition. In response, colleague Elizabeth Thomas warned O'Reilly about the dangers of wealthy women in the WTUL: "If the help of benevolent ladies is to be bought at the price of free speech," she noted, "then it comes high!"[74] O'Reilly also hesitated to endorse Morgan and Belmont because she worried that it would cede control to them, since it was too difficult to disagree with them.[75] Straight drew less ire because she was generous but not demanding. When her second husband pushed her to consider how she wielded her fortune for good (or not), Dorothy replied, "I have always been on my guard against the danger of associating wealth with power. I mean, I have always been conscious of the terrific evil inherent in wealth when it is used for power and I have probably leaned over backwards in the effort to dissociate myself from controls."[76] Her donations to the WTUL came without any restrictions or demands.

After this important strike, the WTUL began to shift its strategy away from a singular focus on direct support of strikes. While still supporting unionization, especially through training women to become union organizers, it broadened its efforts to include publication of a journal, *Life and Labor*;

increased activism in the woman suffrage movement; and lobbying for protective labor legislation.

The involvement of the WTUL and women like Belmont and Morgan in the 1909 strike captured the possibilities and problems of the WTUL writ large: while allies gave important support and financial assistance, they also caused significant discomfort and conflict. Robins and Dreier faced this quandary over the course of their work with the WTUL. From its inception, the WTUL was intended to be different from other women's organizations, like Dodge's Working Girls' Societies, because it was committed to trade unionism and because, to a greater extent than the clubs, it aimed to create a cross-class alliance of equals. The WTUL even inscribed this idea into its constitution, which required that the majority of the nine executive board members had to be female trade unionists.[77] According to Dreier, "Broadly speaking, the organization worked on the principle of helping industrial women to help themselves. It was a new concept of social service for remedying industrial evils. Up to this time work had been done for working women by socially-minded women and men of other classes; now, however, they were co-operating with working women, developing leadership among the working girls themselves, democratizing social service in this field."[78]

Such cooperation could only be possible if the allies and working women understood each other. Biographical sketches praise Robins for her understanding of women workers.[79] Her speech on domestic service, which pointed out the difficulties endured by domestic workers, reveals her ability to relate to the point of view of domestic workers rather than that of only the elite women of her own class who hired them.[80] Such an outlook came from her religious beliefs as well as her idea of democracy. Robins thought that divisions by wealth worked against democracy, which functioned best when workers had their own say.[81] She believed that industrial freedom was necessary to fulfill ideals of religious and political freedom in the nation. She reminded WTUL members "that the potency of light, that the power of life, that the spirit of God is hidden in each human heart, [and] that we are seeking to set it free."[82] She explained that the WTUL was "not a work of charity. It is not a work of endowing some one with a gratuity. It is started so that the girls and the women may be placed in a position where they may be helped to help themselves."[83]

Yet despite these ideals, and belying the coalition of worker and ally in the WTUL, distrust abounded. Robins often talked about women workers as "younger sisters" or "young girls" who needed the assistance of women in the

WTUL to understand the benefits of unionization.[84] Her sister expressed frustration at the lack of trust and friendship between the allies and the workers. Dreier complained that the women workers who were leaders in the book-binders union "never take us into their confidences or ask our advice. . . . They are not exactly on the square with us, never regarded us as friends really."[85] She found it difficult to work with working women because they were worn out from their wage work, and "there isn't any energy left or effective work at the end of the day." Dreier thought this hampered their ability to effectively nominate and elect the best officers in their union, but she faced resistance when she tried to interfere. A disagreement over leadership in ILGWU Local 25 in 1911 led Dreier to complain, "Everybody else is up in arms against us for fear we are butting in on a proposition which does not belong to us." The union, she feared, would "go to pieces" or be "smashed up" without the WTUL's intervention, but the working women "cry out in holy horror at the League usurping authority."[86] Clearly, workers and allies struggled to get along.

Dreier exposed her lack of empathy and condescending attitude when she wrote her sister that some of the workers were "giggly girls whose sole interest in life was boys and how to attract them, . . . oversexed and unwholesome, and I don't like them."[87] Notably, she lacked the sympathy expressed by Dodge when noticing differences in sexual moral standards, even if Dodge's attitude was laden with condescension.

Cultural differences in manners were also an overwhelming problem. There were ethnic, religious, and language differences among the Irish, Russian, Italian, and other women. In order to create the desired shared sisterhood based in common gender identity, the WTUL first had to overcome cultural differences and social discomfort between the wealthy and the workers. Historian Sharon Dye argues that the Sunday teas held for the groups to get to know one another were awkward for both groups.

The fact that allies sometimes seemed to prioritize manners and culture over labor activism was another barrier, just as it had been with the working girls' clubs and YWCA's initial interests.[88] Gertrude Barnum complained that she had come to the WTUL searching for a focus on wages and hours but had found even there that some allies prioritized cultural programs.[89] For example, ally Laura Elliot insisted on arranging singing classes, a chorus, and visits to an art museum for the working women. Despite O'Reilly's disapproval, Elliot held her ground. "You cannot push me out and you cannot make me afraid of my working girl sisters or render me self-conscious before them," she wrote to O'Reilly.[90] Although Elliot refused to change, her fight with O'Reilly reveals the consciousness of class that each woman had and the difficulty of creating a classless society within the WTUL despite best intentions.

Dodge's solution, establishing personal relationships, did not suffice. O'Reilly, despite her deep friendship with Dreier, sometimes still had difficulty overcoming the vast differences between them. This was especially true early in their relationship, when O'Reilly wrote her mother during a visit to the Dreiers' home that she was with "one of the loveliest families that ever existed. . . . Yet," she explained, "my whole soul seemed to burn with the old rebellious spirit. The inequality as expressed in the two modes of life: that of the 'old Man' with barely enough to eat," in contrast to the abundance of the Dreiers. "It seemed to rush up and crowd out every kindly feeling in my heart. For a spell it seemed as if I must get home by the next train. Yet what good would that do? And how it would hurt dear beautiful Mary Dreier."[91] O'Reilly's deep class identity interfered with her desire to forge bonds across class. It was difficult for her to look past Dreier's wealth.

Realizing that the differences between them could derail the organization, O'Reilly thought it crucial that allies avoid condescension. She noted that the WTUL had to reach wealthy women using "an appeal to altruistic principles for human affairs" rather than "the attitudes of lady with something to give to her sister," which she insisted must be dropped. "We must never get where we do *for* the T[rade] U[nion]. We must do *with* them" (italics added).[92] Her conviction was clear. She warned that for working women, "Contact with the Lady does harm in the long run. It gives the wrong standard."[93] The "wrong standard" referred to ways of living (including dress) that the working women could never afford. O'Reilly knew firsthand that for workers in the WTUL, developing close relationships with allies was fraught with tension.

O'Reilly's belief that the division between the two classes was hard to overcome was evident in her suffrage activism as well. The WTUL established and financed the Wage Earners' Suffrage League (formed in 1908 as the East Side Wage Earners' League). As president, O'Reilly told Robins, "We are the only people who can make the W.W. [working woman] understand her own relations to the vote and as well make the leisure-class women understand the workers' point of view—we must get wage-earning women to work it up and there's the rub, for really and truly the other women with the best intentions in the world rub the fur the wrong way, they really don't speak our language and so they use the W.W. and then throw them over."[94] Thus, the problem went beyond a lack of understanding or difficulty communicating. O'Reilly believed that even when allies tried to understand the working women's point of view, they couldn't get along with working-class women, and even worse, they did not truly want to connect with working women. Instead, they used them to argue for suffrage only to abandon them afterward. Notably, the Wage Earners' Suffrage League kept the power to determine its agenda in the hands of working women, who were the only ones allowed to join as voting members.[95]

Rose Schneiderman was also skeptical when she first heard about WTUL. "I had reservations about the organization because of its membership," she later recalled. "I could not believe that men and women who were not wage-earners themselves understood the problems that workers faced."[96] Similarly, Pauline Newman said, "The 'cultured' ladies may be very sincere. . . . I don't doubt their sincereity, [*sic*] but because their views are narrow and their knowledge of social conditions limited, they cannot do as well as some of us can."[97]

Given the distance between allies and workers, and the difference in wealth and age (allies on average were twelve years older than the workers), it is not surprising that there were many clashes among members of the WTUL.[98] Often the lines were drawn between working women and allies, although at other times the disagreements reflected differences in philosophy, age, or personality.[99] Working women's experiences as women working in male-dominated unions left them feeling isolated and unwelcome in unions; their experiences with other women in WTUL could be equally problematic.[100] O'Reilly resigned from the WTUL twice—in 1905 and 1914—and both Schneiderman and Newman also considered leaving.

The power of money was perhaps the biggest obstacle to a cross-class coalition. Had annual dues been paid equally by workers and allies to fund the WTUL, some of the problems besetting it might have been avoided. Dodge attempted to avoid this problem by requiring Working Girls' Society members to pay dues. In the WTUL, O'Reilly suggested to *Life and Labor* editor Stella Franklin that "the money question" had caused gossip about WTUL workers. She suggested that working women pay a per capita tax to create a fund that could then be used by them for their WTUL expenses; this method, she thought, would avoid the question of salaries and create a system in which working women effectively paid for themselves.[101] This suggestion was never put into practice. The big problem for the WTUL was that the major source of funding was the Dreiers. This posed a critical question: If the Dreier sisters and other wealthy women funded the WTUL, did they have the power to decide its agenda despite the equal distribution of allies and workers in positions of leadership as defined by the constitution?

At their father's death in 1899, the sisters each inherited $600,000, the equivalent of nearly $16.7 million in 2016.[102] They quickly began using the money for causes in which they believed. In November 1906, Margaret became concerned that a controversy over the Chicago school board, of which both her husband, Raymond, and Jane Addams were members, would result in fund-raising difficulties for Addams. Robins wrote her, "My father left me a comfortable fortune. I believed he earned every dollar of his fortune honestly and I know that he believed in fair play. I never earned a dollar of it and I recognize that I hold it in trust. I want to and do hereby guarantee that for every dollar lost to Hull House, directly or indirectly, as the result of your work on the Board of Education for the years 1906 and 1907 I will subscribe to the support of Hull House dollar for dollar up to the sum of $20,000."[103] Robins's assertion that her money was honestly earned (as opposed to that of someone like Andrew Carnegie, who paid low wages and did not allow his workers to unionize) was an essential part of her identity. Furthermore, her understanding of the power of money is striking. By giving the money herself, she intended to free Addams from the influence of other donors who might not have agreed with Addams's actions. Having a substantial inheritance also freed Robins to set her own agenda without having to placate other donors when she assumed leadership of the WTUL.

In 1907, Robins became president of the national WTUL and gave a considerable amount of her fortune to its treasury. According to WTUL minutes, she paid "practically the entire expense of the National" WTUL herself the first year. Historian Elizabeth Payne found that "she paid her own traveling expenses as president, conducted the League's business out of an office in her Chicago home, and paid the salaries of two employees of the League; later she underwrote payments to union organizers and provided the seed money for *Life and Labor*, the journal of the WTUL."[104] Most years she underwrote $13,000–$17,000.

She understood that only because the WTUL relied on her money was she able to use her talent and skills on its behalf. "There are times when it makes me quite heart sick," she wrote to Dreier in 1908, "to realize that it is my money which alone enables me to carry out the plans [of the league], and that whatever character or intelligence I have would be utterly useless were it not for the fact that I have the money."[105] Despite some assistance from others, including Julius Rosenwald and Abby Aldrich Rockefeller, Robins felt that it was ultimately up to her to ensure the funding for the WTUL. The responsibility grated on her. "I feel as if I were nothing but a money machine," she complained as late as 1921.[106]

Robins also gave generously to the Chicago branch of the WTUL, and Dreier played a similar role in New York, where "over a third of the contributed money—enough to cover almost all the staff's salaries—came from the Dreier family," according to historian Meredith Tax.[107] Their sister Dorothea also gave to the WTUL. Robins and Dreier even solicited each other. In 1915, Robins asked Dreier to donate a "few hundred dollars" to the national WTUL, in addition to her gifts to the New York branch.[108] When the Dreier sisters no longer gave substantial gifts, the WTUL rapidly declined.[109]

Fund-raising was difficult. Dreier complained that the New York branch "failed" to raise any additional funds for the national WTUL.[110] In 1915, she claimed that the New York League was "busted too—only $55 for all bills due" the next month. "No one," she claimed, showed any concern except her. "Such lack of interest is appalling. . . . I wish we could get a Finance Committee of rich women who see the vision to support us and help the girls—but it's a pretty big vision and person who will give the money to help work out a democratic industrialism and not wish to control it," she concluded.[111] The problem was that Robins and Dreier were not always capable of being that "big person" themselves.

Dreier was so accustomed to she and her sister subsidizing the league that she found it incomprehensible that women in Boston would not do the same. The league there, she wrote her sister, would never amount to much unless one of the wealthy leaders, Elizabeth Glendower Evans or Mary Kehew, gave a more substantial donation. Kehew claimed to be "subsidizing" the branch there with a $25 monthly donation, an amount so small that Dreier thought it was "absurd." She told Evans that "the League would not amount to much in Boston, unless someone guaranteed to give between $2,000.00 and $3,000.00 a year."[112]

Even as Robins claimed she felt uncomfortable with the league's dependence on her generosity, working women who held office in the WTUL complained that she wielded her money powerfully, using it to control the priorities and spending of the WTUL. Newman complained to Schneiderman, "Mrs. Knefler [president of the St. Louis League] is perfectly right when she says the League is owned and controlled by one person." Newman understood that despite Robins's good intentions, her financial control stifled staff freedom and forced them to comply with her desires. "Mrs. Robins means well I am sure, but in the end it is bound to suffer. She does not give the girls a chance to use their brains, she does not want them to think, but wants them to agree with everything she does. And unfortunately they do; they have to; she pays their salaries." In the end, the arrangement meant that the league could not escape being labeled a charitable venture instead of a labor organization. "The girls here are not imbued with the spirit of Unionism—but philanthropy. What would become of the League as an organization were Mrs. Robins to leave them—is easy to imagine," she concluded.[113]

Robins's priorities included a training school for women workers to become union organizers and the *Life and Labor* journal. Some historians have complained that when Robins began to finance the school and the journal in the 1910s, her shift in funding priorities moved the WTUL away from its initial focus on unionization. At the same time, the league began to increase its emphasis on winning protective labor legislation and woman suffrage, which required collaboration with middle-class feminists and reformers rather than union organizers.[114]

Historian Diane Kirkby found that Robins explicitly used her funding to control the content and purpose of *Life and Labor*.[115] Robins pledged $2,500 annually for three years when she founded the journal. She poured much more money into the journal as it floundered: $11,000 from 1911 to 1916. But she was unhappy with the editors, Alice Henry and Stella Franklin, and ultimately withheld funds in order to force them out in 1915. The contest between Henry and Franklin and their benefactor centered on how to define and best reach their readership. Robins wanted articles designed to encourage philanthropy from allies as well as appeals to working women, while the editors thought the primary audience should be other working women. Yet at the same time, Robins did not think they were doing a sufficient job awakening the working class. She condescendingly thought their writing was too intellectual and that the journal should be simpler, modeled after appeals to "children." Furthermore, Henry and Franklin, though more middle class than the factory workers, depended on the wages they earned at the WTUL and complained about their working conditions there.

As a result, Robins withheld funding, and she wrote to Dreier not to send any money until instructed.[116] Robins suspected that Franklin used money intended for the printer to pay salary instead, leaving a $200 publishing bill unpaid. "It looks to me now as if L.&L. must go under,—I see no way out unless I accept full responsibility & this I refuse to do," she wrote. Not wanting Dreier's sympathy to undermine her determination, Robins implored her, "Please do not give anonymously to L.&L. till we know where 'we are at.'" Robins called the "money questions serious but other matters in regard to L.&L. still more serious."[117] She even considered closing the magazine. Instead, Henry resigned, then Franklin. Robins began a fund-raising campaign to pay for the now smaller staff and reduced the number of pages in each issue, then reinstituted funding.[118] According to Franklin, after she quit, Robins resumed funding "now that she had got her own way."[119] Financial statements show that the magazine continued to struggle.[120]

This incident reflects the problems Robins's financial power caused despite her best intentions. Historian Elizabeth Payne concluded that Robins was "overgenerous and self-centered, affectionate and domineering." Used to getting her own way, both as the oldest in a home where she was encouraged to lead and as a married woman in a household where servants followed her commands, it was difficult for Robins when those in the WTUL did not allow her do the same.[121]

Perhaps the quieter and less confident Dreier was better aware that the power of the purse was unfair because she watched her sister Robins exercise it. Dreier commented on the money situation in another organization, commending the YWCA for resisting the temptation to yield to the wealthy. She recalled that in 1920, Robins attended a YWCA convention where the eight-hour day was up for discussion. The convention voted in favor of it even though a wealthy contributor who had been giving $10,000 annually threatened to stop giving.[122] Mary's relative awareness of the power of money, along with other aspects of the sisters' personalities, may have led to the perception among some working women that Mary was well loved while Margaret was not.[123]

The tension over money went beyond the WTUL budget. It was complicated because some women received annuities or stipends from other women. Early on, O'Reilly believed that the Dreier sisters were motivated to their good deeds by their religious faith, calling Mary a "Fairy Godmother" to a girl in need.[124] Dreier became O'Reilly's own fairy godmother when she began providing her with a stipend in 1908. Notably, however, Dreier understood and rejected the potential for control that providing the stipend could give her. She wrote to O'Reilly and her mother that the money would allow O'Reilly to use her talents, making it clear that the money would be forthcoming even if she and O'Reilly disagreed on matters.[125] Dreier also began giving her partner, Frances Kellor, a lifetime annuity the same year.[126] Individual donors also sponsored paid positions in the YWCA (as well as at Hull House, a settlement house in Chicago).

FEMINISTS HAD RECOGNIZED ECONOMIC dependence as part of women's oppression for many years. Chief among them was Susan B. Anthony, who in 1869 debated Frederick Douglass at the Equal Rights Association meeting in New York. Though the issue at hand was whether women should support the

Fifteenth Amendment to give black men the right to vote, Anthony's argument rested on the problems that women's economic dependence caused. Men, she argued, "think that women are perfectly contented to let men earn the money and dole it out to us. We feel with Alexander Hamilton, 'Give a man power over my substance, & he has power over my whole being.' There is not a woman born, whose bread is earned by another, it does not matter whether that other is husband, brother, father, or friend, not one who consents to eat the bread earned by other hands, but her whole moral being is in the power of that person."[127]

Wealthy women understood the power of money. They saw what it could achieve for the men in their families, that it bought not only material possessions but also political influence and power. Some naively thought that women who earned wages, despite their overall poverty, obtained a certain measure of power, too. Many wealthy women romanticized self-supporting women, even though most working women either were married or lived with parents or other relatives whom they helped support and thus, in reality, could not always control their wages.[128] Yet wealthy women may also have been aware of the tradition within many working-class immigrant families of husbands turning paychecks over to wives, who spent money on housekeeping and doled out an allowance to men for spending money. As WTUL ally Gertrude Barnum wrote, "Thank God working girls have a chance to be themselves because they earn their own wage and nobody owns them. I am pretty sure you are somebody, because you are self-supporting."[129] Feminist teacher and reformer Henrietta Rodman, founder of the Feminist Alliance in 1914, expressed a similar sentiment, saying, "Our sisters of the poorer class have the most fundamental right for which we are struggling—the right for economic independence, the right to continue their chosen work after marriage."[130] This romanticized vision of working women's lives (that factory workers had the "right" to work and enjoyed economic independence as a result) reflected the naiveté of the wealthy.

Allies romanticized work and the independence they believed working-class women had due to their wages. Expected to spend their days in leisure and consumption, allies imagined working women's lives to be more meaningful. When wealthy women were limited in their ability to spend money or make financial decisions as wives and daughters, they struggled to gain some control. When they did have financial independence, especially as widows or single women, they thought this made them more similar to wage-earning women despite the vast disparity in the funds at their disposal.[131]

Allies also thought of themselves as workers or self-supporters even if they were not of the working class. Like Dodge, who had asserted that her wages were just paid in advance, the wealthy women who made volunteer work a profession saw themselves as workers because they spent hours at work for an organization, often in an office (even if it was located in their home) with a secretary to assist them.

But even though allies sought sisterhood through an imagined bond of self-supporting womanhood, most laboring women did not share the sentiment. While they appreciated the financial assistance and publicity, they expressed distrust and hesitated to cede control to women who did not necessarily share their social or political views. They recognized that their ability to lead themselves could be compromised if upper-class women led them (or were perceived as leading them). Theresa Serber Malkiel, in a fictionalized account of a luncheon at the Colony Club organized by Anne Morgan during the 1909 Shirtwaist Strike, had her striker declare, "They've brought me to their fashionable clubhouse to hear about our misery. To tell the truth, I've no appetite to tell it to them, for I've almost come to the conclusion that the gulf between us girls and these rich ladies is too deep to be smoothed over by a few paltry dollars; the girls would probably be the better off in the long run if they did not take their money. They would the sooner realize the great contrast and the division of classes; this would teach them to stick to their own."[132]

GRACE DODGE, MARGARET DREIER ROBINS, and Mary Dreier each cared deeply about working-class women. Driven by religious and political ideas that fostered their sense of sisterhood, they sought to know working-class women personally, to aid them, and to enable them to help themselves. As they came to understand the problems working-class women faced, they expanded their agenda to include education and suffrage. They developed and led organizations and, more importantly, financed these organizations with their own inherited fortunes. Their sense of sisterhood was critical to their engagement with working women.

Ultimately, however, the power that their money granted Robins and Dreier hindered the ability for sisterhood to flourish within their organization. "Money-rule" was potentially more divisive than a cultural or social divide. As was the case with wealthy women in the suffrage movement, although they realized the potential for resentment from less wealthy women, it was difficult to prevent. The conflicts in the WTUL, an organization expressly designed to promote cross-class coalition and avoid tilting the balance of power toward wealthy allies, illustrate the enormous power of money. Even when women used their money to benefit other women, they engendered conflict. While Dodge explicitly tried to avoid the appearance of power in the YWCA, Robins seemed unaware of how much resentment her desire to control the WTUL agenda caused.

The experiences of Dodge, Robins, and Dreier also illustrate wealthy women's common concern for enhancing women's economic independence, whether motivated by their contacts with working women or their desire to control their own finances. Education and access to the professions, the right to vote on labor legislation, and the right to control reproduction were essential to economic independence. Women who paid taxes but could not vote began to think of themselves as similar to women who worked but could not vote on labor laws. Even someone like Dodge, whose father did not allow her to go to college or work in the family business, wanted to help working women, claiming that her own wages had been paid in advance. Though not all women made the effort that Dodge, Robins, and Dreier did to truly know and work alongside working-class women, many women philanthropists looked outside themselves to think broadly about the experiences of women in society and became determined to use their money to fight for women's rights. Education, many realized, was another critical component to empowering women, one to which the women in chapter 4 gave generously.

CHAPTER FOUR

An Education for Women Equal to That of Men
Funding Colleges for Women

When Sophia Smith founded Smith College with a bequest totaling just over $393,000 (the equivalent of over $7 million in 2016), she accompanied her donation with a strong statement about the power of education to change women's lives. "It is my opinion that by the higher and more thorough Christian education of women," her will specified, "what are called their 'wrongs' will be redressed, their wages adjusted, their weight of influence in reforming the evils of society will be greatly increased. As teachers, as writers, as mothers, as members of society, their power for good will be incalculably enlarged."[1] Along with other women founders of colleges for women, Smith understood that education, employment, and independence for women were linked, and that women's rights in society depended on increased access to higher education.

Opportunities for higher education for American women in the late nineteenth and early twentieth centuries depended in large measure on the generosity of women like Smith, who gave their money to found colleges for women. Just as they shaped the trajectory of the suffrage movement, a small but significant number of monied women were determined to provide access to college for young women, who were still shut out of many of the nation's universities. Creating separate colleges for women ensured access for women to schools promoting rigorous standards of scholarship while emphasizing a classical or liberal arts education alongside practical training for women to become teachers, artists, or professionals. Like suffragists and supporters of labor activism, they promoted women's independence through education and professional training. Despite their enormous influence, this small group of wealthy women have occasionally had their legacy diminished by administrators or historians who portrayed them as weak, elderly, and infirm women of little import, rather than the fiercely determined women dedicated to bettering women's lives that they were.

Smith's bequest came at the end of the nineteenth century, just as a wave of wealthy male industrialists turned their attention and their fortunes to education. Jonas Gilman Clark, Ezra Cornell, and John D. Rockefeller founded Clark, Cornell, and the University of Chicago, respectively, while Cornelius

Vanderbilt and Benjamin Duke gave millions to transform small colleges into strong centers of academic excellence. These donations were notable for their size—often millions of dollars—and, in some cases, for the educational vision of the donors. Cornell, for example, ensured that his school would emphasize engineering and applied science as well as liberal arts.

In 1965, historians Merle Curti and Roderick Nash examined the influence of philanthropy on higher education and dedicated a chapter to the expansion of women's higher education.[2] However, the chapter provides the impression that men were the primary force behind women's colleges. The authors cover in some detail the Seven Sisters (Vassar, Mount Holyoke, Smith, Bryn Mawr, Wellesley, Radcliffe, and Barnard), known for academic rigor and considered the equivalent of the Ivy League for men. Curti and Nash highlight industrialist Matthew Vassar, who founded Vassar College; physician Joseph Taylor, the primary benefactor of Bryn Mawr; and Henry Durant, who cofounded Wellesley College. However, they do not discuss dean and president M. Carey Thomas's role in transforming Bryn Mawr into a college focused on academic excellence, nor do they explore Pauline Durant's role at Wellesley. Smith College founder Sophia Smith is marginalized in favor of her preacher, John Greene, who as college trustee later took credit for the idea for her donation. Even less attention is paid to women's colleges beyond the Seven Sisters. Outside the Northeast, Indiana Fletcher Williams, Ellen Scripps, and Josephine Newcomb merited only brief mention for their roles in founding colleges. While the authors found that individual donors were important to the opening of women's colleges at the turn of the century, they praised administrators, such as Greene, and hands-off donors like Vassar, who allowed male college presidents to direct the education (and again ignored female president Thomas at Bryn Mawr).[3] Other historians have also downplayed the role that some women played in founding and running their colleges, instead emphasizing the ways their gender and age incapacitated them and necessitated strong male advice and direction.

Rejecting studies that portrayed women founders as frail, weak women, whose gifts and colleges were shaped by the influence of male presidents and advisers, this chapter adds to several recent works that have just begun to capture the importance of these women and their gifts.[4] It traces the ideas of five women founders about women's education and women's rights, and explores their own vision for why they gave, what they wanted their colleges to be like, and how they believed education would benefit women. It argues that the schools they founded were particularly crucial because they provided access to education for women around the nation, in the Northeast, South, and

West. While men debated the propriety of coeducation and the capabilities of women, these women put their fortunes behind their strong belief in women's empowerment through education.

Women's colleges were crucial to women's ability to access higher education because opportunities for women to attend a college offering a rigorous academic program were still hard to find in the late nineteenth and early twentieth centuries. Few colleges were coeducational, especially in the Northeast and Southeast, and even then the top private colleges—Harvard, Princeton, Yale, Amherst—were for men only. With completely integrated coeducation still controversial and limited, and relatively few men interested in women's education (notwithstanding those mentioned in Curti and Nash), it was crucial for women of means to found women's colleges that could offer a rigorous academic program on par with that at the best men's colleges.[5] A small but significant group of women made their mark by founding women's colleges. Others created "coordinate" colleges: a college for women within a larger university. In so doing, they created a parallel structure of women's institutions and women's power.[6]

This chapter explores why Sophia Smith, Indiana Fletcher Williams, Josephine Newcomb, and Ellen Scripps founded Smith, Sweet Briar, Newcomb, and Scripps colleges, respectively. In addition, the chapter examines Jane Stanford, a rare female cofounder of a coeducational university, who shared many of the characteristics and experiences of the other founders under consideration. Stanford was dedicated to offering women an equal opportunity for education, though she later questioned the propriety of coeducation. Because she insisted that Stanford admit women when she and her husband founded it, and took over as the school's ruling trustee two years later, at her husband's death, she shaped the school at its founding, as did the other women in this chapter. (Chapter 5 considers women who used a donation to force an already established school to become coeducational or more welcoming to women.)

The depth of women philanthropists' influence on the development of higher education for women becomes even more apparent when these five women are examined together. The reputation these schools achieved for academic excellence was essential to proving women's intellectual capabilities. Furthermore, this group of founders is significant for their regional breadth: they brought a higher standard of academic rigor to the South and West, as well as to Massachusetts, home of America's first college, Harvard.

These women had strong visions of women's potential, even though they varied in their support of the woman suffrage movement and other organizations promoting the rights of women. Although each of these women had distinct ideas regarding women's rights, they all believed that an education was the best preparation for women's independence, whether she would marry, work, or both. As stewards of large fortunes, they knew from their own experience how important it was to control one's own finances. Each ultimately asserted her independence and decision-making powers, even if she did not seek to do so.

Women founders of colleges were particularly important because they embodied the independence they hoped education could provide to other women. For many years, Smith College students paid their respects at the grave of the college's founder, Sophia Smith. Women at Sweet Briar College could see the personal effects of college founder Indiana Fletcher Williams preserved at the college and annually paid respects to her daughter's grave. Even though founder Ellen Scripps never saw the campus of Scripps College, the first class of students made a pilgrimage to her house to visit her. Students at Newcomb College and Stanford University met Josephine Newcomb and Jane Stanford at formal receptions and teas hosted by the founders, as well as through informal interactions on campus. Although each of these colleges had a male president, they were all founded by women, and knowledge of these women founders and the example they set of what women could achieve had a strong positive influence on their early graduates, as well as the wider public. Women founders helped legitimize women's higher education. The founders' vision was embodied in the young women at their schools, who were proving women's intellectual abilities and making their mark on society.

Their gifts are even more notable because they deviated from the norm, in that most wealthy women who had funds at their disposal and were interested in education gave to men's colleges in order to honor fathers, husbands, or sons. In complaining that wealthy women did not give enough to the suffrage movement, for example, Matilda Joslyn Gage asked, "Is it not strange that women of wealth are constantly giving large sums of money to endow professorships in [men's] colleges yet give no thought to their own sex—crushed in ignorance, poverty and prostitution—the hopeless victims of custom, law and Gospel, with few to offer the helping hand, while the whole world comes to the aid of the boy and glorify the man?"[7] The atypical donations that these founders made were critical to women's education, as well as the larger feminist agenda.

As historian Andrea Walton notes, studies of educational institutions and the women who shaped them help us understand "the ways philanthropy enabled women to cross certain boundaries—to participate in the life of the university and to transcend or enlarge upon certain expectations of 'woman-hood.'" Walton's article—on Grace Hoadley Dodge's role in founding Teachers College of Columbia University, and Elsie Clews Parsons's support for anthropology at Columbia—is one of the few studies that focuses on women's philanthropy for women's higher education. She argues that "engaging in philanthropy itself was educative and liberating; it enabled them to invest personal meaning, including gender-specific concerns, into giving. Educational philanthropy was an avenue by which women might pursue and promote personal, intellectual, and social goals."[8] The creativity, passion, and determination of the five founders are evident in their giving.

As will be evident, while their own access to formal education varied, with Smith and Stanford attending formal schools only briefly, Newcomb living abroad in France, and Williams and Scripps going to college, they all expressed intellectual curiosity and were avid readers, and most were enthusiastic travelers. Similarly, the women in chapter 5, whose donations funded coeducation rather than single-sex women's colleges, had a range of formal education but a common dedication to learning. Some of these donors compensated for their own lack of formal education, while others wanted to ensure that as many women as possible could share the experience they had. They fulfilled their own personal goals, such as promoting social change and expanding access to education and employment. Ultimately, the result was increased independence for women.

Significantly, the "feminism" of these women was not as widely recognized as that of many of their contemporaries, who were leaders in the suffrage, birth control, and labor movements. For example, while Stanford and Scripps supported women's right to vote, especially with financial donations, they did not take leadership roles in suffrage organizations. Collectively, these five women left no fiery speeches about women's equality and did not march in parades or picket the White House. Yet the evidence shows they were all dissatisfied with women's place in society and believed education would broaden opportunities for women. All were concerned that women be able not only to attend college but also to gain employment if desired, with education providing the necessary training. While Newcomb College became known for its pottery classes, designed particularly to enable women to earn money through art, the other founders also expressed concern about "practical" training.[9] In the more than five decades between Smith's death and bequest in 1870 and Scripps's donation to found the college in 1926, the need to increase educational opportunities for women continued, as did the determination of wealthy women to do so.

The fact that the women founders were all elderly, were unmarried (Smith and Scripps) or widowed (Newcomb, Williams, and Stanford), and either had never had children (Smith and Scripps) or had lost an only child to an early death (Newcomb, Williams, and Stanford) is crucial because it means that they had the power to dispose of their fortunes as they pleased. The largest benefactors discussed in chapter 5 were also single (Mary Garrett) or widowed (Katharine McCormick and Phoebe Hearst). While men figured in their decisions as advisers, it was ultimately the decision of the women themselves to champion women's education through the power of their money. They primarily focused on enabling women students, with limited attention to hiring women administrators and teachers.

This chapter explores how these women came to control fortunes ranging from hundreds of thousands to tens of millions of dollars. It also demonstrates how their personal experiences as wealthy independent women shaped their ideas about women's rights and education, whether or not they were well educated themselves. The desire to use their money for a significant purpose led them to contemplate a philanthropic gift, while their desire to empower women convinced them that a college for women (or, in the case of Stanford, open to women) was the best choice for their donations.

IN THE FIRST HALF of the nineteenth century, academies and seminaries for young women began to proliferate around the country. While providing serious academic studies, they offered a curriculum roughly similar to that of the first two years of a modern high school, rather than the classical curriculum leading to a bachelor's degree offered by colleges for men. True women's colleges did not emerge until after the Civil War, with the opening of Vassar in 1865, and Wellesley and Smith in 1875.[10] Newcomb and Stanford followed in the 1880s, Sweet Briar in 1906, and Scripps in 1926.

Whether or not these five women founders had formal schooling, they were well-read and intellectually curious women. Most had large personal libraries. Their biographies reveal differing family experiences because they were raised and lived in various regions of the country. Yet they all had a common desire to promote higher education for women.

Sophia Smith was the first of these women to found a women's college intended to be as good as the best men's colleges. Born in 1796, Smith, the daughter of a Massachusetts farmer and merchant, was the only woman discussed in this chapter who did not move far from her birthplace. She lived virtually her entire life in Hatfield, Massachusetts, with her sister Harriet and

Sophia Smith, n.d. Lovell, Northampton. Used with permission from Smith College Archives, Smith College.

her brother Austin, all unmarried. The only time she lived away from home was when she traveled out of state for one term of school. For the rest of her formal education, Smith attended the Hatfield School, where boys attended in the morning and girls in the afternoon.[11] Her leisure travels were limited to New York, Boston, and Washington, D.C. Smith was quiet, serious, and introspective. By the time she began to consider the idea of founding a women's college, Smith was an elderly and partially deaf woman, living alone after Harriet's and Austin's deaths. She died in 1870.[12]

Indiana Fletcher Williams and Josephine Newcomb had much in common. Both women experienced the death of their young daughters—Daisy Williams at age sixteen and Sophie Newcomb at age fifteen—and the death of their husbands, leaving them alone to manage the investments that made them wealthy women. Both were southern women who spent much of their adult lives traveling and living outside the South, yet they maintained great affection for and close ties with their homes in the South.

Indiana Fletcher Williams. Used with permission from Sweet Briar College.

Born and raised in Lynchburg, Virginia in 1828, Indiana Fletcher Williams was the daughter of Elijah and Maria Fletcher. Her father was a businessman, a slaveholding farmer, an investor, and a land speculator who served as mayor of Lynchburg. He valued education, sending his sons to Yale and his daughters to Georgetown Visitation Convent in Washington, D.C. After graduating with honors from Georgetown, Indiana also attended St. Mary's Hall in Burlington, New Jersey, and traveled extensively throughout Europe and the Holy Land as a teenager. She married James Henry Williams, a minister. They moved to New York, where James gave up the ministry, and they began running boardinghouses and residency hotels. Their only daughter, Daisy, died in 1884. After James died in 1889, Indiana decided to sell their New York properties and move home to the family's farm in Sweet Briar, Virginia, where she lived until her death in 1900.[13]

Josephine Louise LeMonnier was born in Baltimore in 1816 to Alexander and Mary Sophie LeMonnier. She spent time in France as a child. When she

Josephine Louise Newcomb. Used with permission from the Newcomb Archives and Vorhoff Library Special Collections, Newcomb College Institute, Tulane University.

was fifteen, her mother died and her father lost his fortune. Josephine went to live with her sister's family in New Orleans. There she met and married Warren Newcomb, a wealthy grocery merchant. In 1855 they had their only child, Sophie, who died in 1870. Newcomb never established a permanent home for herself after Warren's death in 1866. She spent months at a time in boardinghouses and hotels in New York City and upstate New York, as well as in New Orleans, where she finally bought a home for the winter months, several years after establishing Newcomb College.[14]

Although they established their colleges on the West Coast, Ellen Scripps and Jane Stanford moved there as adults. Born in England in 1836 to Ellen and

James Moggs Scripps, Ellen Browning Scripps lived in Rushville, Illinois, with her father and five siblings after her mother's death. James and his new wife, Julia, had five additional children, including Edward Wyllis, founder of the *Penny Press* and E. W. Scripps Company. Ellen graduated from Knox College in Galesburg, Illinois, and taught school for eight years. She never married but maintained extremely strong relationships with her family, especially Edward, despite the eighteen years between them. When another brother, James, started the *Detroit Evening News* in 1873, Ellen invested her savings in the new business and moved to Detroit to help. She worked as a proofreader, copyeditor, and columnist for the paper, and then for other newspapers founded by her brother Edward. In the 1890s, Ellen retired and followed her siblings to California, where she eventually bought land and built a home in La Jolla. Although she had traveled extensively in the 1880s, including to Egypt, she was elderly and no longer able to travel by the 1920s, when she founded Scripps College.[15]

Born in 1828, Jane Lathrop Stanford was raised in upstate New York, one of seven children born to Jane and Dyer Lathrop. Her father was a merchant. At age twelve, Jane spent one year at the Albany Female Academy. She moved with her husband, Leland Stanford, to California. He was a lawyer and merchant, invested in railroads, building the first transcontinental railroad and serving as president of Central Pacific and Southern Pacific Railroads, and served as governor of California and then a U.S. senator. The Stanfords had a large home in San Francisco and a farm and vineyard outside the city that would become the campus of Stanford University. They also had a home in Washington, D.C., from 1885–1893 when Stanford was a senator. Jane traveled extensively throughout Europe, as well as to Hawaii and Egypt.[16]

Each of these founders had a fortune that she needed to manage, whether earned or inherited. This financial independence was extremely important in driving not only their ability to found a school but also their desire to prepare women for work and financial independence, whether independence was achieved by choice or through widowhood. All these women, except for Stanford, were without close male family members later in life, due to death (Smith's and Scripps's brothers died before them) or to having severed connections with their relatives (Williams and Newcomb). Each forged her own way, advised by ministers, lawyers, or investors.

Smith, Newcomb, and Stanford all inherited their fortunes. Smith and her three surviving siblings each inherited $10,000 from their father. Her brother

Jane Stanford with her son, Leland Stanford Jr. Used with permission from the Stanford Historical Photographs Collection, Stanford University Archives.

Austin successfully invested in stocks, creating an estate worth over $400,000. As the last surviving sibling, Sophia eventually amassed close to a half million dollars from her own and her siblings' fortunes (worth over $9 million in 2016). She managed her investments from Austin's death in 1861 until her own death in 1870 with the assistance of a local lawyer, George Hubbard.[17]

When Warren Newcomb died, his estate of $513,000 was split equally between Josephine and Sophie, their only child. Wisely invested, this inheritance grew rapidly. Newcomb initially relied on her brother for investment advice, although she kept close tabs on his decisions. After a falling out with her siblings, she grew to rely on her bankers, the Pomeroy brothers, with whom she had extensive correspondence regarding her investments.[18]

Jane Stanford also had a brother, Charles Lathrop, whom she trusted for advice, although she took a direct role in her former husband's business affairs. When her husband died, Leland's will gave Jane responsibility for managing the entire estate, including his interests in the railroad businesses, the farm, and the vineyard, as well as for overseeing the college, which had opened only two years earlier. Longtime friend Susan B. Anthony was thrilled to see how much power Jane had.[19] Because of her husband's trust in her, Stanford refused to give power of attorney to one of her husband's business partners. She remained sole executor of her husband's estate, despite the tension this caused between herself and his partners.[20] The court allowed her to spend up to $10,000 monthly to run Stanford University until the estate and lawsuits on it (pertaining to the railroad business) were settled. She had to manage the properties in order to earn that sum. She transformed the vineyards from a money-losing to a money-making business.

Like Stanford, Williams and Scripps earned as well as inherited their fortunes. Williams was known as an astute businesswoman. Having earned a "certificate of merit" from Georgetown in bookkeeping, she kept meticulous records of business transactions of the boardinghouses and hotels she ran with her husband. Furthermore, she made shrewd decisions—for example, selling Confederate notes, which would later become worthless, and investing in tobacco early during the Civil War, which she later sold and invested the profits in securities, earning great dividends. After her husband's death, she sold the New York boardinghouses and hotels and invested in bonds. She also increased her wealth through investing in railroads, banks, and gas companies, as well as renting property in Virginia. She inherited properties after the death of her brother and sister, both childless, in addition to $100,000 from her husband.[21]

Ellen Scripps was also a businesswoman with years of experience in journalism and money management. Her brother noted, "Ellen B. Scripps has always been a working woman. From her girlhood she maintained herself without being any expense to her father or any member of the family. During her whole life, even from the days when she was teaching school, she had contributed to the support of the other members of the family."[22] Ellen had saved money from her salary as a teacher, which she was then able to invest in her brothers' newspaper ventures. In addition to the stock she purchased in the family businesses, she also worked as an editor and journalist, proofreading the paper and writing columns.

Her brother Ed credited her with a strong understanding of the newspaper business and claimed that it was she who advised him, rather than the other way around. According to Ed, "There has never been a moment in my life that I can remember when I have not had almost absolute confidence in, and respect for, my sister Ellen's business ability and her judgment."[23] In addition to her own substantial stockholdings, which were worth millions by the time

Ellen Scripps. Used with permission from the Ella Strong Denison Library, Scripps College.

of her death in 1932, she inherited approximately $600,000 worth of her brother George's stock in the *Cleveland Press* when he died in 1900. She gave the bulk of the proceeds from his stock to the Scripps Institution of Oceanography.

Stanford, Newcomb, and Smith were especially religious women, who prayed for guidance in carrying out their responsibility to better society with their wealth. Smith's journals reveal her self-examinations, resolution, and prayer for self-improvement. She often noted the "solemn responsibility" and "high destination" she felt after inheriting her brother's much more substantial estate. She sought advice from her pastor, John Greene, about how best to use the money. Before her death, Smith gave a $30,000 contribution to Andover Seminary to help train poor men in the ministry, as well as a small fund for the purchase of books for a local library.[24] When Newcomb reflected on the school she founded, she claimed that a college was the most fitting memorial to Sophie and that she was grateful to God "for giving me the will, with the means," to do something of permanent value, "to do that for my sex, which he alone can remove by affliction or death."[25]

Stanford also expressed great stress and concern over her responsibility for the university as well as more broadly for protecting her estate and honoring her husband and son. While a few newspaper articles about Jane Stanford, especially those written while her husband was alive and serving in the United States Senate, referred to her lavish parties and expensive jewels, most articles focused on her charitable works, especially her support for kindergartens and her role as "mother" of Stanford University. Although she gave substantially to kindergartens, the bulk of her fortune went to Stanford University, both during her lifetime and at her death.[26]

While less religious, Scripps also carefully considered the ethics of the enormous wealth her investments provided. Scripps realized as early as 1890 that wealth for personal enrichment was useless to her. She wrote her brother Ed, "I shall feel worthy of being damned if I make no better use of my talents and opportunities, than to leave no other proof of my success after I am dead than a pile of money and an example that money getting was the chief object of my existence."[27] By 1918, Ed shared the same attitude. His money was "piling up," he said, and he wanted the two of them to give it to public institutions. He noted that if he were to outlive her and inherit her money, he would give it away, so she should do so herself.[28] Ellen agreed there was no use "hoarding my money for future possible contingencies which may never come—and if they do won't make much difference to me." Having money did not make her want more. Rather, she wanted to use her money wisely to better society.[29] She was frugal in her spending on her own needs but generous with institutions she believed in, including a hospital, a playground, a library, and many other community projects in La Jolla, as well as many of San Diego's cultural institutions, in addition to Scripps College. After giving away millions of dollars during her lifetime, she died with an estate still worth over $2 million (over $28 million in 2016).

Given their position as unmarried or widowed women in charge of a large fortune, it is not surprising that these women developed strong ideas about women's place in society. Although Smith, Williams, and Newcomb left few direct statements about their beliefs regarding gender equality, there are enough clues to indicate that they contemplated the position of women in society and viewed their schools as an opportunity to improve it.

Apart from her will, evidence about Williams's ideas on women's rights is slim. She may have been influenced to build a school for girls by her father, who was the first in his family to go to college, after which he helped pay for his sister's education. "I think female education is too much neglected," he wrote in 1810. "They are the ones who have the first education of the children and ought to be qualified to instruct them correctly." He also stated, "A good education is the best fortune we can give our children."[30] In addition to her own education, Indiana ensured that her daughter was well educated in private school in New York.

Smith's strongest statement about women also came in her will's specifications for Smith College. Historian Quentin Quesnell, however, also found that her journal and her library reveal that she read widely about women and education. According to her journal, she read Madame de Staël's novel *Corinne*, with its independent, political, and brilliant heroine. After reading the life of French revolutionary Madame Roland, she noted that Roland "found a never failing resource in her richly cultivated mind." Her personal library, though dominated by religious books, included a biography of the founder of Mount Holyoke, Mary Lyons, and *Eminent Women of the Age* (1868), which has biographies of educator Emma Willard, suffragist and feminist Elizabeth Cady Stanton (with a section Stanton wrote on the women's movement), and other prominent women. In biographies of men including Ben Franklin, her only comments were on the few passages within the books on women.[31]

Reverend John Greene claimed that he sent her "Woman: Her Work in the Church" by George Washburn, an article about the need for a college for women in Massachusetts from the *Springfield Republican*, and T. W. Higginson's famous article "Should Women Learn the Alphabet?" (which Higginson answered with a resounding yes).[32] Smith also noted in her journal an interpretation of the disciple Paul's ideas on women that differs from the usual stress placed on his call for women to be submissive to men. She recorded that Professor George Stowe teaches that "Paul treats woman upon two planes, one of which is the natural and physical one in which she is made dependent and subordinate; the second plane is the intellectual and moral one where she is placed in exact equality with man."[33] Given her reading, journal entries, and ultimate decision to provide a women's college with a rigorous curriculum, she must have agreed with the more liberal ideas espoused by these authors.

Furthermore, in addition to founding Smith College, Smith left $75,000 in her will to build an academy in Hatfield that was to serve girls and boys equally, with a preceptress and principal, an equal number of scholarships for girls and boys, and an equal number of female and male teachers.[34] Smith, however, did not extend that requirement to Smith College, which had a largely male faculty. The Hatfield endowment reflected Smith's own ideas about women's education. Even though part of Smith's endowments came from the money her brother left to her, she did not make them to please him. Rather, one of Smith's biographers argues that in founding both Hatfield Academy and Smith College, Smith defied her brother by using the money she inherited from him to support women's education, a cause he did not believe in.[35]

Like Smith, it is difficult to pinpoint Newcomb's exact ideas about women's education and, indeed, women's equality before founding Newcomb College. However, several clues exist. Her personal book collection, like Smith's, indicates she was thinking about women's place in society and the role education could play in shaping it. One notable book is *Woman's Place Today*, written by Lillie Devereux Blake and obtained by Newcomb in 1883. Blake's book consists of a series of lectures in which she argued for women's education and woman suffrage. Newcomb marked several passages and wrote in the margins of the book "good" at various places.[36]

Most importantly, Newcomb was concerned about opportunities for education for women because her daughter Sophie had been a bright and successful student at seminaries in Baltimore and New York.[37] Newcomb regularly reported on her progress, writing her sister, "I desired a brilliant education for Sophie, who I think has the capacities and abilities, to receive one."[38] Sophie excelled academically: a typical report on Sophie's progress noted that she received "the Excelsior or Certificate, as being *first* in all her Classes, & the premium (a copy of Tennyson Poems) for French & Latin."[39] Especially notable is Sophie's achievement in Latin: though Greek was necessary for a bachelor's degree, her study of Latin at her age indicates a fairly rigorous education, one that had become more widely available at girls' academies and seminaries only in the early 1800s.[40] Given Newcomb's own independent situation and her pride in her daughter's academic achievement, it is not surprising that she funded a women's college. She understood the importance of education to a woman's ability to live independently.

Scripps was an independent woman in every sense of the word, and her lifestyle reflects her political beliefs and feminist ideology. Unmarried, she was beholden to no one but herself. Descriptions of Scripps from those who knew her best—her brother, friends, and lawyer—all stress her independent but careful thinking. Scripps supported causes she believed in no matter how unpopular. She declared herself for Progressive Party candidate Robert La Follette and also supported socialism. She responded with a $100 contribution when solicited by Theodore Dreiser to assist the Scottsboro boys, young black men accused of rape.[41]

Scripps was also devoted to women's rights. She was a suffragist, donating to local and national organizations.[42] A generous contributor to the La Jolla Woman's Club, she held meetings at her home before donating the funds to build its clubhouse. As an officer, she spoke to the club on many occasions, stressing women's role in progressive social reform and care for children. In an address on women's place in society, she argued that women needed to consider the universe as their home, thus justifying the extension of their role beyond their own individual homes. She explained that women's clubs were a training ground for women. The papers they wrote and discussions they had at club meetings on many literary, historical, and political topics prepared women for the service they rendered during World War I and as voters. Scripps asserted, "You are better fitted for public service than many who now sit in high places; that you would make wiser legislators, better judges, more efficient public officials. You know that you have the knowledge, the power, the constructive ability and the spirit of justice." While valuing women's roles as mothers and homemakers, she clearly envisioned a much larger role in society for women and exhorted other women to do the same.[43]

According to Mary B. Eyre, a young woman Scripps financially supported in graduate school for psychology, Scripps wanted education and employment for women. She agreed with the idea that women had the right to work and needed the training to prepare for employment. Like George Bernard Shaw, Scripps believed that "women, like men, are entitled to just such rights as they are able to utilize to advantage." Although Scripps thought women could enter any profession, she did assume that they were more naturally fitted for some, such as nursing and medicine. Eyre stressed that Scripps wanted women to use their education to develop and make use of all their talents. Although Scripps College was founded as a four-year undergraduate institution, she also wanted women to attend graduate school for professional training. She supported the creation of a graduate school to be affiliated with Scripps and Pomona Colleges, the first two colleges in what became the Claremont University Consortium.[44] Scripps's strong beliefs in professional roles for women underlay her donations to women's education at Scripps College.

Jane Stanford clearly articulated her interest in issues concerning women's equality, traceable in part through her relationship with Susan B. Anthony, which dated to the early 1870s. In 1871, Anthony signed Stanford's autograph album of famous people with the quote from Alexander Hamilton on the inability to remain independent when another has power over one's subsistence.

By the mid-1890s, the suffrage movement was in full swing in California, and Stanford assisted Anthony by providing railroad passes for suffragists. She invited national leaders Anna Howard Shaw and Carrie Chapman Catt to speak at Stanford University.[45]

Stanford realized that despite her wealth and her control over her dead husband's portion of his business investments, she was discriminated against because of her sex. In 1896, for example, when she again attempted to give Anthony railroad passes, one of her husband's partners, Charles Crocker, denied her request, and she had to involve her brother. Stanford directly connected the powerlessness that she felt when dealing with Crocker to her support for suffrage. Stanford claimed she was for woman suffrage because it was her sex that limited her ability to write the passes herself and forced her to beg for them instead, despite her role as executor of her husband's estate. She complained that she did not have the same power as her husband had had *"because of being a woman.* Could I vote and wear *trousers* I would enjoy more rights," she memorably told Anthony (emphasis in original).[46]

After her husband's death, Jane struggled to assert the power and responsibility that her control over his estate and the university brought her. She was forced to make decisions and to hold firm to them when she disagreed with Leland's business partners or Stanford University's president. Her letters reflect her deep sense of responsibility, her belief that her faith would guide her in her decisions, and the resulting firm hand she used to ensure that her demands were met. Like the other women in this chapter, her choices reflect her strong commitment to education, the betterment of society, and women's rights.

As their backgrounds make clear, these five women were all well-read, serious-minded women who saw their wealth as giving them the opportunity and responsibility to do good. The amount of formal education each woman obtained varied, with Smith, Newcomb, and Stanford receiving little or no formal education, and Williams and Scripps obtaining extensive education for women at the time. Yet despite this difference, each woman believed in the value of education for women. Collectively they read widely, traveled extensively (except for Smith), and thought deeply about the need for women's education. Given their personal independence as widows or unmarried women and their interest in women's rights, it is not surprising that they looked to invest in women's education. In a position to make changes in the lives of other women, these five women each chose to found a college and promote higher education as a means of empowering and enabling other women.

Specifically, their visions of education had two major components: most stressed a combination of academic excellence and equal opportunity for the best education then available to men, as well as some measure of preparation for work and its resulting independence for women. Their own educational attainment did not matter when it came to the type of education they promoted. They wanted women to be fluent in philosophy, art, history, and literature as they were, formal education or not. They did not want limitations placed on women's intellectual strivings. Due to their age and health, it was not the most educated—Williams and Scripps—but Stanford and Newcomb who had the most direct influence on curriculum at their schools. For example, Newcomb supported the pottery and arts training her college offered. In large measure, however, the women founders set a vision and allowed administrators to make decisions about curriculum.

Notably, some of these women founders did not intend their college to include women of color. Two, Newcomb and Williams, specified an education for "white women," while the other women did not address race in their founding documents. The Seven Sister colleges had a mixed record on admitting African American students, with Vassar, Mount Holyoke, and Bryn Mawr excluding blacks until decades into the twentieth century (with the exception of black students unknowingly admitted), and Wellesley and Radcliffe admitting African American women beginning in the 1880s and 1890s. Sophia Smith did not mention race in her plans for Smith, and its first black student graduated in 1900.[47] Jane Stanford is therefore notable, because she apparently ensured that an African American she knew, Ernest Johnson, was admitted to the school in 1891. He was Stanford's first black student, and was likely an exception, as whether any other blacks followed for several decades is not clear.[48]

While it is not surprising that Newcomb and Williams followed southern law and social norms at the end of the nineteenth century (in fact, it would have been shocking if they had not) by inscribing race into their founding documents, these women limited their own visionary gender ideals. Even as Newcomb challenged common expectations for women's dependence, she was unable to challenge racial norms. Envisioning the school as educating young women like her daughter—southern, white—she excluded African American women. Newcomb was a coordinate college of Tulane University, which Paul Tulane founded for white males only. It was not until 1963 that the university desegregated and black women as well as men were welcome.

When Elijah Fletcher died, he left Sweet Briar Plantation to his daughter Indiana and divided the sixty-seven African Americans he enslaved among three of his four children, Indiana included. Although she spent most of her adult life in the North, she retained a servant who had been enslaved and the descendants of others to work for her on the plantation. The racial segregation embedded in Williams's will, which founded Sweet Briar for white women only, was later contested in 1964, when the school decided to integrate and admit African Americans; the court overruled her desire to exclude them, and the school desegregated in 1966. In 2003, Sweet Briar College rededicated the plantation burial ground, which contained over fifty gravestones, with a new marker reading "Sacred Resting Place of Unknown Founders Who Labored to Build What Has Become Sweet Briar College We Are in Their Debt."[49] These women's ideas about moving toward improving the lives of women were for the most part limited to white women, severely diminishing the possibility for an inclusive notion of sisterhood.

The specific stories that follow of how each woman founded her school show how each woman thought about the importance of women's education. As will be evident, these women depended on male administrators to fulfill their wishes. They focused primarily on their vision for students and, for the most part, had little to do with the hiring of faculty (Stanford was a notable exception). Thus, they did not promote women as faculty or administrators the way that several of the donors to coeducational institutions featured in chapter 5 did.

Sophia Smith founded Smith College with a bequest totaling just over $393,000. As noted in the opening to this chapter, Smith's will made it clear that she believed education could have a profound impact on women's lives, ending discrimination against them, increasing their wages, and expanding opportunities for employment and social reform.[50] She founded Smith "with the design to furnish for my own sex means and facilities for education equal to those which are afforded now in our Colleges to young men." However, she was still careful to caution that she did not want "to render my sex any the less feminine."[51]

Although John Greene and his daughter later claimed that Greene encouraged Smith—who was by then, according to Greene, nearly helpless and infirm—to found the school based wholly on his ideas and advice, historian Quesnell argues that her contemporaries recognized her as the visionary. Her stamp on the educational vision for the school is evident from Smith College president Seelye's claim at its opening that "the character of the institution has already been determined by its Founder. . . . By the provisions of the will which gives us our authority as trustees, we are bound. . . . The Founder of the College has fixed the standard for us."[52] Furthermore, Quesnell found that the college catalog for the first twenty years described the school as "founded by Miss Sophia Smith of Hatfield, Mass., who bequeathed funds for that purpose; defined the object and general plan of the institution; appointed the trustees; and selected Northampton as its site." Only later did catalogs begin to credit Greene with a larger role in its creation, after he and then his daughter began to promote him.[53]

Although Greene was clearly an influential adviser to Smith, she did not agree with all his suggestions, most notably that she donate instead to the already established Amherst College and Mount Holyoke Seminary. She also did not take his first suggestions for trustees for the college, and the two debated the location for the school. She sifted through his ideas and her own before instructing her lawyer, Hubbard, on what the final will should say before she signed it. Smith's will funded the college, chose its location and trustees, and specified its high academic standards. Smith was inspired by her religious motivation to do good and her intense desire to aid women.

Smith was fortunate that the trustees and president Seelye carried out her vision and offered the same standards as were found at the best male colleges, as specified in her will. The president of the board of trustees, W. S. Tyler, emphasized the need for a liberal education for the development of the whole person, regardless of sex (even though he did not support coeducation). Under Seelye, the school developed a reputation for top-notch academics. It had a primarily male faculty for its first decades.

Like Smith, Williams founded Sweet Briar College through a bequest at her death in 1900. She left the bulk of her property, approximately $750,000 (over $21 million in 2016), to a board of male trustees to found a women's college on the Sweet Briar property. The will was unsuccessfully challenged by relatives with whom Williams had had a poor relationship and had purposely excluded from sharing in her estate. Williams left few specifications for the school, writing that it was to be "for the education of white girls and young women. It shall be the general scope and object of the school to impart to its students such education in sound learning and such physical, moral and religious training as shall be in the judgment of the directors best fit them to be useful members of society." Williams also noted that she hoped the directors would establish scholarships for needy students.[54]

Williams specifically called for women to be "useful members of society" rather than seek an education as potential wives and mothers. This left the door open to training women for careers in teaching or other occupations. In addition, her attention to needy students suggests that she thought education could offer a woman a chance to earn a living if necessary and thus become financially independent.[55]

THE OTHER THREE FOUNDERS in this chapter founded colleges with donations made while they were still alive, though elderly. They continued to donate to the schools until their deaths, when their estates gave further contributions. Thus, they were able to continue to exert at least some pressure through their donations to shape the schools according to their vision and priorities.

Ellen Scripps founded Scripps College as one of the colleges within an Oxford University–style group of affiliated residential colleges, now known as the Claremont University Consortium. She was influenced by James Blaisdell, president of Pomona College (the original college before the consortium was created), who approached her with the vision of a group of colleges, including a women's college. However, Scripps had her own ideas about the purpose of a college, which she set in motion for Scripps College, leaving Blaisdell, her lawyer J. C. Harper, college president Ernest Jaqua, and the board of trustees to carry out. It was her vision—for Scripps College to "prepar[e] young women for lives of usefulness" through training in independent thinking—that drove the nearly $2 million (nearly $28 million in 2016) she donated to the college.[56]

Scripps's interest in women's education began when she and her sister Virginia donated money and land to the Bishop's School, established by Episcopal bishop Joseph Johnson, to prepare young women for admission to the best women's colleges in the Northeast. Scripps told her lawyer, "I feel more than assured that I have embarked in an undertaking that is almost limitless in its scope and power for good." The school emphasized community service and progressive reform as well as rigorous academics, leading Scripps to comment in 1920, "It is so good to find women 'doing things' instead of spending their time in cooking dainties and embroidering underwear."[57]

Blaisdell then approached Scripps to contribute to Pomona, a coeducational liberal arts undergraduate college, for a lecture fund in honor of Bishop Johnson in 1914.[58] Reporting to her on that fund, Blaisdell told Scripps that Pomona had nowhere to house its women students: some stayed in a "hotel" style dorm, but the majority had to find rooms in private homes in the neighborhood. Scripps agreed to buy land for a women's campus, originally conceived of as a place for female Pomona students to live.[59]

Correspondence among Scripps, Blaisdell, and Harper remained focused on a women's campus through March 1922. Blaisdell, however, was alarmed by the overwhelming number of applicants to Pomona, and rather than enlarging the school beyond a small college, he began to envision a cluster of small residential colleges in the same style as Oxford University in England. The women's campus soon became a women's college in the cluster, and Scripps provided money to purchase the land, the majority of the funds for four dormitories to house all two hundred students, and an endowment for the college.[60]

Notably, the elderly Scripps did not try to micromanage the college. Instead, she set the vision for Scripps College as a school focused on independent thinking and the search for knowledge and truth.[61] Scripps explained, "It is an experimental age, and we don't want to be too sure that we are even on the right track."[62] Rather than a professor lecturing at students from a lectern, she envisioned students sitting in a circle with the professor, discussing and learning together. Scripps posited that the purpose of a college should be to "develop in its students the ability to think clearly and independently, which ability will enable them to live confidently, courageously and hopefully." Scripps College took this directive seriously. It offered a broad humanities curriculum and refused to exert too much control over students' social lives. Harper claimed that Scripps never interfered with faculty hiring or firing except on one occasion in which she championed a controversial figure. Despite the fear shared by some board members that the professor's views were potentially harmful to the new college, Scripps insisted that colleges had to be "free" to face just such views.[63] As she did not specify whether women needed to fill faculty or administrator roles, men dominated the faculty, despite attempts by women on the board of trustees to require half of the faculty to be women. Scripps's example—her open mind, regard for the truth, and tolerance for controversial viewpoints—shaped the college.

Scripps heard regularly about happenings at the college from the president, Jaqua, as well as through her lawyer, Harper, who noted on many of Jaqua's letters the date he read them to Scripps, and kept memorandums of their discussions regarding the school.[64] Given her physical infirmity, it was left to Harper to fight Jaqua to protect her money and her interests. The correspondence between the two suggests that Jaqua wanted to build up the physical campus, moving forward with plans for grounds improvement, athletic facilities, and faculty housing, while Harper continuously pleaded with him to focus instead on increasing the endowment and funding for faculty salaries. The situation was exacerbated because the college opened in 1926, not long before the Great Depression hit. Investments began to yield much smaller dividends, and donors grew less generous. Scripps, Harper cautioned, could not be counted on to give additional gifts, so Jaqua would have to cut spending instead.[65]

Harper intimated to Jaqua that Scripps had originally begun supporting the college out of her appreciation for the residential college cluster system rather than her desire for a women's college, and after having given all the money needed to fund the dormitories, she ultimately left only a relatively small legacy to Scripps College in her will (a $100,000 endowment gift out of a $2-million-plus estate). But given her support for women's rights, her speeches to the La Jolla Woman's Club, her own experiences as a business-woman and philanthropist, and her initial desire to purchase the land for a woman's campus, it is also clear that Scripps would not have given nearly $2 million to Scripps College before her death if it were a residential college for men and not a women's college. Women, she knew, needed education to think independently and to prepare for whatever career they chose, whether it was motherhood or a job outside the home. She wanted women to have a liberal arts education and to be able to train for all sorts of careers, from med-icine to law. She even said she wished that she herself had studied medicine.[66]

Josephine Newcomb also sought to obtain what she called "literary" as well as "practical" education for women. Brokenhearted when her daughter, Sophie, died of diphtheria, Newcomb initially considered founding a Protes-tant orphan asylum in New Orleans in memory of her daughter. It was not until 1886 that she decided to fund a college for white women in New Orleans after being approached by Colonel William Preston Johnston, the first presi-dent of the new Tulane University. Eager to find a donor who would enable him to open a college for women within Tulane, Johnston was guided to New-comb by a mutual friend, Ida Richardson, who knew that Newcomb wanted a memorial to her daughter in New Orleans.[67] "If you think $100,000 will start it I will give you a check for it," Newcomb wrote him.[68] Thus, she wrote the first of many checks to the new H. Sophie Newcomb Memorial College.

Newcomb College began as a coordinate college at Tulane owing to the connection between Newcomb and Johnston rather than out of a prefer-ence by Newcomb for a coordinate college over a completely separate single-sex college. Johnston wanted a coordinate college for women because he believed both that women should have a distinctive curriculum and that this would be a means of educating women at his university without spending any of the money from Paul Tulane: if a donor could be found to finance the women's college, all the money given by Paul Tulane could remain with male students.[69] In fact, founding a women's college within a male university later challenged Newcomb's ability to keep her money dedicated to women's education. Newcomb was anxious to keep her fund separate from the general funds at Tulane.[70]

Once Newcomb made the decision to found the college, she was devoted to the idea of providing higher education to women in New Orleans. She declared it was to be a first-rate college, not just a preparatory school. She shared Johnston's concern that the preparatory school, initially created at Newcomb College to prepare students for the college course, be temporary. She wrote him to agree that "a College should not devote itself to the work of the high schools lest its own progress be retarded."[71] Furthermore, according to the testimony of a friend in court transcripts, she wanted Newcomb to rank with Wellesley, Smith, and other women's colleges then considered to be the best in the country, schools she often referenced in her correspondence.[72]

In her letter to the administrators of the Tulane Educational Fund endowing the school, Newcomb explained that her desire to found a college came from her "deep personal sympathy with the people of New Orleans and a strong desire to advance the cause of female education in Louisiana." She specified only two things: that there be a chapel or room for daily Christian but nonsectarian worship (a liberal attitude at a time when many Christian colleges were sectarian) and that "the education given shall look to the practical side of life as well as to literary excellence."[73] Thus, she was intensely interested in education for girls, and she understood that some girls might need vocational skills to earn independent livings.

In addition to the classical and literary departments, the scientific and industrial departments offered bookkeeping and arts (including pottery) aimed at enabling women to support themselves financially.[74] Newcomb emphasized the respectable nature of the school and its students.[75] Therefore, she did intend for students to learn skills to earn a living if necessary, but through respectable occupations such as bookkeeping, art, or teaching. In this sense, Newcomb—herself a widow managing her financial affairs—broadened her ideas about respectable womanhood to include wage earning and financial independence.

First through her correspondence and then through her extended stays in New Orleans each winter beginning in 1892, Newcomb oversaw changes and additions to the campus. She gave many donations, including additions of $50,000 and $100,000 to the endowment. She wrote a check for $5,000 for a library and one for $125,000 for a chapel, art building, and dormitory. Newcomb carefully vetted all building plans, especially the chapel, for which she selected the furnishings herself—including brass candlesticks—and for which she commissioned Tiffany stained-glass windows.[76] She did not influence faculty hiring, although the college did employ over 60 percent female faculty in its early decades. Despite her enormous interest in the development of the school, Tulane University historian Dyer dismissed her, incorrectly claiming that it was really her male companion, Frank Callender, whose ideas influenced Newcomb College.[77]

Newcomb constantly worried that her money would not be used as she intended for Newcomb College. Knowing the university's financial difficulties, she eventually came to desire a separation from Tulane, especially after its founder, Paul Tulane, died without leaving additional money to the school.[78] Newcomb made a series of proposals designed to ensure that her funds would remain with her college and not be subsumed into Tulane. Ultimately she dropped these demands and her will remained intact, leaving her money to the Tulane Educational Fund for the funding of Newcomb College. The proposals were a result of her long-standing fear that others (her relatives, Tulane) wanted her money for their own purposes.[79]

In the end, Newcomb was right. Newcomb College president Brandt Dixon had a difficult time protecting her money from the larger university. Tulane trustees devised ways to claim some of the money—for example, by taxing Newcomb College for women graduate students and charging the college $2,000 per year toward the salary of the president of the university.[80] The college became less independent over the course of the century. The contentious relationship between Newcomb College and Tulane has continued to the present. As part of a larger reorganization plan after Hurricane Katrina, Tulane moved the Newcomb endowment, worth $40 million, to a new Newcomb College Institute of Tulane University, which supports programming and research on women's issues. This resulted in a recent court case contesting the move by some of Newcomb's remaining relatives.[81] Newcomb's fight to keep her money supporting her goal of education for women has continued into another century.

Although women founders of coeducational institutions at the turn of the century were rare, in 1885, Jane and Leland Stanford together founded the Leland Stanford Junior University as a memorial to their fifteen-year-old son, who died in 1884. The school opened in the fall of 1891.[82] After her husband's death two years later, and against the advice of the trustees to close the school, Jane shepherded the university through a financial crisis until a suit brought against her husband's estate was settled and she could provide a cash endowment.[83] Moreover, the university charter reserved to the founders "the right to exercise all the functions, powers and duties of the trustees," a power she assumed after her husband's death and did not relinquish until 1903, at the age of seventy-five. This caused conflict between Stanford and university president David Starr Jordan, who pushed for years to grow the faculty and the number of students while she refused to raise the payroll, claiming she could not afford to do so.[84] When the court case was dismissed and the estate finally settled, Stanford was freed to donate millions to the school. She focused on building the physical campus—irritating Jordan, who referred to the first decade of the university as the "stone age."

Although Leland dictated the by-laws himself, the couple worked together to found the university. In fact, Harvard president Charles Eliot, who was adamantly opposed to the admission of women at Harvard, nevertheless gave Jane Stanford full credit for her role in the creation of Stanford University. "I thought too," he wrote, "that she had done much more thinking on the subject than [Leland Stanford]."[85] Although they had their differences in priorities, Jordan also recognized Jane's important role at the founding. Jordan claimed that Leland did not give his full estate directly to the university before or at his death if it were to come before hers (as it did) because he wanted Jane to carry out the creation of the school. "His wife was his equal partner as well as his closest friend," Jordan noted.[86]

Not surprisingly, given her support for woman suffrage and women's rights, Jane revealed that it was her idea that women be admitted to the university on equal terms with men, rather than having an all-male university or a separate women's college within it. In 1900, she wrote, "The conception of having the sexes united and put upon an equality in the institution was the result of my own suggestion to my husband." He disagreed at first, but after a day decided that "as I was a coworker with him, signing away as much property to the institution as himself," he should consider the suggestion.[87]

Jane Stanford later told a newspaper reporter, "I favor the education of women, believe in coeducation and, in fact, believe fully in the right of women to have the franchise. Nobody appreciates more than I do the advances of an education of those of my sex. Nor does anybody realize more than I do the effect on society of an educated and enlightened womanhood. A woman can be educated and even vote, if you please, and still be a womanly woman."[88] She insisted that women had to enter as equals to men. She demanded that the school open with both male and female students in the first year. When construction slowed on the women's dormitory, they used a temporary facility so that both sexes would have housing. Stanford ignored calls to create a separate school for women. According to a faculty wife's memoir, "The founders intended that women should be admitted to the University from the first, Mrs. Stanford shrewdly observing that if the men came first and the young ladies came afterwards 'the young ladies might be considered as interlopers.' "[89]

Stanford stated that not only were women to be admitted but they were to "have equal advantage" with male students and to have "every employement [*sic*] opportunity suitable to their sex." This would enable them to be better mothers and better employees who would increase national productivity.[90] Stanford defended women's right to education whether they intended to remain in the home or assume professions outside the home. She declared that women should be allowed to vote, hold office, and work, although she believed there was no higher role than that of wife and mother.[91]

And yet after opening Stanford University as a coeducational university, Stanford later tried to ensure that the number of women students would never equal the number of men because, she said, her husband had wanted the college to be primarily for men. The number of women students grew rapidly, from about one-third of the first class to 51 percent in 1895. A member of the pioneer class noted, "The most logical assumption is that Stanford is better suited for ladies than other colleges. This would seem to point to the possibility that within twenty years Stanford may become the Vassar of the Pacific Coast."[92] Stanford, however, was not about to let that happen. The university, she insisted, "must not change its character as primarily an institution for young men," and in 1899, she established a limit of five hundred women students.[93]

Susan B. Anthony wrote a scathing letter to Stanford when she heard the news: "This sends a chill over me—that this limitation should come through a woman and that one my dear Mrs. Stanford to whom I had looked for the fulfillment of our dream of perfect equality for women in her university," she scolded. Anthony suggested that specifying that the proportion of male and female students should remain equal would have been a better choice, while the quota limited women's opportunity for education and suggested that their presence on campus was detrimental to the university.[94] Stanford University was eventually able to enroll more women by keeping the number of male and female students proportional (approximately one-third women, as it had been when Stanford was alive) until the court granted the school permission to admit students without regard to sex in 1973.

Why Stanford took such a hard stance is not clear. She claimed that she was being true to her husband's desires. She may have thought that because Stanford was a memorial to her son, it should be predominately for boys.

Most importantly, she became disillusioned with coeducation, what she termed an "unsolved question," because she was becoming increasingly worried about the social interactions of male and female students at Stanford. In late 1904, she complained that the girls' dormitory was not properly supervised, and "the free and familiar intercourse between" male and female students in the dormitory and the sorority houses was a concern to her. "You and I are already aware that many things have happened that we pray God may never happen again," she cryptically wrote to Jordan.[95] Stanford was at the forefront of a backlash against coeducation taking place at schools around the country where women were beginning to grow in numbers and academic accomplishment.[96]

This later questioning of the value of coeducation may have led to the common view today that it had been Leland's idea to admit women in the first place. According to her longtime secretary's memoir, written in 1935, Jane wanted it to be a boys' school as a memorial to her son, and her husband had to persuade her to allow women to enter. The memoir also claimed that she thought coeducation might cause social diversions, detracting from the highest level of academics. However, she did not express concerns about preventing immoral behavior among coeducational students until 1899, undergirding her contention that the original decision to admit women to Stanford had been hers, not her husband's.[97]

As the sole decision-making trustee of the university until 1903, it was up to her to determine matters of importance to the university, including whether or not women should be admitted. Though the president had the right to hire and fire faculty, Stanford asserted her position on certain faculty members, resulting in the firing of two professors and controversy over the lack of academic freedom for faculty under Stanford. While she did not insist on hiring women faculty, there were six in the first decade of the university. She fought Jordan on salaries, spending, and campus priorities. She had the most say in how the school was run out of all the women founders in this chapter. Stanford carefully controlled the makeup of the board of trustees, even though they had limited power initially. She depended on her brother, the college treasurer, to help her manage spending. She oversaw the building of the campus, following elements of the original campus plan designed when her husband was alive, but deviating from the plan for certain buildings according to her own wishes. Her determination to shape the college led to extensive criticism from early-twentieth-century historians, who deplored her "meddlesome . . . mothering" of the university and interference with academic freedom.[98]

At age seventy-five, Stanford changed the university charter, ceding her powers as sole trustee to the board of trustees, who elected her president. She left California, traveling to Egypt, though she did not give the board free reign to run the university without her. Instead, she tried to retain power on campus through correspondence with influential board members. The board largely followed her dictates of keeping the number of faculty steady. It also worked to limit the president's power in hiring and firing and add faculty governance. Stanford died unexpectedly while in Hawaii, the victim of strychnine poisoning. Who might have killed her or why remains unanswered today.[99]

THE LIVES OF THESE five women clearly show that as widowed or single women of great means, they felt a great responsibility to invest wisely and ultimately spend their fortunes for the good of the community. Although they had male advisers—brothers, lawyers, college presidents—each ultimately had to make decisions as to how best to invest her money for the good of others. Each of these women, as is evident by their donations to the woman suffrage movement, speeches to women's clubs, and books by and about women, was concerned with women's rights and desired to improve opportunities for women. As women who had to make independent decisions and care for themselves, as well as take charge of their investments and businesses, they realized the need for women to obtain an education that would better enable them to earn money through employment and thus assert their independence in society. Therefore, they founded colleges where women could obtain "sound learning," achieve "literary excellence," and search for knowledge and truth.[100] In addition to providing the means for women to improve their "wages" and their employment, these schools allowed women to benefit from the "practical side" of learning.[101] In this way, women were enabled to become "useful members" of society and to increase their "power for good."[102]

These colleges were explicitly connected to their founders' concepts of equal rights for women, tied not just to their belief in women's employment but also to women's political rights and their desire for women to "live confidently, courageously and hopefully." As Sophia Smith wrote, she endowed a college to offer young women the "means and facilities for education equal to those which are afforded now in our Colleges to young men."[103] The founders each exerted their power to create such a college, sometimes struggling to continue to promote their vision of each school. They did not, however, insist on having a female faculty for the women students.

The two southern founders, Newcomb and Williams, explicitly limited their schools to white women and their vision for combating gender inequities by race. The silence around race from Scripps, Stanford, and Smith when it came to their schools allowed African Americans to attend, especially in the case of Stanford; however, these schools admitted few women of color until later in the century. In this sense, their extraordinary vision of new opportunities was limited to gender, not race.

Chapter 5 further explores the possibilities and limitations of philanthropy by turning from college founders to donors (alumnae, trustees, and others) who had a more specific goal: gaining admission and better conditions for women at coeducational universities. Could women use dollars to force the doors of colleges open to women?

Using Mammon for Righteousness

Funding Coeducation through Coercive Philanthropy

In 1891, M. Carey Thomas dashed off an angry letter to Mary Elizabeth Garrett: "Mr. Gilman is working against us tooth & nail," she fulminated.[1] The Johns Hopkins University (JHU) president Daniel Coit Gilman was determined to prevent women from admittance not only to the undergraduate college but also to the medical school the university was seeking to open. Garrett and Thomas, along with a group of women they recruited from around the country, had initially offered $100,000 if the medical school would admit women. Garrett then used her own money to increase the gift to the full $500,000 needed to establish the medial school (over $13 million in 2016).[2] Faced with the choice between no medical school or a coeducational medical school, Gilman swallowed his resistance and accepted Garrett's gift with her uncompromising conditions.

Donations could force a school in desperate need of funds to open its doors to women. Money could also provide the necessary tools to make a coeducational university more welcoming to women by providing scholarships for women or constructing a women's dormitory or a women's building for social and recreational activities. This chapter documents the enormous importance of women's philanthropy to the growth of higher education for women in the late nineteenth and twentieth centuries by exploring what happened when women approached already existing schools (rather than founding their own) and sought to change them in ways that would benefit women, through either becoming coeducational or improving the campus experience for women at an already coeducational school. In both this and chapter 4, women with money and vision sought to increase access to higher education for women in order to develop their capabilities and independence.

This chapter focuses on the explicit ways in which wealthy women used the strength of their dollars to force male administrators to open their doors to women. A needy college hesitated to say no to a gift of hundreds of thousands or millions of dollars, and although some resisted, others were willing to make concessions regarding women students in order to obtain the money. As doctor and suffragist Mary Putnam Jacobi remarked, "It is astonishing how many invincible objections [to coeducation] on the score of feasibility, modesty, propriety, and prejudice melt away before the charmed touch of a few thousand dollars."[3]

Although Garrett's role at Johns Hopkins is most familiar, in general, women's contributions to higher coeducational institutions have not been emphasized in the field of educational history.[4] The difficulties Mary Garrett faced, along with Oliva Sage's foiled plan to develop a college for women at New York University, demonstrate the enormous hurdles those in favor of coeducation encountered from some of America's best universities. Furthermore, failed efforts at Harvard, as well as Susan B. Anthony's arduous struggle to make the University of Rochester coeducational, showcase fund-raising efforts by groups of women. These stories reveal the potential power of money—and its limits.

The chapter then turns to Phoebe Hearst and Katharine McCormick, who did not attempt to force an institution to become coeducational—the University of California (UC) and Massachusetts Institute of Technology (MIT) already accepted women. Instead, through their generous donations for women's dormitories and other services for women, they pushed these schools to create a more welcoming atmosphere for women and increase their enrollment. MIT's long history of coeducation (since 1883) shows that the battle was not necessarily won when the doors opened to women. A lack of residential facilities (dormitories were single sex through the 1960s) automatically limited the number of women students who matriculated, as MIT (and other schools) restricted the number admitted to those who would fit in scarce campus housing. Furthermore, women in the late nineteenth and first half of the twentieth centuries often felt unwelcome on coeducational campuses, where male students and faculty openly harassed or ignored them. They were excluded from positions in many organizations and from social life centered on sports or hazing. Thus, a women's building, which provided separate social and recreational facilities, could make women feel more comfortable on campus and ironically enhancing women's sense of belonging on coeducational campuses was sometimes achieved by separating them from men.[5] Both women's dormitories and women's buildings were essential for increasing women's admissions at coeducational universities. This chapter shows how the fight for coeducation continued for decades after JHU acceded to Garrett's demands.

IN THE LATE NINETEENTH and early twentieth centuries, not everyone considered higher education for women necessary or appropriate. In particular, coeducation was deeply controversial. Historian Patricia Butcher notes,

"Coeducation was won neither early nor easily. Women attained their right to joint education of the sexes by relentlessly overcoming numerous and mercurial blockades."[6] Arguments against coeducation centered on several key points, including women's mental or physical inferiority, and the idea that the male curriculum was not fit for women's preparation for marriage and motherhood. In addition, commentators at the time claimed that both female and male students would be distracted and "de-sexed" in coeducational schools. Continued resistance came from male faculty, students, and alumni.[7]

Although in many cases male founders and male presidents decided to institute coeducation at their colleges, often pressure from women was behind that decision. Early feminists, including Elizabeth Cady Stanton, Susan B. Anthony, and Lucy Stone, advocated for coeducation as early as the 1850s.[8] Individual young women forced administrators to consider their applications, women's clubs petitioned for women's admission, and, as will be evident, female philanthropists got the attention of decision makers by offering substantial gifts in order to bring about coeducation. Colleges also considered size and economics: there was a growing need for teacher training (mostly women), and it was less expensive for states to build one college than two (a factor, it should be noted, that did not stop southern schools from racial segregation).[9]

Entrée to medical schools was particularly important to women who wanted to increase the number of women doctors but even more difficult to achieve than admission to undergraduate colleges. Historian Margaret Rossiter states that at the same time more women were gaining access to higher education, the fields of science and medicine were beginning to establish standards for these professions and, in so doing, erected barriers to women's careers in science or medicine.[10] Most medical schools did not admit women, so women had to attend women's medical colleges or study abroad. When they were admitted to a coeducational school, they endured harassment.[11] A relatively large number of women doctors in the 1890s resulted in a backlash that reduced their numbers for decades. Historian Mary Roth Walsh argues that women faced barriers because "the medical establishment made a conscious effort to minimize the number of women physicians."[12]

Given this resistance, women turned to "coercive philanthropy," a term coined by Rossiter, with restrictions on gifts that required access for women at educational institutions.[13] Money did not always enable women to push schools to admit or accommodate women, but it held considerable sway. The women in this chapter and the gifts they gave demonstrate the power of money and the creative ways it could be used to gain women access to education and the professions. The efforts of women to improve opportunities for other women were part of the movement for equality. Like the women's college founders in chapter 4, the wealthy women who hoped to force colleges to welcome women believed that women were capable of the same intellectual achievement as men and that providing greater access to education would broaden women's lives and empower them to become independent women.

Moreover, enabling women to attend schools like JHU, MIT, and UC was particularly important, as these schools were already beginning to be perceived as among the best in America. Successful coeducation at these schools signified that women's intellectual and professional capabilities were equal to men's.

The prestige of these universities gives the women in this chapter a particular significance in the history of women's philanthropy. Historian Kathleen McCarthy found that women philanthropists who supported art museums were unable to make significant enough donations or gain powerful positions at elite museums like the Metropolitan Museum of Art in New York or the Art Institute of Chicago. Instead, women were most successful at creating separate museums to legitimize decorative and modern art. Thus, she concludes that their money did not give them legitimate power in an already established institution.[14] This chapter shows that the field of education provided some space for women to wield power commensurate with their wealth, giving donations and gaining more access for women at top universities in the nation. They used their money to make change at these powerful institutions to promote education for women.

Significantly, many of the first wave of young women who attended these universities understood how important their benefactors were, just as had students at women's colleges. Women students were well aware of who had made their university experience welcoming. The recipients of Hearst scholarships at UC, nicknamed the "Phoebes," and all women students gathering in Hearst Hall encountered Phoebe Hearst often, while Katharine McCormick made a point of meeting women students living in McCormick Hall dormitory at MIT. Students at the University of Rochester not only invited Susan B. Anthony to a reception but also served as honorary pallbearers at her funeral.[15] They understood that with few men interested in women's education, it was women who were determined to push schools into admitting women so they could gain access to higher education in preparation for professional employment, especially in the sciences and medicine.

The best known example of coercive philanthropy is Mary Elizabeth Garrett's success in forcing JHU to open its medical school to women students.

Mary Elizabeth Garrett. Used with permission from Bryn Mawr College Special Collections.

Only by doing so would JHU obtain a $500,000 gift desperately needed to fund the opening of the medical school. Born in Baltimore, Mary Garrett was the daughter of Rachel and John W. Garrett, owner of the B&O Railroad and other commercial ventures. She worked closely with her father, providing secretarial services and learning about his business. She was exposed to the art of negotiation, which would later serve her well as a forceful philanthropist.[16] Following the death of her parents in 1883, Mary inherited nearly $6 million (over $186 million in 2016), making the unmarried Garrett one of the wealthiest women in the country.[17] Yet despite the money, Mary resented her lack of power within her family: her brothers had been allowed to attend college and take over the company business while she, the only daughter, could do neither. Furthermore, she began a long series of lawsuits against her brother's wife and the administrators of the estate, who, she claimed, made decisions resulting in financial loss for her.[18]

Garrett had made friends with a group of young women in Baltimore who shared her passion for education and also wanted to obtain more opportunities for women. She grew closest to M. Carey Thomas, who had earned a PhD in Zurich in 1882 and would become the dean and then president of Bryn Mawr College. The two ultimately began a romantic relationship that lasted until Garrett's death.[19] These like-minded women shared a love of learning that led Garrett to disdain the idea that women should be educated only to provide conversation with their husbands. "No!" she exclaimed. "Knowledge is power and I for one am going to do my best to gain it."[20] Despite her own lack of a formal college education, she understood its great importance for other women.

Garrett first succeeded in educating other women at the Bryn Mawr School for Girls, a college preparatory school founded by Garrett and her friends in 1885 to prepare girls for a top women's college like Bryn Mawr. The school offered its students the same curriculum found at the best boys' preparatory schools. The girls were trained to pass Bryn Mawr College's entrance examinations. These exams were the same as those given for entrance into the best men's colleges. Garrett paid for the construction of a new campus for the school scarcely three years after it opened, spending more than $400,000 (nearly $10 million in 2016).

Garrett's health also led her to an interest in women's medical education. Suffering from a variety of ailments, she sought out Drs. Mary Putnam Jacobi and Elizabeth Blackwell.[21] These doctors, while creating and staffing women's schools and hospitals, agreed that women ultimately needed to gain admission to the better equipped and funded male schools. According to Jacobi, "There is no manner of doubt that . . . coeducation in medicine is essential to the real and permanent success of women in medicine. Isolated groups of women cannot maintain the same intellectual standards as are established and maintained by men." Men's schools, she thought, were where research and scientific thinking were advancing, and women needed access to those same facilities.[22]

John Garrett's friend Johns Hopkins died in 1873, leaving $7 million to be divided between a university, which was to include a medical school, and a hospital. Due to a decline in investment income, despite having recruited faculty and opened the hospital, by 1890 there were still not enough funds for the medical school.[23] JHU president Gilman therefore needed a large donation to open the medical school originally envisioned by Johns Hopkins. He began seeking a donor who could provide $100,000.[24]

Thomas and Garrett had found their bargaining chip. They immediately began to plot to raise the money themselves and bribe JHU into admitting women into the medical school.[25] Garrett and Thomas eventually created the Women's Medical School Fund. The national structure of the fund included branch committees in Baltimore, Washington, Philadelphia, and New York, as well as in St. Louis, Chicago, Milwaukee, and the Pacific coast. The committees included a number of prominent women, including philanthropists, doctors, educators, and First Lady Caroline Harrison.[26] They used their informal social networks as well as formal networks of women, such as the General Federation of Women's Clubs.

Garrett and Thomas had many details to sort out as they began their campaign, starting with how best to work together. In 1888, Garrett had the money, while Thomas had the education and the academic prestige as dean at Bryn Mawr. The two had already worked together to create and run the Bryn Mawr School. Both had connections to JHU through their fathers, who had served on the board of trustees together, and both were headstrong and determined. With her own father now deceased, Garrett depended on Thomas to gain inside information through her father, who still served on the board of trustees. Thomas could also speak to Gilman from a more equal vantage point (two college officials). In addition to her own money, Garrett had connections to other wealthy women.

Thomas encouraged Garrett to use her wealth for good. As early as 1884, she wrote to her, "I am so glad, Mary, to think that you will have money someday. Here is so much good to do, and what some of us do in another way you can do in that way, and after all it is rarer than the other ways and does not exclude them."[27] The campaign pushed Thomas to think about their abilities: Garrett, she noted, had "the power that money gives to the very few that have it and have at the same time the power to see things that are needed—and I for a certain power I think I have . . . to make other people care for what I care for."[28]

Even though Thomas was supportive of Garrett, she was also rankled by the fact that Garrett exerted control through her money. With Garrett holding the purse strings, Thomas felt the need to assure Garrett that she would not make decisions without Garrett's approval.[29] She later wrote Garrett that she had "contempt for a board controlled by its pockets. . . . It is well for our friendship you had made me care for you before you had money of your own because I do not think I could have cared for you afterwards."[30] Her difficulty dealing with the power that money brought Garrett echoed the resentment expressed by women in the suffrage movement and women's cross-class labor coalitions about their donors. Promoting women's access to education, professions, and independence while remaining dependent on her most intimate partner was not easy. Yet as much as it bothered Thomas, she also realized the potential of Garrett's wealth and encouraged her to use it to good purpose. Given the stressful negotiations that took place with Gilman, Thomas's encouragement was crucial to Garrett. As their correspondence makes clear, however, Garrett ultimately made her own decisions.

With committees in place and money coming in, their desire to succeed increased. Thomas commented, "I shall feel unable to hold up my head again if after we have aroused everyone the [JHU] trustees would refuse it. It would do harm to women's medical education too. We simply must carry it thro' now. Whatever happens they must *not* refuse it."[31] Thomas and Garrett believed that success at JHU would bring women into one of the country's best universities as well as potentially open up opportunities elsewhere.

The Women's Medical School Fund made its first official offer to JHU in the fall of 1890: $100,000 on the condition that "women whose previous training has been equivalent to that of the preliminary medical course of the university be admitted to the school, whenever it shall open, on the same terms as men."[32] Garrett had provided $47,787.50, or nearly half the total amount. The board of trustees on October 28, 1890, agreed to accept her condition and the money and invest it until they raised the remaining balance of the total $500,000 they now declared was needed to open the school.[33] Garrett and Thomas had heard rumors of the larger figure earlier that spring. The half million dollars would make up for a dramatic decline in the price of B&O Railroad stock, JHU's major investment, and cover the new increased estimates for the amount needed to open a first-rate medical school.[34]

Despite the acceptance of their first offer, the battle was far from over. They still had to raise another $400,000. The real problem, according to Thomas, was that Gilman simply did not want to admit women. She later accused him of trying to prevent the board from accepting their offer.[35] "Of course," she raged in a letter, "he would much much rather *never* have the medical school than have it with women. Nothing is to be done with him."[36] While the women struggled to raise the additional funds, Thomas warned, "Mr. Gilman is working to get a majority to rescind the whole action & return the $115,000. Money is nothing to them. If your $100,000 lapses [without the total of $500,000 raised], as it will, unless we can think of some plan, the next move will be to have the women's fund returned. You do not realize Mr. Gilman's grim determination; it is with him a death struggle & money weighs nothing with him."[37] To Hannah Smith, Thomas wrote, "Many of [the trust-ees], and President Gilman, above all, preferred never to have a medical school at all rather than to have one to which women were to be admitted." The trustees were fighting "in the dark with treachery and false reasons. Trustees, doctors, professors (Mr. Gwinn and Father leading our forces) became involved in the tangle of hatred, malice, detraction that beggars description."[38]

When it became clear that the university had not raised the additional funds, Garrett upped the ante.[39] On December 22, 1892, she noted that the original $100,000 donated by herself and the Women's Medical School Fund had increased to $193,023 due to subsequent donations and interest earned, leaving $306,977 to complete the half-million-dollar total. Garrett pledged the entire $306,977 herself, bringing her total contribution to $354,765 (well over $9 million in 2016).

The new half-million-dollar offer retained the original demand that the school admit and treat women on the same conditions as men. Garrett shrewdly specified that if the medical school were to stop admitting women, or if "women studying in the Medical School do not enjoy all the advantages on the same terms as men, or are not admitted on the same terms as men, to all prizes, dignities or honors that are awarded by competitive examination, or regarded as rewards of merit," the money would revert back to her.[40] Fur-thermore, Garrett cleverly added a requirement that a women's committee, consisting of six women, be created to advise female students directly and provide input to the university on the character of women applicants and nonacademic discipline issues for women students. She named the six mem-bers of the committee, which included herself and Thomas.[41]

Garrett did more than coerce JHU into admitting women to the medical school. She also forced the school to adopt her vision of what standards a university medical school should follow. By early 1893, trustees were willing to admit women but did not want to accede to the additional requirements on entrance requirements and curriculum. They accepted her gift, then spent the next six weeks debating the stipulations, hoping she would withdraw or modify her demands, prompting Thomas to advise that if they did not ac-quiesce, Garrett should save the money for "a better object. They must think you a fool to believe you, or indeed we, can be hoodwinked that way—there seems to me no need for any excitement on your part—even being a woman you have the whip hand for once and can afford to be absolutely immove-able."[42] Garrett was persistent; she hung on, forcing JHU to accept her inno-vative policies.

With these additional demands, Garrett single-handedly shaped what would become one of the best medical schools in the country. She insisted that the medical school provide a four-year course leading to the degree of doctor of medicine, and that incoming students complete the preliminary medical course at the undergraduate level offered at Hopkins or its equivalent. At a time when most medical schools around the country had few standards and no rigorous curriculum, the faculty feared this would limit the number of students applying.[43] Ultimately, JHU and Garrett finally agreed on the high admissions standards, with minor modifications.[44] Historian Alan Chesney points out that these requirements were not invented by Garrett— they had already been articulated in reports and speeches on the potential medical school dating back to the 1870s. However, he concludes, her "contribution consisted in securing the adoption of these requirements though the use of *force majeure*, or perhaps it would be more nearly correct to say through *force monnetaire*."[45]

Beyond the question of how rigorous the requirements should be lay a more central issue: whether a donor had the power to dictate admissions and graduation requirements. Gilman and university faculty tried to reserve the power for the university, but Garrett outmaneuvered them with her $500,000 donation. As Gilman wrote, "The affair seems to me so entangled that the only relief will be in a distinct recognition by all parties of this fundamental principle, namely: The University reserves to itself the exclusive right to determine on what conditions students may be admitted, discharged, and graduated. I do not know of any institution of good standing in which this principle is not established."[46] The medical faculty and academic council adopted resolutions with similar language. Despite all these concerns, in the end the university wanted a medical school, and Mary Garrett could pay for it. Garrett wrote a letter clarifying her language. Acquiescing to her demands, the medical school was opened to women on equal terms and set the highest standards in admissions requirements and curriculum in the country.

Garrett was so successful that the donation was barely accepted before she was making another offer to another institution that also could not afford to refuse her. Thomas had worked hard to install high standards of academic excellence at Bryn Mawr College as dean. Thomas employed a major system similar to that of JHU and offered graduate fellowships, as she worked to create "a great university of women scholars where publication and investigation etc. by women shall prove [their] original thinking power." For Thomas, leadership at Bryn Mawr was a means for her to "help women get free materially and intellectually."[47]

With Bryn Mawr seeking a second president, Garrett offered $10,000 a year if Thomas were promoted from dean to president. At the time, this represented about 10 percent of the college's budget. The sum was apparently enough to overcome the reluctance of the trustees to appoint a woman. "They are terrified at the thought of putting a *woman* in sole power," Thomas reported.[48] She was thrilled to learn of Garrett's offer, which she called a "sweet and clever attempt to use Mammon for righteousness." Thomas proclaimed herself "delighted to have this argument also—inducement, bribe—to use too," to insist on both the presidency and a place on the board of trustees.[49] In appreciation for her support, Garrett was appointed a director of the college, and she eventually gave approximately $450,000 to the school for various projects, including new buildings.[50]

Garrett, with hundreds of thousands of dollars at her disposal, found that she could set conditions for her donations. Her gifts, which came with strings attached, made her a powerful woman, powerful enough to force one of the leading universities in America to accept her demands, if they were to fulfill the desires of JHU's founder to open a medical school. But even with her money and her connections, Garrett still struggled to get a male president and board of trustees to accept her requirements. Garrett used the influence of a national network of powerful women as well as the influence of her friends' fathers, who were trustees friendly to her proposition. She used the media to her advantage, publicizing her fund and then, once the offer was accepted, demanding that JHU publish the agreement annually, along with the requirement that the money would revert back to her if the school ever reneged on its agreement concerning the admission of women on completely equal footing with men.

As the daughter of a multimillionaire railroad owner, she could buy any worldly goods she wanted—mansions, travel, jewels. But as the only daughter, she had not been allowed to go to college or take over her father's business, as her brothers had. Money, she realized, had to be wielded carefully and used to benefit other women who sought independence only made possible through an education and a career.

Other women also tried "bribing" universities to open their doors to women, often using gifts raised from groups of women. Perhaps due to her timing, Carrie Pollitzer was able to leverage a much smaller donation for coeducation at the College of Charleston. Her success came despite the fact that state universities in the socially conservative South had generally resisted coeducation much more than those in the Midwest and West.[51] The College of Charleston still had no women students when the shortage of male students during World War I provided an opening wedge for Pollitzer. One of three daughters of Gustave and Clara Pollitzer, Carrie and her sisters were all feminists, suffragists, and activists. She led the campaign for coeducation at the College of Charleston through the Charleston City Federation of Women's Clubs, holding a petition drive in the spring of 1917. The college required $1,200 for facilities and a matron for women students, so Carrie organized a mass meeting at which she raised more than $1,500.[52] President Harrison Randolph, though not in favor of coeducation, accepted the donation and admitted women. He said that the outbreak of World War I required that women be trained to meet "increasing demands" and new "conditions."[53] Pollitzer admitted that it had not been easy. "You should have seen the expressions when I asked that women be admitted," she later recalled. "I felt like Henny Penny telling them the sky was falling."[54] Pollitzer saw the coeducation and suffrage campaigns as related. "The women of today," she wrote, "as the coworkers, partners, and guardians of a precious civilization, are to be accorded the same opportunities accorded only to men."[55]

Despite the success of Garrett and Pollitzer, even the promise of funding was not enough to convince all schools to open their doors to women. Harvard, for example, despite offers of funding, refused to admit women. In 1869, Harvard president Charles Eliot declared, "The world knows next to nothing about the natural mental capacities of the female sex." Therefore, he concluded that Harvard was not interested in educating women.[56] Boston and Cambridge women, however, wanted access to Harvard and formed the Woman's Education Association (WEA) of Boston in 1872. Despite the women's family connections to Harvard, Eliot was staunchly opposed to allowing women into Harvard and to a proposed plan to grant degrees to women who could pass Harvard examinations. Instead, the Harvard Annex was a program of private instruction offered by Harvard professors and organized by the WEA's Elizabeth Agassiz.[57]

Still hoping to gain full admittance for women, the WEA began an endowment drive with Pauline Agassiz Shaw, Mary Hemenway, Ellen Mason, Thomas Appleton, and the George O. Hovey estate, each giving a $5,000 donation. The $75,000 they ultimately raised, however, was not enough to entice Harvard to admit women, so they began to look for an additional $250,000. Eliot suggested that if the Annex were self-supporting, Harvard might consider taking it over, which was encouraging. In 1893, despite offering the Annex endowment and property valued at $150,000 total to Harvard, Agassiz's hopes that women might obtain an actual Harvard degree were dashed. Instead, a coordinate college, Radcliffe College, was born, with its own diploma, only countersigned by the Harvard president.[58]

Women undergraduates attended Radcliffe, not Harvard, for over five decades, and were not admitted to Harvard until the 1960s. Over one hundred years after it was first deployed, alumnae in the 1990s resurrected the coercive giving strategy. At the time, the number of women faculty was slowly beginning to grow at colleges and universities around the nation. Unhappy with the small number of Harvard women faculty, the Committee for the Equality of Women at Harvard raised money but refused to give it to the university until changes were made to encourage the hiring of women professors. Elizabeth Agassiz would undoubtedly be pleased to know that opportunities for women at Harvard have continued to expand, and in 2007, Harvard chose its first female president, historian Drew Faust.[59]

Women made a similarly unsuccessful effort to break down the barriers for entry into Harvard University Medical School. By the 1870s, the school was ready to expand both its curriculum requirements and its campus. Women saw this as an opportune time to tempt the school with the promise of a donation. Jacobi thought it right to use money to sway opposition.[60] In 1878, Marion Hovey of Boston offered $10,000 from her father's estate to the school if it would use it to educate women on equal terms with men. Although a five-man committee voted in favor, the following year the faculty voted against it. Leaving the door open to coeducation in the future, they demanded a $200,000 endowment if the school were to admit women. Keeping the idea alive, Eliot encouraged the possibility that a large sum could pay for additional faculty and classrooms. The New England Hospital Society raised $50,000, which it offered with the promise of additional funds. However, when the board of overseers appeared willing to accept the offer, the medical school faculty threatened to resign, so the overseers voted against it in 1882. The medical school did not open to women until 1945.[61]

Even if a college accepted a restricted gift, it did not mean it necessarily abided by the terms specified. Troy Seminary graduate and wealthy heir Olivia Sage was unable to enforce her intentions at New York University (NYU). The widow of financier Russell Sage, she inherited millions of dollars at his death and gave most of it away, including establishing the Russell Sage Foundation.[62] NYU seemed open to women's education in the 1880s and 1890s, when the Woman's Legal Education Society founded a Woman's Law Class, which NYU chancellor Henry MacCracken supported. The Woman's Law Class continued, even when women were admitted into the university law school in 1890. Olivia Sage's friend and protégé Helen Miller Gould, daughter of railroad tycoon Jay Gould, graduated from the Woman's Law Class in 1899 and then became vice president of the Woman's Legal Education Society. The University Council then created a Women's Advisory Council to advise the university on opportunities for women.[63] Both Gould and Sage were appointed to membership on the council.

But women seeking a bachelor's degree fared worse at NYU. Despite a chancellor in the 1870s who advocated coeducation and an effort by the women's professional club Sorosis to petition for women's entrance, NYU's main University Heights undergraduate campus was for men only until 1959 (in 1914, undergraduate women were admitted to the Washington Square campus). Recognizing Sage's interest in NYU and her generous donations to other colleges, MacCracken began to solicit the Sages to donate money to create a women's coordinate college at NYU. "If we use our plant and our professors somewhat as Radcliffe College uses Harvard or Barnard College uses Columbia you could tell Mrs. Sage to organize here the best woman's college in the world," he wrote to Russell Sage.[64]

Soon after her husband's death and following several visits from Mac-Cracken, she gave $294,250—then the second largest gift to NYU (over $7.7 million in 2016)—to purchase land, with the specification that "some part of the property at least will be used by New York University as a center for women's working and living, for a women's building, or other University activities in connection with women." Once enough money for an endowment was raised, MacCracken told her, the Olivia Sage College would be established on par with the best women's colleges of the day, like Bryn Mawr, Vassar, and Smith. Instead, NYU decided to build an engineering school on the property, while MacCracken's successor was simultaneously, though unsuccessfully, soliciting her for more money. Sage was more successful at Cornell, where her $300,000 donation built the university's second dormitory for women, named Risley Hall after her mother-in-law, Prudence Risley. Despite her interest in women's education, her gifts to men's schools heavily outnumbered those to women's or coeducational ones.[65]

Women in New Orleans also could not convince school officials to open a Tulane University Medical School for women despite dangling the promise of a $150,000 donation. Caroline Merrick, Evelyn Ordway, and Dr. Mary A. G. Dwight wrote to university administrators offering to raise $150,000 to open a school for women, noting that there was no women's medical school south of the Ohio River. When the board ignored their proposal, women in New Orleans regrouped and asked the medical school to admit women. Ironically in this case, a generous woman philanthropist, Ida Richardson, rejected the idea, arguing that her husband, a noted doctor and faculty member, was against it. After years of resistance from the faculty, the school finally began to admit women in 1914.[66]

The success that Mary Garrett had at JHU is all the more remarkable given these failures. Moreover, shortly after her donation was accepted, a backlash against coeducation hit several major universities, persisting through the first decades of the twentieth century. The increased number of women students and their excellent academic performance threatened men (faculty, students, and alumni), who feared that women were feminizing campuses and would eventually drive male students away. At the same time, Teddy Roosevelt conflated the strenuous life, manliness, and white civilization, and complained that industrialization was threatening American masculinity. Roosevelt also organized college football in 1905, helping to create the National Collegiate Athletic Association in order to save the increasingly popular sport from ·complaints regarding its violence and resultant deaths. Reflecting this crisis in masculinity, even as some schools opened their doors to women, other schools formerly open to women decided either to no longer accept women or to limit the number of women students, as Jane Stanford had done at Stanford. In 1912, for example, after forty years of coeducation, Wesleyan College, under pressure from alumni, graduated its last four women until 1968, when women were once again admitted.[67] Women were outperforming men academically, and with a proliferation of New England colleges, Wesleyan wanted to guard its prominent reputation built on football.

Even schools that continued to admit women did not provide adequate access to dormitories, classes, or the gymnasium, and sometimes considered segregating them either in separate classes or at a separate campus. Cornell had been coeducational since 1872, after donor Henry Sage offered $250,000 to build a dormitory for women. However, his growing concern that the dormitory serve to protect women's virtue pushed the university to require women to live in the dormitory (whereas men did not have a similar requirement). This ultimately restricted the number of women students for decades to those who could be housed in the one dormitory for women.[68] The University of Wisconsin's president suggested offering separate course sections for men and women in 1908, due to concerns that women were overcrowding and feminizing the humanities. Protests against this proposed policy stopped it from being enacted.[69]

The University of Chicago, though coeducational from its beginnings in 1892, also experienced a backlash. President William Rainey Harper was personally opposed to coeducation but had to follow the charter. He hired a dean of women and several women faculty members. Several women even gave $250,000 to build four residence halls for women. The welcome that these residences provided to women students was not to last, however. When women students made up almost half the student population and more than half of Phi Beta Kappa membership, the administration and faculty attempted to separate them from the men by offering separate classes for freshman and sophomore males and females. Although few students actually attended the separate classes, women were made to feel generally unwelcome.[70]

University of Chicago dean Marion Talbot helped women students weather the difficulties through her efforts to treat them as the intellectual equals of men students. She also pushed for a women's organization—the Women's Union—and a women's building—Ida Noyes Hall—which contained a clubhouse, lunchroom, gymnasium, and swimming pool. Talbot oversaw social activities at Noyes Hall that included men and required them to behave according to the women's rules.[71] These efforts on the part of Talbot were essential to keeping women enrolled at the University of Chicago and enabling them to succeed and feel welcome there.

Rochester University provides the best example of both the coercive power of women's giving and its limits in the face of the backlash to coeducation.[72] Susan B. Anthony; Kate Gleason; and other suffragists in Rochester, New York, had been trying to convince Rochester University to admit women for years. When Cornell and Syracuse admitted women in the 1870s, Rochester held out, with most male students happy with the decision. One student complained that coeducation would "necessitate undesirable curricular changes, . . . impose limitations on professorial freedom of expression in the classroom, and distract males from serious academic work," as well as damage the "delicacy" of womanhood.[73]

Women in the local Fortnightly Ignorance Club began raising money in the 1880s to entice the university to admit women. In 1890, 225 citizens of Rochester signed a petition circulated by the club demanding coeducation. Women began attending lectures on Saturdays or as auditors. A female student enrolled in classes in 1893, with her fees paid by Anthony and friends, though without formally matriculating for a degree. Whereas the president and some trustees seemed amenable to women students, protests continued from male students and alumni who did not want their campus feminized.

In 1898, the university finally agreed to admit women, but only if the women donated $100,000 to fund a new gymnasium. Anthony exclaimed triumphantly, "Glory, Hallelujah! This is better news to me than victory over Spain. It is a peace-victory, achieved only by the death of prejudice and precedents." But by 1900, Anthony had solicited only $40,000. In response, the trustees lowered their demand to $50,000. Anthony raised all but the last two thousand, which was "guaranteed" by a donor but not in hand, leaving her to pledge her life insurance to make up the difference. Women were finally admitted that year. After her death, suffragists briefly entertained the idea of raising $75,000 for a women's dormitory. However, after raising $27,000, they decided to use the money for the suffrage movement instead.[74]

The victory at Rochester, however, was bittersweet. There were separate yearbooks and alumni lunches, anti-coeducation articles in the yearbooks and newspapers, and other signs that women were not welcome as fully participating students. Rochester president Rush Rhees was also against coeducation, stating, "The two groups of students are distinct by nature and no educational theory can abolish the distinction." In 1912, the board of trustees decided to raise $250,000 for a separate college for women, and in 1914, the faculty voted to separate large elective classes and all classes for underclassmen. The university built a separate gymnasium—Susan B. Anthony Memorial Hall—and a separate academic building for women in order to create a women's coordinate college. In 1921, the college decided to build a new campus for men and to convert the entire old campus to women, thus completely separating women from men. It was not until 1955 that women were integrated back into the university and the college for women was closed.[75] Women had gained admittance to the University of Rochester after Anthony raised the necessary $50,000, but they were made to feel unwelcome and ultimately segregated into a separate campus. Here, they had more adequate facilities, but a sense of inferiority lingered. Women were left wondering if it was better to feel unwelcome on the main campus or welcome in their own smaller, older campus.

THIS RESISTANCE TO WOMEN at coeducational colleges and universities led Katharine Dexter McCormick to another strategy: enticing schools to become more welcoming to women on campus through the donation of funding for women's dormitories, women's buildings, and women's scholarships. At the University of Rochester, women went from sharing campus space to being relegated to the older campus. But separate spaces could also offer women benefits. Recognizing the difficulties women faced on coeducational campuses, donors like McCormick, as well as deans of women like Talbot at the University of Chicago, sought to create female spaces, which would enable more women to attend universities (admissions policies were sometimes predicated on the number of women who could be housed on campus) and to feel comfortable at an institution that was often unwelcoming. Facing harassment and exclusion from male students and faculty, women needed a place to study, socialize, and exercise. Fund-raising and advocating for such resources was often a top priority for the new deans of women being hired at coeducational universities. A wealthy alumna like McCormick was crucial to transforming a university that admitted women to a university that welcomed women students and enabled their success.[76] The irony was that a women's building promoted separation and inclusion simultaneously.

McCormick was a passionate supporter of women in science and medicine, and like Garrett, she believed that women deserved the same opportunities for education and career as men. McCormick was one of the first women to graduate from MIT with a degree in biology more than three decades after MIT admitted its first woman student, Ellen Swallow, as a "special" (nondegree) student in chemistry in 1871. A small stream of women followed Swallow, first as students in the Women's Laboratory she opened there, and then in 1883, as regularly admitted students.

As a female student in the late 1890s and early 1900s, McCormick had access to a women's lounge and bathroom, built with $8,000 raised by Ellen Swallow and fellow alumnae in 1882, and located in the university's new chemistry building. The lounge was controversial because it provided room for women students to eat lunch separately from the male students, a "privilege" not all observers agreed with. But as there was still no housing for women on campus, McCormick lived at home in Boston when she attended MIT from 1896 to 1904.[77]

For the next several decades, little changed at MIT for women students. Women made up only about 1 percent of the student body through the 1940s, and the university made minimal efforts to accommodate women's presence on campus. A lack of facilities limited the number of women students who could enroll. The women's bathroom was remodeled and enlarged several times, finally as the Margaret Cheney Lounge for women in 1939. However, there continued to be no housing for women on campus. In 1945, MIT opened the Bay State Road house for a few dozen women students in a location thirty minutes from campus by trolley or subway. The building was too small and poorly located. The lack of facilities for women made it easy for admissions officials to limit the number of female students, even rejecting qualified applicants on the basis of lack of housing.

When McCormick's husband, Stanley, died in 1947, she inherited over \$35 million. Almost immediately, MIT began to court one of its wealthiest alumni. President Compton was advised that he should "send her [a] sympathy card and then try to talk to her about MIT." He initiated the first of many conversations with McCormick about her interest in MIT, asking if she would be interested in funding a new laboratory (suggested by an old classmate) or a dormitory for women students (suggested by President Compton's wife).[78] McCormick was slow to respond to MIT's overtures, claiming that she was unable to give yet due to her inheritance taxes.[79] Finally, McCormick established a taxi fund for young women living at the Bay State Road building to get to class. Even with the taxi fund, Bay State was still inadequate. MIT's women students desperately needed a dormitory on campus.

While courting McCormick, MIT finally became increasingly interested in making MIT more welcoming to women. Many skeptical school officials had raised doubts about the wisdom of having women students in a school designed for science and engineering in the first place.[80] While World War II opened opportunities for women to study science and engineering, Cold War pressures to educate more scientists in the late 1940s and 1950s made the presence, albeit small, of women at MIT more noticeable. Although the Commission on the Education of Women promoted national attention on women's education and employment in this time period, ambivalence remained. Were these women taking spaces that should be used to turn out male scientists and engineers? Officials decided they should "eliminate women students . . . , or, decide we really want women, plan an adequate set up, and then deliberately go out and get more good girls."[81] MIT chose the latter. The university commissioned a report on women's status at MIT that appeared in 1959, dovetailing with McCormick's interest, and presidents James Killian and Julius Stratton began to support the growth of female enrollment.[82] Essential to their plans was a new dormitory for women, which was now possible due to McCormick's largesse.

McCormick initially promised \$1.5 million to fund a women's dormitory (over \$12 million in 2016).[83] "I believe, if we can get [women] properly housed," she noted, "that the best scientific education in our country will be open to them permanently. Then I can rest in peace."[84] Thus, McCormick did not consider a women's dormitory as a building that would segregate women on campus but rather as a space that would enable more women to attend MIT. A women's residence hall would also provide an all-female space where women could feel comfortable, which was "preferable to [the] second-class status" they were made to feel on the rest of the campus—classrooms or the library, for example.[85]

When it came to the building, McCormick had very specific ideas. According to a memo she wrote, McCormick was more concerned about the details than the cost. Her lawyer, William Bemis, reported to MIT officials that after meeting with the architects, McCormick approved the concept and estimated cost of $2 million. However, she had concerns about the design of the building, a potential second half to the building, and the landscape and interior decoration. While the architects were willing to compromise on some issues, they complained that she had a "fixation" about details they did not want revised.[86] McCormick responded with a twelve-page, single-spaced typewritten response to the president's checklist for the women's dorm. "I have studied this list with care and checked it against ideas I have in mind for the same building," she wrote, before detailing everything from ceiling height to space for ironing, and individual towel racks (warning against racks "so small that air cannot circulate and towels and washcloths do not dry properly and so become sour").[87] Despite these issues, McCormick Hall opened in 1963, the first dormitory on the MIT campus for women.

Pleased with the results of her first gift, McCormick also wanted to provide housing for women graduate students and began discussions with MIT about adding a second building.[88] This time, however, there were more significant differences between McCormick and the institution. MIT had a broader vision than McCormick. Therefore, the first problem to resolve was the scope of the project. MIT officials wanted to add housing for an additional 250 women students as well as women's athletic and recreational facilities, including a pool. The projected cost was around $5 million. Believing that McCormick was unwilling to donate that amount, officials debated whether to cut the number of students housed, the recreational facilities, or just the swimming pool. Official correspondence reveals that some desired to move forward with the university vision, whether or not McCormick would donate the money. "It is certainly our hope that rather than tailor the buildings and program of the women's residence to Mrs. McCormick's beneficences and personal taste," MIT's dean of student affairs for women, Jacquelyn Mattfield, wrote to former president James Killian and current president Julius Stratton, "M.I.T., having decided to build and support the program for one undergraduate women's house . . . will approach Mrs. McCormick with firm plans, and the attitude that if Mrs. McCormick should not be able or willing to assume all of the costs involved, other foundations or individuals' support will be sought to supplement those parts which she would like to underwrite." She called McCormick's gift "despotic benevolence." But despite her complaints, McCormick's money won out, and the addition housed only 110 additional undergraduates without a swimming pool in order to accommodate the building size she preferred and the amount of her donation.[89]

A series of differences over the architecture also arose, more contentious than the requirements McCormick imposed for the first building. After McCormick's secretary Sara Delaney explained that McCormick was "unalterably opposed" to a building taller than the first, the university agreed but continued recommending that the building be set back and configured differently, rather than be a copy of the first building. The next major stumbling block was that McCormick was determined that the new building also be located on Memorial Drive, which necessitated moving a hospital, Sancta Maria, and the row houses of nuns from the hospital, as well as the Non-Resident Student Association and other groups, a process which would set back construction by at least two years. This plan would also dramatically slow the university's ability to increase its women student population during that time. McCormick's lawyer cautioned that she was "adamant" and "inflexible" about where the building was to be located, and was willing to meet any additional costs that this requirement caused. In the end, the university gave in.[90]

McCormick's most generous gift to MIT was still to come. She bequeathed the majority of her estate to MIT, stating, "Since my graduation in 1904, I have wished to express my gratitude to the Institute for its advanced policy of scientific education for women. This policy gave me the opportunity to obtain the scientific training which has been of inestimable value to me throughout my life."[91] In addition to the approximately $5 million she donated for the two dormitories, MIT also received most of her estate (after bequests to individuals and other organizations).[92] This money has gone to the general endowment and to various building funds.

Though the amount of her bequest was greater than her dormitory gifts, the directed giving for the dormitories had a greater impact on life at MIT in that it dramatically increased the number of women students, and allowed the school to move forward with its plan to attract even more women students. McCormick was undoubtedly pleased with the Conference on Women in Science and Engineering held at MIT in 1963, and the impressive growth in the number of female students that the dormitories allowed. When she attended the school, there were only 44 women (including nondegree students). In 1959, there were still only 61 undergraduates out of the 158 women total (including special and graduate students). The presence of the dormitory freed the school to admit more women students, and by 1967, there were 404 women total enrolled.[93]

McCormick was pleased, writing to Stratton that she was "happy to hear of the increase. . . . I have been so grateful for all I received from the Institute that I realize how much Tech will mean to them, and I am happy to think that perhaps the women's dormitory has been a factor in this increase" in women students.[94] The office of the dean of student affairs concluded, "The importance of McCormick Hall in the history of women at MIT can scarcely be exaggerated. Again and again in personal interviews in the Dean's office individual girls say how much it means to them to live in such attractive quarters." The report found that far more significant than these physical benefits, however, was "the overall lift it has given the morale of the women. . . . It symbolizes in a very real sense President Stratton's statement at the dedication of McCormick Hall that MIT has accepted its 'unique opportunities and special responsibility to contribute to the education of women in our modern world.' "[95] By 2013, women represented 45 percent of undergraduates.[96]

The building, however, did not maintain its stellar reputation due to several factors. A lack of maintenance funds marred the building, and the closing of the dining hall in 1996 made it less desirable to undergraduates. In 2000, O. Robert Simha, emeritus director of planning at MIT, concluded, "We now realize that it would have been possible to accommodate substantially more women on the site in a different design for the building." Yet in 1961, he admitted, excitement over receiving McCormick's donation, coupled with the inability to imagine that women would become 40 percent of the undergraduate student body, led to a building that did not have long-term success as a residence.[97] MIT, it seems, compromised its vision for a dormitory that would have held over twice as many female students in order to please its donor and meet her demands.

McCormick, with her interest in biology and original plans to become a doctor herself, used her philanthropy to further the opportunities for women in science and medicine in other ways as well. She provided financial backing to the New England Hospital (NEH) during her lifetime and left it $25,000 in her will. Founded in 1863 to train women physicians, NEH was staffed by only women doctors for decades. Protesting the addition of male doctors in 1950, Blanche Ames Ames and other women took control of the board of trustees, moved male doctors out of regular staff positions, and struggled to keep the hospital solvent when the local United Community Services (UCS) rescinded its funding in response.[98] Ames, who knew McCormick from the suffrage and birth control movements, asked her for a large donation to support a women's hospital for women—both women patients and women doctors.[99] McCormick responded to her emotional appeal with a $30,000 donation, noting that her gift was inspired by the fact that it "provides for the most adequate development of the professional services of women physicians and surgeons."[100] The hospital remained open with only female doctors due to McCormick's annual donations of $80,000–$100,000, making up for the lack of assistance from UCS.[101]

After six years, the female head of Obstetrics and Gynecology resigned unexpectedly and was replaced by an interim male doctor, leading to further hiring of men. The medical staff then changed the by-laws to admit men to active staff. As a result, McCormick resigned and withdrew her financial support.[102] Ames implored McCormick to continue her interest in women and medicine. "We women who went through the fight for suffrage and for birth control and for all the other good causes to which we were mutually devoted," she wrote, struggled with the decisions made at the hospital. Ames suggested that a women's medical foundation could grant scholarships and stipends to women medical students, interns, and residents.[103] McCormick, while agreeing with the sentiment, had already found a new institution to carry on her goals; she told Ames that she had decided to give money to Stanford Medical School so that more women could attend school there.[104]

McCormick left Stanford University Medical School $5 million (approximately $36 million in 2016), to be used "in aid of women students attending the school of medicine and more generally for the encouragement and assistance of women in pursuing the study of medicine, in teaching medicine, and in engaging in medical research." (McCormick had originally planned to leave $10 million, but she later lowered it in a codicil to her will.) Although she left the details to the trustees, she noted that she "would be pleased" if the money was used "not only for scholarships but also for the employment of women in teaching positions and in medical research," or for a dormitory for women or a school of nursing.[105]

After receiving the McCormick bequest, the school formed the Joint Committee on the Status and Tenure of Women, which looked at both women students and women faculty and set a goal of equalizing the classes to 50 percent women, a feat finally accomplished in the 1990s, with women outnumbering men in 1997.[106] The money she bequested is now used by Stanford to fund McCormick Faculty Awards, given to junior faculty women for career advancement or to junior faculty men or women who support the advancement of women in medicine through research; postdoctoral fellowships and postdoctoral travel grants for men or women; and the McCormick Lectureship for distinguished women scientists.[107]

McCormick was interested in enabling more women to become medical doctors. This is why in the 1950s, when women doctors in Boston had their best opportunity for employment at a hospital run and staffed by women, she generously supported NEH. But when NEH hired male doctors, she ceased her annual donations and left them only $25,000 in her will. She decided instead in 1959 to dedicate a large percentage of her fortune to push for more opportunities for women in coeducation at MIT and Stanford Medical School, spending approximately $10 million on the residence halls and Stanford bequest combined. Education at these schools, she thought, would best prepare women to begin a career in science or medicine. Notably, with her gift to Stanford, she sought to pay for both training and career opportunities: not only to attend Stanford medical school but also to do research at its hospital and teach there. This was her first directive that her philanthropy enable women faculty. She had not made this demand at MIT, where her focus was on students, not on broadening opportunities for women faculty or administrators. Her experience with the hospital may have opened her eyes to the need to focus on faculty as well. Given her decision to finance the development of the birth control pill after decades of monetary support for the birth control movement, McCormick may also have wanted to empower women doctors who could help women access birth control.

By making her donations to MIT and Stanford Medical School, McCormick chose prestigious institutions that already admitted women, thus avoiding the fight for coeducation that Mary Garrett fought at JHU. Although these institutions were coeducational, women did not have an equal opportunity for education in science and medicine. The lack of dormitories and other services meant that women students were scarce and did not generally feel welcome. McCormick understood that admission was only part of the battle for higher education for women, and that her substantial donations could significantly improve opportunities for women. By the late 1950s and early 1960s, university officials at MIT shared her desire to increase the number of women students and gladly accepted her gifts. They did, however, still make compromises in order to gain the significant funding, allowing their donor to make decisions about where the buildings were to be located, what they would look like, and how many students they would house.

McCormick was not the first wealthy woman to push an already coeducational school to improve conditions for its women students. Other women

Phoebe Apperson Hearst and University of California, Berkeley, president Benjamin Wheeler. Courtesy of Library of Congress Prints and Photographs Division, LC-B2-2472-10.

donors also chose to improve opportunities for higher education for women, most notably Phoebe Apperson Hearst. Hearst was particularly important because she served as the first female regent in a significant state university system: the University of California. Thus, she could combine financial influence with official power as a university trustee.

Phoebe Hearst was one of the most significant and wealthy women to bring her agenda for women's education to a coeducational university. Born in 1842, Phoebe Apperson was the daughter of farmers who struggled to make a living. She was educated at Reedville Academy in Steelville, Missouri; worked as a tutor for a wealthy family; and then, at age nineteen, married George Hearst, who made his fortune in the mining, oil, real estate, and publishing businesses. Their son, William, was born in 1863, and Phoebe traveled abroad extensively with him (while George remained in the United States, fostering Phoebe's independence), educating herself and her son about art and culture. When George died in 1891, she inherited his estate, worth over $18 million (nearly $475 million in 2016).[108] At age forty-eight, she began a philanthropic career in which she became personally involved in the organizations and institutions she supported.

Due to her belief in the power of education as a means of enabling social mobility, education became her primary area of philanthropy. She consistently tried to ensure that "those excluded or marginalized from America's mainstream, especially women," would benefit from her wealth.[109] Hearst helped develop and fund the kindergarten movement in San Francisco and around the nation, including donating over $200,000 to the Golden Gate Kindergarten Association. Notably, Hearst extended her attention to African Americans as well. She paid for three kindergartens in Washington, D.C.—two for white children and one for black children—and, more importantly, funded the Phoebe Hearst Kindergarten Training School in Washington, D.C., for African American teachers. This suggests that she saw education not only as a means of mobility for children but also as a way for the black women who attended the school to get "respectable" jobs as teachers with the training they received, at a time when most African American women in the South worked in the fields or in white homes as domestic servants.[110] In addition, Hearst provided kindergartens in the poor mining towns that enriched her family's wealth.

Many of the educational institutions she funded were for girls and women. She gave $250,000 to start the National Cathedral School for Girls in Washington, D.C., and helped found the National Congress of Mothers (later known as the Parent Teacher Association), donating liberally to it in its earliest days. In the 1890s, Hearst donated money to the Association of Collegiate Alumnae to fund American women forced to seek a graduate education in Europe due to the lack of opportunity in the United States.[111] She also supported San Francisco Homeopathic Hospital (like NEH, this hospital was staffed by women doctors who trained women to become doctors), trying to ensure it kept women in positions of power after it merged with Hahnemann Hospital, which was run by male doctors.[112] She also donated to Mary Garrett's Women's Medical School Fund for Johns Hopkins. She was a longtime supporter of the YWCA, and although a late convert to the cause, she donated thousands to the woman suffrage movement.[113]

Hearst supported all these institutions and organizations for women in part because she believed that education and vocational training could be ennobling, providing women with purpose, energy, and character. Although she did not have a college education herself, she took her travels and exposure to opera and art seriously, as means of self-education. She became fascinated with anthropology, which she studied as she financed the anthropology department at the University of California. Moreover, her experiences managing her estate and working with educated women in progressive organizations helped her understand the benefits of education for other women. According to Susan B. Anthony, Hearst told her in 1896 that managing the estate helped her understand that women needed financial *and* political power. She explained to Anthony that she planned to help further women's education.[114]

Hearst's concern for women and education led her to her first donation to the University of California, which was chartered in 1868 and admitted women in 1870. Despite their longtime presence, women made up only 30 percent of students in 1891.[115] Hearst gave $1,500 to create five annual scholarships for girls, upping the number to eight in 1892. She did not choose the winners of the scholarships herself but specified that they have "noble character and high aims," and that the scholarships be based both on financial need and academic merit.[116] Hearst maintained contact with the scholarship winners, nicknamed "Phoebes," and one recipient even invited Hearst to her wedding.[117]

Although the money that Hearst donated to UC to benefit women dovetailed with her overall philanthropic interests in improving opportunities for girls and women, she also donated money to the university for general purposes. Most significantly, she created an international architectural competition to design a new comprehensive campus plan (underwriting $200,000 in expenses for the competition). She also donated the money for a mining building and its addition (well over $700,000 total), and gave over $100,000 for the anthropology department.[118]

Such significant giving led Hearst to become the first female regent of the University of California. School officials continued to court Hearst, hoping for additional donations and ultimately a bequest at her death. Hearst's position on campus meant that she established a close relationship with UC president Benjamin Wheeler, who constantly wrote her updates about campus issues. Hearst was on the committee that chose Wheeler. He realized her importance even before arriving on campus. In fact, he responded to his job offer by stating that he wanted to meet Hearst first, to find out her plans regarding "endowment and equipment," as he intended to come to California as long as he had "cordial, united *continued* support." After meeting Hearst, he accepted the position.[119] Cultivating her affection for the university, long letters from Wheeler updated Hearst on campus happenings, his family, and issues under consideration by the regents, especially needs on campus.

Armed now with the power gained through these donations, Hearst decided to improve accommodations for women on campus. Having been in contact with the Phoebes for years, she understood there was no place on campus where they felt they belonged. While neither sex had dormitories on campus, men had an easier time finding rooms in boardinghouses or forming residence clubs close to the campus. Women had difficulty participating in extracurricular activities dominated by men, and even if they wanted to organize their own activities, they had no building in which to house them. Although they were members of and paid dues to the student government association, women could not join its executive committee and argued that it did not represent their interests. They were excluded from much of the social life of the school, which focused on class hierarchy (freshmen through seniors) and hazing.[120]

In 1901, Hearst donated the land and $40,000 for a women's building and gymnasium, named Hearst Hall, and $5,000 dollars for a women's swimming pool. In her typical hands-on way, she first leased a house right next to campus, so she could oversee the building, and she hired architect Bernard Maybeck to ensure that it would be beautiful and functional. Hearst Hall had beautiful furnishings and artwork, and hosted concerts and teas for students and the community. Wheeler called it a "home and refuge, as well as gymnasium, for the women students," noting that the women previously had no place to gather, socialize, and exercise. The building helped them achieve a sense of belonging on campus and improved their social lives.[121] Faced with exclusion and second-class treatment, having a separate facility enabled women to find a welcome on a campus that did not always seem to want them. It was a strategy that enabled women to thrive at the university for decades, until they were able to join equally in activities and social life in the late twentieth century.[122]

Hearst's presence on the board finally led the regents to consider hiring women teachers or a dean of women. President Martin Kellogg directly argued that "since the coming of Mrs. Hearst onto the board of Regents, the question has often been asked, why not allow women a representation on the faculty?" Kellogg advocated for a dean of women, whose role would be more directed toward counseling and less to teaching. In 1898, Hearst began to pay a part-time salary for Dr. Mary Bennett Ritter to serve as a physician for women students, a lecturer in hygiene, and an all-around adviser to female students. Ritter began by offering medical examinations, which the university required before students could access the gymnasium. Ritter recalled that as the only woman offering lectures to women students, she felt like a "pariah" on campus. The university refused to assume the expense after Hearst stopped paying Ritter's salary in 1904. Instead, UC finally hired its first woman faculty member and then a dean of women in 1906.[123]

Ritter also encouraged Hearst to take an interest in residential opportunities for women after discovering that some students were malnourished and living in unsanitary boardinghouses. Hearst paid Ritter's expenses to travel to the East Coast in the summer of 1900, where she visited women's colleges, inspected women's cooperative housing or residential women's clubs, and spoke to deans of women. Ritter's report convinced Hearst to finance two residential clubs, each housing fifteen students with a housemother. The initial success of these two clubs led to a permanent university committee that sponsored additional clubs.[124] Hearst later established the Hearst Domestic Industries, a boardinghouse and sewing enterprise where young women of "good moral character" could live and work in order to earn their way through UC.[125]

The percentage of women increased from 30 percent in 1891 to 46 percent in 1899–1900. Women students appreciated the personal attention shown to them by Hearst, who held receptions and otherwise interacted with them.[126] Students wrote to Hearst for advice on everything from marriage to careers. She personally assisted several with medical and travel expenses.[127] Known as their "fairy godmother," Hearst's "interest in the women students was deep and abiding."[128]

Because she had funded an architectural competition for the campus, paid the architect's salary, and donated the Hearst Memorial Mining Building, Phoebe Hearst was a powerful figure on the UC campus, a regent, and a confidante of the president. She wielded power to build the women's building—named Hearst Hall in her honor and decorated with her portrait—and to push for greater acceptance of women on campus. Although her donations earmarked for women were dwarfed by those allocated to the campus in general, her decision to build Hearst Hall reflected Hearst's larger pattern of giving dedicated to women and girls at a myriad of educational organizations and institutions. She understood that the best way to assist women students was with her checkbook. The university, perhaps hoping for a financial windfall when she died, was eager to please her, and the women's building was thus built and named for Hearst.

COERCIVE PHILANTHROPY AS PRACTICED by the women in this chapter was often successful in forcing universities and medical schools to open their doors to women and to welcome them with dormitories and other services. The fact that some institutions refused to accept the money with the restrictions imposed by the women donors indicates just how much resistance to coeducation there was at the turn of the century. Garrett's remarkable success at JHU is even more meaningful when examined alongside the difficulties women philanthropists faced at Harvard, NYU, and the University of Rochester.

Notably, they also understood that barriers went beyond admittance. Just because UC and MIT were coeducational did not mean that women had opportunities equal to men on campus. The lack of female dormitories, recreational and social space, and other services meant both that fewer women were admitted and that they often did not feel welcome for decades after a school became coeducational. Therefore, Hearst and McCormick used their significant financial largesse to force schools to become more accommodating to women through women's buildings. These buildings served the practical needs of women for housing, dining, socializing, and other services, even as they symbolically stood as a permanent reminder that women belonged on campus. Having a separate space on the main campus could also ironically serve the purpose of better integrating women on a coeducational campus. Across over eight decades, wealthy women continued their commitment to widening access to higher education for women, providing further evidence of women's continued work for women's rights after the Nineteenth Amendment and before the height of the women's liberation movement of the late 1960s and early 1970s.

Garrett, McCormick, and Hearst each parlayed their fortune into a powerful tool of persuasion. They did much to expand opportunities for other women because they understood the importance of education and career for women's independence. These monied women, who gave to the suffrage movement as well, wanted to enable other women to gain the education they believed could lead to economic independence and the political power necessary to free women from men's control. As women fought for political and economic freedom, some came to realize that these would be meaningless if women could not control their own bodies and when and if they had children. These women would join the birth control movement—the most controversial part of the women's movement and the subject of chapter 6.

CHAPTER SIX

Margaret Sanger's Network of Feminists

Funding the Birth Control Movement

On December 2, 1921, Juliet Barrett Rublee, a wealthy society woman, was arrested while testifying at a hearing in New York. Almost three weeks earlier, acting on the orders of Roman Catholic archbishop Patrick J. Hayes, the police had arrived to shut down a lecture titled "Birth Control: Is It Moral?" the culminating event of birth control advocate Margaret Sanger's first American Birth Control Conference. The *New York Times* claimed, "Hundreds of men and women, many socially prominent, derided the police and urged the speakers to defy the order not to speak." Rublee was one of several women who jumped up on the stage to protect Sanger, but despite their efforts, Sanger was arrested. Rublee and fellow society women were among those who followed her to the police station and the courtroom as witnesses before gathering at Rublee's home after Sanger was released in the custody of her counsel. The *Times* article concluded with a list of many of the "prominent" people on the committee who had planned the conference.[1] Three weeks later, Rublee testified at a hearing as a witness against the police for shutting down the meeting.[2]

Rublee's defense of Sanger led to her own arrest when the hearing was halted and she was "taken in her limousine . . . to the Elizabeth Street [Police] Station." As Rublee put it, "Apparently my crime consisted in having read Section 1142 of the Penal Code [which banned dissemination of information on birth control] and having read it, in attending the Town Hall meeting on November 13th; or perhaps my crime lay in expressing the opinion that the Section 1142 is unwise legislation." The incident ended quickly. Rublee was immediately released, the complaint was dismissed, and the assistant district attorney admitted there were no grounds for the arrest.[3]

Rublee and the wealthy women dedicated to the new birth control movement in the 1910s were willing to risk the approbation of society and, as with those women who picketed the White House for woman suffrage, arrest. The dissemination of birth control information and devices was still illegal under the federal Comstock Act, which prevented the distribution of obscene materials through the mail, including those related to birth control, and under various state laws that banned the distribution or use of birth control. Moreover, birth control's association with sex made it scandalous for prominent women to discuss in public.

Despite the risks, Rublee and other wealthy women supported the birth control movement as they had woman suffrage, labor activism, and higher education for women. Their financial contributions paid for offices, publications, and conferences, as well as lawyers and other costs associated with Sanger's arrests. In the late 1910s and early 1920s, Sanger could not count on men's support; instead, she relied on these committed wealthy women to fund her new movement.

These women were critical to the birth control movement, not just for their dollars but also, more importantly, for their ideas. They advocated for birth control on the basis of women's independence and freedom (as opposed to limiting family size or overpopulation concerns). Sanger's supporters, whether or not they called themselves feminists, articulated a radical vision for women's equality that attracted them to a movement originally conceived by Sanger to be about a woman's control over her body and thus her liberation.[4] As nineteenth-century suffragist Matilda Joselyn Gage put it, "Woman must first of all be held as having a right to herself."[5] Economic and political independence would be incomplete without control over reproduction as well as the right to sexual pleasure. Feminism for Sanger and her supporters was ultimately a "quest for self-realization," which required the ability to control one's body and sex life.[6]

A fearless and determined leader of the movement for decades, Sanger has dominated our understanding of the fight to legalize birth control and expand access to effective means of contraception. But Sanger was not a lone crusader. She surrounded herself with a network of wealthy women who supported her movement. The role these women played is crucial to understanding Sanger herself.

Although Sanger initially became active in labor issues through the Socialist Party in New York, by the late 1910s she had dropped her participation in socialist politics to focus solely on birth control as a tool for women's empowerment. She began to seek financial assistance from wealthy women rather than working-class socialists. As she continued to advocate for birth control, however, she increasingly emphasized infant and maternal health. By the late 1920s and 1930s, she also associated with those in the burgeoning eugenics movement, and she worked to legalize birth control in part by promoting it as a medical treatment. In the 1950s, she sometimes claimed that birth control was the best means of dealing with population growth concerns.

Some historians have blamed her "conservative" turn away from socialism on her desire to cultivate wealthy donors and medical doctors, whereas others argue that while her rhetoric changed to appeal to her audience, she never abandoned her central goal of empowering women by providing them with control over their reproductive choices.[7] Thus, more precise definitions of her radicalism or conservatism are necessary. She may have discarded her radical political embrace of socialism but not her equally radical feminism. Sanger toned down her rhetoric concerning women's control over their bodies with a new emphasis on family planning, but she never abandoned the need for women to control fertility nor for women to enjoy sex (though she no longer mentioned sex outside marriage). Even as she courted doctors because she thought they could help increase women's access to birth control, she continued to prioritize clinics staffed by women, often nurses, serving other women.

In fact, biographer Ellen Chesler asserts that Sanger's abandonment of socialism hinged on her feminism, arguing, "At the heart of this political conversion was the maturing of her consciousness as a feminist. Sanger lost confidence in the power of working people to unite for change but decided to invest in the collective potential of women."[8] According to Chesler, Sanger's first book, *Women and the New Race* (1920), was "a manifesto that demands the democratic dissemination of birth control as a fundamental right of women. The book proposes that political and economic enfranchisement will not alone guarantee an end to discrimination—that medicine and science must also be harnessed to secure women an equal right to experience the full range of human possibility."[9] Thus, though over many decades she could and did justify birth control for health, eugenic, and overpopulation reasons—depending on her audience—a 1930 *New Yorker* profile of Sanger captured her continued feminism: "From time to time," the article asserted, "Mrs. Sanger has let herself go and revealed a feminism so violent as to scare half her supporters out of their wits if they thought she meant it."[10]

Turning away from Sanger herself, this chapter examines the strong feminist support that she received from her wealthy supporters, particularly from 1916 through the 1920s. As Sanger eased herself out of the socialist movement, where she found inadequate support for birth control, she turned to a group of very wealthy women. Rather than leading Sanger to a more conservative ideology, these women sustained her continued radical feminist goals. This chapter shows how and why they encouraged Sanger to keep her focus on women's need for reproductive control, even if she toned down her rhetoric or sought legitimacy through the support of the medical profession. They did not drive Sanger to abandon her radical ideas about feminism. Espousing similar ideas, they supported Sanger because of her feminist position, not in spite of it.

This chapter weaves several of Sanger's wealthiest and most loyal followers—Jessie Ashley, Elsie Clews Parsons, Gertrude Pinchot, and Juliet Rublee—into the story of her developing career. It follows Sanger's first and second arrest and the creation of the Committee of 100, the American Birth Control League (ABCL), and other organizations in the 1920s. The women running these organizations were feminists who believed, like Sanger, that women needed control over their bodies as the most important step toward independence and equality. Many first came to advocate for women's rights through participation in the woman suffrage movement. This chapter examines the feminist beliefs that drove these women to go beyond support for suffrage or higher education for women to rally behind birth control, the most radical movement for women at the time. Their feminism elucidates Sanger's continued commitment to women.

Putting the spotlight on these women also makes it clear that Sanger's success in soliciting funds for the birth control movement came in large measure from her ability to tap into the social networks connecting many of these women.[11] They knew one another from suffrage associations as well as from a variety of clubs, ranging from the unconventional Greenwich Village Heterodoxy Club, devoted to the open discussion of liberal ideas, to the tony Colony Club, a social club formed by New York socialites. This chapter brings to the forefront the connections among many of the women who have appeared elsewhere in this book, demonstrating the importance of social capital as well as financial support.

As with others throughout this book, some of the women discussed in this chapter were more independent than many women of their day because they were single (or lived as if they were): Jessie Ashley never married, and Helen Reid's husband was an alcoholic. Though married when she met Sanger, Gertrude Pinchot soon divorced. However, perhaps because birth control's connection with sex was too controversial for most single women to embrace in the 1910s and 1920s, many of the vocal activists were married. Juliet Rublee, for example, was fortunate in having a husband who shared her enthusiasm not just for the birth control movement but also for women's equality more generally, while Herbert Parsons granted Elsie Clews Parsons the freedom to participate in the birth control movement as well as to spend time in the field doing anthropological research. Edith Hooker, Katharine Hepburn, Charlotte Delafield, Frances Ackerman, and Ida Timme were also married.[12]

Although these women had a variety of educational backgrounds, a disproportionate number were extraordinarily well educated for women in the late 1910s: Ashley had attended New York University Law School, Hooker and Hepburn had attended Bryn Mawr College, Reid had graduated from Barnard, and Elsie Parsons had earned a PhD from Columbia.

Upper-class women were crucial to the success of the birth control movement. They injected much-needed money into the movement, keeping Sanger financially afloat. Sanger had to pay for publications and clinics, both of which were expensive. Because Sanger was so dynamic, she seemed to advocate for birth control on the strength of her ideas alone. The reality was that she worked within a series of organizations that had officers, paid staff, rented offices, and publication and mailing expenses. Thus, as with suffrage and higher education, wealthy women financed the movement and affected its trajectory of success.

Society women also brought additional attention from the press due to the controversial nature of their supporting such a contentious topic. The headlines they could garner as elite women helped draw attention to this controversial issue. As with suffrage, they made it fashionable to stand in court and back Margaret Sanger. Yet even more significantly, they helped legitimize support for a cause that was not just opposed by many but illegal.

Sanger sought the help of wealthy women, and they orbited around her, giving funds and aid. There was none of the resentment or power struggle between Sanger and the women donating money that existed, for example, between Alva Belmont and suffrage officers who begrudged her desire for control. Birth control donors were content to provide monetary support for Sanger's leadership and ideas. They did not tie their donations to their own ability to shape strategies or tactics. This is not to say that the movement was without tension. Indeed, Sanger had rivals, including Mary Ware Dennett. Sanger also later left the ABCL during a struggle for power with Eleanor Jones. But her difficulties were with her rivals for leadership, not with her wealthy donors, with whom she cultivated long friendships.

Always in need of money, Sanger acted first and raised money later. In 1952, she boasted to a colleague, "As you know I have usually been able to find friends who would give some financial support or contributions for anything I wanted to do."[13] Sanger's second marriage to Noah Slee, a wealthy businessman, also enriched her movement because he underwrote it for several years, until he lost much of his fortune in the Great Depression.[14] When the John Price Jones Corporation compiled a report on the Margaret Sanger Research Bureau in 1930, it attributed the success of fund-raising to Sanger herself, writing that the supporters who gave the year before were likely to give again "due to the personal hold which Mrs. Sanger has on the Clinic's supporters."[15] This was because Sanger and her early supporters passionately fought for a woman's right to control her own body.

MARGARET HIGGINS SANGER WAS born in 1879 in Corning, New York. Her father, Michael, was an Irish-born stonecutter, and her mother, Anne, suffered ill health from tuberculosis and too-frequent pregnancies (eighteen pregnancies in twenty-two years, with eleven children born). Educated at Claverack College, Margaret married William Sanger, an architect and painter, and became a nurse. They had three children, including a daughter who died at age six. Margaret eventually divorced William, married Noah Slee, and had a series of affairs with men, including Havelock Ellis. In her autobiography, Sanger claimed it was the influence of seeing her mother's medical struggles with frequent pregnancy and ill health, as well as witnessing the same problems among poor immigrant women while working as a nurse, that led her to begin her work advocating birth control.[16]

The Sangers lived in Greenwich Village, New York, where she and William became active in labor struggles and the Socialist Party. Sanger, however, grew frustrated with socialists who did not prioritize the problem of reproductive freedom. In fact, Sanger recalled that Industrial Workers of the World (IWW) union leader Bill Haywood spoke of a future where women "could have without fear of want all the babies they pleased," completely misunderstanding her concerns. She complained that at the heart of labor strikes was the desire for a higher "breadwinner" wage for men to support their families, without any examination of gender roles or sexism.[17] Yet a frustrated Sanger also argued that suffragists and other feminists were too focused on economic and political freedom (i.e., strikes and suffrage), while she wanted to prioritize woman's "biological subservience to man, which was the true cause of her enslavement." She stressed the need "to protect women from ill health as the result of excessive childbearing and, equally important, to have the right to control their own destinies."[18] Even after she left the Socialist Party, Sanger continued to be concerned for working-class women due to her awareness that poor women had less access to birth control information and devices than did wealthy women. She was determined to achieve reproductive freedom for all women.

Notably, Sanger was also influenced by Havelock Ellis to advocate for women's sexual pleasure. Writing for Sanger's *Birth Control Review* in 1918, he asked, "Is the wife entitled to an equal mutual interest and joy in this act with her husband?" Emphatically arguing yes, Ellis posited that women have an "erotic right" as much as men.[19] Sanger's early writings echoed this perspective.

Sanger's most well-known argument is that "no woman can call herself free who does not own and control her body. No woman can call herself free until she can choose consciously whether she will or will not be a mother." Although she thought that men and women should ideally deal with contraception together, she knew the reality was that it was up to women to practice methods they could control. "She will never receive her freedom," Sanger concluded, "until she takes it for herself."[20]

Given her belief that only birth control could deliver emancipation to women, Sanger grew frustrated with suffragists, whose movement was gaining momentum at the same time that Sanger became active. Suffrage leaders Carrie Chapman Catt and Alice Paul focused on political and legal rights, and like Sanger, each saw her own movement as the one pursuing the single most important issue affecting women.[21] However, by widening the lens to focus on suffragists and birth control supporters beyond Sanger, Paul, and Catt, the connection between the two movements comes into focus. Sanger's circle of wealthy donors were almost all involved in the suffrage movement, where many began to articulate the need for women's equality.[22] Rublee and most other ABCL officers were suffragists, with Rublee even serving as grand marshal of the suffrage procession organized by the Congressional Union in 1914.[23]

Sanger benefited from her supporters' suffrage activism in that they came to her with a history of organizing and speaking out about women's rights and the inequality women faced in society. These women had experience marching and giving speeches and had faced violence and arrest. For many, it was a short distance from woman suffrage parades to birth control rallies. Many also supported working-class women, most notably during the Shirtwaist Strike of 1909, where they encountered violence and arrest as they marched and picketed with women garment workers. The movements used similar tactics. In 1917, Sanger's sister went on a hunger strike after being arrested for birth control distribution, and just months later, suffragists who were jailed following White House protests began hunger striking as well.[24]

One of the first wealthy suffragists to follow Sanger was Jessie Ashley, a Mayflower descendant whose father was president of the Wabash Railway. Her father, Ossian D. Ashley, worked to admit women to the New York University School of Law, where she was one of the first woman graduates. Sanger recalled that the wealthy Ashley "was one of the most conspicuous of the many men and women of long pedigree who were revolting against family tradition. . . . Her peculiarly honest mind was tolerant toward others, but uncompromising towards herself."[25] Ashley had money of her own to spend on the birth control movement Sanger was just creating.

Moreover, Ashley understood the importance of fund-raising. While treasurer of the National American Woman Suffrage Association (NAWSA) in 1911, she pushed for a $75,000 campaign to bring the budget in line with what English suffragists were spending on literature and organization. Frustrated with the pace and politics of NAWSA, she left. Her experience in NAWSA was critical to Sanger, who needed someone aware of the tools for publicity and the costs of campaigning for women's rights.[26]

After her work at NAWSA, Ashley turned her attention to the plight of laborers, supporting the Lawrence strike along with Sanger, and the hotel workers' strike in 1913, as well as offering free legal services and bail money to working women who were arrested for their labor activism. According to a tribute after her death, "The money with which she might have lived in idle luxury went constantly into the battle for freedom of the workers, particularly the women workers."[27] Despite her wealthy background, Ashley was a socialist and had an affair with IWW leader Haywood.[28] According to Sanger, a "socialist in practice as well as theory, [Ashley] spent large portions of her income in getting radicals out of jail, and her own legal experience she gave freely in their behalf."[29]

Ashley came to her support for birth control through her suffrage background, her socialist and labor connections with Sanger, and, most of all, through her strong feminist beliefs. In an editorial written for the *Birth Control Review*, Ashley focused on the need for women to have "power, power to control ourselves," an argument she declared to be "fundamentally sound."[30]

Ashley was quite liberal in her views. Beyond her embrace of birth control, she suggested that the institution of the family needed to undergo dramatic change and advocated that all healthy women, married or not, should be "free to have children."[31] This was an extraordinary statement at the time, and not one she made in public. But Ashley was not afraid of controversy. Like Rublee, Ashley was arrested for her role in the birth control movement. She was convicted of distributing and selling birth control pamphlets, fined fifty dollars, and released. She considered it a "privilege to be persecuted" for the cause.[32]

Sanger's relationship with Jessie Ashley was especially important. Ashley had many connections with women from the suffrage movement and insight into fund-raising. She and Sanger shared a socialist background and feminist ideas regarding birth control. Ashley helped her make connections with wealthy women who helped fund Sanger's transition from the Socialist Party to new organizations created to support her and the birth control movement.

Ashley and Sanger both lived in Greenwich Village for a time, where they socialized with other liberal women and men, especially at Mabel Dodge Luhan's salon, a meeting spot for liberals in the Village.[33] Ashley and Luhan loaned Sanger the money to start the *Woman Rebel*, her first magazine, with which she began her advocacy of birth control. In it, Sanger boldly declared the need for complete freedom for women, including knowledge of birth control. It also advocated socialism.

In 1914, Sanger was invited to address the Heterodoxy Club, to which Ashley and Luhan belonged. This was a women's lunch club that brought together women activists, artists, and professionals for lectures and discussion. The club was known for its unorthodoxy. A couple dozen of the women in the Heterodoxy Club were active suffragists, and at least ten of the women were birth control supporters.[34] The Heterodoxy Club and Greenwich Village thus provided a social network that Sanger used for ideology, contacts, and financial support.

The bohemian nature of Greenwich Village was critical to the support that Sanger received there. The Heterodoxy Club encouraged free-wheeling discussion. Moreover, Greenwich Village was a place where "freedom of thought and action and 'the removal of the barriers between the sexes' went hand in hand," as well as barriers to sexual expression and fulfillment. Modern women wanted to control their bodies—both through the enjoyment of sex within and outside marriage and through control over reproduction.[35] Luhan claimed that Sanger "was the first person I ever knew who was openly an ardent propagandist for the joys of the flesh."[36] The feminism espoused by many of her supporters, like Ashley, was radical for its time in its inclusion of sexual freedom. Even if they did not agree with these ideas, society women who embraced Margaret Sanger could not dissociate themselves from such radical ideas—and talk—about sex in the late 1910s.

Elsie Clews Parsons was another member of the Heterodoxy Club with society connections, who supported birth control and proposed radical ideas about sex and gender relations. The daughter of Lucy and Henry Clews, a wealthy New York banker, Elsie defied expectations for women of her class and went to Barnard, then received her PhD from Columbia University. She claimed she went to Barnard because she did not want to think about her appearance and "dress all day long." She later married Robert Parsons, a congressman and ally of Teddy Roosevelt. While at Barnard, she founded a chapter of the College Settlements Association and later helped found the

Speyer School for immigrant schoolchildren. An admirer of nineteenth-century suffragist Lillie Devereux Blake, she attended the New York State Woman's Suffrage Association meeting in 1894, writing her then boyfriend, Sam Dexter, that she imagined a family with two heads so that women could have a role, too. Parsons was a generous donor to the New York suffrage referendum campaign. However, she believed that the right to vote would never be enough to liberate women who could not control their bodies.[37]

A noted anthropologist who studied Native American tribes, she grounded her support for women's rights in anthropological comparisons of Western women with women in Indian and Mexican societies, arguing that alternative gender models existed in other societies.[38] When Parsons discussed women's oppression, she focused on many factors, including social taboos that hindered women's freedom, such as the ability to go out alone, oppressive clothing, and, most important, reproductive rights.[39] She claimed that women were realizing that "ability and freedom to work are indispensable to a talent for life."[40]

Moreover, she wrote about the importance of birth control within marriage. Parsons argued that "birth control makes possible such clear cut distinctions between mating and parenthood," separating sex from reproduction, that it was likely to force new conceptions of relationships and family. Thus, like Ashley, Parsons made clear the radical implications of birth control for gender dynamics and family.[41] Parsons carried out her ideas in her personal life, with an unconventional marriage in which she spent months at a time away from her husband in the field researching. She also had several intimate relationships with other men while married.[42]

Parsons was among the first wealthy women to support Sanger after her first indictment. Although Sanger did not give explicit contraceptive instructions in the *Woman Rebel*, she was indicted for breaking obscenity laws in August 1914 and escaped to Europe rather than face trial. She returned from Europe in the fall of 1915, ready to face the court. Now a cause célèbre, on January 17, 1916, Sanger began to court rich women like Parsons with the assistance of Henrietta Rodman, a feminist teacher, suffragist, and Heterodoxy Club member. Rodman graduated from Teachers College, taught in the public schools for years, and organized the Feminist Alliance, an organization that intended to build housing for women that would mechanize housework and relieve women of its burden.[43]

The evening before Sanger's trial was scheduled to take place, Rodman and other supporters gave her a dinner at the Hotel Brevoort, where, among others, Parsons spoke. Sanger told her audience, which included many wealthy women and social reformers, that the *Woman Rebel* had been such a radical (i.e., socialist) magazine because she needed to draw attention to birth control. She asked wealthy women to take up the cause now.[44] The following day, Ashley accompanied Sanger to her hearing. However, it was postponed to January 24, then to February 14, 1916. According to the *New York Times*, the Sanger Defense Committee was thrilled when charges against Sanger were finally dropped. They quickly organized a celebration.[45]

Parsons recognized just how difficult it was to get women to support such a controversial issue publicly. In March 1916, she wrote a letter to the *New Republic* revealing how notable the society women were who put themselves forward to support Sanger. She explained that she tried to get a group of New York women to sign statements attesting to their approval of publishing birth control articles, that this information should be "readily accessible," and that they themselves had "imparted birth control information" and "have practiced birth control." She approached about fifty women she thought to be "liberal minded" but could only get six women to sign the first three statements and only three women to sign all four. Parsons was most dismayed by the fact that so many women refused to sign because their husband (or sons) did not approve.[46]

Yet despite Parson's difficulties early in 1916, Sanger and her colleagues soon succeeded in drawing these women into the movement. Wealthy women either ignored opposition or embraced the controversy associated with birth control. Luhan explained that the upper-class women who "stood on street corners" advocating birth control and labor unions had to become "careless about adverse publicity. Booing and hissing . . . became a regular feature of their public meetings."[47]

Sanger's next bold move was to open the first birth control clinic in America on October 16, 1916, in the Brownsville section of Brooklyn. She was scarcely in business ten days before she and the others from the clinic were arrested. The clinic closed for good the following month. These charges were not dismissed. Sanger; her sister Ethel Byrne, a nurse in the clinic; and Fania Mindell, a volunteer, all faced trial in January 1917.[48]

In response to the arrests, Rublee and another monied woman, Gertrude Minturn Pinchot, formed the Committee of 100 on November 28, 1916, to support those arrested and contribute funds to their defense, including $500 bail each.[49] Sanger had grand ambitions for the Committee of 100, which she described to the *New York Tribune* as "one hundred women who . . . will take turns operating the clinic, and as soon as one is arrested another will take up her work."[50] However, the Committee of 100 had no plans to operate the

Gertrude Minturn
Pinchot. Courtesy of
Library of Congress
Prints and Photo-
graphs Division,
LC-B2-1234.

clinic without Sanger, instead seeing itself as providing financial and moral
support to Sanger and her sister during their trial as well as to the larger
movement as a whole.

The very wealthy and prominent Gertrude Minturn Pinchot, who hosted
the inaugural meeting of the Committee of 100 in her home, was also crucial to
Sanger's team. Sanger described her as "aristocratic of bearing, autocratic by
position, she was one to command and be obeyed, and was easily a leading
personality in the philanthropic smart set in New York."[51] Gertrude was born
in 1872 to Susanna Shaw and Robert Browne Minturn Jr., a shipping and mercantile businessman and railroad investor.

Gertrude Minturn came from a socially elite and affluent family of social
reformers. Her aunt Eliza Theodora Minturn was a member of the New York
Local Committee on Harvard Examinations for Women, the Woman's Education Association of Boston, and the Association for Promoting the Higher

Education of Women in New York, who unsuccessfully pressed Columbia to admit women.[52] Another aunt—philanthropist and reformer Josephine Shaw Lowell, a suffragist who founded the organized charity movement, the Woman's Municipal League, and the New York Consumers League—was a major influence on Gertrude and her sisters. Like Josephine, Gertrude's mother and sisters were early supporters of woman suffrage, traveling to Albany in 1894 to assist in the presentation of a suffrage petition. Her sister Edith Stokes would eventually follow their aunt's footsteps and preside over the Municipal League, while her sister Mildred Scott was a pacifist and socialist. Despite this activism, Gertrude and her three sisters were not allowed by their mother to attend college.

Gertrude married Amos Pinchot in her late twenties, a wedding attended by Elsie Parsons and her parents among other New York elites, and with Amos had two children. Amos was a lawyer, progressive reformer, and publicist, whose parents and grandparents had made their fortune in lumbering, land speculation, and real estate. He was drawn into politics through his older brother Gifford Pinchot, an ally of Theodore Roosevelt. Amos's politics, however, veered toward a more progressive tradition as a champion of individual liberties and of the working class, despite his own wealth and privilege. Gifford's wife, Cornelia Bryce Pinchot, was also devoted to women's rights, favoring suffrage and birth control as ways to gain women's freedom, and supporting working-women's issues; and Cornelia's sister, Edith Clare Bryce Cram, was a pacifist and birth control supporter.[53]

Despite these progressive family members, Amos's biographer, Nancy Pinchot, described Gertrude as "sanctimonious" and sexually inhibited due to a conservative upbringing. Their marriage was not happy, eventually ending in divorce in 1918.[54] But before the divorce, according to Nancy Pinchot, Amos drew his wife into the Greenwich Village social and political network, where they attended Luhan's salons together. There she came to embrace labor unions, suffrage (she was a member of the CU), and birth control. Along with Sanger and Ashley, she supported the Lawrence, Massachusetts, textile strike in 1912, and even traveled to Lawrence to meet strikers and write about her experience in the *New York Sun*. She also chaired the New York branch of the Woman's Peace Party. Even if she had been sanctimonious or sexually inhibited, by 1915 she had thrown herself fully into supporting Sanger and birth control, at a time when both were focused on women's freedom and women's pleasure.[55] Like Sanger, Pinchot argued that birth control was more important than suffrage: "No amount of votes women ever get," she said in 1917, "will do as much as the solution of this age-old problem."[56]

By the time of the trial, Pinchot had already been supporting the Sanger family in many ways for several years. Pinchot aided Sanger after her arrest for publishing the *Woman Rebel*, attended William Sanger's trial (also for obscenity charges), and wrote checks to William to ease his economic distress while Margaret was in Europe (and not earning a salary for the family).[57]

As the press covered the trial, it drew attention to the wealth and status of Rublee, Parsons, Pinchot, and others. On January 3, 1917, the *New York Times* article "Escort for Mrs. Sanger" revealed that "women of prominence in this city" would assemble for breakfast at the Women's City Club and then travel by automobile to Brooklyn for the trial. The paper named twelve prominent women who would be at the trial and invited other interested women to attend.[58] The celebrity status of these elite women who supported Sanger was crucial to defending her, given the controversial nature of Sanger's activity.

Sanger's sister Byrne was tried first, found guilty, and sentenced to thirty days in jail, where she went on a hunger strike. In response, the Committee of 100 met and decided to pass a message to Byrne that she was "too valuable to lose" as well as to telegram Governor Charles Whitman on her behalf. Pinchot and Sanger eventually traveled to Albany, where they obtained the offer of a pardon if Byrne would pledge not to break the law again. After visiting her sister, Sanger decided her health was at risk and accepted the pardon on behalf of Byrne, carrying her out of prison wrapped in Pinchot's fur coat. As Sanger recalled, "Mrs. Pinchot imperiously called her hands, and in a voice of command insisted that they lay [Byrne] down on the floor and bring a stretcher. The result was like magic. The word of command from this quarter was not to be ignored." Fania Mindell, who was tried next, was also found guilty on obscenity charges. Pinchot paid her $50 fine. When Sanger, too, was found guilty, she chose to spend thirty days in jail like Byrne rather than pay the $5,000 fine. Her appeal, however, was successful in that Judge Frederick Crane's interpretation of state law opened the door for doctors to prescribe contraception on general medical grounds (as opposed to only for venereal diseases) in New York.[59]

After the trial, Sanger continued to rely on Pinchot for all means of support, including financial. Pinchot sent frequent checks to Sanger, helping, for example, to pay for pamphlets to be published in Polish and Lithuanian. Due to her long-standing support, Sanger was reluctant to share Pinchot with another birth control organization, the National Birth Control League (NBCL), founded by Mary Ware Dennett while Sanger was in Europe after her arrest. Pinchot and several other people were members of both groups. With Dennett now a rival, Sanger complained to Pinchot in April 1917 about the confusion caused by the existence of two birth control organizations, with some members in common. After thanking Pinchot for a $25 contribution and the help of the Committee of 100, Sanger suggested that donations intended for Sanger were mistakenly being sent to the NBCL office because Pinchot had paid for an office for that group, and thus her name was associated with both groups. When Pinchot dashed off a denial of any misappropriation of funds, Sanger had to back down. She told Pinchot she would try to find the letters from supporters on which she based her assumption that donations were going to the wrong office. More importantly, she wrote, "In the meantime I trust we will not let this matter too greatly interfere with matters which are more properly due for first attention. I think it should especially be borne in mind that any indiscriminate discussion of the subject will injure our cause, and give rise to a useless and painful controversy."[60] Clearly Sanger realized she wanted to assuage Pinchot and maintain her support.

Juliet Barrett Rublee, another prominent leader of the Committee of 100, was also a crucial supporter of Sanger and her closest lifelong friend.[61] Born in Chicago in 1875, she attended Miss Porter's School in Farmington, Connecticut. Heir to the Barrett Company (a Chicago roofing supply and tar manufacturer) fortune, she married George Rublee in 1899. George was a lawyer and political adviser to Dwight Morrow, and a Wilson appointee to the Federal Trade Commission in 1899. Although as an adviser to Wilson George sought to gain American public support for entering World War I, Juliet was a pacifist, picketing outside the White House against war. Like Pinchot, Rublee belonged to the NBCL, where she served on the first executive committee, but she quickly changed her loyalty to Sanger.[62]

Rublee was a passionate feminist and free spirit. According to her nephew, she had the "gall of a brass monkey." Rublee was a modern dancer—a contemporary and acquaintance of Isadora Duncan, who revolutionized American dance with her free style and expression.[63] Duncan's adventurous spirit moved Rublee to lead a diving expedition for treasure in the Mediterranean Sea, for which she drew praise from Sanger for proving her abilities, independence, and decisiveness (although she was ultimately kidnapped by the crew and had to be ransomed by her husband). She also produced a silent film on the Mexican Revolution and was a member of New Hampshire's Cornish Colony of artists. A suffragist, she was president of the Cornish Equal Suffrage League and a supporter of the more militant CU. Rublee had energy, time, and money to devote to the cause. She loved being part of the birth control movement and was always seeking a new challenge. Rublee's feminism derived from her "personal search for satisfaction in life and also a

Juliet Rublee, woman suffrage parade. Courtesy of Library of Congress Prints and Photographs Division, photograph by Harris & Ewing, LC-DIG-hec-04146.

general search for harmony, happiness and perfectability of people. She did not want to live an unfulfilled life."[64]

Sanger and Rublee remained friends for decades. Rublee became less active in the movement by the late 1920s, when she turned her attention to archaeology and filmmaking, but she was no less a friend to Sanger, corresponding and traveling with Sanger until they were elderly. She also continued to send her checks for the movement and for Sanger's personal expenses. Sanger wrote about Rublee in her autobiography, "All the way through the years she has never wavered from my side. No more inspired idealist was ever initiated into a movement. The imagination of this picturesque, romantic wife of a conservative lawyer had been so fired that she dedicated to it her entire devotion, loyalty, partisanship."[65] Sanger depended on Rublee for support when times were rough. When the NBCL refused to support Sanger's magazine, the *Birth Control Review*, she turned to Rublee. "Were it not for your friendly spirit I'm afraid I should have run away this week," she groaned. "The task before me seems so colossal to undertake alone."[66]

Rublee thought birth control was necessary for women's liberation. She suggested to Sanger that Sanger's first book, *Woman and the New Race*, be advertised as "Margaret Sanger's Call to the World for the Freedom of Women." Rublee asserted that the book was crucial because "you see you are speaking for the *hearts* of women, all over the world—the book will help to free them—inside—to make them think for themselves, to give them courage to trust & to follow *their own* feelings, instead of accepting the stupid decrees of men & the church & a false tradition."[67] Influenced by Rublee, Sanger suggested instead " 'The Door to Woman's Freedom,' or some name suggesting B.C. as the key to her liberation or as the foundation for human emancipation."[68]

Rublee was remembered by Mary Ferguson, a president of Planned Parenthood of America in the 1950s, as a proponent of women's sexual pleasure and free love, an attitude Ferguson did not even ascribe to Sanger, whom she believed supported birth control as a social reform aimed at helping the poor. Rublee read Havelock Ellis and believed women needed sexual pleasure as much as men. Her biographer speculates that she may have had an extramarital affair with Hugh de Selincourt, one of Sanger's lovers. Ferguson thought Rublee was courageous to support Sanger. "It was not always popular you know, people made fun of these leaders," she recalled.[69] In 1925, Rublee breathlessly exhorted Sanger to hurry and win legality for birth control, which led women to want to "control their own bodies," so they could move on to help women "become Goddesses" as they awakened to the "desire & will to Freedom & free imagination & aspiration."[70]

Sanger was eager to discuss feminism with Rublee and to use the *Birth Control Review* as a medium to bring their ideas to the public. She explained to Rublee that she was trying to publish an issue of the *Birth Control Review* "expressing woman's ideas and feelings on Birth Control," and looked forward to meeting with Rublee to "chat and bring about the *emancipation of womanhood!*"[71] She asked Rublee for suggestions on creating an editorial board for the *Review* made up of women who could discuss "all problems related to woman's freedom."[72] Thanking her for a check, Sanger told Rublee that they were unable to mail the *Birth Control Review* because it had a review of Marie Stopes's book *Married Love*. "So you see dear Lady," Sanger exhorted Rublee, after World War I "we will need you to help us wage a big fight here in U.S.A. for womans [sic] liberty." She thanked Rublee for helping to put the *Birth Control Review* on good footing.[73] A year later, she asked Rublee for a contribution toward "a woman's number" of the *Review*, which would be especially "sympathetic towards feminism."[74] Still conversing with each other about feminism, Sanger wrote to Rublee in 1953 that she was reading Simone de Beauvoir's *The Second Sex*, which became a feminist classic.[75]

Articulate about her support of birth control, Rublee was responsible for writing the statements and resolutions of the Committee of 100 declaring their desire to decriminalize the dissemination of birth control information. Rublee stressed the need for women to have reproductive control over their bodies. She wrote, "We believe that the question as to whether or not, and when, a woman should have a child is not a question for the Doctors to decide, except in cases where the woman's life is endangered, or for the State legislators to decide, but a question for the woman herself to decide." The Committee of 100 also called for the establishment of clinics, run by nurses under the guidance of doctors, to distribute birth control. Drawing on a variety of arguments, Rublee also stated that there would be a decrease in abortion and protection for women from "too frequent pregnancy."[76]

The committee also helped plan a rally at Carnegie Hall on January 29, 1917.[77] The rally raised $1,000 and resulted in a series of resolutions, written by Rublee and signed by those in attendance, which pledged "moral and financial support" for the movement, as well as for Sanger and Byrne, and condemned the laws and prosecutors against birth control.[78]

Hoping to increase attention to the cause, Sanger organized the first American Birth Control Conference, held in November 1921 in New York. This conference was to culminate in a mass meeting at Carnegie Hall, but instead, it was shut down and resulted in the arrest of Sanger and Rublee. Following the conference, Rublee and Sanger founded the American Birth Control League, which took the place of the Committee of 100 as Sanger's birth control organization.[79]

In the speech Sanger wrote for the conference, she remained true to the feminist rhetoric shared by Ashley, Pinchot, Parsons, and Rublee. She argued against abstinence, noting that women were not free to deny their husbands their bodies, and that sexual relations for married couples should be to express love as well as for procreation. "I have never yet met a real argument against birth control," she declared. "And why? Because it is the one need of the people, because this subject belongs mainly to women. It is the first step that woman must take to have her real emancipation. It is the first step that we must take to free our children."[80] The ABCL released a statement of principles that declared that the "function of motherhood should be elevated to a position of dignity" and that "children should be 1. conceived in love; 2. Born of the mother's conscious desire; 3. And only begotten under conditions which render possible the heritage of health."

Rublee continued to write impassioned statements for birth control based on women's need to control their own reproduction. She drafted a letter for the Birth Control Legislative Committee in 1921 in which she asserted that birth control would decrease abortion, increase spacing between children's births, and promote healthier babies and families. Her letter than asked, "Is this a subject on which men should dictate to women, and decide what they should know and what they should not know? Is not the chief burden and suffering upon women, and have they not a right to this knowledge?"[81]

WHEN SANGER LOOKED BACK on her experience in jail in 1917, she claimed that it led her to strategically begin to try to appeal to "the club woman" for assistance. Although her sister Ethel resented the involvement of Pinchot, her sister-in-law Cram, and other wealthy women who wanted to know birth control women while wearing "thousands of dollars worth of elegance," Sanger was more sympathetic. She wrote Byrne, "It is true that the fashionable seem far removed from the cause and its necessity. But we cannot doubt that *they* & they alone dominate when they get an interest in a thing. So little can be done without them." She realized that working-class women did not have the time to help, the prominence to be influential, nor the wealth to donate. "The answer was to make the club women, the women of wealth and intelligence," she decided, "use their power and money and influence to obtain freedom and knowledge for the women of the poor." Women with leisure time, wealth, and influence, she concluded, had to be convinced to become active and donate funds to the movement. It was a sound strategy that capitalized on wealthy women's power to provide funding, draw publicity, and legitimize Sanger's cause.[82]

Sanger hoped that they would legitimize the cause through the weight of their social prominence and ultimately help lead it to its legalization. For example, Sanger told Pinchot in 1917 that a legislative hearing in Albany was "a failure, we were discriminated against shamefully." She concluded, "I do so wish that Mrs. Rublee and yourself could have been with me; in that case we might at least have received more polite consideration."[83] The women understood how valuable their upper-class status was. Rublee, for example, claimed that when she was arrested, the assistant counsel gave false testimony suggesting he had heard her confess to a crime when she had only said that she had read the law. Her husband and other men wrote a letter of protest to the mayor, resulting in her release. "My experience has made me realize keenly how difficult it must be for the poor," she said, "who have no friends to defend them, to obtain justice from certain members of the police force."[84] Rublee's arrest and her reaction to it show her understanding of the resources and social capital a wealthy woman like herself could bring to the movement.[85]

Engaging other monied women was crucial to Sanger's success. Rublee agreed with Sanger's strategy to recruit wealthy women like herself. She wrote to Sanger that another birth control advocate who did not approve of Rublee's committee to raise money for birth control did not understand that it had taken "a lot of work to get all those good names behind it." Rublee concluded, "Such a crowd representing money and brains and influence will do a lot to help the cause it seems to me."[86] Along these lines, in 1917 the Committee of 100 published a pamphlet on the birth control movement that focused largely on defending and legitimizing the movement by naming notable men and women who endorsed birth control, including judges, professors, doctors, social reformers, and prominent society women.[87]

Sanger agreed with how important this influence was. She wrote Rublee that she disagreed with those who did not approve of her "'going to the rich.'"[88] Instead, Sanger praised Rublee for her role in recruiting society women. "Others had rallied their own personal friends around the idea," she later wrote in her autobiography, "but Juliet's influence brought in her husband's associations—the Cravaths, Morrows, Lamonts, Dodge and Blisses," all very wealthy families.

Sanger thought the trial enlarged the circle of monied women who supported birth control from a select few wealthy but "radical" women like Ashley, who was associated with socialism. Thus, she expanded her recruitment of affluent women, begun at the Hotel Brevoort dinner, to include elite women who were not socialists but who still embraced liberal causes and women's rights, especially woman suffrage. This meant, she contended, that "the subject was in the process of ceasing to be tagged as radical and revolutionary, and becoming admittedly humanitarian."[89]

Pinchot and Rublee worked their social networks to build a Committee of 100 and then the ABCL, which was a who's who of New York society. One measure of the high social status of many of the ABCL members was their crossover with the Colony Club, founded in 1907 by Florence "Daisy" (Mrs. J. Borden) Harriman and Helen Hay Whitney, sister-in-law to Dorothy Whitney Straight. The Colony Club was the most prestigious social club for New York women, holding events on many issues and causes, including woman suffrage. According to a history written by one of its members, "most members," led by Alva Belmont and Katherine Duer Mackay, were suffragists.[90] The significant overlap of nineteen women who belonged to both the Colony

Club and the ABCL meant that the ABCL was able to use the club membership list for recruitment, and later even asked for a list of prospective new members, hoping to recruit those women as well.[91]

Not surprisingly, given their membership in the Colony Club, many of the women in the Committee of 100 and its successor, the ABCL, were frequently featured in the society pages of the *New York Times*. Friends and neighbors, they attended the same luncheons, dinners, and balls; traveled together to Europe and other destinations; and frequented the same entertainments, weddings, and society events. Self-confident enough to publicly support such a controversial topic, they signed on when many women were afraid to get involved.

Colony Club member Dorothy Whitney Straight was a key new donor to the ABCL. Straight noted, "I wanted to use my money to serve the causes in which I believed," and she gave money to many of the women's organizations and causes prevalent at the time: the suffrage movement, the WTUL, and the YWCA. The ABCL turned to Straight to host parlor meetings in 1922.[92] She gave $2,500 to Sanger to rent the space where Sanger opened the Birth Control Clinical Research Bureau. Opened in 1923, this clinic was staffed by doctors rather than nurses, because the New York court decision in Sanger's trial had opened a loophole, making it legal for doctors to prescribe birth control in that state. Another donor to the clinic was Addie Wolff Kahn. The daughter of banker Abraham Wolff, Addie married Otto Kahn, an extremely wealthy banker in New York City in 1896. She was at the 1921 meeting when Sanger was arrested. Throughout the 1920s she wrote checks to the ABCL, hosted meetings at her mansion, and visited birth control clinics in Manhattan.[93]

Edith Houghton Hooker, her sister Katharine Houghton Hepburn, and her friend Katherine Day also contributed time and money to the movement. Like Sanger, the sisters grew up in Corning, New York, where their grandfather started Corning Glass. After both were educated at Bryn Mawr College, Edith attended Johns Hopkins Medical School, where she met classmate Donald Hooker and dropped out in her senior year to marry him. Through Donald's research on venereal disease, both Edith and Katharine became interested in social hygiene, prostitution, and unmarried mothers. This moved them to advocate for both suffrage (to pass necessary laws) and birth control. Sanger remembered that Hepburn was a supporter as early as 1916, present at the Hotel Brevoort dinner.[94]

Hooker was a substantial suffrage donor before spending thousands of dollars annually on *Equal Rights* magazine, the publication of the National Woman's Party (formerly the CU), which she edited in the 1920s.[95] Dedicated to equal rights for women in legal, economic, and social areas, Hooker's editorials explained the negative consequences for a society that held back half its population.[96] Sanger quickly realized that Hooker was a useful source of funding. She asked ABCL secretary Anne Kennedy to round up further financial support from Baltimore and Washington, writing, "Can you make some personal calls upon people in Washington and Baltimore and get some money. . . . Can't Mrs. Hooker give us $500? There must be some important Baltimore and Washington contacts where you could get money."[97]

Meanwhile, Katharine worked with friends and neighbors from Hartford, Connecticut, Katherine Day and Annie Porritt. She and her friends were suffragists and served on the board of directors of the ABCL.[98] Porritt was secretary of the ABCL and chaired the editorial board for the *Birth Control Review*. She could not afford to give money like Day, however, and Sanger complained about having "poor workers like Porritt" on the board.[99] Day, the wealthy widow of a Hartford manufacturer, was a substantial contributor and spoke out publicly for birth control.[100] The Houghton sisters and their friends demonstrate the reach of Sanger's circle of wealthy supporters to suffrage and social networks beyond New York City.

The Committee of 100 and later the ABCL understood that they were expected to donate money themselves and raise funds from their friends. In addition to recruiting others, Rublee was a major source of funding herself. Sanger asked Rublee directly for money as well as hinted—she often would explain what she could accomplish if only she had the money. In a typical letter, she told Rublee that she had gotten Harold Cox to agree to attend her conference, but lamented, "Heaven only knows where the money is to be got to pay his expenses. But it has always come when I have gone ahead before so I continue to trust the Universal Provider in this too." Rublee did not seem to resent being Sanger's own "Universal Provider."[101] Indeed, Rublee gave her a loan to tide her over until her book on birth control was published.[102] In 1919, Rublee spent the first money she had ever earned (for writing an article on birth control) to buy shares of the *Birth Control Review*.[103] She underwrote expenses for the clinic, earning appreciation from Sanger, who noted, "You are the only one that has contributed to it's [*sic*] upkeep."[104] Rublee paid Sanger's rent for her office and sent her money for her personal spending. In 1923, Rublee donated the money Sanger needed to print and mail letters. She also helped fund the 1925 conference on birth control.[105] Rublee seemed to personify exactly Sanger's contention that "the more you ask of people who can give, the better they love to give."[106]

Minutes from the Committee of 100, which met at Gertrude Pinchot's home, indicate that fund-raising was a priority for the group. Drawing on the success of the suffrage movement's "parlor meetings"—private meetings held in homes so that society women would feel comfortable—they planned meetings during which Sanger could speak about birth control. Their understanding of the significance of funding was immediately apparent at one of the first meetings, on January 21, 1917. Not only did they agree to pay Sanger $25 per parlor meeting, but they also pledged a monthly sum for the cause. Passing the hat, they collected over $700, which the women decided should be spent on printing and mailing birth control movement pamphlets, and paying any legal fees or fines assessed to Sanger and Byrne.[107] The Committee of 100 also solicited funds from members of the Colony Club. A fundraiser at the club in early 1919 yielded $1,300 in subscriptions to the *Birth Control Review*, as well as cash contributions collected on the spot and additional donations received over the course of the next several months.[108]

Even with these donations, financing the *Birth Control Review*, conferences, and other efforts was expensive. It cost a significant amount of money to plan the 1922 conference, for example. An office for headquarters had to be rented, a stenographer and typist hired, printing and postage paid, and travel expenses covered for speakers. The costs added up to $10,605 for the new ABCL. Publishing expenses of the *Birth Control Review* were also high, with bills from the printer coming in just under one thousand dollars. Sanger was printing the magazine, getting billed, and then desperately trying to cover the costs. In December 1917, for example, a $100 check from Pinchot cleared costs for the December issue and left Sanger with funds toward January.[109]

In response to these high costs, Rublee incorporated the New York Women's Publishing Company in 1918 with the goal of selling $10,000 worth of stock in groups of ten shares, an idea that Ashley had suggested to Sanger earlier. This had also been tried in the suffrage movement, when the Literature Company was formed to run the *Woman's Journal*. The stock scheme began with a plan for a $500 initial investment. Records show that forty-eight initial shares were sold, including ten each to Ashley, Frances Ackerman, and Mary B. Knoblach. Ackerman and Knoblach were suffragists and birth control supporters. Ackerman's activism dated back to the Hotel Brevoort dinner, while Knoblach was a Heterodoxy Club member.[110]

However, selling additional stock was difficult. Ashley worried that too many supporters were simply writing checks for a $2.50 membership and not purchasing stock for ten dollars. This may have been because they did not see the stock offer due to its placement at the bottom of the subscription forms.[111] Constantly fretting about funds, Ashley wanted Ackerman and Knoblach to approach Sanger to criticize her for overspending on the *Review*. She called the financial situation "alarming" and feared that the board of directors did not contain an angel capable of funding it: Pinchot she described as "pretty well bled" and herself as "dead broke."[112] A luncheon hosted by the board of the publishing company gathered $8,874 in pledges from 450 guests and greatly helped the cause.[113]

Like Ashley, Sanger was a bit frustrated with the pace of recruiting wealthy supporters and fund-raising. She grumbled that women's clubs sometimes seemed more interested in socializing than in her message: "The continued apathy of such organizations disappointed me intensely; the desire to build up a structure appeared to dominate them all."[114] Accustomed to passionate feminists like Rublee, Ashley, and Pinchot, Sanger seemed surprised that not everyone shared her vision.

Throughout the 1920s, ABCL officers worked hard to raise funds and draw crowds at gatherings.[115] Fund-raising was done informally and guided by the ABCL office in New York, which provided members of the board of directors lists of potential donors from a particular state, from the Colony Club, or from other sources of likely contributors.[116] Fifty-four people gave over one hundred dollars in 1925, only ten of whom were men (including Sanger's husband, Noah Slee).[117] While substantial, these donations were dwarfed by at least twice as many women who gave $1,000 or more to the suffrage movement in the 1910s.

ABCL director and suffragist Ida Timme was one of its most successful fund-raisers.[118] Known as a "strong feminist," she married Dr. Walter Timme, a Columbia University professor and expert on nervous and mental diseases, who supported race hygiene (eugenics) due to his work on inheritable physical and mental defects.[119] Describing Timme's strong, forceful style, Sanger gratefully noted, "More than once our bank account would have faded to a mere wraith had it not been for Ida Timme's money-raising talents."[120] Working in Washington and soliciting large contributions of $4,000 and up, as well as smaller gifts, Timme drew on the feminist themes Sanger had been articulating for a decade. In a fund-raising letter, Timme wrote, "Do you, a woman, realize that true emancipation and acknowledgement of an equal status for women can never be realized until motherhood is by choice and not by chance? This is the first time in the world's history that an organized drive at race betterment, through conscientious intelligent, forward looking parenthood, is being launched and women must lead the way since women are the mothers of the race."[121] Timme married her husband's support for eugenics with her own feminism, resulting in a support for birth control that spoke to ending sexism at the same time as it offered a strategy for eugenics.[122]

Sanger went to Europe in 1926 to plan an international birth control conference, to be held in Switzerland the following year, leaving Eleanor Jones in charge of the ABCL. Jones, the wife of lawyer and college professor Frederick Robertson Jones, had also been a suffragist. She reorganized the ABCL while Sanger was gone, notably taking power away from its president (Sanger) and firing the executive secretary.

Sanger later complained that the ABCL grew staid under Jones because she was unwilling to embrace controversy. It became, Sanger wrote, a " 'pink tea social center for pleasant conversation and gossip,' run by 'drawing room lizards.' "[123] Additionally, conflict boiled over concerning finances, with Sanger complaining that Jones was incapable of raising enough funds to support the organization. Jones admitted as much but argued that she was hampered by the fact that Sanger overshadowed the movement and was able to make successful personal appeals that Jones could not.[124]

On her return, angry at her loss of power, Sanger eventually resigned from the ABCL. Rublee's letters to Sanger reveal the machinations that took place during the conflict. Describing Jones and several officers as "hand and glove, hard as nails and determined as iron," Rublee met with others and then reported their positions to Sanger.[125] Given all this acrimony, Sanger took special note of her loyal followers—Rublee, Ackerman, and Charlotte Delafield—in her resignation letter, thanking them for standing by in the early days when supporting birth control carried such great risk.[126] She brought Rublee and Ackerman with her to the board of managers of the Birth Control Clinical Research Bureau. Without Sanger, the ABCL could not survive. Eventually it merged with the bureau to become the new Birth Control Federation of America, later renamed Planned Parent Federation of America (PPFA).[127]

Notably, Jones also took the rhetoric and purpose of the ABCL in explicitly racist and eugenicist directions, arguing that inferior stock should not have children. While the vast majority of Rublee's writings focus on women's freedom, she did occasionally use the language of the growing eugenics movement. For example, she wrote that birth control could serve to limit the "birth of the unfit" and provide "economic relief" for the poor. In a pamphlet likely from 1921, the ABCL emphasized the need for women to control their reproduction in order to retain their health and become the best mothers possible. It then called for sterilization "of the insane and feeble minded and the encouragement of this operation upon those afflicted with inherited or transmissible diseases."[128] Sanger used similar language and has been correctly criticized for her willingness to collaborate with eugenicists to promote birth control as a tool of eugenics. However, overemphasizing this rhetoric is to mischaracterize Sanger, Rublee, and her other wealthy followers' primary motivation for birth control, which stemmed from their strong feminism. Throughout the 1920s, the ABCL and Sanger used a variety of arguments, including those related to eugenics, even as they maintained the focus on women's freedom.

The controversy over Sanger's use of eugenic arguments and association with leading eugenicists of the 1920s has been linked to two of her efforts to promote birth control among African Americans: a clinic opened in Harlem in 1930, and the Negro Project, begun in 1939 to reach black women in southern states. Both efforts were simultaneous with the opening of clinics for whites across the country and educational campaigns for poor southern white women. In both cases, Sanger sought African American leadership and support, soliciting the approval of leading blacks, including Mary McLeod Bethune, and looking to black doctors and black nurses to win the trust of black patients. These efforts were consistent with Sanger's lifetime of support for poor women to exercise control over their reproduction to improve their health and wealth as well as to empower them as women.[129]

The documents produced by Rublee and the ABCL suggest that while the birth control movement broadened its rhetoric to include health, poverty, and even eugenics, wealthy women like Rublee, Pinchot, and the women they recruited to the movement—many of whom had been involved in suffrage—still promoted the primary importance of birth control as a tool for women's liberation. They understood that even with the vote and education, without birth control, women would not be truly free to control their employment and career, nor could they enjoy the freedom of sexual pleasure without procreation.

FOR JUST OVER THE decade when the Committee of 100 and the ABCL were active, Sanger was able to attract a group of wealthy feminist women, most of whom were also suffragists, to the movement for birth control, which focused on the need for women to be able to control their own bodies. These women were wealthy enough to give hundreds, and sometimes thousands, of dollars to the cause. The great wealth of some of Sanger's richest supporters also enabled them to do as they pleased, their status insulating them. These women were willing to lend their names to publications, attend meetings, make speeches, lobby Congress, and otherwise work for birth control. Her most significant supporters—Jessie Ashley, Elsie Parsons, Gertrude Pinchot, Juliet Rublee, Edith Hooker, and Katharine Hepburn—passionately embraced feminism, with Ashley, Parsons, and Rublee promoting ideas about sexual freedom that were radical for the time. Many others—including Dorothy Straight, Frances Ackerman, Addie Kahn, Helen Reid, Mary Knoblach, and Charlotte Delafield—expressed their desire for women's rights as they fought for woman suffrage as well as birth control.

Sanger was proud of her association with such prominent women. She purposely looked to them to support her desire to create a single-issue organization dedicated to enabling women to gain access to birth control information and devices. Their money paid for her travels, her conferences, her magazines, her speeches, and her rallies, as well as, eventually, research on birth control methods. Their social prominence never threatened her famed position as the leader of the movement. Rather, their status drew publicity to the movement and helped legitimize Sanger's cause.

As the movement matured, the composition of her supporters began to shift. Just as in 1916, Sanger broadened her network beyond the radical women she had met in the Socialist Party to more mainstream but feminist and liberal wealthy women, especially suffragists, by the 1930s, when she once again looked for new donors. Unfortunately for Sanger, Jessie Ashley died in 1919, Elsie Parsons was busy with her fieldwork, and Pinchot's activism faded after her divorce, leaving Sanger without three of her strongest supporters. Juliet Rublee remained a devoted friend for life, though she moved away from an active role in the movement (to pursue other ventures) and could no longer bankroll Sanger when she had to cut her expenses due to the Great Depression. By the 1930s, many of the women who had been prominent in the Committee of 100 disappeared from Sanger's correspondence and the rolls of birth control organizations through death, divorce, aging, and attrition.

Moreover, with the passage of the woman suffrage amendment in 1920, women's organizations changed to some extent. Many women continued to use single-sex associations to promote women's rights, especially the needs of working women, but in some ways these groups lost their prominence as women succeeded in forcing government and other organizations to take on the social welfare concerns that they had advocated for during the Progressive Era. The major remaining women's organizations—the National Woman's Party, the League of Women Voters, and the Children's Bureau—were unwilling to support birth control.[130] Birth control as a single cause did not unite as many women around the same cause as suffrage had, perhaps due to its relationship to sex.[131]

Due to these changes, while Rublee, Pinchot, Ashley, Parsons, and many other of the women active in the late 1910s and early 1920s maintained Sanger's focus on feminism and the need for birth control to secure the liberation of women, this rhetoric receded from her newer supporters' discourse and, to a lesser extent, from Sanger's own rhetoric in the 1930s and 1940s. Philanthropists Doris Duke, Dorothy Brush, and Mary Lasker, as well as Amy du Pont and Abby Aldrich Rockefeller, became significant benefactors. These women had a different orientation from Sanger's first set of supporters. Although in their personal lives, many of the women were fiercely independent and believed in women's capabilities, they were not associated with organizations dedicated to women's equality, such as the woman suffrage associations had been. They were more concerned about poor women, children, and health, and less outspoken about women's equality.[132]

Doris Duke, heir of the tobacco fortune from her father's company, American Tobacco Company, inherited approximately $30 million plus millions more in trust when her father died in 1925. Duke was a prolific philanthropist, giving to a variety of causes, many of them for women. Although Duke and Sanger had met, Duke's contributions were anonymous. Duke annually gave $15,000, and in 1942 she gave an anonymous contribution of $15,000 to go to Sanger's project on birth control for African Americans in the South. Her total contributions to PPFA between 1934 and 1951 were $80,500, out of the $201,440 total her foundation spent on health and mental health organizations in those seventeen years. Her interest in birth control may have stemmed from a concern for women and women's causes, but Duke could not be counted on to publicly represent the birth control movement as a feminist cause.[133]

Dorothy Brush—cousin of Juliet Rublee and daughter of inventor and businessman Charles Francis Brush—was a wealthy widow and close friend of Sanger's. Although dedicated and generous to the International Planned Parenthood Federation, Brush focused more on population control than women's rights, and her father's foundation was explicitly pro-eugenics.[134]

Mary Reinhardt Lasker was a clothing pattern designer. Along with her husband, Albert, an advertising executive, she worked to increase health research and awareness, most notably through the creation of the National Institutes of Health and the American Cancer Society. She and her husband were generous donors to Planned Parenthood, although their focus was health rather than feminism. Before they married, Mary was secretary of the Birth Control Federation of America, and in 1939 she successfully helped Sanger solicit Albert for a donation to the project for African Americans in the South. In an interview two decades later, Lasker focused on her interest in birth control as a health issue, claimed that it was her husband's idea to change the name from the Birth Control Federation of America to PPFA, and explained that she left PPFA and shifted her focus to fighting cancer and other health concerns due to her frustration with lack of progress in the birth control movement in the early 1940s.[135]

With the help of Rublee, Sanger was also able to convince the wives of several top New York financiers, including William K. Vanderbilt, J. P. Morgan, and Thomas Lamont, to sit on her board in the 1930s. But their support was limited to donations; they did not help run her organization, fund-raise, or lobby for birth control the way that the first generation of wealthy women had.

Sanger herself was conflicted during these decades, annoyed that the movement had moved from women's rights to family planning yet responsible in part for the shift, through her appeals to the medical profession, her relationship with eugenicists, as well as her solicitations of these new donors.[136] The movement had been grounded in feminism when she had feminist supporters; now she had few left. However, Sanger did continue to focus on building clinics, which were often run locally by women for women.[137] Her feminist language still came through, as when she argued that doctors or priests should not "have the say and decisions as to who shall have knowledge or information which may mean happiness and health to women."[138]

After leaving the ABCL, she focused on the Birth Control Clinical Research Bureau, which ultimately reunited with the ABCL in 1939 as the new Birth Control Federation of America and was renamed Planned Parenthood of America in 1942. For the first time, the leading birth control organization in the nation was led by a man, Kenneth Rose, who worked with doctors to shift away the rhetoric away from birth control to child spacing and family planning. Sanger complained to Rose, "If I told or wrote to you that the name Planned Parenthood would be the end of the movement, it was and has proven true. The movement was then a fighting, forward, no fooling movement, battling for the freedom of the poorest parents and for women's biological freedom and development. The P.P.F. has left all this behind and has no interest in any fight."[139] Therefore, monied women gave the money necessary for expenses and legitimized the birth control movement as they did other phases of the women's movement, but in the case of birth control, their promotion of its feminist implications and rhetoric was even more significant than their financial donations. The feminist thrust to the movement faded considerably when they left.

Sanger herself, however, never abandoned feminism as a key issue. Perhaps the most important link between Sanger's first decade of activism, during which she was supported by a group of wealthy feminist advocates for birth control, and her last decade of activism was Katharine Dexter McCormick, an original member of the Committee of 100 who inherited over $35 million in the late 1940s. Together they recognized and acted on the continued need for women's activism after the passage of the woman suffrage amendment in 1920 and throughout the decades leading to the women's liberation movement of the late 1960s and 1970s. In the 1950s, she and Sanger worked to fund research for a more effective and more accessible form of birth control that would be controlled by women: the hormonal birth control pill. If women were to continue the fight to legalize birth control and make it more reliable, accessible, and easy to use, they would continue to need the financial support of women like McCormick.

CHAPTER SEVEN

Feminism and Science

Funding Research for the Pill

In February 1954, Katharine Dexter McCormick wrote birth control advocate Margaret Sanger a three-page, single-spaced typewritten letter in which McCormick blasted the Planned Parenthood Federation of America (PPFA) and its head, William Vogt. Seven months earlier, McCormick and Sanger toured the laboratory of Gregory Pincus, the lead scientist researching a possible oral contraceptive pill, at the Worcester Foundation for Experimental Biology (WFEB) in Shrewsbury, Massachusetts. After a recent visit to the PPFA offices, McCormick boiled with frustration at Vogt and the PPFA's lack of support for Pincus's research. "I seemed to be the only person really interested in an oral contraceptive," she concluded. "I believe that now I should give up trying to cooperate with the Research Committee of the P.P. Federation [PPFA] and concern myself with the Shrewsbury Laboratory work." With that, McCormick began directly funding Pincus and John Rock, the gynecologist who led the clinical and field trials for the pills developed by Pincus, rather than funneling her contributions through PPFA.[1]

For the next seven years, until FDA approval of the first hormonal birth control pill in 1960, McCormick paid approximately $100,000–$150,000 annually to fund the research of Pincus, Rock, and their assistants, Celso-Ramón García and Min-Chueh Chang.[2] At the time of her death seven years later, she was still writing generous checks to fund Pincus's continued research refining the pill as well as his program to teach doctors around the world about it. Without both her dedication to the idea of reproductive freedom for women and her money, the pill would not have been developed in the 1950s.

Not only was Planned Parenthood uninterested, but pharmaceutical companies, the government, and foundations were also reluctant to fund this controversial research, which occurred at a time when birth control was still illegal in many states. The New York appeals court had opened a loophole in 1918 for doctors in that state to prescribe birth control for medical reasons. Similarly, a federal court decision in 1936 determined that federal law could not prevent physicians from prescribing birth control, leading the American Medical Association to approve the distribution of birth control by doctors.

However, by the 1950s, thirty states still had laws restricting access to birth control. Massachusetts and Connecticut were the strictest, with Massachusetts prohibiting the dissemination of birth control information and Connecticut criminalizing its use. The FDA approved the pill in 1957 for menstrual disorders and in 1960 for contraception. By this time, a half dozen or so states still prohibited birth control. The Massachusetts and Connecticut laws were not struck down until *Griswold v. Connecticut* in 1965 established the right of married couples to use birth control, and *Eisenstadt v. Baird* in 1972 extended that right to all Americans.[3] Despite its illegality in Massachusetts for almost her entire life, McCormick was determined to improve birth control by making it more effective and accessible.

McCormick single-handedly shepherded in the invention of the first truly new means of contraception. Although people have used some form of condoms, diaphragms, douching, or withdrawal for hundreds of years, these methods were often ineffective. Regulating hormones to prevent conception was an entirely new approach to birth control, one that was made possible only through advances in hormonal research, research paid for by McCormick.

MCCORMICK'S PASSIONATE DEDICATION TO developing the pill came when she was a seventy-eight-year-old widow. McCormick was the only major birth control advocate to support Sanger based on her feminist activism in the 1910s and 1920s who was still backing the movement in the 1950s. Although the other leaders in the Committee of 100 and the ABCL discussed in chapter 6, such as Jessie Ashley, Elsie Parsons, Gertrude Pinchot, and Juliet Rublee, no longer bankrolled Sanger, McCormick remained committed to birth control for decades, providing evidence for the continuity of women's activism between the suffrage movement and the women's liberation movement of the late 1960s and 1970s. McCormick continued to make donations through the 1920s and 1930s, remained in correspondence with Margaret Sanger, and launched her extensive campaign to fund development of the pill between 1952 and 1953, well before the "second wave" of the women's movement. Like many other women in this book, she did not rest after women won the right to vote but continued to fight for a more expansive vision of women's rights.

McCormick's feminism was essential to her continued support for birth control and her decision to fund research for the pill. The pill was particularly important to McCormick because it enabled women to control their own reproduction. In fact, McCormick claimed she didn't "give a hoot" about a male pill.

This feminism was crucial because most men were not interested in advancing research that would make birth control more effective or easily accessed. McCormick encountered significant resistance from the leading but by then male-dominated birth control organization in the country, PPFA. Like the other women in this book who faced opposition to their philanthropy and vision, McCormick was willing to battle anyone who got in the way of her goal: reproductive freedom for women. McCormick wanted women around the world to gain control over their bodies through a more effective birth control method. She went around PPFA to fund the research directly. Once Pincus and Rock developed the pill, she paid for clinics and other means to distribute the pill despite birth control's still illegal status in many states. She helped pay to educate doctors from countries ranging from India to Switzerland about the pill. Most importantly, she wanted it to be priced cheaply enough for widespread use among poor women as well as wealthy women. In addition, she financed medical education for women, ensuring that women doctors would be in a position to continue to help other women.

Through her philanthropy, McCormick exemplified the power that women had to bring about significant change for women in society, including political equality, professional opportunity, and reproductive freedom, and the necessity for women to make change for women. By the time McCormick bankrolled the development of the pill in the 1950s, she had spent decades using her money to support causes in which she believed. A suffragist leader and treasurer of the National American Woman Suffrage Association, McCormick understood the necessity of fund-raising to promote suffrage. She also had provided financial support for scientific research due to her efforts to help scientists find a cure for her husband's mental illness. McCormick well understood how to harness the power of her money to fulfill her passionate desire for the development of a more effective means of contraception that women could control.

McCormick consistently focused on women's reproductive control as a means of empowering and freeing women. By the 1950s, McCormick, like Sanger, was alarmed by population growth. She clipped articles on the population problem, often expressing her strong frustration that most people were not using birth control as a solution to the crisis.[4] However, this later embrace of population control never overshadowed her feminist beliefs.

KATHARINE DEXTER MCCORMICK WAS born in 1875 to Wirt and Josephine Dexter of Dexter, Michigan, a town named for the family. As a young child, Katharine was raised in Chicago, where her father was a lawyer who headed the prestigious Chicago Relief and Aid Society. After his sudden death in 1890, Katharine, her mother, and her older brother moved to Boston. Unfortunately, tragedy struck again, and her brother also died unexpectedly. Katharine remained close to her mother, living with her until her mother's death in 1937.[5]

McCormick was fiercely independent, strong willed, and unafraid of confrontation. Although she was featured in the *New York Times* society columns, she eschewed fashionable dress and had a serious demeanor. As she got older, she stood out "not only because she was often the smartest person in the room but also because her dress and comportment harked back to Victorian times, while her outlook and opinions were thoroughly modern."[6]

Katharine decided she wanted to be a scientist and attend the best college open to women at the time. Radcliffe offered inadequate facilities—she was told they did chemistry in the bathroom—so in 1896 she entered the Massachusetts Institute of Technology (MIT). McCormick was classified as a special student, meaning she had to take preparatory classes before she could enter a degree program in biology, with her ultimate goal to become a surgeon. While at MIT, McCormick protested the policy that women students had to wear hats to chemistry lab, and succeeded in changing it. Ambitious, smart, serious, yet capable of irreverent humor, these qualities enabled her to maintain excellent grades and succeed as a woman at MIT, graduating in 1904 with a bachelor's degree in biology.[7]

McCormick, who once said biochemists would "inherit the earth," believed science could help usher in reproductive control for women. Understanding McCormick as a scientist and a feminist sheds light on why she and Margaret Sanger were willing to work with the male-dominated medical profession to legalize birth control. Sanger began trying to recruit doctors to her cause, opened clinics staffed by doctors and nurses, and relied on legal decisions that would allow the medical profession to distribute contraception as a means of legitimizing and legalizing it. This association with primarily male doctors seemed at odds with her interest in birth control as a means to women's liberation.[8] Turning the spotlight on McCormick elucidates why the two women looked to scientists and doctors to create a pill, available to women only through medical professionals, as the best means to provide women access to effective birth control. McCormick cherished her degree from MIT; read and understood the scientific research in birth control; and wholly agreed with Sanger, who argued that only doctors could "force open the doors of the laboratories where our chemists will give the women of the twentieth century reliable and scientific means of contraception hitherto unknown."[9] She also supported medical education for women. Their vision can be seen as a feminist technology, defined as "tools plus knowledge that enhance women's ability to develop, expand, and express their capacities."[10]

McCormick's scientific education had a significant impact on her role as the woman behind the development of the pill. As a biologist, McCormick was comfortable with matters of the body, reproduction, and sex. Her desire to develop a better form of birth control also developed because she believed that the sex drive was powerful, that sex should be pleasurable, and that the purpose of sex was not limited to procreation. To take control of their lives and reproduction, women needed a better form of birth control that would enable them to enjoy sex without fear of pregnancy. A story about Laura Pincus, daughter of Gregory Pincus, captures McCormick's views. Laura Pincus worked on the pill trials held in Puerto Rico, and on her return to Boston, she went to meet McCormick. As recounted by David Halberstam, "Laura Pincus was, in her own words, rather naive about sex and she got a little flustered talking to this old woman about the experiments taking place. But Kate McCormick did not become unsettled: she talked openly and frankly. The sex drive in humans was so strong, she kept insisting, that it was critical that it be separated from reproductive functions. She followed that with a brief discussion of the pleasures of sex."[11]

Notably, Laura Pincus remembered that McCormick "added rather casually that sex between women might be more meaningful. This was spoken dispassionately, not suggestively. Nonetheless, young Ms. Pincus was stunned."[12] The reference to "sex between women" may be a reference to a possible lesbian relationship with her close friend, Jennie Roessing. Roessing was a Pennsylvania suffragist, who married (and later divorced) Frank M. Roessing, a civil engineer. The two women met in the suffrage movement in 1910 and worked together in NAWSA. Roessing stayed with Katharine in Santa Barbara frequently and was present at the trial over Stanley's guardianship, sitting with Katharine. The exact nature of their relationship is not documented.[13]

McCormick's statements to Laura Pincus highlight her comfort discussing the body and sexual intercourse. She could even joke about it. Anne Merrill, one of the scientists who worked with Pincus, remembered that McCormick told Merrill and others that on a recent trip—at age eighty—she had birth control pills for someone else in her suitcase. "She put them in something like a box of crackers," Merrill recalled, "and the custom men dumped them out and said 'what are these?' She said they were birth control pills. They said, 'good for you, lady!'"[14]

McCormick believed that contraception should not interfere with sexual pleasure. She did not think withdrawal, the most effective means of birth control at the time, was appropriate. Further, she told Sanger she agreed that abstinence was "neither harmless nor acceptable."[15] When the pill was finally achieved, McCormick wrote to Pincus, "The oral contraceptive inaugurated and maintains a new era of sexual relations for mankind,—fundamentally it is a sex revolution for human beings."[16] Taken together, her statements demonstrate that McCormick, the matter-of-fact biologist, desired birth control in order to separate sex from reproduction and thereby promote sexual pleasure for women without fear of pregnancy.

DURING HER SENIOR YEAR at MIT, Katharine encountered an old acquaintance from Chicago, Stanley McCormick. The son of the McCormick reaper inventor, Stanley was a Princeton graduate and the comptroller of McCormick–International Harvester Company. They shared interests in art and athletics, and married in Switzerland in September 1904. Given the rarity of married women doctors at the time, McCormick may have believed she had to make a choice between a medical career and marriage; whatever the reason, she no longer pursued a medical degree after her wedding.

Stanley's mental illness may also have been the cause of this decision. The signs of erratic behavior, self-denigration, and obsession over sexual potency that Katharine had noticed in Stanley before their marriage increased as his mental state began to deteriorate further after they married. Two years after their wedding, he was hospitalized with dementia praecox, now considered a form of schizophrenia.[17] Katharine and his family decided to move him to a family home in Santa Barbara, where he was confined for the next four decades while she primarily resided in Boston. This meant that McCormick grew more independent (rather than less) after her marriage due to Stanley's confinement.

Some historians have wrongly attributed McCormick's interest in birth control to her concern that she would become pregnant and pass on her husband's mental illness to any children they would have. Sanger biographer Madeline Gray even speculated that despite her alleged fears, "since he was very demanding, she undoubtedly continued to have marital relations with him." Others expanded on Gray's assertion: historian James Reed noted how much time she spent with Stanley on his Santa Barbara estate, and John Rock biographer Loretta McLaughlin claimed that McCormick was having sex with Stanley until his death in 1947.[18] But the historical record does not support these assertions. When Katharine and Stanley were first married, he was impotent, and doctors prescribed some months without sex for the couple.

His breakdown occurred after only two years of marriage, and he was soon isolated in Santa Barbara. On the advice of his doctors, who believed that his insanity was related to sexual problems, including impotence, Katharine was not allowed to visit him for twenty years. By the time she was allowed to see him again, she was fifty-two years old and saw him only for short periods of time at his house, with others present, often one of his brothers. Katharine clearly had little reason to be concerned about becoming pregnant and passing Stanley's mental illness to their children. Given her initial desire for an heir, his impotence, and her lack of access to him for twenty years, her support for birth control was not about her fear of passing his schizophrenia to the next generation but about her feminism.[19]

Katharine remained dedicated to Stanley and her marriage despite his mental breakdown. Although she and her mother were well-off themselves, Katharine stood to inherit millions more if she remained married to Stanley and refused his family's attempts to entice her to divorce him. However, her continued concern for his treatment and determination that she knew best how to help him suggest that her interest in Stanley was not for his money. McCormick spent nearly three decades trying to understand and treat her husband's disease. This was not the medical career she envisioned for herself when she entered MIT, to be sure. Nevertheless, she read the latest in scientific journals and interacted with leading doctors across the country, insisting on particular approaches to treatment for her husband.

Her decades-long battle with Stanley's siblings and doctors over his care shows her willingness to do whatever was necessary to achieve her goals. She fought his siblings to retain control over his medical treatment, even suing for sole guardianship over Stanley (which she shared with his siblings). The Mc-Cormick family papers are replete with acerbic single-spaced typewritten letters from Katharine to the McCormick siblings, explaining point by point her views on Stanley's care and documenting situations that arose in Santa Barbara. Meanwhile, Stanley's siblings were writing letters to each other using code to identify family members, doctors, and others, as they tried to wrest control from her. His psychiatrists' reports portray her as a controlling, dominating woman who emasculated Stanley, causing his impotence and mental collapse.[20] Although such strong-mindedness on the part of Katharine Mc-Cormick was problematic as far as Stanley's doctors were concerned, it reflected her feminist independence and served her well in her work in the suffrage and birth control movements.

McCormick believed science could help Stanley, and she was willing to pay for it. McCormick's first foray into financial support for medical research came in 1908, when she persuaded Dr. Hamilton, a researcher on apes and sexual behavior, to accompany Stanley to Santa Barbara. She promised Hamilton she would pay for a laboratory and apes for research, which she and Hamilton hoped might lead to insights into Stanley's illness.[21] Quickly she became convinced there was a physiological cause and treatment for Stanley's disease (though she also supported psychiatric counseling).[22]

At the same time that she began to support scientific research for Stanley, McCormick became active in the fight for woman suffrage. McCormick was a passionate feminist. Beginning around 1908, as an officer in the Massachusetts and national suffrage associations, she argued that women without the vote were denied their "political freedom," and that woman suffrage was essential for human equality. After having fought so hard for her undergraduate degree at MIT but then given up a professional career when she married, McCormick found personal satisfaction in her suffrage activism, as did many other educated women of her day.[23] She held office in the leading national suffrage organization from 1912 until ratification in 1920.

Soon, McCormick began to merge her interest in feminism, honed in the suffrage movement, with her belief in the possibility of scientific research, developed in her support for Stanley, into a new cause: birth control. The movement was just beginning to grow under Sanger. With hindsight, it almost seems inevitable that McCormick would come to believe that science could provide the key to reproductive freedom for women. McCormick spent a decade immersed in the woman suffrage movement, fighting for women's political equality. She came to see that women also needed reproductive freedom to achieve full equality. By financing the research for the pill, she combined her desire for better birth control to her conviction that science could produce it. Her determination in the face of opposition sustained her not only when she opposed her husband's family and his doctors but also when she pioneered open-air suffrage rallies in Massachusetts in 1909 (considered scandalous at the time) and smuggled diaphragms into the United States from Europe in the 1920s.[24]

The scientists who worked with her recognized the importance of her feminism. Celso-Ramón García described her as "a most remarkable woman. . . . [Her] philosophy [was to] relieve women [from the] burden [of] childbearing, fear of pregnancy; [she was an] original suffragette."[25] When McCormick was honored by the Planned Parenthood League of Massachusetts (PPLM), Pincus noted her lifelong devotion to birth control and her friendship with Sanger. He stated that her aid was "now making the difference between misery and happiness for millions of women in this world." García and Pincus thus underscored the needs of women as the driver of her motivation for funding development of the pill.[26]

McCormick wanted women to have access to birth control in order to be free to regulate their own lives, echoing Sanger's declaration, "No woman can call herself free who does not own and control her body. No woman can call herself free until she can choose consciously whether she will or will not be a mother."[27] Evidence of McCormick's beliefs comes from a comment she made years later. McCormick told the director of the archives at Radcliffe, Barbara Solomon, that the only money she would consider giving to Radcliffe would be for a birth control clinic there, going "into a long soliloquy in which she expressed great resentment over woman's biological burdens, denouncing not only the discomforts and risks of childbearing, but menstrual periods also. Solomon later speculated that menstruation may have been for McCormick 'a constant reminder of the barriers to equality for women.' "[28] McCormick may have resented her own choice not to pursue a career as a doctor after she married, and believed that pregnancy limited women's choices.

McCormick wanted a simple birth control method that was controlled by women, not men. In this way, birth control would become a means to freedom for women. She did not think that men understood the problems with the forms of birth control prevalent at the time, particularly diaphragms, which Sanger and the PPFA advocated due to their relative effectiveness over other methods. She wrote to Pincus, "The oral contraceptive vitally concerns women and their bodies. I think that women do not care to have mechanical gadgets of one kind or another introduced into the innermost parts of their bodies, and that is solely a man's point of view that they do not object to this procedure."[29] Moreover, she thought that because women were the ones to get pregnant, they had to be the ones to control their reproduction. She wrote to Sanger, "I didn't give a hoot for a male contraceptive, that it was the sure female one that concerned me."[30] These comments suggest that McCormick saw in science the possibility that women could regulate their own bodies and thus provide themselves with freedom from reproduction if they wanted. With so few female scientists doing medical research, male scientists needed to be pushed into working on contraceptive research, and McCormick had the money to tempt them.

McCormick's first recorded act in support of the birth control movement came in the winter of 1916–17, when, along with her friend Elsie Clews Parsons, McCormick joined the Committee of 100 to support Sanger after her arrest.[31] Parsons was the feminist anthropologist who, as a young woman, had been engaged to Samuel Dexter, Katharine's brother.[32] Though he died before they could marry, Parsons remained close friends with Katharine. They corresponded for years, traveling in Europe together and even camping in 1910. After both serving together as committee chairs in the College Equal Suffrage League, they worked together in support of birth control. After they joined the Committee of 100, the group put out a statement arguing that it is for "the woman herself to decide" whether or not, and when, to have a baby.

Like Parsons, many others in McCormick's circle of colleagues from the suffrage movement also supported birth control, including Blanche Ames Ames and Juliet Rublee, with whom she corresponded for years. Decades after the passage of the Nineteenth Amendment, McCormick was still in touch with Mrs. Guy Stantial, a former suffragist who promised to send McCormick a copy of a letter stating that women's rights advocates Lucy Stone and Angelina Grimke "believed in Birth Control" in the 1850s. "It is certainly amusing . . . her [Grimke's] foresight was remarkable," commented McCormick when she received it. This continued friendship and note demonstrate the link between suffrage, birth control, and women's rights that also influenced McCormick.[33]

McCormick's friendships indicate that she was drawn to and surrounded herself with other like-minded feminist women throughout her life, beginning with Elsie Clews Parsons. The relationships she cultivated with other women were extremely important to McCormick. Her father and brother had died when she was a teenager, her husband was confined in Santa Barbara, and she fought his family members rather than looking to them for support and friendship. McCormick was therefore free from male control—no father, brother, or husband. She and her mother ruled their household with only the advice of lawyers—lawyers who eventually came to include Newton Baker, secretary of war under Woodrow Wilson and a committed suffragist.[34] McCormick undoubtedly also realized, as she worked with other women in the suffrage and birth control movements, that living without a spouse or dependent children freed her to dedicate long hours to these movements.

When the suffrage movement ended with success in 1920, McCormick maintained her focus on birth control and on Stanley's illness. She remained dedicated to scientific research for him, and she continued to fight his family over his treatment. In the mid-1920s, Katharine brought Roy G. Hoskins, a research endocrinologist, to Santa Barbara to test Stanley for endocrine factors, over the objections of his siblings and his psychiatrists.[35] Even though Stanley was being treated by the most prominent doctors in the field, Katharine was not afraid to criticize their approach and demand changes.[36]

To support research on potential causes and treatments for Stanley, Katharine founded the Memorial Foundation for Neuro-Endocrine Research (originally called the Stanley R. McCormick Memorial Foundation for Neuro-Endocrine Research) in 1927, with Dr. Hoskins on the board.[37] The work of this foundation was directly related to Katharine's later support of the pill research due to the circle of doctors and scientists she met through the foundation and the direction of the research funded by it, which included a focus on the possible relationship between sex hormones and mental disease. Hoskins, along with scientist Hudson Hoagland, did hormone research; the board discussed Pincus's research on rabbit egg fertilization; and board member Walter Cannon communicated with John Rock regarding his research.[38] Foundation correspondence was among (or about) key players in the development of the pill: Hoagland, Hoskins, Pincus, Rock, and Chang.[39] Notably, Mrs. Cornelia Cannon and Mrs. Gertrude Hoskins were both suffrage and birth control supporters who eventually became officers in the Massachusetts Birth Control League.[40]

McCormick also maintained her interest in Sanger and birth control throughout the 1920s. She joined the American Birth Control League (ABCL), a successor to the Committee of 100. Although McCormick rebuffed solicitations to join its board of directors several times in the early 1920s, by the mid-1920s she had joined the ABCL's national council. She was a member of the conference committees for the First American Birth Control Conference, held in New York in 1921, and the Sixth International Neo-Malthusian and Birth Control Conference held in 1925, both organized by Sanger.[41] McCormick was also a member of the Hospitality Committee for the World Population Conference held in Geneva, Switzerland, from August 30 to September 2, 1927, where Sanger hosted a dinner at McCormick's chateau.[42]

Many of the doctors who examined and treated Stanley also participated in the conferences on birth control organized by Margaret Sanger in the 1920s, including Dr. Walter Timme, an endocrinologist, whose wife Ida was active in the ABCL. Sanger's magazine, the *Birth Control Review*, even featured the article "The Relation of Endocrinology to Birth Control" in 1925. Given her membership in birth control organizations, McCormick was likely a subscriber.[43] These relationships indicate that McCormick knew about sex hormone research as early as the 1920s, was interested in its application to mental illness for the potential treatment of Stanley, and possibly already understood its implications for contraception. McCormick's scientific background had led her to push for medical research into her husband's condition, which ultimately gave her an understanding of endocrinology few other women would have had at the time.

Although from the late 1920s through the late 1940s McCormick and Sanger corresponded only intermittently, their extant correspondence indicates that McCormick was already interested in increasing scientific research to create better birth control methods—more effective, more accessible, and more affordable. In 1928, Sanger unsuccessfully asked McCormick for a $2,500 contribution to support research. She was rather vague about who the scientists were and just what it focused on.[44]

Sanger tried to involve McCormick more heavily in the 1930s but had to be content with $50 contributions from McCormick in response to her requests. After a phone call in early 1937, Sanger wrote, "It is encouraging to know that you are coming back to the movement and it especially delights my heart to have you interested in research." Responding to McCormick's suggestion that they map out a five-year research plan, Sanger noted that such a long-term approach would free scientists to explore without the pressure of producing immediate results. Sanger asked McCormick to clarify her ideas and her financial offer, delicately writing, "It would not be necessary to have financial assistance immediately but if we could find sufficient assurance of financial backing, we could at least begin soon to pick our men for the future."[45]

Sanger was not yet to benefit from McCormick's largesse, however. Sanger had resigned from the ABCL and was instead running the Birth Control Clinical Research Bureau. She received only a $100 contribution from McCormick in response to a form letter soliciting funds. However, McCormick was still sending $1,000 to the ABCL. Noting McCormick's interest in research, Sanger tried to interest McCormick in funding rural birth control dissemination. Because they would be using a different method of birth control at the rural clinics, Sanger called it a "really practical piece of vital research." McCormick, who was focused on scientific research for new birth control methods, not research into the efficacy of current methods, was not fooled by Sanger's rhetorical sleight of hand, and declined to contribute to the bureau.

Not easily discouraged, Sanger tried again, sending information to McCormick about research at the bureau and pointedly asking her what research the ABCL was conducting "that has aroused your interest." After the merger of the ABCL with the bureau in 1939 to form the Birth Control Federation of America (changed in 1942 to the Planned Parenthood Federation of America [PPFA]), McCormick gave her annual $1,000 contribution to the new organization.

When Katharine inherited $35 million (over $376 million in 2016) after Stanley's death in 1947, Sanger tried again to draw McCormick more fully into the movement. Sanger reminded McCormick of her role at the Geneva conference and asked her to help the Massachusetts federation.[46] By this time, McCormick and Sanger had drifted far enough apart that McCormick expressed appreciation to Sanger for remembering her, and declared, "I still feel, as I have felt from the first, that there is nothing more important than birth control." However, she claimed that her hands were tied financially until the estate was settled and she paid inheritance taxes. Biding her time, Sanger gracefully replied, "The important thing is that you are with us in this ever harder struggle and there are times when good will and good wishes are stronger than money."[47]

With her financial affairs finally in order in 1950, McCormick wrote Sanger, asking her "what the present prospects are for further Birth control research, and by research I mean contraceptive research."[48] What is notable here is McCormick's consistent insistence that the most important priority in the birth control movement was research—research, that is, into a new method of contraception that would be safe, effective, and controlled by women.

Furthermore, the depth of her commitment to birth control is evident throughout her letters in the 1950s. "My greatest worry," she wrote Sanger, was over "a lack of easy and adequate contraception" and a "foolproof method . . . over which I chafe constantly."[49] Sanger noted to a friend that McCormick felt strongly about birth control: "She is such a dear—speaks of the BC work as 'we' and 'our.' "[50] Sanger and McCormick grew friendlier, exchanging more personal information in their letters. Sanger even began staying at McCormick's guest house in Santa Barbara on trips to California.

When Sanger responded to McCormick's letter in 1950 with an elaborate plan for research, McCormick backed off, claiming that her financial affairs were still not in order. But a month later McCormick sent a $5,000 check, in addition to her annual $1,000 contribution to Planned Parenthood. Sanger used the $5,000 to fund an international conference in London. Inspired by McCormick's fierce determination that research could produce a better contraceptive, Sanger sent William Vogt, head of the PPFA, to see McCormick when he was in California. Her gambit paid off, and Vogt reported the news that McCormick gave an additional $8,000 to PPFA for research. In addition, she was planning an additional donation for a medical director's office to oversee research at the PPFA.

Significantly, Vogt also reported to Sanger the optimism at the California Institute of Technology about the development of an oral contraceptive—information he likely shared with McCormick also, which perhaps prompted her larger donation. In response, Sanger warned Vogt that McCormick was to be dealt with carefully. Her money, Sanger said, needed to be spent according to McCormick's wishes, because McCormick would follow through to ensure her money was being used as she intended. Sanger took all the credit for McCormick's PPFA donation, writing to another friend, "I sold her on Vogt a year ago—& have kept her well informed on all the news. I have had sent her letters on the four research doings which Dr Stone sent me after high pressure from me to get them. This did the trick & she sent $8,000 last year & now $10,000—Pretty good for an old friend."[51]

At the same time that McCormick was asking where birth control research was headed, Pincus was attempting to find the money to expand his research on the study of the effect of progesterone on the fertilization of rabbit eggs. In 1949, he received $7,500 from the National Committee on Maternal Health and the National Research Council's Committee on Human Reproduction, which were collaborating for two years with the PPFA.[52] In 1950, the PPFA did not recommend continued support for Pincus, claiming that his study was too "far afield from the main interest of the federation" and that the amount needed was too large.[53] Undeterred, in 1951 and 1952 Pincus applied to the Robert L. Dickinson Memorial Research Fund of the PPFA but received only a total of $6,500 in funding for oral contraceptive research on rabbits using progesterone.[54] Planned Parenthood's Vogt was not impressed with Pincus and doubted his research had any practical application, a concern he continued to express until after FDA approval of the pill almost a decade later.[55] The Planned Parenthood News update on research in the fall of 1952 concluded that the idea of the pill was more "academic than practical value" and that it was "doubtful" a daily medication would ever become an acceptable form of contraception.[56] Given this lack of interest from PPFA, Pincus, who had already conceived of the pill, was stymied by a lack of funds and unable to do the necessary research until he received substantial funding from McCormick.[57]

When McCormick wrote to Sanger in 1950 to ask about the state of research into contraception, she was already aware of Pincus and his research on hormones from her work with the Foundation for Neuro-Endocrine Research she had funded to research mental illness.[58] Meanwhile, after meeting Pincus at a dinner at her home in 1951, Sanger wrote to McCormick in March 1952 to tell her about him and his latest research, which was now focused on human contraception. McCormick's old friend Roy Hoskins arranged for McCormick to visit Pincus's laboratory later that year. Afterward, she complained to Sanger that she was "rather surprised that the Pincus plan does not receive more attention. Perhaps it is considered too long ranged and complicated." McCormick, however, was impressed, and she sent a $17,500 contribution through Planned Parenthood to fund Pincus, her first contribution earmarked specifically for him to fund research for the birth control pill.[59]

Sanger credited McCormick with having the vision to support him so early on. "You must, indeed, feel a certain pride in your judgment," she wrote McCormick. Noting that Pincus had been working for years on reproductive research with very little money, she added, "Then you came along with your fine interest and enthusiasm—with your faith and wonderful directives— things began to happen and at last the reports . . . are now out in the outstanding scientific magazine and the conspiracy of silence has been broken." Two years later, she concluded that "at least 90 percent" of Pincus's success was due to McCormick's "financial support as well as moral encouragement."[60]

Sanger and McCormick began exchanging letters expressing discontent with Planned Parenthood almost immediately in 1952. Under the male leaders who took over the organization in 1939, the PPFA was beginning to focus on social science research into birth control knowledge and opinion rather than scientific research into birth control methods. As early 1949, PPFA's annual report asserted that it would have to wait to fund full-scale research until the organization was stronger and wealthier. It also cut back on opening new clinics and focused instead on birth control education through publications. This frustrated Sanger, who argued that the PPFA would be better off cutting overhead expenses and educational planning so that they could focus instead on contraceptive research.[61] Sanger was also upset with Vogt because the PPFA was taking 15 percent of all contributions before passing the rest on to specific projects—including Sanger's new organizational home, the International Planned Parenthood Federation.[62]

Vogt confidentially admitted to Sanger in June 1952 that he thought the pill would cost $1 million, perhaps as much as $5 million, to produce. This may account for his reluctance to support it. A year later, the new medical director, William Esty, wrote Sanger's colleague Abraham Stone that although the medical committee thought that Pincus's work "may never have applicability to our problem," they essentially had no choice but to allow McCormick to continue to fund it and to focus their own funds elsewhere.[63] In addition, a strained relationship between Vogt and Paul Henshaw, PPFA's first medical director, limited PPFA's interest in Pincus. While McCormick would have approved of Henshaw's attempts to "move research away from more traditional spermicide and occlusive methods and to biochemical, hormonal, and botanical agents," Vogt did not.[64] His opposition may have been owing to the fact that if an over-the-counter drug was produced, it would cut into the profits of diaphragms, the central birth control method sold at PPFA clinics. At the time, it was not clear that the pill would be prescription only.[65]

This lack of support on the part of Vogt, Esty, and others in the PPFA accounts for the growing frustration of McCormick and Sanger with the organization. In 1952, Sanger wrote to Vogt to complain that she had received a letter from McCormick saying that "she sent her contributions to the RL Dickinson Memorial Fund for research but is keenly disturbed, feeling that not much is being done."[66] A year later, McCormick groused to Sanger that Vogt had been in Boston but did not see Pincus and Rock. "He left me very puzzled as to what he really considered the worth of progesterone," she wrote.

On June 8, 1953, McCormick returned to visit Pincus for a second time, this time with Margaret Sanger and Gertrude Hoskins. She immediately offered an additional $10,000 for a new medical lab, and in November she donated $40,000 for a new building.[67]

These initial donations were funneled through the PPFA, but her frustration with their lack of support caused her to change her plans. Her complaints culminated in the 1954 three-page, single-spaced typewritten letter in which she gave up on Vogt and the PPFA. A visit to their offices had left her frustrated and bewildered. Vogt had told her that he did not think her donation for an animal laboratory was "necessary." McCormick had had enough. If Vogt would not support Pincus's research, she would have to do it herself. She stopped sending money to PPFA and instead began sending checks to Pincus and Rock through the WFEB.[68] After this, Pincus and his colleague Rock presented her with annual budgets, which she supported through direct cash donations as well as donations of McCormick–International Harvester stock, totaling between $100,000 and $150,000 annually. These funds covered salaries (for Chang, clinical trial directors, and many other laboratory and clerical assistants); materials such as animals, chemicals, and instruments; laboratory testing; and travel.[69] These contributions lasted until her death, when she left $1 million to the WFEB in her will. Given Vogt and PPFA's lack of support for Pincus, McCormick's decision to finance the research by herself was essential to the development of the pill and well reflected her decades-long support for women's rights and scientific research. As with the woman suffrage movement and higher education for women, women had to fund changes for women, and it took a woman to finance a reliable and easily obtainable form of birth control.

As late as 1958, McCormick still complained to Sanger that the PPFA "is doing nothing about" funding the studies on Enovid (the brand name) and oral contraception.[70] Vogt still doubted the research of Pincus and Rock, reporting to PPFA's board of directors that it was doubtful that they were going to be able to develop a birth control pill.[71] This infuriated McCormick, who wrote Sanger that she had "felt his hostility to 'the pill' before now, but have never seen it so clearly expressed." Sanger wrote on the report "jealous." Despite these disagreements, Katharine resumed her contributions to the organization once it began to support the pill. When PPFA clinics became a prime venue for women to access the pill, she left the organization $5 million in her will, significantly more than the $1 million she left to the WFEB.

McCormick's great attention to detail and her passionate interest in both birth control and science meant that she followed research for the pill closely. In the summer of 1954, McCormick visited Pincus on July 1, called Dr. Stone at the Margaret Sanger Research Bureau in New York on July 4, and wrote Sanger on July 13 to tell her that she had just spoken twice with Pincus. Sanger and McCormick wanted to begin a study in Japan, but a misunderstanding occurred about who would run the study because Sanger did not realize the potential problem using a doctor from a government-controlled university could cause—Pincus and Rock did not want the Japanese government involved until they had proven the efficacy and safety of their drug. Desperately backtracking, McCormick sent a telegram to Sanger two days later to reiterate the need for a "non-governmental approach." She saw Pincus again on July 15 and Rock on July 16. McCormick admitted to Sanger that she had previously not completely understood how the testing was run, misconceptions that Rock cleared up in a two-hour conversation. After talking to Rock, McCormick explained to Sanger that Rock and Pincus preferred expansion to Puerto Rico instead of Japan or Hawaii because it was close enough for them to visit and bring specimens back to Massachusetts for testing.[72] Following up on this conversation, McCormick went back to see Hoagland and Pincus on July 20, talked to Rock again, and wrote two letters to Sanger on July 21 to reiterate their desire to do the additional testing in Puerto Rico.[73]

Pincus asked McCormick to visit the field-test sites in Puerto Rico and Haiti repeatedly. Although she was not willing to travel, McCormick clearly relished her collaboration with Pincus. She told him, "I was really sitting on the edge of my chair waiting to hear about it, so you can realize how grateful I was to you for describing so fully both situations [testing sites]."[74] McCormick's dedication to the project seemed to know no bounds. She remained all year at her primary residence in Boston, no longer moving to Santa Barbara each winter. "Freezing in Boston" for the pill was worth it to her, because there were so many issues to deal with, and she had to be in Boston to keep an eye on the project. "I do so like to be near the works and to Pincus and Rock so as not to miss the details that arise," she wrote.[75]

She expected the same level of commitment from Pincus and Rock. She complained every time they left town, even for science conferences (the only exception was Puerto Rico). Rock, for example, was not able to attend the International Birth Control Conference in Tokyo in 1955. Rock requested $5,000 in funding from McCormick to attend with his wife. The normally generous McCormick refused to pay for him, writing a long explanation of how important both Pincus and Rock were to the project and concluding that they could not both be away at the same time. She wrote Sanger, "If I possibly can I want to keep everybody's nose to the grindstone until we get further along toward reaching our end point."[76]

Rock benefited from McCormick's largesse in other ways. When he turned sixty-five and faced mandatory retirement from Harvard, they found a build-ing for him right near the hospital but in need of work. Renovations were made slowly, transforming "the hovel" into a "palace." McCormick told Sanger she "vetoed" Rock's concerns about the cost and forced him to agree to it. This was an exception for her, she admitted, as she was loathe to spend money "on bricks and mortar instead of brains and experiments." McCormick was reluctant to spend money on anyone or anything that she perceived as being nonessential to progress on the pill.[77]

Another reason McCormick was crucial to the development of the pill was that she was willing to support a controversial issue. Other potential donors were reluctant to sponsor birth control research in Massachusetts, where it was against the law (and had to be presented as research in reproduction, menstrua-tion disorders, or fertility, rather than contraception).[78] Alan Guttmacher, who succeeded Vogt as president of the PPFA, even cabled Rock and Pincus, warn-ing them to keep quiet and avoid publicity when reporters contacted them.[79] But McCormick was not concerned. She encouraged Pincus and Rock to share their results as soon as possible, delighted in the publicity, and was willing to do whatever it took to get their research accomplished.[80] Furthermore, as historian Lara Marks argues, McCormick was flexible in her giving. She was willing both to give more if she considered it necessary and to allow the scientists to present revised budgets according to their progress, something that pharmaceutical companies and the federal government could not do.[81]

McCormick's dedication to the cause is evident from her frustration about the slow pace of the research. She became even more impatient when the scientists prepared to conduct human trials because she was so eager to have it ready for use. In 1956, she wrote Sanger, "In spite of the growing hullabaloo over Population Increases no one but ourselves seems to want to get out of the laboratory and in to the clinic for practical attacks on the real problems, so apparently we must inch along as we are doing, but it certainly is a slow business."[82] She never wavered in her belief that the pill was right around the corner.

McCormick earned both the gratitude and the respect of the men with whom she worked, not just for her money but for her genuine interest in the science and medicine they practiced. As Pincus biographer Leon Speroff wrote, "What at first must have been uncomfortable meetings viewed with a sense of obligation by Pincus and Rock, rapidly became an interchange of ideas and thinking that traveled in both directions, earning Katharine the respect of the scientists and clinicians establishing her rightful place as a true collaborator."[83] When Pincus wrote to her to thank her for her financial contributions, he stated, "More important to me is your understanding interest in the investigative work. It is this interest which sustains us in the difficult and complicated task."[84] Though she may have been controlling and demanding, she also proved her dedication to the cause and her confidence in the scientists. Pincus dedicated his book, *The Control of Fertility*, to McCormick "because of her steadfast faith in scientific inquiry."[85]

Pincus and Rock and the Searle Corporation applied for FDA approval of Enovid, first for menstrual disorders, approved in 1957, and then as a contraceptive. The latter application languished for months, due to concerns about providing healthy women with a daily pill that would effectively separate sex from reproduction. Rock even traveled to Washington in an attempt to reassure regulators. Finally, in May 1960, FDA approval was announced.

Together McCormick and Pincus continuously looked ahead to the next phase of the research. Even before the final approval, in 1958 Pincus explained to McCormick that because the pill was in field trial, he was ready to interest doctors in other countries in the pill and to investigate additional compounds that might be less expensive to use. By 1959, he had determined his three goals: continuation of studies of the long-term medication of Enovid, development of additional compounds to lower costs, and training of doctors to prescribe the pill around the world.[86]

McCormick found the third aspect of Pincus's vision compelling. She had a home in Switzerland, had been an officer in the International Woman Suffrage Association, and had supported the International Birth Control Conference that Sanger organized in 1927. Such an international outlook led her to support efforts to spread the testing and use of the pill all over the world. McCormick initiated many of these international efforts through her own travels and contacts in Europe. She offered to pay the expenses of a doctor whom Pincus had met in London to visit the Shrewsbury laboratory, asking Pincus, "Do you think it would be helpful to the progress of the oral contraceptive in England to do this? I am disturbed by their lack of initiative there and believe it comes from not being in close enough touch with our efforts in this country."[87] When the Ford Foundation granted the WFEB millions to have doctors from all over the world train in reproductive medicine at WFEB, McCormick donated thousands of dollars to pay for the living expenses of fifteen fellows per year.[88]

After the FDA approved the birth control pill in the spring of 1960, McCormick remained dedicated to expanding access to the pill. Rock biographers Margaret Marsh and Wanda Ronner argued that McCormick lost interest in supporting birth control research and shifted her focus to her donation of a women's dormitory to MIT. This was because McCormick was no longer "Lady Bountiful" to Rock (as he nicknamed her).[89] But in fact McCormick was still promoting the pill and birth control even though she did not support Rock's new research.[90] She was not interested in funding his new approach to contraception through immunology, an antisperm inoculation for limited sterilization of women, and a simple home test to figure out ovulation (which could be used for the rhythm method or for increased fertility).[91] McCormick may not have fully warmed up to Rock owing to his Roman Catholic faith (as the Church was against the pill); his continued interest in fertility treatment, while her consuming interest was in birth control; and his view of birth control as a tool for couples to limit and space children rather than "an instrument of women's autonomy."[92]

Despite her lack of enthusiasm for Rock's new interests, McCormick's letters reveal that she never lost interest in expanding access to birth control. She told Sanger she had three projects. Although one was planning a dormitory for women at MIT, the other two were related to the pill: keeping up with oral contraceptive research and paying for the housing for the fifteen international fellows training in reproductive medicine.[93] McCormick was not content to have been instrumental in the creation and approval of the pill. She wrote to Sanger that Pincus was investigating the potential of a once-a-month pill or a long-lasting injection, research she continued to support. As to the injection, McCormick added, "I think we'll get it too, quicker than the oral one. I'm waiting for it!!"[94]

McCormick also focused on broadening access to the pill through hospitals and clinics. She paid for Massachusetts hospitals to have clinics give out pills for "menstrual disorders" when contraception was illegal there. She wrote John Rock to ask if any hospitals in Boston would dispense Enovid "as a 'menstrual regulator' for such patients who might be in need of it." She was concerned about "women in the poorer parts of this city especially those who cannot afford the trip to Rhode Island," where they could legally obtain a prescription for birth control.[95]

As a member of the board of the Planned Parenthood League of Massachusetts (PPLM), she worked to arrange for clinics at several Boston area hospitals. McCormick suggested that if Enovid could be distributed for menstrual disorders, a nurse could then "*tell* the patient to take the Enovid tablets every day for contraception." Despite their concerns with such a strategy (including the ethical problem for nurses), McCormick and PPLM executive director Mrs. Maurice Sagoff tried to follow through with this plan. They decided to approach Beth Israel Hospital first because there were no Catholics on the board, though this plan took two years and a new director of Obstetrics and Gynecology to come to fruition.[96] Meanwhile, McCormick donated funds for "steroid research" (rather than "contraception," thus keeping it legal), establishing clinics at Boston Lying-In and Peter Bent Brigham Hospitals, where doctors could study women's responses to Enovid.[97] In 1962, Sagoff suggested trying to expand the program to Massachusetts General Hospital. After the hospital refused, McCormick flatly denied a fundraising request from Mass General, saying that she was not willing to support a hospital that would not distribute birth control, a policy she called "indefensible in a medical profession dedicated to the vital maintenance of humanity."[98] As late as 1967, McCormick was still expanding her support to Boston area hospitals, paying for a new clinic at Boston City Hospital with Spanish-speaking and African American nurses and social workers. Clearly, McCormick wanted all women, whether they were rich, poor, white, black, Hispanic, or Catholic, to have access to birth control.[99] McCormick also was concerned that the cost of the pill was too high. In 1960, after the FDA announced its approval, she wrote an old friend from the woman suffrage movement that "everything is O.K. with 'the pill,' but the price is still too high."[100]

All her efforts indicate that McCormick embraced a scientific-research approach to improving the efficacy of birth control by developing a new method, rather than widening distribution of already existing methods. When this goal was accomplished, she moved on to improve access to that new, more effective method. In the early 1950s, when she began her contributions, her optimism and faith in science may have blinded her to the fact that the pill would be difficult for some women to obtain due to the need to see a doctor and obtain a prescription. As soon as possible, she began working to remedy the problem of limited access to the pill.[101]

McCormick and Sanger shared the belief that science held the answer for reproductive freedom for women and would provide families the ability to limit the number of children they had. As with the issue of insanity, she gave her money to research that would achieve the ends she sought: a cure for her husband and an effective method of contraception that women could control.

McCormick's decision to seek a solution through science and with the help of doctors in no way compromised her desire for women to control their own reproduction and to widen access to birth control to all women. It is therefore ironic that as the feminist movement of the 1970s developed, it included a negative critique of the pill. Feminists criticized the pill for putting the burden of birth control on women rather than men and for its safety concerns and side effects. McCormick, of course, wanted a method that women could control; she thought keeping contraception in women's hands provided them with control rather than burdened them with more responsibility Admittedly, she, Pincus, and Rock were so focused on developing the pill that they dismissed the significance of the side effects.

Feminists and others also criticized McCormick and the scientists for conducting trials in Puerto Rico. The historical disregard for the health and safety of people of color in medical experimentation warrants this suspicion, as does Margaret Sanger's affiliation with eugenics in the 1920s and 1930s. Since most federal regulations concerning human subjects were not put into place until the mid-1960s, well after the trials were completed, it is also true that Pincus and Rock did not adhere to today's standards of informed consent with their test subjects.[102]

However, Pincus and Rock chose to conduct field trials in Puerto Rico not out of racist disregard for the safety of Puerto Rican women in the trial but for practical reasons. The first human clinical trials were conducted in Massachusetts on fifty of Rock's infertility patients and nurse volunteers. This initial group was highly motivated to follow a protocol that required daily vaginal smears and temperature measures, forty-eight-hour urine specimen collections, and, for some, monthly endometrial biopsies. The next two groups to participate were not actually free to consent. They were small groups of nursing students in Puerto Rico, who were pressured to comply with the testing protocol under threat that their grades would suffer, and mentally ill patients at Worcester State Hospital, whose relatives granted permission for them. McCormick approved of the latter group due to her familiarity with testing there: decades earlier, doctors she'd worked with from the Foundation for Neuro-Endocrine Research had also experimented there.

As Pincus and Rock moved from clinical trials to field trials, which involved much larger numbers of women and required only that the women adhere to taking the daily pill and reporting on pregnancy (or lack thereof), they deliberated over where to hold the new trials. They considered, at one time or another, India, Japan, Haiti, Mexico, New York, Los Angeles, Hawaii, Boston, Sweden, Rome, China, Jamaica, and Puerto Rico. Pincus and Rock eventually convinced McCormick and Sanger that Puerto Rico was the best choice: birth control was legal there, they personally knew a doctor who could oversee it, and it was close enough to bring specimens back to Massachusetts for testing.

Furthermore, they correctly believed that they would be able to recruit enough Puerto Rican women who wanted access to birth control. Contraceptive pilot programs on the island that preceded the pill trials had drawn volunteers who relied primarily on sterilization for birth control. Rather than seeing their poverty as a reason to push birth control on them for eugenic reasons, McCormick assumed that all women, regardless of class, wanted reproductive control. In this case, she correctly predicted that poor women in Puerto Rico had the desire necessary to fulfill the requirements of the study.

Did Pincus, Rock, Sanger, and McCormick take advantage of Puerto Rican women's desire for birth control to inflict unsafe testing on a group they saw as inferior? None of them believed the pill had safety issues of concern. Instead, they saw the trial as primarily testing efficacy. They gave pills to white, middle-class women in Boston and Europe as well as to women of color in Puerto Rico, both before and after FDA approval. McCormick herself purchased the pill for a friend when it was still only approved for menstrual disorders.[103] In their desperate drive to produce a pill that was effective, they lost sight of the very women they were trying to help and did not prioritize comfort or safety concerns. Thus, when many Puerto Rican women complained about side effects, especially nausea, the doctors mostly dismissed the complaints as unimportant.

While it would be incorrect to attribute racially liberal ideas to McCormick, my reading of the correspondence among McCormick, Sanger, Pincus, and Rock in 1954 and 1955 indicates that she did not agree to finance trials in Puerto Rico due to a racist disregard for the women living there. Her statement that it would be nice to have a "cage of ovulating females" has been taken out of context. Rather than racism, it reflected her impatience with human subjects who traveled, forgot, or otherwise broke protocol, slowing down the time-consuming trials.[104] Indeed, she implicitly recognized Puerto Rican women's humanity when she groused that they could not be controlled. She originally did not even want the trials to be in Puerto Rico, having plans with Sanger that focused on Japan. The key was finding somewhere it would be legal to conduct the trials and a group of women willing to follow the protocol. Like the scientists, McCormick was blinded by her single focus on finding an effective pill; at most she can be accused of wanting to believe in the pill so badly that she, along with Pincus and Rock, was willing to ignore any negative findings, such as side effects, that might have derailed its approval and dissemination to women everywhere.

Katharine McCormick's decision to personally underwrite the development of the pill with over a million dollars reflects her lifelong commitment to women's rights and her understanding of the power of money. As a suffragist, she gave thousands of dollars to the cause while holding office in the national association. She also gave millions of dollars to widen opportunities for women in higher education in science and medicine, donating about $5 million to her alma mater, MIT, to build women's residence halls there; hundreds of thousands of dollars to New England Hospital to support women doctors on staff; and $5 million to Stanford University Medical School for women students and faculty. Perhaps she thought women scientists and doctors would be more likely to support birth control and other needs of their women patients. McCormick understood that in order to be equal to men, women needed access to education, professions, the vote, and control over reproduction. McCormick knew that women had to claim their own freedom. When the male-run PPFA was uninterested in better birth control and in fact resisted research efforts, McCormick went around them and funded Pincus and Rock directly. Because of her feminist beliefs, McCormick used her money to fund groundbreaking change for women: the ability to control reproduction on their own terms.

Epilogue

For nearly one hundred years—from 1870, when Sophia Smith died, founding Smith College in her will, through 1967, the year in which MIT's second McCormick residence hall for women opened and its donor, Katharine McCormick, died—a number of wealthy women donated millions of dollars to make changes for women in American society. Their contributions made it possible for women to gain the right to vote, to control their reproduction, and to have access to better educational and employment opportunities. Money was an effective tool to force change in a society that was highly patriarchal. Affluent white women who, despite their class and race privilege, still experienced sexism seized the opportunity to use their fortunes to benefit women. Their ideas about sisterhood, equality, and freedom are important to the history of American feminism.

By 1967, although much had changed for women, much remained the same. By the late 1960s, women were once again marching in the streets, demanding rights in what became known as the women's liberation movement. With "the personal is political" as a rallying cry, women continued to work on employment and legal rights even as they turned their attention to such issues as rape and domestic violence.

Women had won the right to vote with the passage of the Nineteenth Amendment in 1920, and by the 1960s, women were running for office in larger numbers. Women now made up nearly 50 percent of college students, and many Ivy League colleges were getting ready to open their doors to women. And women were about to begin entering professional schools in larger numbers.[1] The Supreme Court declared the right to privacy that made birth control legal for married couples in 1965 and for non-married people in 1972, striking down the few remaining state laws banning birth control.

Yet even with the growth of women's economic power, opportunities, and rights, women still have not yet achieved equality in American society. Nearly fifty years after the start of the women's liberation movement, the glass ceiling remains in many corporations and industries. Women are still not paid as much for the same work as men, and single mothers are disproportionately mired in poverty. Women are still underrepresented in government. Hard-won rights to abortion and birth control are now under assault. There is still an enormous need for women to fund movements that will continue to benefit women and women's rights.

Women are also still underrepresented in philanthropy, both as donors and as beneficiaries. Women donors and fund-raisers have tried to address this discrepancy through the development of women's funds, political action committees (PACs), and social science research on women's philanthropy. Through these efforts, women's giving for women has dramatically increased since the 1960s. Women's funds usually require a minimum donation annually, from $1,000 up, while PACs usually take smaller donations. However, both rely on a smaller group of major donors for much of their funding.

Women's funds promote philanthropy by soliciting women's donations and prioritizing the giving of grants to organizations and efforts that benefit women and girls. These funds direct money toward social change as well as social services. They are similar to community or general foundations in that they function as a clearinghouse that collects donations and distributes grants. PACs pool money to support women candidates for political office. Women's funds and PACs illustrate both historical continuities and new trends in women's giving. The objects of women's giving remain much the same as they were in the early twentieth century: political equality for women, assistance to working-class women and their children, educational and training opportunities, and reproductive rights. However, some of these new organizations are working to avoid the resentment and power struggle that plagued the suffrage movement. Women's funds call for shared power between grantor and grantee. They also pool funds to widen their impact and simultaneously diminish the role of any one giver.

Swanee Hunt, a major philanthropist, recently declared that for women to have more political power, "Money is key. At all levels we must go beyond the traditional envelope-stuffing and phone-bank managing to supporting political change with the power of the purse. When serious women support serious issues with serious money, that's serious change."[2] The best known of the women's PACs is Emily's List (an acronym for "early money is like yeast"), which advocates for political equality for women, continuing the work of suffragists by working to elect women to public office. It was founded with the intent to provide pro-choice Democratic women candidates with early money to establish their candidacy and attract additional money from other donors and PACs. For several years, Ellen Malcolm—whose great-grandfather cofounded IBM—had been making charitable donations anonymously, due to her discomfort with her wealth. She finally decided to reveal her identity, hosting an event in 1985 to launch this group along with California senator Barbara Boxer and former Texas governor Ann Richards. The need for women candidates was high: there were only twelve women Democrats in the House at the time. By bundling small contributions, Emily's List has significantly increased the power of women donors as well as the number of women candidates, helping dozens of women win election to Congress. The organization also has staff with expertise in running political campaigns.[3]

Women have created other organizations to recruit and train women to run for political office, including Emerge America, a training program for Democratic women aspiring to run for office, and WomenCount PAC, to mobilize women around issues of concern to women. Both organizations were founded by Susie Tompkins Buell, founder of Esprit clothing company. Two other organizations looked to the ultimate goal of a woman president. The White House Project, led by the Ms. Foundation, focused on training women for leadership from 1998 through 2013; and the Barbara Lee Family Foundation trains women to run for governorships in order to create a pool of viable presidential candidates.[4] The Susan B. Anthony Fund supports pro-life women congressional candidates, while pro-choice Republican women support candidates through the WISH List (Women in the Senate and House). Regarding funding, all of these organizations share the sentiments of WISH List advocate Jennifer Stockman: "Money drives the political process whether we like it or not. . . . If women are to have a powerful voice in electoral politics," then women must begin to "write substantial checks."[5]

While PACs focus on political representation, women's funds generally steer their grants toward social change and social services. Although the first women's funds appeared in the 1970s, their number began to grow dramatically in the 1980s. According to nonprofit expert Marsha Rose, women's funds arose from three trends: "The second feminist movement [of the 1960s], shifts in the distribution of wealth, and reaction to the economic and social policies of the Reagan administration." Women began to want "to exercise more control over their money."[6] They also hoped to address some of the criticism of the women's liberation movement for being white, middle class, and exclusionary by developing funds that would be inclusive in both their makeup and their programming by addressing low-income women's needs as well as women's equality more generally. In 1985, representatives organized the National Network of Women's Funds, now the Women's Funding Network—a federation of 160 women's funds, cultivating women donors to give to programs that benefit women and girls and encourage gender equality in twenty-five countries.

These funds have led to increased power for women. First, women run the funds, as CEOs and board members. This is still rare, because despite the high number of women volunteers around the country, few general foundations are run by female CEOs or female board members. Second, women and girls benefit from the funds. While all U.S. foundations have begun to increase funding for women and girls, general foundations still direct less than 10 percent of total grant dollars to programs for women and girls. Women's funds, on the other hand, direct all or most of their funds to benefit women and girls, often addressing such issues as violence, sex trafficking, and anti-poverty and economic self-sufficiency for women.[7] Third, women donate to the funds. Nearly all contributions come from women donors.

Founded in 1972 by Gloria Steinem and others, the Ms. Foundation was one of the earliest funds to create programs that addressed the social and economic status of women. It is known for offering grants as well as assistance, so that grantees can learn strategies for fund-raising. Two notable priorities of the Ms. Foundation since its inception have been promoting reproductive rights and combating racial prejudice. By the 1980s, it also began to focus on domestic and sexual abuse, including that of children, as well as programs for low-income women.[8] It initiated the Take Our Daughters to Work program in 1993 to encourage girls to learn about employment opportunities. The Ms. Foundation has been supported by both small and major contributions. Today, there are funding circles of donors who contribute at least $20,000 to a particular program.

Most women's funds try to address the inequity of power that caused resentment in the suffrage movement. That is, as feminist organizations, they explicitly strive to be "non-hierarchical and function by means of processes that attempt to preserve nondifferentiation, collaboration among all members, and equal attention to means and ends."[9] These funds often include grantees and community activists on the committees or boards that make decisions regarding grants. A study of the Boston Women's Fund, for example, found that when it faced an increasing number of grant proposals that did not meet its criteria, the fund engaged in dialogue with grantees, which led it to make changes in the criteria.[10] Not all funds, however, have been successful at achieving their democratic ideals. Some allow donor-directed giving, keeping the decision making in the hands of the donor, or are not inclusive in their boards or in their committees.

Building on the growth of women's funds, in 2006 sisters Swanee Hunt and Helen LaKelly Hunt created the Women Moving Millions campaign to increase million-dollar gifts from individual women to women's funds for women's benefit, with the goal of raising $150 million to push women's funds' assets over $1 billion.[11] After exceeding its initial goal during its first phase in 2009, the effort continued, inspiring over 207 donors to make gifts over $300 million from 2009 to the present. The idea motivating the Women Moving Millions campaign is that women need to give bigger gifts in order to have more impact and create greater change. As one donor said, "We women must play big to maximize our power."[12]

Unfortunately, due to the paucity of history of women's philanthropy, women philanthropists today are often unaware of the history of women donors who came before them. They may be familiar with a couple of the women, such as Mrs. Frank Leslie, or know that leaders like Susan B. Anthony had to work tirelessly to raise money for the suffrage movement. But many women today lack knowledge of the significant contributions made by the women who came before them.

The personal stories of the women donating to the Women Moving Millions campaign are striking. Many of the women are married. Their million-dollar gifts come with the support of their husbands but also with the recognition that they had previously been making smaller donations, held back by a lack of knowledge of their assets or because their husbands were the primary earners.[13] Their stories echo the lack of control over finances that many women in the early twentieth century also experienced.

Furthermore, many of these women experienced sexism themselves, despite their fortunes, as did the women discussed throughout this book. Alice Young was a member of the first undergraduate class at Yale to include women, Sheila C. Johnson refused to be told she could not do things "because I was female," and Margot Franssen was not allowed into a training program for stockbrokers because she was told that "women can't pass" the program requirements.[14]

Their feminist beliefs inspired them to give to the campaign. Lynne Rosenthal explained that she became interested in supporting feminism after reading *Ms.* magazine while she was a young mother. She gave the Ms. Foundation a check for $25 when it was founded, and when she later inherited money from her father, she made the Ms. Foundation her first million-dollar recipient.[15] Many women also cite their suffragist grandmothers as providing a powerful role model for women's activism.[16]

Their stories echo the social science research on women's giving conducted in the last several decades by academics at philanthropy institutes, like the Women's Philanthropy Institute at the Lilly Family School of Philanthropy at Indiana University, as well as by fund-raising professionals. These efforts try to understand women's philanthropy and, in particular, compare it to men's in order to understand why and how women give. The studies investigate whether women need a personal connection to a cause, which organizations women are more likely to give to, and their reasons for giving. A survey from 2001, for example, found that more men than women were motivated by tax and estate laws to give; more women gave to social causes in which they believed; and women were more likely to support organizations focused on health, homelessness and poverty, and the elderly, while men were more likely to donate to arts and political organizations.[17] Studies by fund-raisers include a yearlong conversation UCLA had with its alumnae in 1994, resulting in the formation of an organization called UCLA Women and Philanthropy, which works to encourage major gifts from women to UCLA. The conversation revealed that many women were not asked to give and not recognized when they did give. Married women felt empowered when they were treated as individuals rather than extensions of their husbands.[18]

These studies reveal that despite the women's movement of the 1960s and 1970s, many wealthy women continue to feel a lack of control over their finances.[19] They also continue to be uncomfortable discussing money. The Ms. Foundation tried to address this discomfort with a conference on "Women, Money, and Power." The conference led to the creation of a program to teach financial literacy to women of wealth and fight what they called the "masculinization of wealth."[20] It is hoped that women will grow more comfortable with money and wealth, especially as the number of women who earn their fortunes, rather than inheriting or marrying into them, continues to grow.

Since the late nineteenth century, women have created enormous social changes in society. Millions of women have marched in the streets, knocked on doors, lobbied legislatures, and otherwise demanded change to improve women's lives. As this book has shown, money has often been key to success, as exemplified by the major gifts to the suffrage and birth control movements, as well as to institutions of higher education. Women of means continue to make a difference for women today through their giving. Katharine McCormick would be pleased to know that Suzanne Perot McGee, along with her sisters and mother, were behind the Perot Foundation's million-dollar gift to Planned Parenthood of Greater Texas.[21] Alva Belmont would rejoice in the knowledge that Susie Tompkins Buell is giving millions to train women for political office. Josephine Newcomb would be happy to see that Leonie Faroll left her alma mater, Wellesley College—one of the few women's colleges still thriving—$27 million when she died in 2005, a gift made possible by successful personal investing over several decades.[22] Mrs. Frank Leslie, the first woman to donate over $1 million to the woman suffrage movement with her bequest to Carrie Catt, would celebrate Peg Yorkin, who in 1990 made the largest gift at the time dedicated to women's rights: a $10 million grant to the Feminist Majority Foundation, which she had helped found. The foundation works for gender equality and, in particular, to protect reproductive rights.[23]

Despite tremendous progress, gender equality has not yet been achieved in the United States. Women are still overrepresented as victims of poverty, violence, and rape, and do not yet have political power equal to their numbers. The U.S. Supreme Court has been curtailing women's access to abortion and birth control. Furthermore, women face inequities due to race, ethnicity, religion, and sexuality. The need for women to give major gifts to fund changes benefiting all women is more imperative today than ever.

Notes

McConnell Papers	McConnell Family Papers, Tulane University Archives, New Orleans, La.
McCormick Papers	McCormick–International Harvester Collection, Historical Society of Wisconsin Archives, University of Wisconsin, Madison, Wisc.
MCT	M. Carey Thomas
MDR	Margaret Dreier Robins
MDR Papers	Papers of the Women's Trade Union League and Its Principal Leaders (microfilm), Series I, Margaret Dreier Robins Papers
MED	Mary Elisabeth Dreier
MEG	Mary Elizabeth Garrett
MS	Margaret Sanger
MS Papers (unfilmed)	Margaret Sanger Papers, unfilmed, Sophia Smith Women's History Collection, Smith College, Northampton, Mass.
MS-CD	Margaret Sanger Papers, Collected Documents, Sophia Smith Women's History Collection, Smith College, Northampton, Mass.
MS-LOC	Margaret Sanger Papers (microfilm), Library of Congress, Washington, D.C.
MS-SS	Margaret Sanger Papers, Sophia Smith Women's History Collection, Smith College, Northampton, Mass.
MWD	Mary Ware Dennett
MWD Papers	Mary Ware Dennett Papers (microfilm), Schlesinger Library, Radcliffe Institute, Harvard University, Cambridge, Mass.
NAWSA Papers	National American Woman Suffrage Association Records (microfilm), Library of Congress, Washington, D.C.
NWP-I	National Woman's Party Papers, 1913–1974, (microfilm), Library of Congress, Washington, D.C.
NWP-II	National Woman's Party Papers: The Suffrage Years, 1913–1920, (microfilm), Library of Congress, Washington, D.C.
NYT	*New York Times*
PAH	Phoebe Apperson Hearst
PAH Papers	Phoebe and George Hearst Papers (microfilm), Bancroft Library, University of California, Berkeley
PPFA	Planned Parenthood Federation of America Papers, Sophia Smith Women's History Collection, Smith College, Northampton, Mass.
PPLM	Planned Parenthood League of Massachusetts Papers, Sophia Smith Women's History Collection, Smith College, Northampton, Mass.
Presidential Papers-KC	Karl Compton Presidential Papers, Massachusetts Institute of Technology Archives, Boston, Mass.
Presidential Papers-S	Julius Stratton Presidential Papers, Massachusetts Institute of Technology Archives, Boston, Mass.

Rublee Papers	Juliet Barrett Rublee Papers, Sophia Smith Women's History Collection, Smith College, Northampton, Mass.
Schneiderman Papers	Papers of the Women's Trade Union League and Its Principal Leaders (microfilm), Series VI, Rose Schneiderman Papers
Smith Papers	Sophia Smith Papers, Smith College Archives, Smith College, Northampton, Mass.
SPMS	*Selected Papers of Margaret Sanger*
Thomas Papers	M. Carey Thomas Papers (microfilm), Bryn Mawr College, Bryn Mawr, Pa.
Welch Papers	William Henry Welch Papers, Alan Chesney Archives, The Johns Hopkins Medical School, Baltimore, Md.
YWCA Papers	Sophia Smith Women's History Collection, Smith College, Northampton, Mass.

Introduction

Epigraph: Karen Stone quotation in Stone, Rice, and Angel, "Women, Money, and Political Clout," 109; Kathleen McCarthy quotation in McCarthy, *Lady Bountiful Revisited*, x.

1. Women's Funds currently continue this vision. Sunny Fischer, "Introduction," 1–9.

2. Cott, *Grounding of Modern Feminism*, 4–5, 15.

3. Ibid.; Freedman, *No Turning Back*, 7.

4. Fisher, "Celebrating the Heroines of Philanthropy," 13–24.

5. Virginia Woolf, *Three Guineas*.

6. McCarthy, *Lady Bountiful Revisited*; Scott, *Southern Lady*; Hewitt, *Women's Activism and Social Change*; Beverly Gordon, *Bazaars and Fair Ladies*.

7. Gross, "Giving in America," 29–48.

8. Scott, *Natural Allies*; Joan Marie Johnson, *Southern Ladies, New Women*.

9. Zunz, *Philanthropy in America*, 2–3. Rather than viewing philanthropy as "an act of kindness as understood in Christianity," Zunz focuses on the ambition, scale, and use of philanthropy to change society for the better. His depiction of modern philanthropy fits the women in this book.

10. Friedman, "Philanthropy in America," 1–9.

11. Stanton et al., *History of Woman Suffrage*, 1:742–43 (hereafter cited as *HWS*).

12. McCarthy, *Lady Bountiful Revisited*, and Walton, ed., *Women and Philanthropy in Education*, include more articles on women's philanthropy of time and talent than on financial contributions. See also important scholarly biographies of philanthropists: Hoffert, *Alva Vanderbilt Belmont*; Sander, *Mary Elizabeth Garrett*; Crocker, *Mrs. Russell Sage*; Bittel, *Mary Putnam Jacobi*. Biographies in the popular press include Fields, *Katharine Dexter McCormick*; Mansfield, *Richest Girl in the World*; and Stuart, *Consuelo and Alva Vanderbilt*.

13. McCarthy, "Parallel Power Structures," 1–31, quotation on 1; McCarthy, "Women and Political Culture," 179–97.

14. McCarthy, *Women's Culture*. See also Gaudiani, *Daughters of the Declaration*.

15. Max Weber's definition of power is quoted in Hammock, *Power and Society*, 5.

16. Sklar, "Who Funded Hull House?," 94–115; McCaskill, "Hull House's Hidden Power," 1–30. On women's financial support for women social reformers, see also Faderman, *To Believe in Women*.

17. Dudden, *Fighting Chance*; DuBois, *Harriot Stanton Blatch*.

18. Payne, *Reform, Labor, and Feminism*; Rossiter, *Women Scientists in America*.

19. Yohn, "Crippled Capitalists," 85–109, quotation on 88; Yohn, "You Can't Share Babies with Bonds," 1–20; Yohn, "Let Christian Women Set the Example in Their Own Gifts," 213–35; Wallach, *Richest Woman in America*.

20. I refer to Mrs. Frank Leslie this way to distinguish her from her husband after she legally changed her name from Miriam to Frank.

21. Yohn, "Crippled Capitalists," 103.

22. Fraser and Gerstle, eds., "Introduction"; Beckert, *Monied Metropolis*. On suspicion of the wealthy and their giving, see Dalzell Jr., *Good Rich and What They Cost Us*. Historians Sven Beckert and Susie Pak emphasize the power of social networks and the conscious ways in which society leaders constantly reformed the boundaries of their class, which in reality was often more porous than they liked. Beckert, *Monied Metropolis*; Pak, *Gentlemen Bankers*. Gilded Age New York, where monied industrialists worked their way into social acceptance, is the subject of many other studies, including Homberger, *Mrs. Astor's New York*, and Jaher, "Style and Status."

23. Remus, *Consumers' Metropolis*; Wiersema, "All Consuming Nature"; Glymph, *Out of the House of Bondage*; Jones-Rogers, "Mistresses in the Making"; Bachand, "Gendered Mobility and the Geography of Respectability"; Merkin, "We Were Much Afraid of Our Voices for a Long Time."

24. Friedman, "Philanthropy in America," 1–9. See also Bremner, *American Philanthropy*. Diana Kendall argues that the women in her study were more focused on their own position and not in interacting with the poor. Kendall, *Power of Good Deeds*. Susan Ostrander also argues that noblesse oblige makes them want to give back to society but not to really solve problems like poverty. Ostrander, *Women of the Upper Class*.

25. On the pleasure women planning fund-raising fairs derived, see Gordon, *Bazaars and Fair Ladies*, 6.

26. Mansbridge, "On the Contested Nature of the Public Good," 3–19; Blum et al., "Altruism and Women's Oppression," 222–47.

27. Daniels, *Invisible Careers*; Ostrower, *Why the Wealthy Give*; Walton, "Rethinking Boundaries," 29–57, esp. 44; Friedman, "Philanthropy in America."

28. Sage, "Opportunities and Responsibilities of Leisured Women," 712–21; Addams, *Democracy and Social Ethics*.

29. McCarthy, "Ms. Foundation"; Ostrower, *Why the Wealthy Give*; Greene, "Study Finds Differences in Giving Patterns Between Wealthy Men and Women," 12–14.

30. Rockwell, "Elite Women and Class Formation," 153–66.

31. Ostrander, "Moderating Contradictions of Feminist Philanthropy," 29–46; Martin, "Rethinking Feminist Organizations," 182–206; Leidner, "Stretching the Boundaries of Liberalism," 263–89; Alter, "Bureaucracy and Democracy in Organizations," 258–71. Betsy Duncan Diehl defines feminism as having three objectives without mentioning women or gender: "the elimination of oppression and oppressive societal hierarchies; the implementation of a collaborative approach to problem solving that involves those who are affected by the problems; and the pursuit of social change that improves and elevates the lives of all members of society." Diehl, "Philanthropy as an Expression of Feminism," 22.

32. Addams, "A Modern Lear," 131–37.

33. For the relationship between donor and recipient and the effect of giving on the donor, see Friedman, "Philanthropy in America," 1–9.

34. See, for example, Hewitt, "Feminist Frequencies"; Meyerowitz, *Not June Cleaver*; Cobble, *Other Women's Movement*.

35. For more on individual women, see biographical information within chapters. College graduates included Katharine Dexter McCormick, Ellen Scripps, Carola Woerishoffer, and Helen Ogden Reid; female seminary attendees included Olivia Sage, Juliet Rublee, Phoebe Hearst, and Indiana Fletcher Williams; Louisine Havemeyer, Josephine Newcomb and Alva Belmont were educated in France; Mary Jacobi had an MD, and Jessie Ashley attended New York University Law School; Hearst, Williams, and Jane Stanford traveled abroad extensively; and Margaret Dreier Robins, Mary Dreier, Grace Dodge, and Mary Garrett all resented their brothers' education because their fathers did not allow the same for them.

36. For more on individual women, see biographical information within chapters. Single women include M. Carey Thomas and Mary Garrett (who were lesbian partners), Emily Howland, Mary A. Burnham, Mary Dreier, Grace Dodge, Carola Woerishoffer, Jessie Ashley, Sophia Smith, and Ellen Scripps; widows (at the time of their greatest activism and philanthropy) include Pauline Shaw, Louisine Havemeyer, Alva Belmont, Phoebe Hearst, Jane Stanford, Indiana Williams, Josephine Newcomb, Olivia Sage, and Miriam Leslie; and unhappily married or divorced women include Gertrude Pinchot, Katherine Mackay, Helen Reid, and Katharine McCormick (whose husband was mentally ill and did not live with her). Women who were married and had the public support of their husbands include Mary Putnam Jacobi, Vira Whitehouse, Margaret Dreier Robins, Elsie Clews Parsons, Juliet Rublee, Edith Hooker, and Katharine Hepburn. Notably, these last four were all supporters of the birth control movement.

37. On social, financial, and intellectual networks among women, see Romney, *New Netherland Connections*; Pal, *Republic of Women*, esp. 2–4; Wellman, "Seneca Falls Women's Rights Convention," 9–37.

38. Joan Marie Johnson, "Black Women and Philanthropy," 474–83; Joan Marie Johnson, *Southern Ladies, New Women*; and Paula Giddings, *In Search of Sisterhood*.

Chapter One

1. Anthony, quoted in Dudden, *Fighting Chance*, 8; Mary Garrett to Phoebe Hearst, Aug. 30, 1906, PAH Papers, reel 21; Mary Beard to Alice Paul, Aug. 21, 1914, NWP-II, reel 1.

2. *HWS*, 5:252.

3. On women and philanthropy, see McCarthy, *Women's Culture* and *Lady Bountiful Revisited*; Crocker, *Mrs. Russell Sage*; Sander, *Mary Elizabeth Garrett*.

4. On economic independence, see Cott, *Grounding of Modern Feminism*, 118–19; Vapnek, *Breadwinners*.

5. Kraditor, *Ideas of the Woman Suffrage Movement*, 43–74.

6. *HWS*; Kraditor, *Ideas of the Woman Suffrage Movement*; Eleanor Flexner, *Century of Struggle*; DuBois, *Feminism and Suffrage*; Buechler, *Women's Movements in the United States*.

7. Faye Dudden explores Susan B. Anthony's and Elizabeth Cady Stanton's desperate need for funding in the 1860s, and Lisa Tetrault examines the wages organizations paid suffrage speakers in the 1870s to 1880s. Ellen DuBois demonstrates how Harriot Stanton Blatch initiated a cross-class alliance in 1908–9 that included very wealthy women as well as working-class women. Although DuBois and Sara Hunter Graham both conclude that upper-class women exercised disproportionate influence in the movement, this was not the central point of their work. Dudden, *Fighting Chance*; Tetrault, "Incorporation of American Feminism," 1027–56; DuBois, *Harriot Stanton Blatch and the Winning of Woman Suffrage*, 106; Graham, *Woman Suffrage and the New Democracy*. Biographies of donor Alva Belmont and NAWSA president Anna Howard Shaw explore the economic power of the donor and the officer who received funding. Hoffert, *Alva Vanderbilt Belmont*; Franzen, *Anna Howard Shaw*.

8. NAWSA's 1913 budget was approximately $38,000. "Facts for Delegates," 1913, NAWSA Papers, reel 58. Conversion to 2016 value on www.davemanuel.com/inflation-calculator.php.

9. "List of Contributors from Beginning of Organization to Dec. 31, 1920," NWP-II, reel 126. The alphabetical list cuts off after Mrs. E. Stoddard but provides the total amount raised. Lists from 1915 to 1917 name donors from the end of the alphabet but not the exact total number of donors.

10. "Annual Report of the New York State Woman Suffrage Party," 1917, NAWSA Papers, reel 72.

11. *National Citizen and Ballot Box* 5 (Aug. 1880): 4.

12. Gross, "Giving in America," 29–48.

13. Daniels, *Invisible Careers*; Mansbridge, "On the Contested Nature of the Public Good," 3–19; Blum et al., "Altruism and Women's Oppression," 222–47.

14. Terborg-Penn, *African American Women in the Struggle for the Vote*. NAWSA, while officially not a segregated organization, was willing to exclude African American women from conventions in the South and otherwise limit their participation.

15. For works that challenge Seneca Falls as a starting point for the women's movement, see Ginzburg, *Untidy Origins*; Zaeske, *Signatures of Citizenship*; Faulkner, *Lucretia Mott's Heresy*.

16. Buechler, *Women's Movements in the United States*; Flexner, *Century of Struggle*; Lunardini, *From Equal Suffrage to Equal Rights*.

17. Dudden, *Fighting Chance*, 8–12, 20–23, 51, 68–70, 90–94, 105–108, 139, 176.

18. Anthony to Jane Stanford, Apr. 23, 1898, JLS Papers, series 1, box 3, f. 5.

19. Harper, *Life and Work of Susan B. Anthony*, 3:1352.

20. *National Citizen and Ballot Box* 5 (Aug. 1880): 4.

21. *HWS*, 1:742–43.

22. *Woman's Journal*, May 31, 1913.

23. DuBois, "Working Women, Class Relations, and Suffrage Militance," 34–58.

24. Bittel, *Mary Putnam Jacobi*, 257–63; Jacobi, "Report of the 'Volunteer Committee' in New York City," 217–20. See also clipping, n.d., Boyer Scrapbooks, vol. 1, p. 48; *HWS*, 4:850.

25. Bittel, *Mary Putnam Jacobi*, 259–61.

26. Waugh, *Unsentimental Reformer*.

27. Lowell, "Relation of Women to Good Government," 435–45, quotation on 439.

28. Waugh, *Unsentimental Reformer*, 213.

29. Crocker, *Mrs. Russell Sage*.

30. Ibid., 154–56.

31. Ibid., 158; *New York Times*, Apr. 15, 1894 (hereafter cited as *NYT*).

32. Crocker, *Mrs. Russell Sage*, 166. Sage's education donations are discussed in chapter 5.

33. Bittel, *Mary Putnam Jacobi*, 264–68; DuBois, "Working Women, Class Relations, and Suffrage Militance," 38–39.

34. Crocker, *Mrs. Russell Sage*, 164, 168.

35. Hanna, "Ethics of Social Life," 53–57.

36. Marilley, *Woman Suffrage and the Origins of Liberal*, 152.

37. Hanna, "Ethics of Social Life"; Sander, *Mary Elizabeth Garrett*, 241.

38. Blanche Ames, "If I Were a Poor Girl," *Boston Sunday Post*, Apr. 18, 1915. The reference to women's parasitism comes from Olive Schreiner, *Woman and Labor* (New York: Frederick A. Stokes, 1911).

39. Fisher, "Celebrating the Heroines of Philanthropy," 13–24.

40. Boyer Scrapbooks, vol. 1, pp. 17, 22, 24; Graham, *Woman Suffrage and the New Democracy*, 36–39.

41. Mead, *How the Vote Was Won*, 68–69, 83.

42. Sander, *Mary Elizabeth Garrett*. See chapter 5 herein for an extended discussion of this effort.

43. Susan B. Anthony to Harriet Upton, Jan. 21, 1906, quoted in Upton, *Harriet Taylor Upton's Random Recollections*, 229.

44. Mary Garrett to Phoebe Hearst, Aug. 30, 1906, and Apr. 13, 1907, PAH Papers, reel 21.

45. *Life and Work of Susan B. Anthony*, 3:1399–1401. See *HWS*, 5:183, for the notation that after Sage's death, her identity as the anonymous donor became known.

46. Sander, *Mary Elizabeth Garrett*, 239.

47. Ibid., 206–10.

48. Horowitz, *Power and Passion of M. Carey Thomas*.

49. Ibid., 397–405; Thomas to Ida Porter-Boyer, Sept. 25, 1902, NAWSA Papers, reel 19; *HWS*, 5:171–72.

50. Carey Thomas, "A New Fashioned Argument for Woman Suffrage," 1908, NAWSA Papers, reel 67.

51. DuBois, *Harriot Stanton Blatch*.

52. Ibid., 3–4, 97.

53. "Funds for Suffrage: Mrs. Blatch Says Money Lying Ready Is Limitless," *NYT*, Nov. 29, 1910.

54. See Harriot Stanton Blatch to Nancy (Anne Miller Fitzhugh), Apr. (n.d.) 1908, and attached "Luncheon—31st March," in Elizabeth Smith Miller and Anne Fitzhugh Mill Scrapbooks, NAWSA Papers, Library of Congress, no. 6, 58.

55. DuBois, *Harriot Stanton Blatch*, 102.

56. Montgomery, *Displaying Women*.

57. Havemeyer, "The Suffrage Torch: Memories of a Militant, first paper," 528–39, quotation on 528.

58. Havemeyer, "The Suffrage Torch: Memories of a Militant, first paper," and "The Suffrage Torch: Memories of a Militant, second paper," 661–76.

59. "List of Contributors," NWP-II, reel 126.

60. Mary Simpson Sperry (Mrs. Austin) to PAH, Sept. 9, 1911, PAH Papers, reel 76.

61. Reyher, *Search and Struggle for Equality and Independence*, 91.

62. *HWS*, 6:445.

63. "Suffragists Hold a Street Meeting," *NYT*, May 14, 1909. See also Daggett, "Suffrage Enters the Drawing-Room," 37–38, 70; Brush, "Society and Working Women March in Suffrage Parade."

64. *HWS*, 6:445.

65. On the movement becoming fashionable, see DuBois, *Harriot Stanton Blatch*, 108–9.

66. "Whitehouse, Vira Boarman, 1875–1957. Papers of Vira Boarman Whitehouse, 1889–1957: A Finding Aid," Schlesinger; Schwarz, *Radical Feminists of Heterodoxy*, appendix; Wolper, "Woodrow Wilson's New Diplomacy," 226–39. Quote from Rich MacAlpine, "Yates Country and Women's Suffrage," Yates County History Center and Museums, Mar./Apr. 2009, http://www.yatespast.com/articles/suffrage.html, accessed Oct. 15, 2016.

67. Whitehouse, *My Year as a Government Agent*, 2–3.

68. Whitehouse donated over $8,000 to the New York campaigns. "Annual Report of the New York State Woman Suffrage Party," 1917, NAWSA Papers, reel 72.

69. Helen Reid to Mrs. Morrow, Jan. 28, 1926, ABCL, f. 312.

70. *Notable American Women*, 4:574–75; John Arthur Garraty and Mark Christopher Carnes, eds., *American National Biography* (New York: Oxford University Press, 1999), 18:306; Kluger *Paper*, 171–81, 201–6.

71. "Annual Report of the New York State Woman Suffrage Party," 1917, NAWSA Papers, reel 72.

72. Eric Rauchway argues that Dorothy saw her marriage to Willard as enabling her to enter politics under the cover of their joint interest. Rauchway, *Refuge of Affections*, 47–59; Young, *Elmhirsts of Dartington*, 33–96.

73. Michael Straight, *After Long Silence* (New York: W. W. Norton, 1983), 31.

74. "Annual Report of the New York State Woman Suffrage Party," 1917, NAWSA Papers, reel 72; Cofer, *Straight Story*, 8; Rauchway, "A Gentlemen's Club in a Woman's Sphere," 60–85; Rauchway, *Refuge of Affections*, 131–32.

75. Cott, *Grounding of Modern Feminism*, 76.

76. On the controversy over spending within households from 1870–1930, see Zelizer, "Social Meaning of Money," 342–77.

77. Crocker, "From Gift to Foundation," 199–215, quotation on 202; Zelizer, "Social Meaning of Money," 354–62.

78. Reyher, *Search and Struggle*, 84. See Zelizer, "Social Meaning of Money," 358, for another story of affluent women resorting to deceit in order to make charitable contributions.

79. Jane Stanford to Susan B. Anthony, Sept. 8, 1896, and Susan B. Anthony to Jane Stanford, Sept. 9, 1896, JLS Papers, series 1, box 3, f. 5.

80. Susan B. Anthony to Jane Stanford, quoted in Gunther Nagel, *Iron Will: The Life and Letters of Jane Stanford*, 8–9.

81. Phoebe Hearst, "California as a Field for Women's Activities," *California's Magazine*, July 1915, 371–73.

82. See Stern, *Purple Passage*; "Mrs. Frank Leslie: New York's Last Bohemian," *New York History*, Jan. 1948; and *NYT*, Sept. 19, 1914.

83. Stern, *Purple Passage*, 27, 39, 44–45, 58–59, 97, 105–8, 162–70.

84. Mrs. Frank Leslie to Carrie Chapman Catt, Oct. 27, 1910, in "Memoranda concerning Mrs. Frank Leslie and Her Connection with Woman Suffrage," NAWSA Papers, reel 45.

85. Stern, *Purple Passage*, 162–63; Stinson, "The Frank Leslies," 12–21, quotation on 20.

86. Hoffert, *Alva Vanderbilt Belmont*, 39–40.

87. Belmont, "Woman's Right to Govern Herself," 664–74; Belmont, "A Girl? What a Pity It Was Not a Boy!"

88. Belmont, "Woman's Suffrage Raises the Quality of Electorate."

89. Hoffert, *Alva Vanderbilt Belmont*, 123; Belmont, "Woman and the Suffrage," 170.

90. *Woman's Journal*, Nov. 22 and Dec. 13, 1913. See Orleck, *Common Sense and a Little Fire*, 87–113.

91. On the connections between financial independence and women's rights in this period, see Vapnek, *Breadwinners*, 1–3.

92. Belmont, "The Ballot Is a Scepter of Sovereignty in America."

93. Rose, "Philanthropy in a Different Voice, 227–42, quotation on 229.

94. Belmont, "Woman Suffrage as It Looks To-Day," 264–67. On the workers' point of view, see Vapnek, *Breadwinners*, 131.

95. See, for example, Grace Dodge in chapter 3.

96. See the series of articles Belmont wrote for the *Chicago Daily Tribune* in 1912, including June 16, 1912. DuBois points out that many wealthy women saw themselves as obligated to work to aid and protect the poor and therefore wanted to demand suffrage for them, whereas Belmont was willing to encourage them to demand it for themselves. Dubois, *Harriot Stanton Blatch*, 109.

97. Geidel, "Alva E. Belmont," 152–56; Terborg-Penn, *African American Women in the Struggle*, 100–102.

98. Geidel, "Alva E. Belmont," 240.

99. Ibid., 528; Lunardini, *Alice Paul*, 51–53, 146–47. Paul was careful not to alienate southern white women, and was dedicated to making suffrage a single-issue campaign that would not get derailed by other concerns, including race. This is evident both in her decision to move African American women to a back position in the 1913 parade, behind men who could defend them if necessary, and in her contention in the 1920s that the NWP be devoted solely to the ERA; the disenfranchisement of African American women, she claimed, was a race issue, not a women's issue.

100. Strom, *Political Woman*, 71; Minutes, 1910–1912, Massachusetts Woman Suffrage Association Papers, Schlesinger.

101. Clipping, n.d.; clipping, *Boston Sunday Herald*, Nov. 2, 1913, both in Ames-WRC, vol. 119; Minutes of the Annual Convention, NAWSA, 1913, 139–42, MWD Papers, reel 11, f. 220.

102. *HWS*, 5:325; "Katharine Dexter McCormick, a Woman Who Is Helping to Make the Suffrage Movement a Big Practical Force for Good," *Woman's Journal*, Sept. 28, 1912, 312; and clipping, *Boston Globe*, Ames-WRC, vol. 119, Schlesinger.

103. "Asks, Should Men Vote?" *NYT*, Mar. 31, 1914, 6.

104. "Katharine Dexter McCormick, a Woman Who Is Helping," 312.

105. Breault, *World of Emily Howland*, quotation on 140; "No Suffragist Violence," *NYT*, Oct. 16, 1908, 12; *HWS*, 4:849; Gaffney, *Emily Howland Papers at Cornell University*.

106. "'Free Love' Charge Held Ridiculous," *NYT*, Feb. 15, 1914.

107. "Mrs. Clarence Mackay," *American*, Sept. 1906, 609–10. See also Wilson, *Harbor Hill*.

108. Harriman, *From Pinafore to Politics*, 92.

109. DuBois, *Harriot Stanton Blatch*, 107–8, 111–12, 129.

110. "Woman Suffrage Convention," *NYT*, Oct. 27, 1909; Blatch, *Challenging Years*, 117–18.

111. "Mrs. Mackay at Work," *Harper's Bazaar* 44 (Apr. 1910): 240–41.

112. "Mrs. Mackay Pleads for Equal Suffrage," *NYT*, Jan. 16, 1909, and "Woman Suffrage Has Helped," Feb. 27, 1909.

113. See "Mrs. Mackay Quits as Suffrage Head," *NYT*, Apr. 13, 1911, for the news that she was stepping down from the presidency. On the affair and divorce, see " Mrs. Mackay Denies Mrs. Blake's Charge," *NYT*, Sept. 26, 1913; "Mackays Obtain Divorce in Paris," Feb. 19, 1914; "Divorces Dr. Blake on Desertion Plea," Nov. 28, 1914.

114. "Mrs. Mackay Pleads for Equal Suffrage," *NYT*, Jan. 16, 1909.

115. Boyer Scrapbooks, NAWSA Papers, reel 63, vol. 8, p. 96.

116. Ibid., 96.

117. Quotation from Horowitz, *Power and the Passion*, 402.

118. Flexner, *Century of Struggle*, 204.

119. See *Woman Suffrage Arguments and Results*; "For Beginners," *Woman's Journal*, June 3, 1911, through Aug. 26, 1911. Kraditor argued that the new expedient argument allowed white suffragists to focus on their moral superiority and thus their fitness for citizenship over immigrant and minority voters. Louise Newman and Alison Sneider instead argue that racism also undergirded the justice argument. Newman, "Reflections on Aileen Kraditor's Legacy," 290–316; and Sneider, *Suffragists in an Imperial Age*.

Chapter Two

1. Ostrander, "Moderating Contradictions of Feminist Philanthropy," 29–46. Historically, many feminist organizations have not been inclusive in terms of class, race, ethnicity, or sexuality, among other divisions. Scholars have been particularly interested in the divisions of race and ethnicity and bringing working-class women into the movement. There has been less historical focus on the divide between wealthy and middle-class women. On racism in the suffrage movement, see Terborg-Penn, *African American Women in the Struggle for the Vote*; Newman, "Reflections on Aileen Kraditor's Legacy," 290–316.

2. Alter, "Bureaucracy and Democracy in Organizations," 258–71, quotation on 259.

3. Crocker, *Mrs. Russell Sage*, 161–62.

4. For the term "money power" and the Pujo investigation in 1912–13, see Pak, *Gentlemen Bankers*, 27–29.

5. Ostrander, "When Grantees Become Grantors," 257–70, esp. 261.

6. Fraser and Gerstle, "Introduction," 1–26, quotation on 1; Beckert, *Monied Metropolis*.

7. Wallach, *Richest Woman in America*.

8. DuBois, *Harriot Stanton Blatch*, 115–21. Blatch moved away from the working class and toward wealthy recruits after the 1909 Shirtwaist Strike ended.

9. Lunardini, *From Equal Suffrage to Equal Rights*; Zahniser and Fry, *Alice Paul*.

10. Dudden, *Fighting Chance*, chap. 1.

11. Tetrault, "Incorporation of American Feminism," 1027–56, quotation on 1027.

12. Fry, "Conversations with Alice Paul", 87–88.

13. Shaw, *Anna Howard Shaw*, 194–95; Anna Shaw to Thomas, Mar. 22, 1909, Thomas Papers, reel 57.

14. Franzen, *Anna Howard Shaw*, 11–12, 96–102, 106.

15. Anna Shaw to Thomas, May 13, 1910, Thomas Papers, reel 159.

16. Sander, *Mary Elizabeth Garrett*.

17. The average is across eight states. Farr and Liles, "Male Teachers, Male Roles," 234–39, esp. Table 2.

18. Tetrault, "Incorporation of American Feminism," 1027–56.

19. Ibid., 1052.

20. *HWS*, 5:211.

21. *Notable American Women*, 3:278–80; *Pauline Agassiz Shaw: Tributes Paid*.

22. Maud Wood Park, "Mary Hutcheson, Supplementary Notes," Mary Hutcheson Page Papers in the Woman's Rights Collection (WRC), f. 653, Schlesinger.

23. *Pauline Agassiz Shaw: Tributes Paid*.

24. *HWS*, 5:404; Shaw, *Anna Howard Shaw*, 296–97; Anna Shaw to Thomas, July 24, 1914, Thomas Papers, reel 160.

25. Pauline Shaw to Maud Wood Park, Apr. 24, 1905, NAWSA Papers, reel 19.

26. Pauline Shaw to Maud Wood Park, Apr. 18, 1915, NAWSA Papers, reel 19.

27. Graham, *Woman Suffrage and the New Democracy*, 8.

28. Upton, *Harriet Taylor Upton's Random Recollections*, 133.

29. Hoffert, *Alva Vanderbilt Belmont*, 39–40.

30. "A Letter written by Mrs. Belmont to a friend," n.d., NWP-II, reel 113.

31. Harper, a Stanford graduate, was a journalist and author/editor of Susan B. Anthony's official biography and three of the *History of Woman Suffrage* volumes. "Inventory, Ida Harper Research Collection," Vigo County Library, Indiana; Franzen, *Anna Howard Shaw*, 119.

32. Hoffert, *Alva Vanderbilt Belmont*, 71–73, quotation on 73; Geidel, "Alva E. Belmont," 76.

33. Stuart, *Consuelo and Alva Vanderbilt*, 43.

34. In a statement given to the press, Belmont claimed to have given $8,200 in 1910 for rent of both national and state headquarters, and well as her own; $8,000 for partitioning and furnishings; and $12,000 for press bureau expenses, including salaries. "What Mrs. Belmont Has Done for Suffrage," *NYT*, Mar. 9, 1910.

35. Geidel, "Alva E. Belmont," 82–83. The donation would be approximately $180,000 in 2016. Franzen argues that it was Shaw's idea to move headquarters and Belmont's to locate it in New York. *Anna Howard Shaw*, 119–20.

36. Clippings, Boyer Scrapbooks, vol. 6, p. 74.

37. Boyer Scrapbooks, vol. 1, pp. 17, 22, 24; Graham, *Woman Suffrage and the New Democracy*, 36–39.

38. Geidel, "Alva E. Belmont," 88.

39. "Miss Malone Quits the Suffragettes," *NYT*, Mar. 27, 1908.

40. Geidel, "Alva E. Belmont," 88.

41. Thomas to Harriet Upton, Dec. 16, 1909, Thomas Papers, reel 149.

42. "Charges Misuse of Susan Anthony Fund," *NYT*, Aug. 20, 1909.

43. Geidel, "Alva E. Belmont," 88–93, 174–75.

44. Ibid., 196.

45. "Votes for Women," *NYT*, Nov. 7, 1909; clippings, Boyer Scrapbooks, vol. 6, p. 69.

46. Quoted in Geidel, "Alva E. Belmont," 87. Clay had herself received a $5,000 bequest from Laura Bruce, a woman from Lexington, which she had invested and then given to state campaigns. However, this money was not enough to compete with Belmont's generous donations, and it did not empower Clay to make demands, as Belmont did. Fuller, *Laura Clay*, 96.

47. Clippings, Boyer Scrapbooks, vol. 6, p. 74.

48. Ibid.

49. [Catherine McCulloch?] to Thomas, July 4, 1911; Jessie Ashley to Catherine McCulloch, July 18, 1911; and McCulloch to the Official Board, July 22, 1911, Catherine McCulloch Papers, Series 6 of the Mary Earhart Dillon Collection, microfilm, f. 102, Schlesinger.

50. Geidel, "Alva E. Belmont," 242–57.

51. "Charges Misuse of Susan Anthony Fund," *NYT*, Oct. 24, 1911; Franzen, *Anna Howard Shaw*, 134.

52. Fuller, *Laura Clay*, 122–24.

53. Minutes, NAWSA Board, Mar. 13, 1912, NAWSA Papers, reel 58.

54. Thomas to Anna Shaw, Feb. 12, 1912, Thomas Papers, reel 123; MWD to Jane Addams, Mar. 16, 1912, and Addams to MWD, Mar. 20, 1912, MWD Papers, reel 10, f. 210.

55. Peck, "Some American Suffragists," 368–73.

56. Thomas to Anna Shaw, Feb. 12, 1912, Thomas Papers, reel 123; MWD to Jane Addams, Mar. 16, 1912, and Addams to MWD, Mar. 20, 1912, MWD Papers, reel 10, f. 210.

57. Anna Shaw to MWD, Aug. 17, 1912, MWD Papers, reel 10, f. 210.

58. Thomas to Garrett, Apr. 14, 1912, Thomas Papers, reel 25.

59. Minutes, NAWSA Board, June 5 and June 29, 1912, NAWSA Papers, reel 58.

60. Minutes, NAWSA Board, June 5, 1912, NAWSA Papers, reel 58; clipping, Nov. 24, 1912, Maud Wood Park Papers, WRC, scrapbook 1, Schlesinger.

61. Minutes, NAWSA Board, June 29, 1912, NAWSA Papers, reel 58; *Woman's Journal*, Dec. 6, 1913.

62. Minutes of the Annual Convention, NAWSA, 1913, 139–42, MWD Papers, reel 11, f. 220. The equivalents are nearly $150,000 in 2016 to pay off the debt, and annual contributions from approximately $20,000 to $45,000.

63. MWD to the Official Board, Apr. 4, 1914, MWD Papers, reel 11, f. 215.

64. Anna Shaw wrote, "It is the business of the treasurer to raise money." Shaw to Thomas, May 13, 1910, Thomas Papers, reel 159.

65. KDM to Antoinette Funk, Mar. 31, 1915, NAWSA Papers, reel 33; Thomas to Mary Garrett, Feb. 6, 1913, Thomas Papers, reel 26.

66. KDM to Antoinette Funk, Mar. 31, 1915, NAWSA Papers, reel 33.

67. "Miss Paul . . . report" [Dec. 1913], NAWSA Papers, reel 33. To avoid confusion, I have referred to the organization as the CU rather than NWP. See also Zahniser and Fry, *Alice Paul*.

68. "On Militant Women," *NYT*, Apr. 23, 1913.

69. Lunardini, *From Equal Suffrage*, 4–5, 21–2; Fry, *Conversations*, 63–64.

70. Lunardini, *From Equal Suffrage*, 24, 181n16; "Miss Paul's report," [Dec. 1913], NAWSA Papers, reel 33; Harriot Blatch to Lucy Burns, Dec. 22, 1913, NWP-II, reel 1.

71. Lucy Burns to Edith Marsden, Dec. 23, 1913, NWP-I, reel 6. Fry, *Conversations*, 66–69; for the cost estimate, see Zahniser, *Alice Paul*, 141.

72. "Miss Paul . . . report"; and Harriot Blatch to Lucy Burns, Dec. 22, 1913, NWP-II, reel 1. The $12,000 would be just under $300,000 in 2016.

73. Alice Paul to Dora Lewis, Jan. 5, 1914, and Jan. 7, 1914, NWP-I, reel 6.

74. Fry, *Conversations*, 309; Zahniser and Fry, *Alice Paul*, 132.

75. Quoted in Adams and Keene, *Alice Paul and the American Suffrage Campaign*, 79, 82.

76. "Miss Paul . . . report"; Fry, *Conversations*, 98.

77. McCormick, "Statement by Treasurer N.A.W.S.A.," NAWSA Papers, reel 33.

78. "Random Notes taken . . . , Feb. 12, 1914," NAWSA Papers, reel 33; Paul to Katharine Hepburn, Feb. 14, 1914, NWP-I, reel 6.

79. "At the last business session" notes, typescript, Feb. 19, 1914, NAWSA Papers, reel 32.

80. Shaw hoped the states would pay the expenses and NAWSA could pay the salary. Anna Shaw to the Official Board, Jan. 14, 1914, Harriet Laidlaw Papers, Schlesinger.

81. McCormick also tabled a resolution calling for an arbitration committee to mediate between the two. "Suffragists Veto Attack on Congress," *NYT*, June 8, 1915. McCormick also complained that CU efforts to fund-raise for the federal amendment in New York hurt the state movement, which was then working for a state referendum. "Women Organize New Suffrage Move," *NYT*, Apr. 1, 1915.

82. *Chicago Tribune*, Jan. 25, 1914.

83. Hoffert, *Alva Vanderbilt Belmont*, 93; Geidel, "Alva E. Belmont," 395, 404.

84. Belmont to Paul, Jan. 23, 1914, NWP-I, reel 6.

85. Beard to Paul, Dec. (n.d.) 1913, and Jan. 8 and Feb. 4, 1914; Beard to Burns, Jan. 9, 1914, NWP-I, reel 6.

86. Crystal Eastman to Burns, Jan. 9, 1914, NWP-I, reel 6.

87. Eastman to Burns, Jan. 9, 1914, NWP-I, reel 6.

88. Anne Martin to Paul, Jan. 14, 1914, NWP-I, reel 6.

89. Katharine Houghton Hepburn to Edith Houghton Hooker, Jan. 15, 1914, and Hepburn to Paul, Jan. 15, 1914, NWP-I, reel 6.

90. Carrie Catt to Mary Page, June 15, 1900, Mary Page Papers, vol. 23a0, Schlesinger.

91. Belmont to Miss Whittemore, Aug. 31, 1915, NWP-II, reel 113.

92. Geidel, "Alva E. Belmont," 456.

93. Burns to Paul, Mar. 12, 1914; Belmont to Burns, Mar. 3, 1914, NWP-I, reel 8. Notably, Harriot Blatch also wanted an office in New York that would open on the ground floor, while Mackay insisted on the fourth or fifth floor. Blatch recalled, as "Mrs. Mackay was to pay the piper, we . . . bowed to her authority . . . [and] started with utterly useless offices." Blatch, *Challenging Years*, 120.

94. Beard to Burns, Mar. 15, 1914, and Burns to Beard, Mar. 16, 1914, NWP-I, reel 8.

95. Geidel, "Alva E. Belmont," 501.

96. Keeler, "Alva Belmont," 25–26; Geidel, "Alva E. Belmont," 124–26.

97. Fry, *Conversations.*

98. Hoffert, *Alva Vanderbilt Belmont,* 98–99.

99. More significant differences did not arise until after suffrage was won, when Belmont assumed the presidency of the NWP and pushed it into international directions, at odds with Paul's new focus on the equal rights amendment. Hoffert, *Alva Vanderbilt Belmont,* 145–74.

100. Douglas Ewbank, "Powelton's Suffragettes," *Powelton History Blog,* Jan. 20, 2014, http://poweltonhistoryblog.blogspot.com/2014/01/poweltons-suffragettes.html; Katzenstein, *Lifting the Curtain,* 135.

101. Katzenstein, *Lifting the Curtain,* 154.

102. Alice Paul to Mary Burnham, June 12, 1914, reprinted in Katzenstein, *Lifting the Curtain,* 136–37.

103. Krone, "Dauntless Women," 169.

104. Ibid.

105. Dora Kelly Lewis to Louise Lewis, Jan. 10, 1919, Historical Society of Pennsylvania, Philadelphia, Dora Kelly Lewis Correspondence, collection 2137, box 1, f.: Correspondence 1919.

106. This ability to assuage donors went hand in hand with her ability to compromise when necessary in order to make expedient decisions, a trait described in Zahniser and Fry, *Alice Paul,* 139.

107. MWD to Anna Shaw, Sept. 1, 1914, in MWD Papers, box 12, f. 214; MWD to the Board, Oct. 15, 1914, in MWD Papers, box 12, f. 213; Shaw to Thomas, Aug. 14, 1914, Thomas Papers, reel 57, and Shaw to Thomas, Nov. 3, 1914, Thomas Papers, reel 160. While NAWSA officially stopped paying Shaw's salary after the Garrett-Thomas fund ended in 1912, it appears that Thomas was still raising money to pay Shaw. Franzen, *Anna Howard Shaw,* 153.

108. KDM to WWD, Oct. 15, 1914, in MWD Papers, box 12, f. 213; KDM to MWD, Feb. 4, 1915, in MWD Papers, box 12, f. 215.

109. Harriet Upton to Cora Smith King, Oct. 21, 1912, quoted in Franzen, *Anna Howard Shaw,* 142.

110. Geidel, "Alva E. Belmont," 78; Keeler, "Alva Belmont," 23.

111. Katharine McCormick to Laura Morgan, Nov. 13, 1915, Laura Morgan and Ethel Howes Papers, box 1, f. 13, Schlesinger.

112. Anna Shaw to Thomas, Easter 1914, and Dec. 2 and Dec. 12, 1916, Thomas Papers, reel 57.

113. See McCormick's report on war work in *HWS,* 5:720–40.

114. Rose Young, *The Record of the Leslie Woman Suffrage Commission, In., 1917–1929,* 58–60; "Statement of Income and Expenses," Minutes, LWSC, vol. 3, reel 45.

115. Harriet Upton to Paul, Sept. 5, 1914, NWP-II, reel 1.

116. Strom, *Political Woman,* 93.

117. DuBois, *Harriot Stanton Blatch,* 162; "Break in Suffrage Ranks," *NYT,* Feb. 26, 1915.

118. Alice Paul to MWD, Dec. 16, 1913, NWP-I, reel 6.

119. [Catt], "To the incorporators," n.d., Minutes, LWSC, vol. 1, reel 44.

120. Minutes, LWSC, vol. 1, reel 44.

121. Harriet Upton to Paul, Sept. 5, 1914, NWP-II, reel 1.

122. Minutes, Nov. 7, 1918, and May 31, 1919, LWSC vol. 2 and Minutes, June 29, 1929, LWSC, vol. 3, reel 45; "Annual Report of the New York State Woman Suffrage Party," 1917, NAWSA Papers, reel 72.

123. Graham, *Woman Suffrage and the New Democracy*, 92–94.

124. Upton, *Harriet Taylor Upton's Random Recollections*, 154.

125. Finnegan, *Selling Suffrage*, 147.

126. [Catt], "To the incorporators."

127. "Leslie Woman Suffrage Commission Services," in Minutes, LWSC, vol. 1, reel 44.

128. June 25, 1917, Minutes, LWSC, vol. 1, reel 44.

129. Katherine Mackay paid for parade costs (see chapter 1) and salaries for three publicity workers. DuBois, *Harriet Stanton Blatch*, 112; Belmont paid Ida Harper's salary (see below).

130. Agnes Ryan to Catt, Aug. 5, 1916, NAWSA Papers, reel 12.

131. Alice Paul to Alice Stone Blackwell, May 7, 1913, and Minnie Brook, "Dear Suffragist," June 23, 1913, NAWSA Papers, reel 32; Lunardini, *From Equal Suffrage to Equal Rights*, 39, 183n22. Interestingly, the WTUL also launched its newspaper, *Life and Labor*, around the same time, and it, too, struggled to make ends meet. Kirkby, "Class, Gender and the Perils of Philanthropy," 36–51.

132. Young, *Leslie Commission*; "Statement of Income and Assets," Minutes, LWSC, vol. 3, reel 45; Ryan, *Torch Bearer*.

133. Minutes, July 17, 1929, and "Statement of Income and Assets," LWSC, vol. 3, reel 45; Young, *Leslie Commission*, 89–94.

134. Fry, *Conversations with Alice Paul*, 201.

135. Peter Geidel, while arguing that Belmont's integral role in the suffrage movement has been largely ignored by historians, concedes that Catt's winning plan and the Leslie bequest made it so that Belmont and the CU played a less significant role in the final push for the amendment. Geidel, "Alva E. Belmont," 586.

136. Graham, *Woman Suffrage and the New Democracy*, 94.

Chapter Three

1. Pauline Newman to Rose Schneiderman, Dec. 9, 1911, Schneiderman Papers, reel 1.

2. Dye, *As Equals and as Sisters*; Jacoby, *British and American Women's Trade Union Leagues*; Deutsch, "Learning to Talk More Like a Man," 379–404.

3. Freedman, *No Turning Back*, 76.

4. Addams, *Democracy and Social Ethics*; Friedman, "Philanthropy in America," 1–9.

5. On economic independence, see Vapnek, *Breadwinners*.

6. Jane Addams discussed these difficulties when she criticized benefactors who did not involve recipients in decision making. Addams, *Democracy and Social Ethics*. See also Ostrander, "When Grantees Become Grantors," 257–70.

7. Fraser and Gerstle, "Introduction," 1–26.

8. On feminism as nonhierarchical, see Ostrander, "Moderating Contradictions of Feminist Philanthropy," 29–46.

9. Gross, "Giving in America," 29–48.

10. Huyssen, *Progressive Inequality*, 1–9; DuBois, *Harriot Stanton Blatch*, 111.

11. Sander, *Business of Charity*.

12. Storrs, *Civilizing Capitalism*; Vapnek, *Breadwinners*, 66–101.

13. Kessler-Harris, *Out to Work*; Chesler, *Woman of Valor*, 81.

14. Tax, *Rising of Women*, 95; Dye, *As Equals*, 63–67.

15. Historians also note that reformers may have mitigated the worst excesses of industrial greed and thus served to perpetuate it. Dawley, "The Abortive Rule of Big Money," 168.

16. On the formation of the bourgeois class, with emphasis on the growing labor unrest, see Beckert, *Monied Metropolis*.

17. Katz, "Grace Hoadley Dodge," 9.

18. Edwin Wildman, "What Grace Dodge Has Done for the Working Girl," Dec. 1910, Dodge Papers, box 1, f. 1.

19. Katz, "Grace Hoadley Dodge," 3, 20–21; Graham, *Grace H. Dodge*, 56–60.

20. Cross, "Philanthropic Contribution of Louisa Lee Schuyler," 290–301.

21. Katz, "Grace Hoadley Dodge," 51–55.

22. Murolo, *Common Ground of Womanhood*, 10.

23. Katz, "Grace Hoadley Dodge," 58.

24. Murolo, *Common Ground of Womanhood*, 18–19.

25. Ibid., 100–43. She argues that Dodge was so "dismayed" by the focus on labor issues that she cut back her work in the association (106).

26. Graham, *Grace H. Dodge*, 270–71.

27. Receipts acknowledging $2,500 from Grace Dodge, May 6, 1907, in Thomas Papers, reel 57. "Not Room for All Who Came, *NYT*, May 4; "Mrs. Schieren Has Signed," May 5, 1894; "Woman and the Public Schools," Jan. 11, 1895. See also "Suffragists Pose in the "Antis' Yard," *NYT*, Apr. 30, 1913, which reported that the Municipal League members who were suffragists included Grace Dodge, Mary Dreier, Margaret Dreier Robins, Josephine Lowell, and Mrs. Richard Aldrich.

28. Grace Hoadley Dodge, *A Bundle of Letters to Busy Girls on Practical Matters* (1887); "Practical Suggestions Relating to Moral Elevation and Preventive Work among Girls," *Association Monthly*, Mar. 1915 (originally written in 1885); "A Private Letter to Girls," (1889), in Dodge Papers, box 2, f. 10.

29. Murolo, *Common Ground of Womanhood*, 33.

30. See, for example, Dodge's letter to the New York YWCA, printed in the *Newburg [New York] Journal*, Feb. 18, 1889, in Dodge Papers, box 2, f. 12.

31. Dreier, *Margaret Dreier Robins*, 35, 116.

32. "Sisterhood and Cooperation," Scrapbook, Dodge Papers, box 3, f. 1, and "Working for the Good of Others," clipping, *National Baptist,* Jan. 4, 1883, scrapbook, Dodge Papers, box 3, f. 1.

33. Quotation in Graham, *Grace H. Dodge,* 98.

34. Annual meeting, Dec. 5, 1907, typescript, Dodge Papers, box 2, f. 10.

35. Katz, "Grace Hoadley Dodge," 3–4.

36. Mabel Cratty, "The Fine Profession of Being a Laywoman," in Dodge Papers, box 1, f. 2. Cratty was general secretary in the YWCA and worked closely with Dodge for ten years.

37. Annual meeting, Dec. 5, 1907, typescript, Dodge Papers, box 2, f. 10.

38. Wildman, "What Grace Dodge Has Done."

39. 1873 report from Conference of Associations in Philadelphia, in Mary S. Sims, *The Natural History of a Social Institution: The Y.W.C.A.* (New York: Womans Press, 1936), 18.

40. Dodge, "Practical Suggestions Relating to Moral Elevation."

41. Katz, "Grace Hoadley Dodge," 65–66.

42. Annual Meeting, Dec. 5, 1907, typescript, Dodge Papers, box 2, f. 10.

43. Graham, *Grace H. Dodge,* 258–61.

44. Dodge, "Wages in Advance," *Independent,* May 7, [?] Dodge Papers, box 2, f. 12; Lagemann, *Generation of Women,* 22–23.

45. Dodge, "Wages in Advance."

46. Cratty, "The Fine Profession of Being a Laywoman."

47. Mabel Cratty, "Miss Dodge in Relation to Those with Whom She Worked," Dodge Papers, box 1, f. 3.

48. Dodge to Miss Thorburn, Dec. 16, 1914, YWCA Papers, box 35, f. 18.

49. Graham, *Grace H. Dodge,* 211–12.

50. Ibid., 263.

51. Andrew Carnegie, "Wealth," *North American Review* 148 (June 1889): 653–65, and "Wealth," *North American Review* 149 (Dec. 1889): 82–99.

52. Murolo, *Common Ground of Womanhood,* 18.

53. Mary Kenney O'Sullivan, unpublished autobiography, typescript, WTUL Papers, series 13, 62.

54. "A Brief History of the YWCA and Its Work with Employed Women," 1953, YWCA Papers, box. 1, f. 7.

55. Dodge to Mrs. J. S. Griffith, Feb. 19, 1906, YWCA Papers, Box 90, f. 10.

56. Her donations from 1907 through 1914 were $48,400, $37,650, $49,985, $56,803, $54,378, $65,112, $94,039, and $98,233. "National Board of the Young Woman's Christian Association of the United States of America, Total Expenditures," in YWCA Papers, box 43, f. 14; "The Grace H. Dodge Memorial Endowment Fund for the National Board of the Young Woman's Christian Association," Dodge Papers, box 2, f. 1.

57. Robertson, *Christian Sisterhood.*

58. *NYT,* Jan. 5, 1915.

59. "National Board of the YWCA Budget, 1907–1908," box 95, f. 1; "To Meet the Budget," 1907, YWCA Papers, box 224, f. 1.

60. See entries in *Notable American Women* for biographical info.

61. Salzman, *Reform and Revolution*, 83.

62. MED to MDR, Jan. 11, 1911, MDR Papers, reel 22. For references to readings on "the great Woman's question," see also Katherine Dreier to MDR, Jan. 11, 1911, MDR Papers, reel 22.

63. Dye, *As Equals*, 122. Mary Dreier, for example, donated $1,425 to the New York referendum campaign. "Annual Report of the New York State Woman Suffrage Party," 1917, NAWSA Papers, reel 72.

64. Margaret Dreier Robins, editorial, *Life and Labor*, Mar. 1911, p. 1; Margaret Dreier Robins, "The Minimum Wage," *Life and Labor*, June 1913, 168–72; Payne, *Reform, Labor, and Feminism*, 123–24.

65. On the strike, see Glenn, *Daughters of the Shtetl*, 167–206; Enstad, *Ladies of Labor, Girls of Adventure*, 84–160; Orleck, *Common Sense*, 53–80; Dye, *As Equals*, 88–109. The link is not surprising, given that Harriot Stanton Blatch, who recruited many wealthy women into the suffrage movement, had been an extremely active member of the WTUL before the strike. DuBois, *Harriot Stanton Blatch*, 93–94, 116–21.

66. Schneiderman, *All for One*, 8. See also "Girl Strikers Tell the Rich Their Woes," *NYT*, Dec. 16, 1909, and "Rich Women's Aid Gives Strikers Hope," *NYT*, Dec. 17, 1909, and "The Rich Out to Aid Girl Waistmakers," *NYT*, Jan. 3, 1910, for coverage that stressed the new hope strikers gained from support of wealthy women including Anne Morgan and Alva Belmont.

67. Orleck, *Common Sense*, 62; Huyssen, *Progressive Inequality*.

68. Ida Tarbell, introduction to *Carola Woerishoffer: Her Life and Work*, by the Class of 1907 of Bryn Mawr College (Bryn Mawr, Pa.: printed by author, 1912), 11–12.

69. Tarbell, introduction, 22–25; Dye, *As Equals*, 43.

70. Class of 1907 of Bryn Mawr College, *Carola Woerishoffer*, 99–100.

71. On the involvement of Morgan and Belmont, see MDR to MED, Nov. 26, 1909, and MED to MDR, Dec. 17, 1909, MDR Papers, reel 21. See chapters 1 and 2 for an extended discussion of Belmont.

72. Dreier, *Margaret Dreier Robins*, 128; for the 1922 campaign for the WTUL headquarters, see Lash, *Eleanor and Franklin*, 280–81. Eleanor Roosevelt, introduced to the WTUL by suffragist Mrs. James Lee Laidlaw, met Rose Schneiderman at a tea given by Straight while fund-raising for the headquarters. Eleanor helped raise the additional $35,000 needed to pay off the mortgage.

73. Enstad, *Ladies of Labor*, 84–118.

74. Elizabeth Thomas to LOR, Jan. 6, [1910?], LOR Papers, microfilm, reel 5.

75. Dye, *As Equals*, 93. Furthermore, historian David Huyssen argues that in contrast to Belmont's mass meeting at the Hippodrome, which had the possibility of uniting women on the basis of their needs as a sex, Morgan's tea at the Colony Club put the strikers on display, soliciting wealthy women for support. "Suffragists to Aid Girl Waist Strikers," *NYT*, Dec. 2; and "Girl Strikers Tell Rich Their Woes," "Girl Strikers Tell Rich Their Woes," *NYT*, Dec. 16, 1909; Huyssen, *Progressive Inequality*, 174–225.

76. Young, *Elmhirsts of Dartington*, 33–96.

77. Dye, *As Equals*, 12, 16.

78. Dreier, *Margaret Dreier Robins*, 22.

79. Olive Sullivan, "Margaret Dreier Robins," MDR Papers, reel 1.

80. MDR, "Domestic Service," MDR Papers, reel 1.

81. MDR, "Democracy," MDR Papers, reel 1.

82. Margaret Dreier Robins, "Presidential Address," *Life and Labor*, Sept. 1911, 278–80, quotation on 280.

83. Clipping, *Brooklyn Eagle*, Mar. 28, 1905, MDR Papers, reel 1.

84. Margaret Dreier Robins, "The President's Report," *Second Biennial Convention of the National Women's Trade Union League of America, Report of Proceedings, 1909*, 4–6.

85. MED to MDR, Jan. 1911, MDR Papers, reel 22.

86. MED to MDR, May 18, 1911, MDR Papers, reel 22; Dye, *As Equals*, 98.

87. Dye, *As Equals*, 46.

88. Jane Addams also initially focused on culture over economics.

89. Dye, "Creating a Feminist Alliance," 25.

90. Laura Elliot to LOR, Mar. 1911, LOR Papers, reel 5.

91. Leonora O'Reilly to "Mother," n.d. (1900), LOR Papers, reel 3.

92. O'Reilly, handwritten notes on the back of English Walling to O'Reilly, Dec. 17, 1903, LOR Papers, reel 4.

93. Dye, "Creating a Feminist Alliance," 28.

94. Dye, *As Equals*, 130–31.

95. Orleck, *Common Sense and a Little Fire*, 96; Vapnek, *Breadwinners*, 144.

96. Rose Schneiderman, *All for One* (New York: Paul S. Eriksson, 1967), 77.

97. Dye, "Creating a Feminist Alliance," 30.

98. The average age of the allies was forty; the average age of the workers, twenty-eight. Payne, *Reform, Labor, and Feminism*, 56–57.

99. Dye, *As Equals*, 45.

100. Dye, "Creating a Feminist Alliance," 34–35.

101. LOR to Lady Franklin, Feb. 22, 1912, LOR Papers, reel 6.

102. Equivalency found using www.davemanuel.com/inflation-calculator.php.

103. Dreier, *Margaret Dreier Robins*, 31.

104. Payne, *Reform, Labor, and Feminism*, 34.

105. MDR to MED, Sept. 18, 1908, MDR papers, reel 20.

106. MDR to MED, May 27, 1921, MDR Papers, reel 26.

107. Tax, *Rising of Women*, 115. Robins gave the Chicago League $1,200 annually. Mary Anderson to Robins, Nov. 14 and Nov. 18, 1915, MDR Papers, reel 23.

108. Dreier to MDR, May 23, 1911, MDR Papers, reel 22.

109. Payne, *Reform, Labor, and Feminism*, 100.

110. MED to MDR, Jan. 1911, MDR Papers, reel 22.

111. MED to MDR, Aug. 18, 1915, MDR Papers, reel 23.

112. MED to MDR, Jan. 31, 1911, MDR Papers, reel 22. Mary Kehew was the daughter of a banker and the wife of an oil merchant. Payne, *Reform, Labor, and Feminism*, 50–51.

113. Newman to Schneiderman, Dec. 9, 1911, Schneiderman Papers.

114. Jacoby, *British and American Women's Trade Union Leagues,* 55, 62; Payne, *Reform, Labor, and Feminism,* 59–60.

115. Kirkby, "Class, Gender and the Perils of Philanthropy," 36–51.

116. MDR to MED, Jan. 9, 1915, MDR Papers, reel 23; Kirkby, "Class, Gender and the Perils of Philanthropy," 43–45; Jacoby, *British and American Women's Trade Union Leagues,* 42–50.

117. MDR to MED, Jan. 17, 1915, MDR Papers, reel 23.

118. MDR to MED, Jan. 22, 1915, and Olive Sullivan to Mary, Feb. 8, 1915, MDR Papers, reel 23. She also reassured Mary on Feb. 13, 1915, that she would not do any fundraising for the magazine in New York but would have to approach Chicago and western donors instead.

119. Quoted in Jacoby, *British and American Women's Trade Union Leagues,* 48.

120. MED to MDR, Aug. 18, 1915, MDR Papers, reel 23.

121. Payne, *Reform, Labor, and Feminism,* 17.

122. Dreier, *Margaret Dreier Robins,* 148. The contributor was Helen Gould Shepard, who withdrew a $4,000 contribution. But Abby Aldrich and John D. Rockefeller announced a $500,000 donation, mitigating the effect of Shepard's decision. Robertson, *Christian Sisterhood,* 74–80.

123. Orleck, *Common Sense,* 44; Dye, *As Equals,* 37.

124. LOR to Mother, July 23, 1903, and July 1903, LOR Papers, reel 3.

125. MED to LOR, Jan. 16, 1908, LOR Papers, reel 4. They did disagree, although they also clearly loved each other deeply. See MED to LOR, May 2, 1910, MED to LOR, Apr. 18, 1911, and Melinda Scott to LOR, May 9, 1910, LOR Papers, reel 5.

126. See entries in *Notable American Women* for biographical info.

127. May 12, 1869, in *The Selected Papers of Elizabeth Cady Stanton and Susan B. Anthony,* ed. Ann D. Gordon, vol. 2, *Against an Aristocracy of Sex, 1866–1873* (New Brunswick, N.J.: Rutgers University Press, 2000), 239–40.

128. Zelizer, "Social Meaning of Money," 362–65.

129. Quoted in Dye, *As Equals,* 56.

130. Dye, *As Equals,* 9; Cott, *Grounding of Modern Feminism,* 118–19; Vapnek, *Breadwinners,* 1–3.

131. Dye, *As Equals,* 9.

132. Malkiel, *Diary of a Shirtwaist Striker,* 132.

Chapter Four

1. Quesnell, *Strange Disappearance,* 67, 127–50.

2. They argued that the influx of philanthropy in education succeeded in transforming colleges into universities, broadening curriculums from the classical to include engineering and business management, and establishing schools for women and African Americans. Curti and Nash, *Philanthropy and the Shaping of American Higher Education;* Goodspeed, *History of the University of Chicago;* Bishop, *History of Cornell University.*

3. Curti and Nash, *Philanthropy and Higher Education*, 89–106. Curti and Nash disapproved of too much intervention by donors, concluding that colleges and universities were better off when being run by their presidents and administrators without too much interference. Of the Seven Sister colleges (seen as the women's equivalent of the then male Ivy League schools), Smith is the only one both founded and funded by one woman. According to histories of Wellesley, founded by Henry and Pauline Durant after the death of their son, both took an active interest in the building and running of the school, although Henry's role overshadowed Pauline's. After his death, she took his position as college treasurer from 1881 to 1895, and until her death, she continued to give generously and attend college events, as well as to make decisions that presidents Alice Freeman and Julia Irvine complained should have been left to the president. Irvine only agreed to take the job in 1895 when Pauline resigned as treasurer. Glasscock, *Wellesley College*, 4–6, 45–47; Florence Converse, *Story of Wellesley*, 6–7, 37–38, 53. Mount Holyoke was founded by Mary Lyon through a fund-raising campaign, as she did not have the means herself. Barnard and Radcliffe were both cooperative efforts established by groups of mostly women and a few men. In New York, Annie Nathan Meyer, not wealthy enough herself to fund the effort, reached out to wealthy women and men to create a women's college at Columbia. For Radcliffe, see chapter 5.

4. For a more in-depth exploration of this approach to Newcomb and Stanford, see Joan Marie Johnson, "College Founders Josephine Newcomb and Jane Stanford: Bereaved Mothers, Grieving Widows, Powerful Women" (unpublished article in possession of the author). For works that diminished their roles, see Hanscom and Greene, *Sophia Smith and the Beginnings of Smith College*, which is based largely on the unpublished journal and notes of John Green; Dyer, *Tulane*; and Orrin Leslie Elliott, *Stanford University*. On the rewriting of Smith's story, see Quesnell, *Strange Disappearance*, and Bradley, "Smith College Trilogy."

5. On women and higher education, see McCandless, *Past in the Present*; Lynn D. Gordon, *Gender and Higher Education in the Progressive Era*; Horowitz, *Power and Passion of M. Carey Thomas*; Solomon, *In the Company of Educated Women*. On women's colleges as incubators of women social scientists, see Dzuback, "Gender and the Politics of Knowledge," 171–95.

6. For an emphasis on using philanthropy (of time and money) as a parallel structure of power and institutions, see McCarthy, *Lady Bountiful Revisited*; Scott, *Natural Allies*.

7. *HWS*, 1:742–43.

8. Walton, "Rethinking Boundaries," 29–57, quotations on 30, 32. See also her edited collection, *Women and Philanthropy in Education*; Sander, *Mary Elizabeth Garrett*; Simari, "Philanthropy and Higher Education."

9. Olivia Sage provides another example of this approach. She gave millions to men's, coeducational, and women's liberal arts colleges, in addition to funding a teachers' college at Syracuse University; supporting the New York School of Applied Design for Women, the Pennsylvania School of Horticulture for Women, and the New York

University Woman's Law Class (see next chapter for more on this); and giving money to institutions that housed working women. Crocker, "From Gift to Foundation," 199–215, esp. 208.

10. Joan Marie Johnson, *Southern Women at the Seven Sister Colleges*, 14–17.

11. She attended school in either Connecticut or Vermont. Quesnell, *Strange Disappearance*, 2.

12. Quesnell, *Strange Disappearance*; Seelye, *Early History of Smith College*; Hanscomb and Greene, *Sophia Smith and the Beginnings of Smith College*; Davis, *Miss Sophia's Legacy*. See also William Greenwood to John Greene, July 27, 1875, and Charles Smith to John Greene, July 29, 1875, for accounts that stress her plainness and submissiveness to her sister, clio.fivecolleges.edu/Smith/origins/beginnings/, accessed July 17, 2014.

13. Whitley, *Indiana Fletcher Williams of Sweet Briar*.

14. Rose Keller, "Josephine Louise Newcomb," typescript, Josephine Newcomb Papers, Newcomb College Archives; Wedell, "Founding Newcomb College."

15. Britt, *Ellen Browning Scripps*.

16. Nagel, *Iron Will*; Orrin Leslie Elliott, *Stanford University*; Nilan, "Jane Lathrop Stanford and the Domestication of Stanford University," 7–30; Jordan, *Story of a Good Woman*.

17. Will and Executive Inventory, Sophia Smith Papers, College Archives, Smith College (Smith Papers), box 25, f. 21. Inflation values to 2016 calculated on www.davemanuel.com/inflation-calculator.php.

18. Wedell, "Founding Newcomb College." Much of Josephine Newcomb's correspondence is reprinted in the bound court volumes from the case surrounding her bequest to Newcomb College/Tulane University, copies of which are located in the archives at Tulane University Law School. Handwritten originals of some of these letters are in the McConnell Papers, Tulane University Archives, New Orleans. The inheritance would be worth nearly $7.5 million in 2016.

19. Susan B. Anthony to Jane Stanford, Jan. 29, 1894; Nagel, *Iron Will*, 6.

20. See letters in Nagel, *Iron Will*, 74–77, 97–101; JLS to Crocker, Feb. 4, 1897, JLS Papers, series 1, box 1, f. 28; Berner, *Mrs. Leland Stanford*, 101–2.

21. Whitley, *Indiana Fletcher Williams*.

22. Britt, *Ellen Browning Scripps*, 85.

23. Ibid., 25.

24. Quesnell, *Strange Disappearance*, 34–37; journal extracts, Smith Papers, box 26.

25. JLN to Johnston, May 8, 1899, and JLN to Brandt Dixon, Aug. 8, 1890, in New York Supreme Court Appellate Division, *Brief on Behalf of Respondent Brandt V. B. Dixon, (NY) in the Matter of the Estate of Josephine Louise Newcomb, Deceased*, Tulane University Law School.

26. See clipping, Stanford Family scrapbooks, University Archives, Stanford University, vol. 2, pp. 4, 13–15, 45; vol. 3, p. 58.

27. EBS to EWS, July 10, 1890, in Scripps Papers, box 1, f. 57.

28. EWS to EBS, Feb. 23, 1918, Scripps Papers, box 2, f. 51.

29. Britt, *Ellen Browning Scripps*, 75.

30. Elijah Fletcher to Jesse Fletcher, Oct. 1810, and Elijah Fletcher to Calvin Fletcher, Mar. 13, 1842, in Maria von Briesen, ed., *The Letters of Elijah Fletcher* (Charlottesville: University Press of Virginia, 1965), 16, 181.

31. Quesnell, *Strange Disappearance*, 38–41, 44–47; Sophia Smith, journal, Smith Papers, box 26.

32. John Greene to Sophia Smith, Mar. 9, 1869, and Apr. 5, 1869; John Greene to Nina Brown, Apr. 1, 1904; and Mary Eastman to T. W. Higginson, Jan. 28, 1890, in the online collection, Smith College Founding Documents, clio.fivecolleges.edu/Smith/origins/beginnings/.

33. Sophia Smith, journal, Smith Papers, Oct. 3, 1869.

34. Quesnell, *Strange Disappearance*, 58–59.

35. Marion Billings, "Sophia Smith," Smith Papers, Smith, box 25, f. 26.

36. Wittig, "Reflections of Sorrow and Hope," 2–3, 11–13.

37. Wedell, "Founding Newcomb College," 27.

38. JLN to "My dear Sister," in New York Supreme Court Appellate Division, *Record on Appeal*, vol. 3.

39. JLN to [brother] William Le Monnier, July 9, 1868, in New York Supreme Court Appellate Division, *Record on Appeal*, vol. 3.

40. Gordon, "Sophie Newcomb and Agnes Scott Colleges," 60.

41. Theodore Dreiser to EBS, June 25, 1931 (handwritten notation: "$100, July 7, 1931"), Scripps Papers, box 25, f. 10.

42. A. M. McCuskey to EBS, Dec. 4, 1908, Scripps Papers, box 25, f.19. See also her donation of $1,250 to the NWP, "List of Contributors from Beginning of Organization to Dec. 31, 1920," NWP-II reel 126.

43. EBS, "Paper Read Before the Club," May 13, 1918, Scripps Papers, box 22, f. 23.

44. "Address of Miss Mary B. Eyre at Scripps College Convocation, 1935," Scripps Papers, box 1, f. 1.

45. Anthony dedication reprinted in Nagel, *Iron Will*, 5; Jane Stanford to David Jordan, Oct. 23, 1896, JLS Papers, series 1, box 2, f. 17.

46. Jane Stanford to Susan B. Anthony, Sept. 8, 1896, and Susan B. Anthony to Jane Stanford, Sept. 9, 1896, JLS Papers, series 1, box 3, f. 5.

47. Joan Marie Johnson, *Southern Women at the Seven Sister Colleges*.

48. "Regarding Ernest Johnson," *Stanford*, Nov.–Dec. 2004, https://alumni.stanford.edu/get/page/magazine/article/?article_id=35525. It is not clear how many black students were admitted between Johnson in 1891 and the 1960s, following a 1957 university commitment prohibiting racial and religious discrimination. Scripps College did not have a policy against admitting black students, and Pomona College had its first black graduate as early as 1904. However, how many blacks attended Scripps in its early days is not clear.

49. "Slave Cemetery," African-American Heritage at Sweet Briar, accessed Apr. 1, 2016, http://tusculum.sbc.edu/africanamericans/slavecemetery.shtml; Whitley, *Indiana Fletcher Williams*, 2, 7.

50. Quesnell, *Strange Disappearance*, 67, 127–50.

51. Seelye, *Early History of Smith College*, 224–25, and *Addresses at the Inauguration of Rev. L. Clark Seelye*, 4, 26, 27.

52. Quesnell, *Strange Disappearance*, xviii.

53. See Quesnell, *Strange Disappearance*, for an explanation of Greene's tactics and motives.

54. "Will of Indiana Fletcher Williams"; Whitley, *Indiana Fletcher Williams*.

55. In spring 2015, the administration of Sweet Briar College announced that despite retaining over $80 million in its endowment, the school would soon be bankrupt and was to be closed. At question in part was whether the decision follows the will of Williams, and how the remaining endowment should be dispersed, according to the terms of the will. The school raised funds and remains open at press time.

56. EBS to William E. Scripps, Dec. 4, 1928; copy in Patricia Schaelchlin Papers, Scripps College Archives, box 39, f. 71.

57. McClain, preface to *The Bishop's School*.

58. James Blaisdell to EBS, Sept. 5, 1914, and EBS to Blaisdell, Sept. 24, 1914, Scripps Papers, box 1, f. 73.

59. Blaisdell to EBS, Oct. 29, 1919, Scripps Papers, box 30, f. 32.

60. "To Trustees," 1926, Scripps Papers, box 31, f. 4. She gave over $1.5 million in donations and one thousand shares of Detroit News stock (1/4 of her holdings) and the approximately $25,000 in dividends it provided annually until her death. The stock was to provide an endowment for the school, while the other donations provided for the land and most of the funding for four dormitories. "Contributions by Miss Scripps," Scripps Papers, box 30, f. 36.

61. Minutes of the Board, 1926, Scripps Papers, box 31, f. 9.

62. EBS to Mrs. Johnson, Sept. 24, 1926, Scripps Papers, box 1, f. 10.

63. Ernest Jaqua, "Annual Report," 1933, Scripps Papers, box 1, f. 10.

64. See, for example, Jaqua to EBS, Aug. 18, 1926; Feb. 10, 1927; and Sept. 15, 1928, Scripps Papers, box 1, f. 93.

65. Harper to Jaqua, Dec. 30, 1930, and correspondence between the two from 1927 to 1932, Scripps Papers, box 28, ff. 14–17.

66. "Scripps College Aims and Needs," 1936, Scripps Papers, box 32, f. 33, p. 51; Harper to Jaqua, Mar. 6, 1931, and Apr. 6, 1931, Scripps Papers, box 28, f. 17.

67. JLN to Ida Richardson, Dec. 28, 1881, in New York Supreme Court, Appellate Division, *Brief on Behalf of Respondent Brandt V. B. Dixon*.

68. JLN to Colonel William Preston Johnston, 8th day of Lent, 1886 New York Supreme Court, Appellate Division, *Brief on Behalf of Respondent Brandt V. B. Dixon*. Worth approximately $2.5 million in 2016.

69. JLN to Johnston, 8th day of Lent, 1886; Tucker and Willinger, "Part I: Beginnings," 3–4.

70. Dixon, *Brief History*, 36–37.

71. JLN to Johnston, June 30, 1892, McConnell Papers, box 40, f. 1.

72. JLN to Johnston, Oct. 18, 1890; June 15, 1891; June 30, 1892; June 28, 1897; and July 10, 1897, and JLN to Dixon, June 15, 1891; June 28, 1897; and July 24, 1899, McCon-

nell Papers, box 30, f. 3. See also the testimony in New York Supreme Court Appellate Division, *Brief on Behalf of Respondent Brandt V. B. Dixon.*

73. JLN to Administrators of the Tulane Educational Fund, Oct. 11, 1886, quoted in Dixon, *Brief History,* 9–11.

74. Dyer, *Tulane,* 58.

75. Tucker and Willinger, "Part 1: Beginnings," 10–13; Tucker and Willinger, "Lives," 271.

76. Dixon, *Brief History,* 11, 35, 85, 89; JLN to Johnston, Tenth Day of Lent, 1887, and Apr. 18, 1888, in New York Supreme Court, Appellate Division, *William H. Henderson et al v. Estate of Josephine Louise Newcomb,* 52.

77. Dyer, *Tulane,* 94. See Johnson, "College Founders."

78. Callender to Dixon, n.d., Brandt Dixon Papers, University Archives, Tulane University, f. 5.

79. Dixon, *Brief History,* 103, 108, 110–13.

80. See letters and also Dyer, *Tulane,* 101, 116–17.

81. Mohr, "Coming Together (and Falling Apart)," 53–92.

82. Berner, *Mrs. Leland Stanford,* 34. Orrin Leslie Elliott, *Stanford University.*

83. Jane Stanford, manuscript, Nov. 1, 1898, in Nagel, *Iron Will,* 60–61.

84. Jane Stanford to David Jordan, Dec. 16, 1899, JLS Papers, series 1, box 2, f. 23.

85. Eliot quoted in Nilan, "Tenacious and Courageous Jane L. Stanford," 3.

86. Jordan, *Story of a Good Woman,* 7.

87. Berner, *Mrs. Leland Stanford,* 45; JLS to Orrin Elliott, Jan. 28, 1900, JLS Papers, series 1, box 2, f. 1. Trustee George Crothers, her dear friend and trusted adviser, claimed that she said she "caused" her husband to admit women. Crothers, *Founding of the Leland Stanford Junior University,* 35. Nagel says that she "had convinced her husband" to admit women. *Iron Will,* 2. Leland assured Jordan there would be space for eighty girls by Oct. 1. Leland Stanford to Jordan, May 21, 1891 (telegram), Leland Stanford Papers, University Archives, Stanford University, series 6, box 1, f. 1.

88. Said in 1901 when NAWSA met in San Francisco and quoted in Nagel, *Iron Will,* 4.

89. Ellen Coit Elliott, *It Happened This Way,* 206–7.

90. Nilan, "Jane Lathrop Stanford," 25–26. Orrin Leslie Elliott, *Stanford University,* 132–33. Jordan claimed that eastern businessmen who had graduated from Harvard or Yale did not favor coeducation, and that Roman Catholics wanted a girls' annex instead, but Jane Stanford ignored both. Jordan, *Days of a Man,* 420–21. Furthermore, Francis Walker, president of MIT, had suggested that they begin with male students and add women in two to three years, which they also refused. Orrin Leslie Elliott, *Stanford University,* 29.

91. Clipping, Nov. 17, 1899, JLS Papers, series 7, box 1, f. 5.

92. Mr. Donald, *Daily Palo Alto,* May 29, 1895, quoted in Orrin Leslie Elliott, *Stanford University,* 133.

93. Jane Stanford to Gentlemen of the board of Trustees, May 31, 1899, and Jane Stanford to David Jordan [1899], in Nagel, *Iron Will,* 143–44; Crothers, *Educational Ideals,* 17. By 1899, women had reached 40 percent of the total enrollment.

94. Anthony to JLS, quoted in Harper, *Life and Work of Susan B. Anthony*, 3:1133–34. The letter may not have been mailed or saved, as I was unable to locate it in Stanford's papers.

95. Jane Stanford to Susan Mills, July 14, 1904, in JLS Papers, series 1, box 2, f. 9; Jane Stanford to David Jordan, Dec. 1904, JLS Papers, series 1, box 2, f. 30. Jordan had previously tried to reassure her that there had been no drunken behavior or improprieties involving the male and female students or between a female and a male professor, Professor Gilbert. Jordan to JLS, Nov. 2 and Nov. 5, 1902, JLS Papers, series 1, box 6, f. 34. Her draft of a statement to the trustees noted that the university stood in as a guardian over the young women, which was especially difficult to do for women living off campus. "Statement to Trustees," JLS Papers, series 5, box 1, f. 13.

96. See the following chapter on coeducation for discussion of this backlash.

97. Berner, *Mrs. Leland Stanford*.

98. Orrin Leslie Elliott, *Stanford University*, 258, 271, 275; Hofstadter and Metzger, *Development of Academic Freedom*, 413–15, 436–37, quotation on 437.

99. Cutler, *Mysterious Death of Jane Stanford*.

100. "Will of Indiana Fletcher Williams"; JLN to Administrators of the Tulane Educational Fund, Oct. 11, 1886, quoted in Dixon, *Brief History*, 9–11.

101. Quesnell, *Strange Disappearance*, 67, 127–50; JLN to Administrators of the Tulane Educational Fund, Oct. 11, 1886, quoted in Dixon, *Brief History*, 9–11.

102. Quesnell, *Strange Disappearance*, 67, 127–50.

103. Ernest Jaqua, "Annual Report," 1933, Scripps Papers, box 1, f. 10; Quesnell, *Strange Disappearance*, 67, 127–50.

Chapter Five

1. MCT to MEG, June 13, 1891, Thomas Papers, microfilm, reel 16.

2. Calculations to today's currency based on www.davemanuel.com/inflation -calculator.php.

3. Quoted in Walsh, *Doctors Wanted*, 169.

4. Eisenmann, "Brokering Old and New Philanthropic Traditions," 148–66.

5. Lynn D. Gordon, *Gender and Higher Education*; Horowitz, *Campus Life*, 41–42, 67–68.

6. Butcher, *Education for Equality*, 36. See also Datnow and Hubbard, eds., *Gender in Policy and Practice*; Lasser, *Educating Men and Women Together*; Gordon, *Gender and Higher Education*.

7. Sewall, "Education of Woman in the Western States," 77–79; Rosalind Rosenberg, "The Limits of Access: The History of Coeducation in America," in *Women and Higher Education in American History: Essays from the Mount Holyoke College Sesquicentennial Symposia*, ed. John Mack Faragher and Florence Howe (New York: W.W. Norton, 1988), 107–29.

8. Rosenberg, "The Limits of Access," 107–9.

9. Thomas Woody points to economics as a factor leading to coeducation, and briefly mentions donations to the University of Michigan (from women in Michigan), Johns Hopkins (from "a woman"), and the University of Rochester (from Susan B. Anthony's fund-raising efforts). Woody, *History of Women's Education in the United States*, vol. 2, 258–59. Sarah Manekin also points to economic factors and the needs of the university in the University of Pennsylvania's decisions to admit or recruit more women students in various schools and departments. Manekin, "Gender, Markets, and the Expansion of Women's Education," 298–323.

10. Rossiter, *Women Scientists in America*, 39–49.

11. Morantz-Sanchez, *Sympathy and Science*, 64–67, 113–14; Bonner, *To the Ends of the Earth*, 26–30; Walsh, *Doctors Wanted*.

12. Walsh, *Doctors Wanted*, xviii.

13. Rossiter, *Women Scientists in America*, 38.

14. McCarthy, *Women's Culture*. See also Gaudiani, *Daughters of the Declaration*.

15. McKelvey, "Susan B. Anthony," 1–24.

16. Sander, *Mary Elizabeth Garrett*; *NYT*, July 14, 1888.

17. Sander, *Mary Elizabeth Garrett*, 110–11.

18. Ibid., 138–42.

19. Ibid., 84–85.

20. Ibid., 80.

21. Ibid., 91.

22. Morantz-Sanchez, *Sympathy and Science*, 67.

23. Chesney, *Johns Hopkins Hospital*, 13–16, 45–46, 75, 80–83, 152.

24. $2.6 million in 2016.

25. MCT to MEG, Nov. 20, 1888, Thomas Papers, reel 15; MEG to MCT, Nov. 19, 1888, reel 42; Thomas to MEG, Nov. 25, 1888, Thomas Papers, reel 15. For ease of reading, I have spelled out words that Thomas abbreviated in her letters.

26. The fund included Frances Morgan, wife of J. P. Morgan; Fanny Villard, daughter of William Lloyd Garrison and a suffragist; Bertha Palmer, president of the board of Lady Managers for the Chicago World's Fair; Ellen Henrotin, president of the General Federation of Women's Clubs; Harriet Blaine, wife of the secretary of state; First Lady Caroline Harrison; Phoebe Hearst; Jane Stanford; Mary A. Burnham and Katherine Bell Lewis, contributors to the suffrage movement; Grace Hoadley Dodge, the YWCA and Columbia Teachers College philanthropist; Emily Blackwell, Mary Putnam Jacobi, and M. E. Zakrzewska, all physicians; Alice Freeman Palmer, Elizabeth Agassiz, and Marion Talbot, all educators; and Marion Hovey. The Women's Medical School Fund, Circular, 4–5, Women's Medical School Fund Collection, Alan Chesney Archives, The Johns Hopkins Medical School.

27. Horowitz, *Power and Passion*, 210.

28. MCT to MEG, Dec. 1, 1888, Thomas Papers, reel 15.

29. MCT to MEG, Nov. 29, 1888, Thomas Papers, reel 15.

30. MCT to MEG, Nov. 1, 1891, Thomas Papers, reel 16.

31. MCT to MEG, Apr. 19, 1890, Thomas Papers, reel 16.

32. Text of letter from the women's committee offering an endowment for the school of medicine. Chesney, *Johns Hopkins Hospital*, appendix, 295. Nancy Morris Davis to George W. Dobbin, May 1, 1891, Women's Medical School Fund Collection, Alan Chesney Archives, The Johns Hopkins Medical School.

33. Gilman Papers, box 4, f. 4.

34. MEG to MCT, Apr. 18, 1890, Thomas Papers, reel 42, and MCT to MEG, Apr. 20, 1890, Thomas Papers, reel 16.

35. Flexner and Flexner, *William Henry Welch*, 217; Chesney, *Johns Hopkins Hospital*, 197–98.

36. MCT to MEG, July 19, 1891, Thomas Papers, reel 16.

37. MCT to MEG, Nov. 22, 1891, Thomas Papers, reel 16.

38. Horowitz, *Power and Passion*, 237.

39. MEG to MCT, Feb. 21, 1892, Thomas Papers, reel 43.

40. Mary E. Garrett to George W. Dobbins, Apr. 27, 1891, and clippings, May 3, 1891, Welch Papers, box 97, f. 23; Charles Gwinn to Daniel Coit Gilman, Dec. 26, 1892, Gilman Papers, box 1.16.

41. Reprinted in *Johns Hopkins Hospital Bulletin*, Dec. 1892, 139–40.

42. Daniel Coit Gilman, "Memorandum," Dec. 24, 1892, Gilman Papers; MCT to MEG, Jan. 26, 1893, Thomas Papers, reel 17. Chesney, *Johns Hopkins Hospital*, 206–21.

43. MEG to the president of the board of trustees, Jan. 30, 1893, Welch Papers.

44. Mary Garrett to the board of trustees, Feb. 15, 1893, Welch Papers.

45. Chesney, *Johns Hopkins Hospital*, 220–21.

46. Quoted in Chesney, *Johns Hopkins Hospital*, 216.

47. Quoted in Cynthia Brown, "'Putting a *Woman* in Sole Power': The Presidential Succession at Bryn Mawr College, 1892–1894," *History of Higher Education Annual*, 1988, 89–90.

48. MCT to MEG, Mar. 10, 1893, Thomas Papers, reel 17.

49. MCT to MEG, Mar. 24, 1893, Thomas Papers, reel 17. See also Horowitz, *Power and Passion*, 257–59.

50. Horowitz, *Power and Passion*, 279.

51. McCandless, *Past in the Present*, 86–102.

52. McCandless, "The Pollitzer Sisters," 740; "Miss Carrie T. Pollitzer, Veteran Teacher, Dies," *Charleston Evening Post*, Oct. 23, 1974.

53. Chaddock, *College of Charleston Voices*, 100–101.

54. "Though Different, Sisters Had Same Goals," *News and Courier*, Oct. 7, 1984.

55. Hutchison, "Handmaidens of History," 98–107, quotation on 101.

56. Schwager, "Taking Up the Challenge," 87–105, quotation on 90.

57. Ibid., 94, 98–99.

58. Ibid., 103–5.

59. Hancock and Kalb, "Harvard Held Up," and Shapiro, "A Radcliffe Girl at Harvard," in Ulrich, *Yards and Gates*, 303–10.

60. Walsh, *Doctors Wanted*, 163–68.

61. Ibid., 169–76.

62. Crocker, *Mrs. Russell Sage*. Similarly, in 1898, the University of Michigan learned that Dr. Elizabeth Bates had left the school $133,000 "provided that they would expand their offerings, especially in clinical instruction, to women medical students (whom they had been admitting since 1871) to make their education fully equal to that of its men students." The university took the money but used it to pay for the Department of Obstetrics and Gynecology, withdrawing university support for that department, which effectively limited its budget to income from the fund while other department budgets grew. It did not expand clinical instruction in obstetrics as was intended. Rossiter, *Women Scientists in America*, 47; Shaw, *University of Michigan*, 866–69.

63. Crocker, *Mrs. Russell Sage*, 242–45; *"For the Better Protection of Their Rights."* Some women entered the university's law school after completion of the Woman's Law Class. The $25,000 endowment fund for the Woman's Law Class came from twelve women and three men, with Helen Gould giving the largest donation, $16,000. *"For the Better Protection of Their Rights,"* 52.

64. Crocker, *Mrs. Russell Sage*, 242–45.

65. Crocker, "From Gift to Foundation," 199–215, especially 208; Crocker, *Mrs. Russell Sage*, 242–45; Christina Zhang, "'The Castle on the Hill': Risley Hall's 100th Anniversary," *Cornell Daily Sun*, Oct. 29, 2013, http://cornellsun.com/blog/2013/10/30/the-castle-on-the-hill-risley-halls-100th-anniversary.

66. Duffy, *Tulane University Medical Center*, 84–85, 133–36.

67. Knight, "This Time We're Here to Stay," 2–6; Bederman, *Manliness and Civilization*, 170–215.

68. Conable, *Women at Cornell*.

69. Nidiffer, *Pioneering Deans of Women*, 113–14.

70. Lynn D. Gordon, *Gender and Higher Education*, 87–112, 118; "Creating Women's Residence Halls," University of Chicago Library, accessed Oct. 10, 2014, www.lib.uchicago.edu/e/webexhibits/building/residence.html.

71. Anya Jabour, "Separatism and Equality: Women at the University of Chicago, 1895–1945," presented at the Societa Italiana Per Lo Studio Della Storia Contemporanea's National Seminar on the History of Universities, "Universities, Institutions, and Society (1914–1968)," Sept. 6, 2014, Pisa, Italy; Nidiffer, *Pioneering Deans*, 45.

72. The following account can be found in Rosenberger, *Rochester*, and Arthur J. May, *History of the University of Rochester* (manuscript edition). Janis F. Gleason, *Life and Letters*, 53.

73. May, *History of the University of Rochester*, chapter 13.

74. Clipping, Feb. 16, 1907, p. 53, NAWSA Papers, reel 63.

75. Rosenberger, *Rochester*, 265, 274–75, 291–94; May, *History of the University of Rochester*. Tufts University attempted a similar move to segregate women in a separate women's college, Jackson College, in 1910 in order to attract more men students. The experiment lasted only a few years, when it was decided that the financial burden was too great. Russell Miller, *Light on the Hill*, 199–207.

76. Jabour, "Separatism and Equality"; Nidiffer, *Pioneering Deans of Women*, 2–3, 30, 67, 92, 96–100; Andrea Radke-Moss, *Bright Epoch*, 2–3, 48–78.

77. She had to complete preparatory classes before matriculating. Bix, *Girls Coming to Tech!*, 47–48.

78. R. M. Kimball to Dr. Compton, Feb. 5, 1947, and Karl Compton to KDM, Oct. 20, 1947, Records of the Office of the President, Karl Taylor Compton and James Rhyne Killian (President's Records-C/K), Institute Archives, Massachusetts Institute of Technology, Boston (MIT), box 141, f. 2.

79. KDM to Mrs. Karl Compton, May 3, 1948, President's Records-C/K, MIT, box 141, f. 2.

80. Bix, "Feminism Where Men Predominate," 24–45, esp. 24–26; Bix, "Supporting Females in a Male Field," 320–45.

81. Bix, *Girls Coming to Tech!*, 228; Bix, "Supporting Females in a Male Field," 325.

82. "The Woman Student at MIT," 1959, Records of the Office of the President, Julius A. Stratton President's Records-S, MIT, box 79, f. 3. Hartmann, "Women's Employment and the Domestic Ideal in the Early Cold War Years," in *Not June Cleaver*, 84–100.

83. *Boston Globe*, Oct. 28, 1962.

84. "Katharine Dexter (McCormick), Class of 1904," MIT Institute Archives and Special Collections, accessed Oct. 18, 2013, http://libraries.mit.edu/archives/exhibits /mccormick.

85. Jabour, "Separatism and Equality," 8.

86. P. A. Stoddard, Memorandum, Jan. 30, 1961, President's Records-S, MIT, box 79, f. 2.

87. KDM to Stratton, June 8, 1960, President's Records-S, MIT, box 79, f. 2.

88. KDM to Stratton, Oct. 10, 1963, President's Records-S, MIT, box 79, f. 2.

89. J. A. Mattfeld to Dr. Killian and Dr. Stratton, Nov. 24, 1964, President's Records-S, MIT, box 79, f. 1; Bix, *Girls Coming to Tech!*, 236.

90. Philip Stoddard, "Confidential Memorandum," Jan. 29, 1965; KDM to Julius Stratton, May 3, 1965; Julius Stratton to KDM, May 7 and June 4, 1965; and Philip Stoddard to Julius Stratton, June 21, 1965, President's Records-S, MIT, box 79, f. 1.

91. James R. Killian, "Remarks," in "A Tribute to Katharine Dexter McCormick, 1875–1967," 1968, President's Records-S, MIT, box 79, f. 1.

92. Treasurer's Reports, MIT.

93. Howard W. Johnson, "Response," in "A Tribute to Katharine Dexter McCormick, 1875–1967," 1968, President's Records-S, box 79, f. 1.

94. Bix, "Supporting Females in a Male Field," 326.

95. "A Program for the Women of MIT: Background for Building the Second Tower of McCormick Hall, Office of the Dean of Student Affairs (written by Jackie Mattfeld and Robert Simha), Mar. 16, 1964," Planning Office, MIT, box 21, f. 3.

96. "Enrollments 2016–2017," MIT Facts, http://web.mit.edu/facts/enrollment .html.

97. Simha, *MIT Campus Planning*, 32–34.

98. Wall, "Feminism and the New England Hospital," 88.

99. Ames to KDM, Oct. 13, 1952, Ames Papers, f. 11.

100. KDM to Ames, Dec. 22, 1952, Ames Papers, f. 11.

101. "Certificate" (KDM gives $50,000 worth of Harvester Company shares to the NEH), 1956, box 2, f. 20, and Eliza Melkon to Blanche Ames, Dec. 4, 1958, Ames Papers, f. 12.

102. Eliza Melkon to Blanche Ames, Dec. 4, 1958, Ames Papers, f. 12; Ames to Melkon, Jan. 6, 1959, Ames Papers, f. 13.

103. "Suggested Copy of Letter to Mrs. McCormick," NAWSA Papers, reel 13, 267.

104. KDM to Ames, Mar. 17, 1959, Ames Papers, f. 13.

105. KDM Will, McCormick Papers, MIT. Why McCormick chose Stanford is not clear.

106. Chen, "Women's Admissions." http://stanmed.stanford.edu/2000fall/woman .html.

107. https://med.stanford.edu/facultydiversity/diversity-resources/mccormick-dis tinguished-lecture-series/katharine-d-mccormick.html.

108. Hearst, "Phoebe Apperson Hearst," 46; Bonfils, *Life and Personality of Phoebe Apperson Hearst*, 14–15.

109. Nickliss, "Phoebe Apperson Hearst's 'Gospel of Wealth,' " 576.

110. Nickliss, "Phoebe Apperson Hearst," 114–18.

111. Bessie Bradwell Helmer to PAH, May 1, 1894, PAH Papers, reel 110.

112. Hearst, "Phoebe Apperson Hearst," 207.

113. *Boston Post*, Dec. 7, 1916, Maud Wood Park Papers, Scrapbook 1, Schlesinger, and "List of Contributors from Beginning of Organization to Dec. 31, 1920," NWP-II, reel 126.

114. Susan B. Anthony to Jane Stanford, quoted in Nagel, *Iron Will*, 8–9.

115. Lynne D. Gordon, *Gender and Higher Education*, 52–58.

116. PAH to Board of Regents, Sept. 24, 1891, Board of Regents Papers, University of California, University Archives, Bancroft, box 26, f. 4.

117. Rose Hermann to PAH, June 15, 1906, PAH Papers, reel 69.

118. "Mrs. Hearst Promotes Higher Education," clipping, n.d. PAH Papers, reel 71.

119. Quoted in Adele S. Brooks, "Phoebe Apperson Hearst: A life and Some Letters" (unpublished manuscript), PAH Papers, reel 129.

120. Lynne D. Gordon, *Gender and Higher Education*, 70–79.

121. "Donations to the University by Mrs. Phoebe A. Hearst, 1897–1918," PAH Papers, reel 66; Acting Secretary of the board to PAH, Aug. 10, 1899, reel 65; Benjamin Wheeler to PAH, Apr. 20, 1901, reel 64; clipping, *San Francisco Call*, Feb. 10, 1901, PAH Papers, reel 65. For the University of Chicago's Ida Noyes Hall, see Nidiffer, *Pioneering Deans*, 45.

122. Jabour, "Separatism and Equality"; Nidiffer, *Pioneering Deans*, 136–37.

123. Lynne D. Gordon, *Gender and Higher Education*, 58–59, Mary Bennett Ritter, *More Than Gold in California, 1849–1933* (Berkeley, Calif.: Professional Press, 1933), 206.

124. Ritter, *More Than Gold*, 208–15.

125. Nickliss, "Gospel of Wealth," 597–98.

126. "Mrs. Hearst's and Other Munificent Gifts," clipping, n.d., PAH Papers, reel 71.

127. Lynne D. Gordon, *Gender and Higher Education*, 57.

128. Ritter, *More Than Gold*, 203.

Chapter Six

1. "Police Veto Halts Birth Control Talk," *NYT*, Nov. 14, 1921.

2. Ibid.

3. "Arrest Mrs. Rublee for Views on Birth Control," *NYT*, Dec. 3, 1921.

4. Cott, *Grounding of Modern Feminism*, 4–5.

5. Quoted in Solinger, *Pregnancy and Power*, 74.

6. Stansell, *Feminist Promise*, 165.

7. For the conservative argument, see Kennedy, *Birth Control in America*; Linda Gordon, *Woman's Body, Woman's Right*. For the view that she was always more conservative, see Susan A. Nicholson, "Margaret Sanger: Rebellion and Respectability," MA, Smith College, 1973, in Sanger Papers (unfilmed), box 20, f. 2. For a focus on her feminism, see Reed, *From Private Vice to Public Virtue*; Chesler, *Woman of Valor*; Holz, "Nurse Gordon on Trial," 112–40, esp. 113–14, 131n2; Meyer, *Any Friend of the Movement*; Coates, *Margaret Sanger and the Origin of the Birth Control Movement*. For the view that she abandoned feminism and took up eugenics, see Caron, *Who Chooses?*, 73.

8. Chesler, *Woman of Valor*, 13.

9. Ibid., 43.

10. "They Were Eleven," *New Yorker*, July 5, 1930, copy in Sanger Papers, unfilmed, box 19, f. 1.

11. On social networks, see Wellman, "Seneca Falls Women's Rights Convention," 9–37.

12. Dorothy Straight was married, though she had inherited her own fortune and was widowed during much of her philanthropy to the birth control movement, between her first husband's death in 1919 and her second marriage in 1925.

13. Sanger claimed, "I don't really know how most of my ventures in this work were ever financed. . . . I do things first and somehow or another they get paid for." Sanger, *My Fight for Birth Control*, 62.

14. Slee made generous contributions from after their marriage in late 1922 to 1931. Chesler, *Woman of Valor*, 254, 317.

15. "Report, John Price Jones Corporation," MS-SS.

16. Chesler, *Woman of Valor*; Sanger, *Autobiography*.

17. Quoted in Chesler, *Woman of Valor*, 81.

18. Sanger, *Autobiography*, 107, 212.

19. Havelock Ellis, "The Love Rights of Women," *Birth Control Review*, June 1918, 3–6.

20. Margaret Sanger, "A Parent's Problem or Woman's?" *Birth Control Review*, Mar. 1919, 6.

21. See Carrie Chapman Catt to MS and Juliet Rublee, Nov. 24, 1920, in Katz, *Selected Papers of Margaret Sanger*, 1:290 (hereafter cited as *SPMS*).

22. Historians have not followed up on this connection pointed out by Reed in 1978. Reed, *From Private Vice.*

23. Photograph in the National Woman's Party Papers, group I, container 1:159, LOC.

24. Cott, *Grounding of Modern Feminism*, 59.

25. Sanger, *Autobiography*, 71.

26. Chen, *Sex Side of Life*, 139.

27. "Jessie Ashley—a Soul That Marches On," *Birth Control Review*, Feb. 1919, 4–5.

28. Chen, *Sex Side of Life*, 139; SPMS, 1:226n5.

29. Sanger, *Autobiography*, 71.

30. Jessie Ashley, "Editorial Comment," *Birth Control Review*, Jan. 1919, 2.

31. Jessie Ashley to Mary Ware Dennett, "Friday," n.d., MWD Papers, reel 2, f. 30.

32. "Fine Birth Control Agent," *NYT*, Oct. 31, 1916; "Jessie Ashley—a Soul That Marches On," 4–5.

33. Chesler, *Woman of Valor*, 90–91.

34. Chen, *Sex Side of Life*, 162; Chesler, *Woman of Valor*, 97; Schwarz, *Radical Feminists of Heterodoxy*, appendix.

35. Stansell, *American Moderns*, 225, 234–41, 273–86.

36. Quoted in Kennedy, *Birth Control in America*, 127.

37. Parsons donated over $2,000. "Annual Report of the New York State Woman Suffrage Party," 1917, NAWSA Papers, reel 72; Rosenberg, *Changing the Subject*, 98–100.

38. Zumwalt, *Wealth and Rebellion.*

39. See, for example, Parsons, "When Mating and Parenthood Are Theoretically Distinguished," 207–216; "Feminism and the Family," 52–58; and Feminism and Sex Ethics," 462–65.

40. Elsie Clews Parsons, "Girls with Nothing to Do," *Charities and the Commons*, Oct. 1905, 124–25.

41. Elsie Clews Parsons, "Press Clippings," *Birth Control Review*, June 1924, 190.

42. Deacon, "Republic of the Spirit," *Frontiers* 12 (1992): 13–38.

43. Adickes, *To Be Young Was Very Heaven*, 74.

44. "Friends Dine Mrs. Sanger," *NYT*, Jan. 18, 1916; speech reprinted in Sanger, *My Fight for Birth Control*, 132–34.

45. "Drops Mrs. Sanger's Case," *NYT*, Feb. 19, 1916. The committee included Mrs. Heaton Force O'Brien, Elsie Clews Parsons, Rose Stokes Pastor, Mrs. J. Sargent Cram (Edith Clare Bryce Cram was Gertrude Minturn's sister-in-law's sister), Mrs. Albert De Silver, Mrs. Florence Woodston, Marion Cothren, Mrs. Allen Dawson, Jessie Ashley, Dr. Gertrude Slight, Henrietta Rodman, Mrs. William Colt, and Helen Todd.

46. Parsons, "Wives and Birth Control."

47. Pinchot, "Amos Pinchot: Rebel Prince," 166–98, esp. 186.

48. "Mrs. Sanger Accepts Bail," *NYT*, Oct. 28, 1916, and "Mrs. Sanger's Writ Fails," Dec. 23, 1916.

49. SPMS, 1:215n7; Sanger, *My Fight for Birth Control*, 161.

50. *New York Tribune*, Nov. 26, 1916.

51. Sanger, *Autobiography*, 230.

52. Rosenberg, *Changing the Subject*, 36.

53. "The Weddings of a Day," *NYT*, Nov. 15, 1900; Pinchot, "Amos Pinchot," 166–198; Zimmerman, *Love, Fiercely*, 53–54, 85–87, 112, 179; Furlow, "Cornelia Bryce Pinchot," *Pennsylvania History* 43 (1976): 329–46; Allison, *Mildred Minturn*, 183.

54. Nancy Pinchot does not indicate whether she is related to Amos. Because the article is written about Amos, it may take his point of view on the marriage. Other sources suggest he was having an affair. On Pinchot's divorce, see MS to Rublee, Dec. 18, 1918, Juliet Barrett Rublee Papers, box 1. Amos's new wife, Ruth Pickering, also supported birth control, though not to the same extent as Gertrude had.

55. Pinchot, "Amos Pinchot," 166–98; "Mrs. Amos Pinchot's 8 Days in Lawrence," *New York Sun*, Mar. 17, 1912. Pinchot's feminism is more difficult to document because she did not leave as many statements about her ideas like those of Ashley, Parsons, or Rublee. For a statement about the Women's Peace Party, see "Woman's Peace Effort," *NYT*, Apr. 18, 1915.

56. "Mrs. Byrne Fasts in Workhouse Cell," *NYT*, Jan. 25, 1917.

57. *SPMS*, 1:214n1; MS to Rublee, Aug. 10, 1918, *SPMS*, 1:234.

58. "Escort for Mrs. Sanger," *NYT*, Jan. 3, 1917.

59. Chesler, *Woman of Valor*, 154–55; Sanger, *My Fight for Birth Control*, 167.

60. MS to Pinchot, Apr. 16, 1917, and MS to Pinchot, May 6, 1917, *SPMS*, 1:213, 215–16, 215n4; Pinchot to MS, Apr. 17, 1917, *SPMS*, 1:216n5.

61. Chesler claims Rublee was essential to Sanger's celebrity status and her now consolidated leadership of the movement was not possible without Rublee. Chesler, *Woman of Valor*, 167.

62. She may have met her at Mabel Dodge Luhan's salon or through her mother. *SPMS*, 1:219–20n1. Grant Sanger claimed that Rublee was infertile due to a gynecological operation and that her mother, after meeting Sanger in Chicago, encouraged Rublee to meet Sanger in New York. Grant Sanger, interview by Ellen Chesler, Aug. 1976, transcript, Sanger Papers unfilmed, box 20, f. 7; Bowers, "Oceans of Love," 4, in Rublee Papers, box 2.

63. See correspondence between Duncan and Rublee in the Mary Desti Collection on Isadora Duncan, Special Collections, University of California, Irvine.

64. Paul Marashio, "A Feminist Voice in N.H.: Juliet Barrett Rublee" (unpublished manuscript), Juliet Barrett Rublee Papers, University of New Hampshire Archives and Special Collections; Sanger to Rublee, Aug. 10, 1920, Rublee Papers, box 1; Arredondo, "From Travelogues to Political Intervention," 79–93.

65. Chesler, *Woman of Valor*, 235; Margaret Sanger, *Autobiography*, 300; MS to Rublee, June 6, 1955, Rublee Papers, box 1.

66. MS to Rublee, Dec. 4, 1917, in *SPMS*, 1:224–25.

67. Juliet Rublee to MS, Aug. 6 1919, in *SPMS*, 1:259.

68. Sanger to Rublee, Aug. 19, 1919, Rublee Papers, box 1; the book was eventually titled *Woman and the New Race*.

69. Oral interview, Frances Hand Ferguson, in the Women's Studies Manuscript Collection from the Schlesinger Library, Series 3, Sexuality, Sex Education and Reproductive Rights, reel 2.

70. Juliet Rublee to MS, Sept. 11, 1925, *SPMS*, 1:429.

71. Juliet Rublee to MS, Oct. 10, 1917, Rublee Papers, box 1.

72. MS to Rublee, Jan. 22, 1918, Rublee Papers, box 1.

73. MS to Rublee, Aug. 10, 1918, *SPMS*, 1:232–33.

74. MS to Rublee, Oct. 10, 1919, Rublee Papers, box 1.

75. MS to Rublee, Feb. 6, 1953, Rublee Papers, box 1.

76. "Statement by Juliet Barrett Rublee in 1916 from which the Committee of One Hundred was formed," MS-SS.

77. "Special Notice," Jan. 8, 1917, MS-SS.

78. "Resolutions Adopted at Carnegie Hall," Committee of One Hundred, Jan. 29, 1917, MS-SS.

79. "Budget [1921]," ABCL Papers, Houghton.

80. Margaret Sanger, Nov. 18, 1921, *SPMS*, 1:328–29.

81. "A Word of Explanation on Birth Control," June 1921 [Rublee?], MS-SS.

82. Sanger, *My Fight for Birth Control*, 190–91; MS to Ethel Byrne, Feb. 14, 1917, *SPMS*, 1:207–8.

83. MS to Pinchot, May 6, 1917, *SPMS*, 1:215.

84. "See Plot by Police to Bar Free Speech," *NYT*, Dec. 10, 1921; "Statement by Mrs. Juliet Rublee," n.d., Sanger Papers (unfilmed), box 33, f. 24.

85. "Mrs. Rublee's Arrest: A Record and a Protest," *Birth Control Review*, Feb. 1922, 5–7.

86. Juliet Rublee to MS, letter fragment, [Mar. 1, 1938?], MS-SS.

87. "The Birth Control Movement," pamphlet, published by the Committee of One Hundred, 1917, MS-SS.

88. MS to Rublee, Dec. 4, 1917, Rublee Papers, box 1.

89. Sanger, *Autobiography*, 212.

90. Members of both the ABCL and the Colony Club, in addition to Pinchot and Harriman, included Mrs. Adams Batchelier, Alva Belmont, Mrs. Karl Bitter, Mrs. Francis H. Cabot, Mrs. Joseph Gilder, Mrs. J. M. Hartshorne, Mrs. F. C. Havemeyer, Mrs. E. R. Mathews, Mrs. Edward McVicker, Mrs. Robert Minturn (mother of Gertrude), Elsie Clews Parsons, Mrs. H. H. Pell, Mrs. W. S. Rainsford, Mrs. Prescott Slade, Mrs. Victor Sorchan, and Mrs. I. N. Phelps Stokes (sister of Gertrude Minturn). Cox, *History of the Colony Club*, 27–28, 39, 50.

91. Mary Ware Dennett's list of potential contributors noted that Colony Club list names were marked with an *X*. [n.d.], MWD Papers, Schlesinger Library, Reel 13. For wait-listed women, see Jones to Mrs. Richard Billings, Apr. 15, 1927, ABCL Papers, Houghton, f. 382.

92. Minutes, ABCL, Nov. 3, 1922, MS-SS. Quoted in Rauchway, "Gentlemen's Club in a Woman's Sphere," 60–85, quotation on 65; Chesler, *Woman of Valor*, 167. Katharine McCormick also gave money to establish the clinic; her philanthropy is discussed in chapter 7. *SPMS*, 1:348.

93. Collins, *Otto Kahn*, 154, 327n53; *Birth Control Review*, May 1924, 156; Addie Wolff Kahn to MS, July 15, 1927, Aug. 30, 1928, and Apr. 16, 1931; MS to Mrs. Kahn, Aug. 1, Sept. 8, Oct. 3, and Oct. 5, 1928; Apr. 14 and Nov. 13, 1931; and Nov. 3, 1932, all in MS-LOC.

94. Leaming, *Katharine Hepburn*, 67, 73, 112–13, 121. Hepburn was the mother of actress Katharine Hepburn. Sanger, *An Autobiography*, 188.

95. Edith Houghton Hooker to Carrie Chapman Catt, June 8, 1915, NAWSA Papers, reel 33; "List of Contributors from Beginning of Organization to Dec. 31, 1920," NWP-II, reel 126.

96. MS to Edith Houghton (Mrs. Donald) Hooker, Oct. 9, 1923, ABCL Papers, Houghton, f. 99; "Edith Houghton Hooker," NWP-II; MS to Anne Kennedy, Jan. 22, 1926, ABCL Papers, Houghton, f. 362.

97. MS to Kennedy, Jan. 22, 1926, ABCL Papers, Houghton, Folder 362.

98. Garrow, *Liberty and Sexuality*, 9; Chesler, *Woman of Valor*, 326; Nichols, *Votes and More for Women*, 13, 24.

99. Katherine Day and Annie Porritt to Carrie Chapman Catt, May 29, 1915, NAWSA Papers, reel 33; Annie Porritt to Alice Blackwell, Oct. 31, 1922, NAWSA Papers, reel 17; "The Story of Annie G. Porritt as told by her daughter Marjorie Blackall," 1976, in Anne G. Webb Porritt Papers, Smith College, box 1. MS to Rublee, n.d. [1920], Rublee Papers, box 1.

100. *SPMS*, 1:370n6 and 388n7; see also Nichols, *Votes and More for Women*, appendix.

101. MS to Rublee, Aug. 25, 1921, *SPMS*, 1:309.

102. MS to Rublee, July 13, 1917, Rublee Papers, box 1.

103. MS to Rublee, n.d. [1919], Rublee Papers, box 1.

104. MS to Rublee, Dec. 4, 1917, *SPMS*, 1:225.

105. Chesler, *Woman of Valor*, 167, 236–37, and ABCL to Rublee, Nov. 27, 1923, ABCL Papers, f. 108; Gray, *Margaret Sanger*, 238.

106. MS to Dorothy Brush, Apr. 26, 1934, PPFA, microfilm, reel 8.

107. Brownsville Clinic/Committee of One Hundred, Minutes, Jan. 21, 1917, MS-SS.

108. Frances Ackerman to Rublee, Mar. 9, 1919, Rublee Papers, box 1.

109. "Budget," [1921], ABCL Papers, Houghton. Sanger's estimate for the 1925 conference was that it would cost $25,000, which the ABCL board did not want to finance due to the high cost and other expenses. Sanger, *My Fight for Birth Control*, 282. On the *Birth Control Review*, see MS to Rublee, Dec. 4, 1917, in *SPMS*, 1:225.

110. Ackerman was a suffragist, philanthropist, and clubwoman from Bronxville, NY. She donated $1,664 to the CU. *SPMS*, 1:388n6; Sanger, *An Autobiography*, 188. Knoblach was a Bryn Mawr graduate and suffragist from New York. Leonard, *Woman's Who's Who of America*. "Certificate of Incorporation," MS-SS; MS to Juliet Rublee, Jan. 22, 1918, *SPMS*, 1:229.

111. Jessie Ashley to MWD, July 9, 1918, MWD Papers, reel 2, f. 30.

112. Jessie Ashley to MWD, Aug. 14, 1918, MWD Papers, reel 2, f. 30.

113. Minutes, Board of Directors, New York Women's Publishing Company, Dec. 10, 1921.

114. Sanger, *Autobiography*, 262–63.

115. Kennedy to Charlotte Delafield, Oct. 2, 1922, ABCL Papers, Houghton, f. 20.

116. Eleanor Jones to Annie Porritt, Jan. 25, 1927, and Eleanor Jones to Charlotte Delafield, Apr. 14, 1927, ABCL Papers, f. 382.

117. "Report from Finance Department," PPFA, MS-SS.

118. Eleanor Jones to Frances Ackerman, Nov. 28, 1927, ABCL Papers, f. 384.

119. Edith Houghton Hooker to Anne Kennedy, Apr. 10, 1925, ABCL Papers, f. 154; Kennedy to Hooker, Jan. 16, 1926, ABCL Papers, f. 309; *SPMS*, 1:439n7.

120. Sanger, *Autobiography*, 417.

121. Anne Kennedy to Mrs. Walter Timme, Feb. 5, 1926, ABCL Papers, f. 316; Anne Kennedy to Juliet Rublee, Feb. 9, 1926, ABCL Papers, f. 318; quoted in Chesler, *Woman of Valor*, 324.

122. Jones to Timme, Sept. 7, 1927, and Oct. 26, 1927, ABCL Papers, f. 384.

123. Baker, *Margaret Sanger*, 195–96, quotation on 258; MS to Clarence Gamble, Apr. 13, 1927, MS-LOC.

124. MS to Eleanor Jones, Aug. 27, 1926, MS-LOC; Eleanor Jones to MS, Sept. 3, 1926, MS-LOC.

125. Juliet Rublee to MS, Nov. 16, Dec. 6, and Dec. 18, 1927, MS-LOC.

126. Sanger's letter of resignation to the ABCL Board of Directors, June 8, 1928, *SPMS*, 1:480–81. Charlotte Delafield, the wife of Lewis Delafield, a prominent New York attorney, was a suffragist who supported the CU. Sanger recalled that despite a fragile demeanor, "she had the spiritual courage to stand by her ideas and ideals in both her public and private life." In 1924, she hosted birth control luncheons in honor of foreign guests. Minutes of the annual convention, NAWSA, 1913, 139–42, MWD Papers, reel 11, f. 220; Sanger, *Autobiography*, 230 (quotation).

127. *SPMS*, 1:416n2; Chesler, *Woman of Valor*, 236–39. Delafield remained in the ABCL with Sanger's blessing.

128. "Aims and Objections," American Birth Control League, 1921 [?], MS-SS. For a discussion of birth control, Sanger, and eugenics, see Chesler, *Woman of Valor*, 122–23, 195–96, 215–16; Engelman, *History of Birth Control*.

129. Chesler, *Woman of Valor*, 295–97, 388.

130. McCann, *Birth Control Politics in the United States*, 42–45, 48–58.

131. Baker, "The Domestication of Politics."

132. Dana S. Creel to Hugh Moore, Mar. 15, 1960, MS-SS.

133. "The Doris Duke Foundation," pamphlet, Sanger Papers (unfilmed), box 50, f. 2; Chesler, *Woman of Valor*, 292; MS to Marian Paschal, Sept. 12, 1936, *SPMS*, 2:367–68.

134. See "Brush, Dorothy Adams Hamilton," *Encyclopedia of Cleveland History*, https://ech.case.edu/cgi/article.pl?id=BDAH; Chesler, *Woman of Valor*, 365; MS to Juliet Rublee, May 17, 1928, *SPMS*, 1:475–76; *SPMS*, 3:18n5; Mary Lasker to MS, Jan. 5, 1943, MS-SS; "The Brush Foundation," pamphlet, explains the mission as combating over-population and pro-eugenics when it was founded; it gave money to support the IPPF. Sanger Papers, (unfilmed), box 50, f. 1.

135. Mary Lasker to MS, Dec. 4, 1950, MS-SS (on the gift of money); Albert Lasker to "Gentlemen," June 1943, PPFA Part 2, reel 6 (on Lasker's interest in contraception for health). Columbia University Libraries, Oral History Research Office, Notable New Yorkers, Mary Lasker, interview by John T. Mason, Oct. 1962. Mary inherited nearly $6 million when Albert died in 1955. *NYT*, Mar. 11, 1955.

136. *SPMS*, 3:xx–xxi.

137. Holz, "Nurse Gordon on Trial."

138. MS to Kenneth Rose, Dec. 11, 1942, *SPMS*, 3:143–44.

139. MS to Kenneth Rose, Aug. 20, 1956, *SPMS*, 3:402.

Chapter Seven

1. KDM to MS, Feb. 17, 1954, MS-SS.

2. Courey, "Participants in the Development," 34; Speroff, *Good Man*. See also Tone, *Devices and Desires*; Marks, *Sexual Chemistry*; Asbell, *The Pill*; R. Christian Johnson, "Feminism, Philanthropy and Science," 63–78; Watkins, *On the Pill*.

3. John Rock to GP, Aug. 11, 1957, GP-LOC; Hoagland, *Road to Yesterday*, 94–95.

4. In May 1956, she sent an article to Sanger about population threatening prosperity. See also KDM to MS, May 31, 1952, MS-SS; KDM to MS, Mar. 1952, MS-SS.

5. Katharine Dexter, "A Brief Account of My Life," Oct. 11, 1899, KDM Papers, box 1.

6. Engelman, *History of the Birth Control Movement*, 88.

7. Fields, *Katharine Dexter McCormick*, 28–33; see also Rossiter, *Women Scientists in America*, and Schiebinger, *Has Feminism Changed Science?*, 70–71.

8. Chesler, *Woman of Valor*.

9. Ibid., 146.

10. Layne, introduction to *Feminist Technology*, 2–3.

11. Halberstam, *The Fifties*, 640.

12. Ibid.

13. According to McCormick's biographer, Armond Fields, McCormick discussed Roessing with her psychoanalyst. I have been unable to corroborate Fields's assertion.

14. Speroff, *Good Man*, 178.

15. KDM to MS, Sept. 14, 1954, MS-SS.

16. KDM to GP, Aug. 8, 1964, GP-LOC.

17. Fields, *Katharine Dexter McCormick*, 47–67.

18. See Reed, *From Private Vice*, 434n5; McLaughlin, *The Pill*, 94; Gray, *Margaret Sanger*, 413. The claim is repeated in Marks, *Sexual Chemistry*, 53, and Tone, *Devices and Desires*, 205.

19. There is also very little evidence that Katharine was interested in birth control because she wanted to avoid pregnancy while having sexual relations with other men, though still married to Stanley (and refusing to divorce him). Stanley's family, who very much wanted her to divorce him so that they could control his care and prevent her from inheriting his money, made several references to the possibility that she had

interests in other men, including Butler Ames, the brother of Blanche Ames Ames and an MIT graduate, whom Stanley had considered a rival before their marriage. However, the references are few and vague. Had they obtained more evidence of such a relationship, they would have likely used it to force a divorce. Harold McCormick to Cyrus McCormick and Anita McCormick Blaine, Dec. 5, 1927, McCormick Papers, box 1; Dr. Kempf to Dr. Rowe, Dec. 5, 1927, box 1. Kempf report to Anita Blaine, Dec. 9, 1927.

20. KDM to Dr. Edward Kempf, Nov. 25, 1927, box 1. See also the box of medical reports in Stanley's papers for references to the marriage and Katharine's domineering role. Given his impotence with Katharine and references to homosexual tendencies in the reports, it is possible that Stanley was homosexual.

21. Fields, *Katharine Dexter McCormick*, 83.

22. KDM to Cyrus Bentley, Apr. 11, 1918, and KDM to Cyrus Bentley, July 8, 1918 (quotation), McCormick Papers, box 474.

23. Quotations from McCormick are from *HWS*, 5:597 and 325; clipping, *Boston Globe*, n.d., Ames Papers, v 119. Stanton, quoted in Stansell, *Feminist Promise*, 122.

24. Alan Guttmacher claimed that McCormick's longtime secretary, Sara Delaney, told him that McCormick smuggled contraceptives for Sanger. "Dear Friend of Planned Parenthood," from Alan Guttmacher, Feb. 10, 1968, PPLM.

25. McLaughlin notes, Loretta McLaughlin Papers, Countway.

26. GP to Mrs. Sagoff, Mar. 26, 1965, PPLM.

27. Margaret Sanger, "A Parent's Problem or Woman's?" *Birth Control Review*, Mar. 1919, 6.

28. Reed, *From Public Vice*, 432n5.

29. KDM to GP, Aug. 8, 1964, GP-LOC.

30. KDM to MS, Apr. 11, 1958, MS-SS.

31. "Statement by Juliet Barrett Rublee in 1916 from which the Committee of One Hundred was formed," MS-CD; "Aims and Objectives, American Birth Control League" (typescript), [Nov. 1921] and "Birth Control—What It Will Do," flyer, ABCL, n.d., in MS-CD.

32. Deacon, "Republic of the Spirit," 13–38, esp. 20.

33. Mrs. Guy Stantial to KDM, June 23, 1958, NAWSA Papers, reel 13. I have not been able to locate correspondence between the two alluded to by Stantial, but Sarah or Angelina Grimke did write in "Marriage" that women had the right "to decide *when* she shall become a mother, how often, and under what circumstances." Degler, *At Odds*, 272.

34. On Baker's suffragist support, see *Woman's Journal*, Mar. 11, 1916. On his progressive politics, see Craig, *Progressives at War*.

35. KDM to Cyrus Bentley, June 9, 1926, and letters between KDM and the McCormick siblings in Sept. 1927, McCormick Papers, box 474.

36. For Stanley's treatment, see Noll, "Styles of Psychiatric Practice," 145–89.

37. Hoagland, *Road to Yesterday*, 77.

38. Minutes, board meeting of the Neuro-Endocrine Foundation, May 19, 1941, Cannon Papers. Although she did not attend this meeting, she certainly would have read the minutes and the reports.

39. Minutes, board meeting of the Neuro-Endocrine Foundation, May 19, 1941; GP to Walter Cannon, Feb. 24, 1934, Cannon Papers, box 121, f. 1694; GP to Walter Cannon, Mar. 12, 1934, Cannon Papers (a three-page letter summarizing the investigations on mammalian eggs); Walter Cannon to Dr. F. O. Schmitt, Feb. 20, 1942, box 144, f. 2035, Cannon Papers. Walter Cannon to John Rock (hereafter JR), Dec. 29, 1937, box 13, f. 165, and JR to Cannon, Dec. 23, 1937, both in Cannon Papers. Pincus and Rock were also corresponding with each other by 1937. Marsh and Ronner, *Fertility Doctor*, 140.

40. "Item 6, Non-charitable Gifts, 1965, 1966, 1967," in KDM Papers, box 2; "For the Family Chronicles," Cornelia James Cannon, Apr. 7, 1965, typescript, Cannon Family Papers, Schlesinger; Schlesinger, *Snatched from Oblivion*, 105–6; Diedrich, *Cornelia James Cannon*.

41. For minutes that indicate that McCormick was asked to join the board, see Minutes, ABCL Board of Directors, Nov. 27, 1923, Dec. 7, 1925, MS-SS; *Program, First American Birth Control Conference*, 1921, MS-SS; *Program, Sixth International Neo-Malthusian and Birth Control Conference*, 1925, vol. 1, pp. 222, 225. Biographer Armond Fields says that McCormick donated seed money for the *Birth Control Review*, although I have been unable to find corroborating evidence for this. Fields, *Katharine Dexter McCormick*, 179–82.

42. Social Programme, World Population Conference, 1927, MS-SS.

43. See programs for the Sixth International Neo-Malthusian and Birth Control Conference, 1925, which included A. Brill and Adolph Meyer, and the program committee for the First American Birth Control Conference, 1921, which included Dr. John Favill. The article stressed the need for birth control for people with endocrine disorders but, in so doing, asserted that endocrines likely affected conception and sometimes caused sterility. William Berkeley, "The Relation of Endocrinology to Birth Control," *Birth Control Review*, Mar. 1925, 75.

44. MS to KDM, July 31, 1928, in *SPMS*, 2:5.

45. MS to KDM, Jan. 8, 1937, MS-CD; KDM to MS, Dec. 28, 1929, MS-CD. During the early 1930s Sanger was more focused on legislative lobbying than research, and dealing with her and her friend Juliet Rublee's husbands' loss of fortune during the Great Depression.

46. KDM to Birth Control League of Massachusetts, June 6, 1942, PPLM. Its president, Mrs. Walter Campbell, later added a handwritten note to a copy of Sanger's letter, letting Sanger know that McCormick refused to see her until June 1953, when McCormick would become involved in the pill research. MS to KDM, Nov. 3, 1948, MS-CD.

47. KDM to MS, Nov. 15, 1948, MS-CD; MS to KDM, Nov. 23, 1948, MS-CD.

48. KDM to MS, Oct. 1, 1950, MS-SS.

49. KDM to MS, Oct. 18, 1951, MS-SS ("greatest worry quotation); KDM to MS, Jan. 22, 1952, MS-SS (chafe quotation); MS to KDM, Oct. 27, 1950, MS-SS; KDM to MS, Nov. 18, 1950, MS-SS; and KDM to MS, Dec. 29, 1950, MS-SS.

50. MS to Dorothy Hamilton Brush Dick, May 12 1952, *SPMS*, v. III, 304–5.

51. Ibid.

52. *SPMS*, 3:267n7 and 268n11.

53. Minutes of the July 19, [1950], meeting of the Research Committee, PPFA, Robert L. Dickinson Papers, Countway, box 2, f. 36.

54. See, for example, Minutes, PPFA, Oct. 23, 1951, MS-SC (Pincus's work is described as "an attempt to discover an oral contraceptive); Mrs. Georgia Furst to Doris Duke, June 19, 1952, MS-SS; GP to Abraham Stone, Jan. 25, 1952, GP-LOC (the Report of Progress to PPFA attached to this letter specifies the testing of oral progesterone); GP to William Vogt, Apr. 18, 1952, GP-LOC; GP to Paul Henshaw, Jan. 28, 1953, GP-LOC; PPFA Minutes of the Board of Directors, Oct. 23, 1951, p. 4, MS-SS; Grants, Jan. 1952 and Apr. 1952, GP-LOC.

55. Grants, Jan. 1952 and Apr. 1952, P-LOC; William Vogt to MS, June 26, 1952, MS-SS.

56. *Planned Parenthood News*, Fall 1952, in Guttmacher Papers, Countway, p. 2.

57. Reed, *From Private Vice*, 433n13; GP to Vogt, Apr. 21, 1952, GP-LOC; box 12 specifies that Pincus and Stone had discussed beginning trials on women.

58. WFEB director Hudson Hoagland, her old friend from the Foundation for Neuro-Endocrine Research, recalled that McCormick visited him to encourage the WFEB to work on contraception in the early 1950s but did not specific what year. Hoagland interview cited in James Reed, *From Private Vice*, 339; MS to KDM, Mar. 10, 1952, MS-SS. In her reply, KDM said that she had "heard nothing re the research and Dr. Pincus" and was grateful for the bulletin on his research. Given the rest of the evidence, I interpret this remark to mean that she did not know about his latest research, rather than that she knew nothing about him at all. KDM to MS, Mar. 13, 1952, MS-SS. See Marks, *Sexual Chemistry*, 282n61, for the claim that McCormick did not know Pincus.

59. Paul Henshaw to GP, May 18, 1953, GP-LOC.

60. MS to KDM, Dec. 12, 1956, and Aug. 19, 1958, MS-SS.

61. MS to Roslyn Campbell Weir, Mar. 2, 1950, *SPMS*, 3:255, 258n9.

62. For the 15 percent, see, for example, MS to KDM, Feb. 23, 1954, MS-SS.

63. William Esty to Abraham Stone, May 17, 1953, in Abraham Stone Papers, Countway.

64. *SPMS*, 3:364n11.

65. Marian Ingersoll to MS, Mar. 5, 1954, MS-SS; Paul Henshaw to MS, Feb. 28, 1954, MS-SS.

66. MS to Abraham Stone, Jan. 24, 1952, *SPMS*, 3:294.

67. Reed, *From Private Vice*, cites GP to Paul Henshaw, June 10, 1953, MS-SS. KDM to MS, May 31, 1952; MS to William Vogt, July 9, 1952; and MS to William Vogt, Aug. 20, 1952, all in MS-SS.

68. KDM to MS, Nov. 13, 1953, MS-LOC; KDM to MS, Feb. 17, 1954, MS-SS.

69. See, for example, "Budgets for Calendar Years of Projects Sponsored by Mrs. Stanley McCormick," Feb. 11, 1957, GP-LOC.

70. KDM to MS, Jan. 28, 1958, MS-SS.

71. KDM to MS, June 26, 1958, includes a typed excerpt from Report of National Director, Planned Parenthood Federation of America, at Board of Directors Meeting, Apr. 9, 1958, MS-SS. See also "PPFA Statement on 'Birth Control Pill' Publicity," July 1957, PPLM, box 95, f. 3, and Frederick Jaffe to William Hull, Dec. 11, 1959, suggesting that Hull take a less enthusiastic position on the pill on an article he was writing, PPFA II, box 110, f. 2.

72. KDM to MS, July 2, 1954; July 4, 1954; July 13, 1954; July 15, 1954 (telegram); and July 19, 1954, all in MS-SS.

73. KDM to MS, July 21, 1954, and July 21, 1954, MS-SS.

74. KDM to GP, Mar. 21, 1957, GP-LOC.

75. KDM to MS, Mar. 29, 1955, and Nov. 1958, MS-SS.

76. KDM to MS, July 5, 1955, MS-SS.

77. Memo to GP, Jan. 31, 1957, and Hudson Hoagland to Crawford, regarding telephone conversation with McCormick and Bemis.

78. Paul Henshaw told Pincus that they had a potential donor, but he did not want them to test in Massachusetts where birth control was illegal. Henshaw to GP, Feb. 17 and Mar. 27, 1953, GP-LOC Papers, box 14.

79. John Rock to GP, June 26, 1957, GP-LOC.

80. Ibid.; John Rock to GP, Aug. 11, 1957, GP-LOC.

81. Courey, "Participants in the Development," 34.

82. KDM to MS, May 8, 1956, MS-SS.

83. Speroff, *Good Man,* 201.

84. GP to KDM, Dec. 2, 1953, GP-LOC.

85. Whereas a donor who asked no questions and simply wrote checks would have been easier for Pincus, perhaps he was flattered by her interest in his work.

86. GP to KDM, Dec. 16, 1958, and GP to KDM, May 6 1959, GP-LOC.

87. KDM to GP, Apr. 21, 1958, GP-LOC.

88. KDM to GP, May 19, 1958, GP-LOC.

89. Marsh and Ronner, *Fertility Doctor,* 201.

90. GP to KDM, Aug. 29, 1960, GP-LOC.

91. John Rock to KDM, May 18, 1961; June 13, 1961; Oct. 4, 1961; and May 27, 1963, and KDM to John Rock, May 31, 1963, in Rock Papers, Countway.

92. See Marsh and Ronner, *Fertility Doctor,* 147, on Rock's view of the purpose of birth control, and John Rock to Mary White, May 9, 1939, PPLM, box 16, f. 35.

93. GP to KDM, June 8, 1960, GP-LOC.

94. KDM to MS, Feb. 20, 1961, MS-SS.

95. KDM to John Rock, Jan. 5, 1960, in Rock Papers, Countway.

96. "Policy Committee Meeting, Jan. 11, 1960," and Mrs. Maurice Sagoff to KDM, Apr. 6, 1961, and Aug. 7, 1962, in PPLM.

97. Mrs. Maurice Sagoff to KDM, Nov. 21, 1961, PPLM.

98. KDM to Dr. John Knowles, May 25, 1962; Mrs. Maurice Sagoff to KDM, May 15, 1962; Mrs. Maurice Sagoff to KDM, May 17, 1962; James Faulkner to Dr. John Knowles, May 18, 1962; and John Knowles to KDM, June 13, 1962, all in PPLM. Sagoff detailed the five "research" clinics to KDM at Brigham, Lying-In, Massachusetts Memorial, and Beth Israel in Mrs. Maurice Sagoff to KDM, Dec. 13, 1962, PPLM. For McCormick's refusal to donate to Mass General, see KDM to Dr. Francis Gray, Dec. 12, 1963, PPLM.

99. Mrs. Maurice Sagoff to KDM, June 27, 1967, in PPLM. The series of letters is consistent; McCormick and Sagoff sought to expand access in every hospital in Boston.

100. KDM to Mrs. Guy W. Stantial, May 16, 1960, in NAWSA Papers, reel 13.

101. My appreciation to Margaret Marsh for pointing out the issue of prescription versus over-the-counter.

102. Marks, *Sexual Chemistry*, 89, 95–96.

103. KDM to GP, Aug. 3, 1959, GP-LOC Papers, box 39.

104. KDM to MS, Nov. 13, 1953, MS-LOC.

Epilogue

1. The National Center of Education Statistics found that women made up 49.8 percent of all college students in 1967 and crossed the 50 percent threshold in 1974. "Table 187," NCES, accessed July 1, 2014, http://nces.ed.gov/programs/digest/d99/d99t187.asp. According to a study by the Russell Sage Foundation, a dramatic rise in graduate school numbers began by 1970, allowing women to equal men by the late 1970s. "The Rise of Women: Seven Charts Showing Women's Rapid Gains in Educational Achievement," Feb. 21, 2013, www.russellsage.org/news/rise-women-seven-charts-showing-womens-rapid-gains-educational-achievement. Although Cornell had been coed since the late nineteenth century, beginning with Yale in 1968, all but Columbia opened to women in the ensuing eight years. Columbia did not admit women until 1983 (maintaining Barnard as the women's college).

2. Swanee Hunt, "She Speaks Serious Change, Carries Big Purse," Sept. 25, 2009, http://womensenews.org/2009/09/she-speaks-serious-change-carries-big-purse.

3. Pimlott, *Women and the Democratic Party*; Vaida and Skalka, "Can Emily's List Get Its Mojo Back?"; Clift and Brazaitis, *Madam President*.

4. Susie Tompkins Buell, "She Steeped Her Support of Women in Watershed Year," Sept. 25, 2009, http://womensenews.org/2009/09/she-steeped-her-support-women-in-watershed-year/; Barbara Lee, "Clarity of Values Stirred Her Political Mission," Sept. 25, 2009, http://womensenews.org/2009/09/clarity-values-stirred-her-political-mission.

5. Jennifer Stockman, "She Raises Stakes That Support the 'Big Tent,'" Sept. 25, 2009, http://womensenews.org/2009/09/she-raises-stakes-support-the-big-tent. On Emily's List and WISH List, see Day, "Gender, Feminism, and Partisanship," 687–700.

6. Rose, "Philanthropy in a Different Voice," 227–42.

7. Rose, "Philanthopy in a Different Voice." For more information, see the website of the Women's Funding Network, www.womensfundingnetwork.org. The network promotes women's leadership and philanthropy, and partners with funds to run a "national campaign to research, prevent and end domestic minor sex trafficking." For an example of unequal funding, in 1990 the United Way allocated almost double the amount of funding to the YMCA and Boy Scouts as to the YWCA and Girl Scouts. McCarthy, "Ms. Foundation."

8. McCarthy, "Ms. Foundation."

9. Alter, "Bureaucracy and Democracy in Organizations," 258–71, quotation on 259; Ostrander, "When Grantees Become Grantors," 257–70; Martin, "Rethinking Feminist Organizations," 182–206; Leidner, "Stretching the Boundaries of Liberalism," *Signs* 16 (1991): 263–89.

10. Ostrander, "Moderating Contradictions of Feminist Philanthropy," 29–46.

11. For more information, see www.womenmovingmillions.org. Swanee Hunt is the founding director of the Women and Public Policy Program at Harvard's Kennedy School of Government, and president of the Hunt Alternatives Fund.

12. Ruth Ann Harnisch, "Journalist Funds a Rewrite of Gender Rules," July 21, 2008, womensenews.org/2008/07/journalist-funds-rewrite-gender-rules.

13. Cecilia Boone, "Giving to Women and Girls Is Her Liberation," Sept. 25, 2009, http://womensenews.org/2009/09/giving-women-and-girls-her-liberation; Lindsay Shea, "After Gaining Financial Savvy, Now She Funds It," Sept. 25, 2009, http://womensenews.org/2009/09/after-gaining-financial-savvy-now-she-funds-it; Helen LaKelly Hunt, "Sharing the Wealth: Female Philanthropists Open Up," Sept. 25, 2009, http://womensenews.org/2009/09/sharing-the-wealth-female-philanthropists-open-2.

14. Alice Young, "Inequality Fueled Her Dreams of Political Change," June 17, 2009, http://womensenews.org/2009/06/inequality-fueled-her-dreams-political-change-2; Sheila C. Johnson, "Knowing She's Powerful, Her Gifts Get Girls to Go," Sept. 25, 2009, http://womensenews.org/2009/09/knowing-shes-powerful-her-gifts-get-girls-go; Margot Franssen, "Helping Women Is Part of a Rebel's Life Story," Sept. 25, 2009, http://womensenews.org/2009/09/helping-women-part-rebels-life-story; Cate Muther, "Her Philanthropic Story Footnotes Virgina Woolf," Sept. 25, 2009, http://womensenews.org/2009/09/her-philanthropic-story-footnotes-virginia-woolf. Ruth Ann Harnisch complained, "I've continued to rail every time boys put the 'no girls allowed' sign on the clubhouse door." Harnisch, "Journalist Funds a Rewrite."

15. Lynne Rosenthal, "Over Time, She Developed Her Theory of Giving," Aug. 18, 2008, http://womensenews.org/2008/08/over-time-she-developed-her-theory-giving.

16. Sue Wieland, "Women's Rights Are Her Family Gifts to Pass Along," Sept. 25, 2009, http://womensenews.org/2009/09/womens-rights-are-her-family-gifts-pass-along; Muther, "Her Philanthropic Story."

17. Greene, "Study Finds Difference in Giving Patterns," 12–14.

18. Dundjerski, "Paying Attention to Women," 31–33.

19. Steinem, "Trouble with Rich Women," 41–43, 78–80.

20. Gary, "Lessons Learned," 117–25; McCarthy, "Ms. Foundation."

21. Michelle Goldberg, "Planned Parenthood's Rich Red-State Backers," *Daily Beast*, www.thedailybeast.com/witw/articles/2013/09/04/ross-perot-s-foundation-gives -one-million-to-texas-planned-parenthood.html.

22. Erica Noonan, "Wellesley Gift to Generate Years of Buzz," May 20, 2005, *Boston Globe*, www.boston.com/news/local/articles/2005/05/20/wellesley_gift_to_generate _years_of_buzz?pg=full.

23. Steinem, *Moving beyond Words*, 194.

Bibliography

Unpublished Primary Sources

Bryn Mawr College, Bryn Mawr, Pa.
   M. Carey Thomas Papers (microfilm)
Harvard University, Cambridge, Mass.
   Countway Library, Harvard University Medical School
      Walter Cannon Papers
      Robert I. Dickinson Papers
      Lawrence Lader Papers
      Loretta McLaughlin Papers
      John Rock Papers
      Abraham Stone Papers
   Houghton Library, Harvard College
      American Birth Control League Papers
      Margaret Sanger Papers
   Schlesinger Library, Radcliffe Institute
      Blanche Ames Ames Papers
      Boston Equal Suffrage League Papers
      Mary Calderone Papers
      Cornelia Cannon Papers
      Mary Ware Dennett Papers (microfilm)
      Susan Fitzgerald Papers
      Edna Gellhorn Papers
      Harriet Laidlaw Papers
      Florence Luscomb Papers
      Alma Lutz Papers
      Catherine McCulloch Papers
      Laura Puffer Morgan Papers
      Mary Hutcheson Page Papers in the Woman's Rights Collection
      Edna Stantial Papers
      Doris Stevens Papers
      Vira Boarman Whitehouse Papers
The Johns Hopkins Medical School, Baltimore, Md.
   Alan Chesney Archives
      Mary Elizabeth Garrett Papers
      William Henry Welch Papers
      The Women's Medical School Fund Collection

Library of Congress, Washington, D.C.
    Gregory Pincus Papers
    National American Woman Suffrage Association Records (microfilm)
    National Woman's Party Papers, 1913–1974 (microfilm)
    National Woman's Party Papers: The Suffrage Years, 1913–1920 (microfilm)
    Margaret Sanger Papers (microfilm)
Massachusetts Institute of Technology Archives, Boston, Mass.
    Katharine Dexter McCormick Papers
    Office of the President, 1930–1959
    Planning Office Papers
    Presidential Papers, Karl Compton and Julius Stratton
Papers of the Women's Trade Union League and Its Principal Leaders (microfilm)
    I. Margaret Dreier Robins Papers
    V. Leonora O'Reilly Papers
    VI. Rose Schneiderman Papers
    VIII. O'Sullivan Autobiography
Scripps College, Pomona, Calif.
    Scripps College Archives, Ella Strong Denison Library
        Patricia Schaelchlin Papers
        Ellen B. Scripps Collection
Smith College, Northampton, Mass.
    Smith College Archives
        Sophia Smith Papers
    Sophia Smith Women's History Collection
        Blanche Ames Ames Papers
        Dorothy Brush Papers
        Grace Hoadley Dodge Papers
        Massachusetts Planned Parenthood Papers
        Planned Parenthood Federation of America Papers
        Annie Porritt Papers
        Juliet Barrett Rublee Papers
        Margaret Sanger Papers (filmed and unfilmed)
        YWCA Papers
Stanford University, Palo Alto, Calif.
    Stanford University Archives
        Jane L. Stanford Papers
        Leland Stanford Papers
        Stanford Family Albums
Tulane University, New Orleans, La.
    Sophie Newcomb College Archives
        Brandt Van Blarcom Dixon Papers
        Josephine Newcomb Papers
    Tulane University Archives

Brandt Van Blarcom Dixon Papers
McConnell Family Papers
Newcomb Family Folder
Tulane University Law School Library
Bound volumes, *New York Supreme Court, Appellate Division, first department, Brief on behalf of respondent Brandt V. B. Dixon, (NY) in the matter of the estate of Josephine Louise Newcomb, deceased Surrogate's Court, County of New York, Opinion of Robert E. Deyo, referee*
University of California, Berkeley
Bancroft Library
Phoebe and George Hearst Papers (microfilm)
Office of the President
Regents Papers
University of New Hampshire, Durham, N.H.
University of New Hampshire Archives and Special Collections
Juliet Barrett Rublee Papers
University of Wisconsin, Madison, Wisc.
Historical Society of Wisconsin Archives
McCormick–International Harvester Collection

ONLINE ARCHIVAL COLLECTIONS

Smith College
Smith College Founding Documents: www.clio.fivecolleges.edu/Smith/origins/beginnings
Sweet Briar College
Cochran Library, Sweet Briar history document: https://archive.org/details/sweetbriarcollege
University of Rochester
May, Arthur J., *A History of the University of Rochester*: www.lib.rochester.edu/index.cfm?PAGE=2437

Published Primary Sources

Addams, Jane. "A Modern Lear." *Survey* 29 (November 2, 1912): 131–37.
———. *Democracy and Social Ethics*. 1907. Reprint, Cambridge, Mass.: Belknap Press of Harvard University Press, 1964.
Belmont, Alva. "The Ballot Is a Scepter of Sovereignty in America." *Chicago Daily Tribune*, October 13, 1912.
———. "A Girl? What a Pity It Was Not a Boy!" *Chicago Daily Tribune*, June 9, 1912.
———. "Woman and the Suffrage." *Harper's Bazaar* 140 (March 1910): 170.
———. "Woman Suffrage as It Looks To-Day." *Forum* 143 (January 1910): 264–67.
———. "Woman's Right to Govern Herself." *North American Review* 190 (November 1909): 664–74.

———. "Woman's Suffrage Raises the Quality of Electorate." *Chicago Daily Tribune*, June 30, 1912.

Blatch, Harriot Stanton. *Challenging Years: The Memoirs of Harriot Stanton Blatch*. New York: G.P. Putnam's Sons, 1940.

Brush, Mary Isabel. "Society and Working Women March in Suffrage Parade." *Chicago Daily Tribune*, May 26, 1912.

Carnegie, Andrew. "The Best Fields for Philanthropy." *North American Review* 149 (December 1889): 682–98.

———. "Wealth." *North American Review* 148 (June 1889): 653–64.

Converse, Florence. *The Story of Wellesley*. Boston, Mass.: Little, Brown, 1915.

Crothers, George. *The Educational Ideals of Jane Lathrop Stanford, Co-founder of Leland Stanford Junior University*. Stanford, Calif.: Stanford University Press, 1933.

Daggett, Mabel Potter. "Suffrage Enters the Drawing-Room." *Delineator*, January 1910, 37–38, 70.

Dixon, Brandt V. B. *A Brief History of H. Sophie Newcomb Memorial College, 1887–1919: A Personal Reminiscence*. New Orleans, La.: Hauser, 1928.

Dreier, Mary E. *Margaret Dreier Robins: Her Life, Letters, and Work*. New York: Island Cooperative Press, 1950.

Elliott, Ellen Coit. *It Happened This Way: American Scene*. Palo Alto, Calif.: Stanford University Press, 1940.

Elliott, Orrin Leslie. *Stanford University: The First Twenty-Five Years*. 1937. Reprint, New York: Arno Press, 1977.

Fry, Amelia. "Conversations with Alice Paul: Woman Suffrage and the Equal Rights Amendment." Suffragists Oral History Project, University of California, Berkeley, 1975.

Gleason, Arthur. "Mrs. Russell Sage and Her Interests." *World's Work*, 13 (November 1906): 8182–86.

Gleason, Janis F. *The Life and Letters of Kate Gleason*. Rochester: RIT Press, 2010.

Hanna, Ione T. "Ethics of Social Life." In *The Congress of Women Held in the Woman's Building, World's Columbia Exposition, Chicago, U.S.A., 1893, with Portraits, Biographies, and Addresses*, edited by Mary Kavanaugh Eagle, 53–57. Denver, Colo.: C. Westley, 1894.

Harper, Ida Husted. *The Life and Work of Susan B. Anthony*. Vol. 3. Indianapolis, IN: Bowen-Merrill Company and Hollenbeck Press, 1908.

Harriman, Mrs. J. Borden (Florence). *From Pinafore to Politics*. New York: Henry Holt, 1923.

Havemeyer, Louisine. "The Suffrage Torch: Memories of a Militant." First paper. *Scribner's*, May 1922, 528–39.

———. "The Suffrage Torch: Memories of a Militant." Second paper. *Scribner's*, June 1922, 661–76.

Jacobi, Mary Putnam. "Report of the 'Volunteer Committee' in New York City." In *1894 Constitutional-Amendment Campaign Year; Report of the New York State Woman Suffrage Association*, 217–20. Rochester, N.Y.: Charles Mann, 1895.

Jordan, David Starr. *The Days of a Man: Being Memories of a Naturalist, Teacher and Minor Prophet of Democracy.* Vol. 1, *1851–1899.* Yonkers-on-Hudson, New York: World Book Company, 1922.

―――. *The Story of a Good Woman: Jane Lathrop Stanford.* Boston: Beacon Press, 1913.

Katz, Esther, ed. *Selected Papers of Margaret Sanger.* Vol. 1, *The Woman Rebel.* Urbana: University of Illinois Press, 2002.

―――. *Selected Papers of Margaret Sanger.* Vol. 2, *Birth Control Comes of Age.* Urbana: University of Illinois Press, 2007.

―――. *Selected Papers of Margaret Sanger.* Vol. 3, *The Politics of Planned Parenthood, 1939–1966.* Urbana: University of Illinois Press, 2010.

Lasker, Mary. Interview by John T. Mason, October 1962, Columbia University Libraries, Oral History Research Office, Notable New Yorkers, www.columbia.edu /cu/lweb/digital/collections/nny/laskerm/audio_transcript.html.

Leonard, John. *Woman's Who's Who of America, 1914–1915.* New York: Commonwealth, 1914.

Lowell, Josephine Shaw. "Relation of Women to Good Government." In *The Philanthropic Work of Josephine Shaw Lowell,* edited by William Rhinelander Stewart, 435–45. New York: MacMillan, 1911.

Malkiel, Theresa Serber. *Diary of a Shirtwaist Striker.* First published New York: Cooperative Press, 1910. Ithaca, N.Y.: ILR Press of Cornell University Press, 1990.

"Mrs. Clarence Mackay." *American Magazine,* September 1906, 609–10.

Nagel, Gunther. *Iron Will: The Life and Letters of Jane Stanford.* Palo Alto, Calif.: Stanford University Alumni Association, 1940.

Parson, Elsie Clews. "Feminism and the Family." *International Journal of Ethics* (October 1917): 52–58.

―――. "Feminism and Sex Ethics." *International Journal of Ethics* (July 1916): 462–65.

―――. "When Mating and Parenthood Are Theoretically Distinguished." *International Journal of Ethics* (January 1916): 207–16.

―――. "Wives and Birth Control." *New Republic,* March 18, 1916.

Pauline Agassiz Shaw: Tributes Paid Her Memory at the Memorial Service. Boston, Mass., 1917.

Peck, Mary Gray. "Some American Suffragists." *Life and Labor,* December 1911, 368–73.

Reyher, Rebecca. "Search and Struggle for Equality and Independence: An Interview Conducted by Amelia Fry and Fern Ingersoll." Suffragists Oral History Project. University of California, Berkeley, 1977.

Ryan, Agnes E. *The Torch Bearer: A Look Forward and Back at the "Woman's Journal," the Organ of the Woman's Movement.* Boston, Mass.: Woman's Journal and Suffrage News, 1916.

Sage, Olivia. "Opportunities and Responsibilities of Leisured Women." *North American Review* 181 (November 1905): 712–21.

Sanger, Margaret. *The Autobiography of Margaret Sanger.* 1938. Reprint, New York: Dover, 2004.

———. *My Fight for Birth Control*. New York: Farrar & Rinehart, 1931.

Schneiderman, Rose. *All for One*. New York: P.S. Eriksson, 1967.

Seelye, L. Clark. *Addresses at the Inauguration of Rev. L. Clark Seelye, as President of Smith College, and at the Dedication of Its Academic Building, July 14, 1875*. Springfield, Mass.: Clark W. Bryan, 1875.

———. *The Early History of Smith College, 1871–1900*. Boston: Houghton Mifflin.

Sewall, May Wright. "The Education of Woman in the Western States." In *Woman's Work in America*, edited by Annie Nathan Meyer, 77–79. New York: Henry Holt, 1891.

Shaw, Anna Howard. *Anna Howard Shaw: The Story of a Pioneer*. 1915. Reprint, Cleveland, Ohio: Pilgrim Press, 1994.

Stanton, Elizabeth Cady, Susan B. Anthony, Matilda Joslyn Gage, and Ida Husted Harper. *History of Woman Suffrage*. 6 vols. New York, 1881–1922.

Steinem, Gloria. *Moving beyond Words: Age, Rage, Sex, Power, Money, Muscles: Breaking Boundaries of Gender*. New York: Simon and Schuster, 1994.

———. "The Trouble with Rich Women." *Ms. Magazine*, June 1986, 41–43, 78–80.

Upton, Harriet Taylor. *Harriet Taylor Upton's Random Recollections*. Edited by Lara Dunn Eisenbraun. Warren, Ohio: Harriet Taylor Upton Association, 2004.

Von Breisen, Maria, ed. *The Letters of Elijah Fletcher*. Charlottesville: University Press of Virginia, 1965.

Whitehouse, Vira B. *My Year as a Government Agent*. New York: Harper & Brothers, 1920.

Whitley, Ann Marshall. *Indiana Fletcher Williams of Sweet Briar*. Sweet Briar, Va. Sweet Briar College, 1992.

Woman Suffrage Arguments and Results: A Collection of Eight Popular Booklets. NAWSA, [1911?].

Woolf, Virginia. *The Three Guineas*. London: Hogarth, 1938. Reprint, New York: Harvest Books, 1963.

Secondary Sources

Adams, Katherine H., and Michael L. Keene. *Alice Paul and the American Suffrage Campaign*. Urbana: University of Illinois Press, 2008.

Adickes, Andra. *To Be Young Was Very Heaven: Women in New York before the First World War*. New York: St. Martin's Press, 1997.

Allison, Leslie Minturn. *Mildred Minturn: A Biography*. Quebec: Shoreline, 1995.

Alter, Catherine. "Bureaucracy and Democracy in Organizations: Revisiting Feminist Organizations." In *Private Action and the Public Good*, edited by Walter W. Powell, 258–71. New Haven, Conn.: Yale University Press, 1998.

American National Biography. 24 vols. New York: Oxford University Press, 1999.

Arredondo, Isabel. "From Travelogues to Political Intervention in Juliet Rublee's *Flame of Mexico*." *Mexican Studies/Estudios Mexicanos* 1 (Winter 2010): 79–93.

Asbell, Barnard. *The Pill: A Biography of the Drug That Changed the World*. New York: Random House, 1995.

Bachand, Marise. "Gendered Mobility and the Geography of Respectability in Charleston and New Orleans, 1790–1865." *Journal of Southern History* 81, no. 1 (February 2015).

Baker, Jean H. *Margaret Sanger: A Life of Passion.* New York: Hill and Wang, 2011.

Baker, Paula. "The Domestication of Politics: Women and American Political Society, 1780–1920." *American Historical Review* 89, no. 3 (June 1984): 620–47.

Beckert, Sven. *The Monied Metropolis: New York City and the Consolidation of the American Bourgeoisie.* New York: Cambridge University Press, 2001.

Bederman, Gail. *Manliness and Civilization.* Chicago: University of Chicago Press, 1995.

Berner, Bertha. *Mrs. Leland Stanford: An Intimate Account.* Palo Alto, Calif.: Stanford University Press, 1935.

Bishop, Morris. *A History of Cornell University.* Ithaca, N.Y.: Cornell University Press, 1962.

Bittel, Carla. *Mary Putnam Jacobi and the Politics of Medicine in Nineteenth-Century America.* Chapel Hill: University of North Carolina Press, 2009.

Bix, Amy Sue. "Feminism Where Men Predominate: The History of Women's Science and Engineering Education at MIT." *Women's Studies Quarterly* 28 (2000): 24–45.

———. *Girls Coming to Tech! A History of American Engineering Education for Women.* Cambridge, Mass.: MIT Press, 2014.

———. "Supporting Females in a Male Field: Philanthropy for Women's Engineering Education." In *Women and Philanthropy in Education,* edited by Andrea Walton, 320–45. Bloomington: University of Indiana Press, 2005.

Blum, Larry, Marcia Homiak, Judy Housman, and Naomi Scheman. "Altruism and Women's Oppression." In *Women and Philosophy: Toward a Theory of Liberation,* edited by Carola C. Gould and Marx W. Wartofsky, 222–47. New York: G. P. Putnam's Son, 1976.

Bonfils, Winifred Black. *The Life and Personality of Phoebe Apperson Hearst.* San Francisco, Calif.: John Henry Nash, 1928.

Bonner, Thomas Neville. *To the Ends of the Earth: Women's Search for Education in Medicine.* Cambridge, Mass.: Harvard University Press, 1992.

Bowers, Jane Elkind Bowers. "Oceans of Love: An Introduction to and Excerpts from Juliet Barrett Rublee to Margaret Sanger." Master's thesis, University of Texas, Austin, 1994.

Bradley, Jacqueline Hack. "The Smith College Trilogy: The Spinster, the Minister and the Academic." Master's thesis, San Jose State University, 2001.

Breault, Judith Colucci. *The World of Emily Howland: Odyssey of a Humanitarian.* Millbrae, Calif.: Les Femmes, 1976.

Bremner, Robert. *American Philanthropy.* 2nd ed. Chicago, Ill.: University of Chicago Press, 1988.

Britt, Albert. *Ellen Browning Scripps: Journalist and Idealist.* Pomona, Calif.: Printed for Scripps College, Oxford University Press, 1960.

Buechler, Steven. *Women's Movements in the United States: Woman Suffrage, Equal Rights, and Beyond.* New Brunswick, N.J.: Rutgers University Press, 1990.

Butcher, Patricia Smith. *Education for Equality: Women's Rights Periodicals and Women's Higher Education, 1849–1920*. New York: Praeger, 1989.

Capek, M. E. "Women and Philanthropy: Old Stereotypes and New Challenges." Monograph series. St. Paul, Minn.: Women's Funding Network, 1998.

Caron, Simone. *Who Chooses? American Reproductive History Since 1830*. Gainesville: University Press of Florida, 2008.

Chaddock, Katherine E., ed. *College of Charleston Voices: Campus and Community through the Centuries*. Charleston, SC: History Press, 2006.

Chen, Constance M. *The Sex Side of Life: The Story of Mary Ware Dennett*. New York: Free Press, 1996.

————. "Women's Admissions." *Stanford Medicine* 17 (Fall 2000), http://stanmed .stanford.edu/2000fall/woman.html.

Chesler, Ellen. *Woman of Valor: Margaret Sanger and the Birth Control Movement in America*. New York: Simon and Schuster, 1992.

Chesney, Alan. *The Johns Hopkins Hospital and the Johns Hopkins University School of Medicine: A Chronicle*. Vol. 1, *Early Years, 1867–1893*. Baltimore, Md.: Johns Hopkins University Press, 1943.

Clift, Elayne, ed. *Women, Philanthropy, and Social Change: Visions for a Just Society*. Medford, Mass.: Tufts University Press; Hanover: University Press of New England, 2005.

Clift, Eleanor, and Tom Brazaitis. *Madam President: Women Blazing the Leadership Trail*. New York: Routledge, 2003.

Coates, Patricia Walsh. *Margaret Sanger and the Origin of the Birth Control Movement, 1910–1930: The Concept of Women's Sexual Autonomy*. Lewiston, N.Y.: Edwin Mellen, 2008.

Cobble, Dorothy Sue. *The Other Women's Movement: Workplace Justice and Social Rights in Modern America*. Princeton, N.J.: Princeton University Press, 2004.

Cofer, Rebecca H. *The Straight Story: An Informal History of Willard Straight Hall, 1925–1990*. Ithaca, N.Y.: Cornell University Press, 1990.

Collins, Theresa M. *Otto Kahn: Art, Money, and Modern Time*. Chapel Hill: University of North Carolina Press, 2002.

Conable, Charlotte Williams. *Women at Cornell: The Myth of Equal Education*. Ithaca, N.Y.: Cornell University Press, 1977.

Cott, Nancy. *The Grounding of Modern Feminism*. New Haven, Conn.: Yale University Press, 1987.

Courey, Renee Michelle. "Participants in the Development, Marketing and Safety Evaluation of the Oral Contraceptive, 1950–1965: Mythic Dimensions of a Scientific Solution." PhD diss., University of California, Berkeley, 1994.

Cox, Anne F. *The History of the Colony Club*. New York: privately printed for the Colony Club, 1984.

Craig, Douglas B. *Progressives at War: William G. McAdoo and Newton D. Baker, 1863–1941*. Baltimore, Md.: Johns Hopkins University Press, 2013.

Crocker, Ruth. "From Gift to Foundation: The Philanthropic Lives of
Mrs. Russell Sage." In *Charity, Philanthropy, and Civility*, edited by Lawrence J.
Friedman and Mark D. McGarvie, 199–215. New York: Cambridge University
Press, 2003.

———. *Mrs. Russell Sage: Women's Activism and Philanthropy in Gilded Age and
Progressive Era America*. Bloomington: Indiana University Press, 2006.

Curti, Merle, and Roderick Nash. *Philanthropy and the Shaping of American Higher
Education*. New Brunswick, N.J.: Rutgers University Press, 1965.

Cutler, Robert W. P. *The Mysterious Death of Jane Stanford*. Stanford, Calif.: Stanford
University Press, 2003.

Dalzell, Robert F., Jr. *The Good Rich and What They Cost Us*. New Haven, Conn.: Yale
University Press, 2013.

Daniels, Arlene Kaplan. *Invisible Careers: Women Civic Leaders from the Volunteer
World*. Chicago, Ill.: University of Chicago Press, 1988.

Datnow, Amanda, and Lea Hubbard, eds. *Gender in Policy and Practice: Perspectives on
Single-Sex and Coeducational Schooling*. New York: Routledge, 2002.

Davis, Gladys Wooley. *Miss Sophia's Legacy*. Oxford: Basil Blackwell, 1950.

Dawley, Alan. "The Abortive Rule of Big Money." In *Ruling America: A History of
Wealth and Power in a Democracy*, edited by Steve Fraser and Gary Gerstle, 149–80.
Cambridge, Mass.: Harvard University Press, 2005.

Day, Christine L. "Gender, Feminism, and Partisanship Among Women's PAC
Contributors." *Social Science Quarterly* 82 (December 2001): 687–700.

Deacon, Desley. "The Republic of the Spirit: Fieldwork in Elsie Clews Parsons's Turn
to Anthropology." *Frontiers* 12 (1992): 13–38.

Degler, Carl. *At Odds: Women and the Family in America from the Revolution to the
Present*. New York: Oxford University Press, 1981.

Deutsch, Sarah. "Learning to Talk More Like a Man: Boston Women's Class-Bridging
Organizations, 1870–1940." *American Historical Review* 97 (April 1992): 379–404.

Diedrich, Maria. *Cornelia James Cannon and the Future of the American Race*. Amherst:
University of Massachusetts Press, 2010.

Diehl Betsy Duncan. "Philanthropy as an Expression of Feminism: Aligning a
Traditionally Masculine Concept with a Decidedly Feminist Ideal." Master's thesis,
Hood College, 2010.

DuBois, Ellen C. *Feminism and Suffrage: The Emergence of an Independent Women's
Movement in America*. Ithaca, N.Y.: Cornell University Press, 1978.

———. *Harriot Stanton Blatch and the Winning of Woman Suffrage*. New Haven,
Conn.: Yale University Press, 1997.

———. "Working Women, Class Relations, and Suffrage Militance: Harriot Stanton
Blatch and the New York Woman Suffrage Movement, 1894–1909." *Journal of
American History* 74 (June 1987): 34–58.

Dudden, Faye E. *Fighting Chance: The Struggle over Woman Suffrage and Black Suffrage
in Reconstruction America*, New York: Oxford University Press, 2011.

Duffy, John. *The Tulane University Medical Center: One Hundred and Fifty Years of Medical Education*. Baton Rouge: Louisiana State University Press, 1984.

Dundjerski, Marina. "Paying Attention to Women." *Chronicle of Philanthropy*, February 23, 1995, 31–33.

Dye, Nancy Shrom. *As Equals and As Sisters: Feminism, the Labor Movement and the Women's Trade Union League of New York*. Columbia: University of Missouri Press, 1980.

———. "Creating a Feminist Alliance: Sisterhood and Class Conflict in the New York Women's Trade Union League, 1903–1914." *Feminist Studies* 2 (1975): 11–25.

Dyer, John P. *Tulane: The Biography of a University, 1834–1965*. New York: Harper & Row, 1966.

Dzuback, Mary Ann. "Gender and the Politics of Knowledge." *History of Education Quarterly* 43 (Summer 2003): 171–95.

Eisenmann, Linda. "Brokering Old and New Philanthropic Traditions: Women's Continuing Education in the Cold War Effort." In *Women and Philanthropy in Education*, edited by Andrea Walton, 148–66. Bloomington: University of Indiana Press, 2005.

Engelman, Peter C. *A History of the Birth Control Movement in America*. Santa Barbara, Calif.: Praeger, 2011.

Enstad, Nan. *Ladies of Labor, Girls of Adventure: Working Women, Popular Culture, and Labor Politics at the Turn of the Twentieth Century*. New York: Columbia University Press, 1999.

Faderman, Lillian. *To Believe in Women: What Lesbians Have Done for America—a History*. Boston, Mass.: Houghton Mifflin, 1999.

Farr, Courtney Ann, and Jeffrey Liles. "Male Teachers, Male Roles: The Progressive Era and Education in Oklahoma." *Great Plains Quarterly* (1991): 234–39, esp. table 2.

Faulkner, Carol. *Lucretia Mott's Heresy: Abolition and Women's Rights in Nineteenth Century America*. Philadelphia: University of Pennsylvania Press, 2011.

Fields, Armond. *Katharine Dexter McCormick: A Pioneer for Women's Rights*. Westport, Conn.: Praeger, 2003.

Finnegan, Margaret. *Selling Suffrage: Consumer Culture and Votes for Women*. New York: Columbia University Press, 1999.

Fischer, Sunny. "Introduction: Women's Values, Women's Vision, The Power of Giving Women." In *Women, Philanthropy, and Social Change: Visions for a Just Society*, edited by Elayne Clift, 1–9. Medford, Mass.: Tufts University Press; Hanover: University Press of New England, 2005.

Fisher, Joan M. "Celebrating the Heroines of Philanthropy." In *Women and Philanthropy: A National Agenda*, edited by Anne I. Thompson and Andrea R. Kaminski, 13–24. Madison: Center for Women and Philanthropy, University of Wisconsin, 1993.

Flexner, Eleanor. *A Century of Struggle: The Woman's Rights Movement in the United States*. Cambridge, Mass.: Belknap Press of Harvard University Press, 1959.

Flexner, Simon, and James Thomas. *William Henry Welch and the Heroic Age of Medicine.* New York: Viking Press, 1941.

"For the Better Protection of Their Rights": A History of the First Fifty Years of the Woman's Legal Education Society and the Woman's Law Class at New York University. New York: New York University, 1940.

Franzen, Trish. *Anna Howard Shaw: The Work of Woman Suffrage.* Urbana: University of Illinois Press, 2014.

Fraser, Steve, and Gary Gerstle. Introduction to *Ruling America: A History of Wealth and Power in a Democracy,* edited by Steve Fraser and Gary Gerstle, 1–26. Cambridge, Mass.: Harvard University Press, 2005.

Freedman, Estelle. *No Turning Back: The History of Feminism and the Future of Women.* New York: Ballantine Books, 2002.

Friedman, Lawrence J. "Philanthropy in America: Historicism and Its Discontents." In *Charity, Philanthropy, and Civility in American History,* edited by Lawrence J. Friedman and Mark D. McGarvie, 1–21. New York: Cambridge University Press, 2003.

Friedman, Lawrence J., and Mark McGarvie, eds. *Charity, Philanthropy, and Civility in American History.* New York: Cambridge University Press, 2003.

Fuller, Paul E. *Laura Clay and the Woman's Rights Movement.* Lexington: University of Kentucky Press, 1982.

Furlow, John. "Cornelia Bryce Pinchot: Feminism in the Post-Suffrage Era." *Pennsylvania History* 43 (1976): 329–46.

Gaffney, Patricia H. *The Emily Howland Papers at Cornell University: A Guide to the Microfilm Publication.* Ithaca, N.Y.: Cornell University Libraries, 1975.

Garrow, David J. *Liberty and Sexuality: The Right to Privacy and the Making of Roe v. Wade.* Berkeley: The University of California Press, 1998.

Gary, Tracy. "Lessons Learned: Strategies for Success in Education and Endowment." In *Women, Philanthropy, and Social Change: Visions for a Just Society,* edited by Elayne Clift, 117–25. Medford, Mass.: Tufts University Press; Hanover: University Press of New England, 2005.

Gaudiani, Claire. *Daughters of the Declaration: How Women Entrepreneurs Built the American Dream.* New York: Public Affairs Press, 2011.

Geidel, Peter. "Alva E. Belmont: A Forgotten Feminist." PhD diss., Columbia University, 1993.

Gettleman, Marvin. "Philanthropy as Social Control in Late-Nineteenth Century America." *Societas* 5 (Winter 1975): 49–59.

Giddings, Paula. *In Search of Sisterhood: Delta Sigma Theta and the Challenge of the Black Sorority Movement.* New York: William Morrow, 1988.

Ginzburg, Lori D. *Untidy Origins: A Story of Women's Rights in Antebellum New York.* Chapel Hill: University of North Carolina Press, 2005.

Glasscock, Jean. *Wellesley College, 1875–1975: A Century of Women.* Wellesley, Mass.: Wellesley College, 1975.

Glenn, Susan A. *Daughters of the Shtetl: Life and Labor in the Immigrant Generation.* Ithaca, N.Y.: Cornell University Press, 1990.

Glymph, Thavolia. *Out of the House of Bondage: The Transformation of the Plantation Household.* New York: Cambridge University Press, 2008.

Goodspeed, Thomas Wakefield. *A History of the University of Chicago: The First Quarter-Century.* Chicago, Ill.: University of Chicago Press, 1916.

Gordon, Beverly. *Bazaars and Fair Ladies: The History of the American Fundraising Fair.* Knoxville: University of Tennessee Press, 1998.

Gordon, Linda. *Woman's Body, Woman's Right: Birth Control in America.* New York: Penguin, 1976. Revised as *The Moral Property of Women: The History of Birth Control Politics in America.* Urbana: University of Illinois Press, 2002.

Gordon, Lynn D. *Gender and Higher Education in the Progressive Era.* New Haven, Conn.: Yale University Press, 1990.

———. "Sophie Newcomb and Agnes Scott Colleges, 1887–1920: From Dutiful Daughters to New Women." In *Newcomb College: 1886–2006, Higher Education for Women in New Orleans,* edited by Susan Tucker and Beth Willinger, 56–79. Baton Rouge: Louisiana State University Press, 2012.

Graham, Abbie. *Grace H. Dodge: Merchant of Dreams.* New York: Woman's Press, 1926.

Graham, Sara Hunter. *Woman Suffrage and the New Democracy.* New Haven, Conn.: Yale University Press, 1996.

Gray, Madeline. *Margaret Sanger: A Biography of the Champion of Birth Control.* New York: R. E. Marek, 1979.

Greene, Elizabeth. "Study Finds Differences in Giving Patterns between Wealthy Men and Women." *Chronicle of Philanthropy* 13 (May 2001): 12–14.

Gross, Robert A. "Giving in America: From Charity to Philanthropy." In *Charity, Philanthropy, and Civility in American History,* edited by Lawrence J. Friedman and Mark D. McGarvie, 29–48. New York: Cambridge University Press, 2003.

Halberstam, David. *The Fifties.* New York: Ballantine Books, 1994.

Hammock, David C. *Power and Society: Greater New York at the Turn of the Century.* New York: Russell Sage Foundation, 1982.

Hancock, LynNell, and Claudia Kalb. "Harvard Held Up. No Female Profs, No Checks." *Newsweek,* December 11, 1995.

Hanscom, Elizabeth Deering, and Helen French Greene. *Sophia Smith and the Beginnings of Smith College.* Northampton: Smith College, 1925.

Hartmann, Susan. "Women's Employment and the Domestic Ideal in the Early Cold War Years." In *Not June Cleaver: Women and Gender in Postwar America, 1945–1960,* edited by Joanne Meyerowitz, 84–100. Philadelphia, Pa.: Temple University Press, 1994.

Hearst, Kathryn P. "Phoebe Apperson Hearst: The Making of an Upper-Class Woman, 1842–1919." PhD diss., Columbia University, 2005.

Hewitt, Nancy. "Feminist Frequencies: Regenerating the Wave Metaphor." *Feminist Studies* 3 (2012): 658–80.

———. *Women's Activism and Social Change: Rochester, New York, 1822–1872*. Ithaca, N.Y.: Cornell University Press, 1984.

Hoagland, Hudson. *The Road to Yesterday*. Worcester, Mass.: privately printed, 1974.

Hoffert, Sylvia. *Alva Vanderbilt Belmont: Unlikely Champion of Women's Rights*. Bloomington: Indiana University Press, 2011.

Hofstadter, Richard, and Metzger, W. P. *The Development of Academic Freedom in the United States*. New York: Columbia University Press, 1955.

Holz, Rose. "Nurse Gordon on Trial: Those Early Days of the Birth Control Clinic Movement Reconsidered." *Journal of Social History* 39 (Fall 2005): 112–40.

Homberger, Eric. *Mrs. Astor's New York: Money and Social Power in a Gilded Age*. New Haven, Conn.: Yale University Press, 2002.

Horowitz, Helen Lefkowitz. *Alma Mater: Design and Experience in the Women's Colleges from Their Nineteenth-Century Beginnings to the 1930s*. New York: Alfred A. Knopf, 1984.

———. *Campus Life: Undergraduate Cultures from the End of the Eighteenth Century to the Present*. New York: Alfred A. Knopf, 1987.

———. *The Power and Passion of M. Carey Thomas*. New York: Alfred A. Knopf, 1994.

Hutchison, James. "Handmaidens of History." *Charleston*, January–February 2005, 98–107.

Huyssen, David. *Progressive Inequality: Rich and Poor in New York, 1890–1920*. Cambridge: Harvard University Press, 2014.

Jacoby, Robin Miller. *The British and American Women's Trade Union Leagues, 1890–1925*. Brooklyn, N.Y.: Carlson, 1994.

Jaher, Frederic Cople. "Style and Status: High Society in Late-Nineteenth-Century New York." In *The Rich, the Well Born, and the Powerful: Elites and Upper Class in History*, edited by Frederic Cople Jaher, 258–84. Urbana: University of Illinois Press, 1973.

Johnson, Joan Marie. "Black Women and Philanthropy." In *Black Women in America: An Historical Encyclopedia*, 2nd ed., edited by Darlene Clark Hine, 2:474–83. New York: Oxford University Press, 2004.

———. *Southern Ladies, New Women: Race, Region and Clubwomen in South Carolina, 1890–1930*. Gainesville: University Press of Florida, 2004.

———. *Southern Women at the Seven Sister Colleges: Feminist Values and Social Activism, 1875–1925*. Athens: University of Georgia Press, 2008.

Johnson, R. Christian. "Feminism, Philanthropy and Science in the Development of the Oral Contraceptive Pill." *Pharmacy in History* 19 (1977): 63–78.

Jones-Rogers, Stephanie. "Mistresses in the Making: White Girls, Mastery and the Practice of Slave Ownership in the Nineteenth-Century South." In *Women's America: Refocusing the Past*, 8th ed., edited by Linda K. Kerber, Jane Sherron De Hart, Cornelia Hughes Dayton, and Judy Tzu-Chun Wu. New York: Oxford University Press, 2015.

Katz, Esther. "Grace Hoadley Dodge: Women and the Emerging Metropolis, 1856–1914." PhD diss., New York University, 1980.

Katzenstein, Caroline. *Lifting the Curtain: The State and National Woman Suffrage Campaigns in Pennsylvania as I Saw Them.* Philadelphia: Dorrance, 1955.

Keeler, Rebecca T. "Alva Belmont: Exacting Benefactor for Women's Rights." Master's thesis, University of South Alabama, 1987.

Kendall, Diana. *The Power of Good Deeds: Privileged Women and the Social Reproduction of the Upper Class.* Lanham, Md.: Roman and Littlefield, 2002.

Kennedy, David. *Birth Control in America: The Career of Margaret Sanger.* New Haven, Conn.: Yale University Press, 1970.

Kessler-Harris, Alice. *Out to Work: The History of Wage-Earning Women in the United States.* New York: Oxford University Press, 1983.

Kirkby, Diane. "Class, Gender and the Perils of Philanthropy: The Story of *Life and Labor* and *Labor Reform* in the Women's Trade Union League." *Journal of Women's History* 4 (Fall 1992): 36–51.

Kluger, Richard. *The Paper: The Life and Death of the New York Herald Tribune.* New York: Alfred A. Knopf, 1986.

Knight, Lucy. "This Time We're Here to Stay." *Wesleyan,* Summer 1990, 2–6.

Kraditor, Aileen. *The Ideas of the Woman Suffrage Movement, 1890–1920.* New York: W.W. Norton, 1981.

Krone, Henrietta Louise. "Dauntless Women: The Story of the Woman Suffrage Movement in Pennsylvania." PhD diss., University of Pennsylvania, 1946.

Lagemann, Ellen Condliffe. *A Generation of Women: Education in the Lives of Progressive Reformers.* Cambridge, Mass.: Harvard University Press, 1979.

——. *Philanthropic Foundations: New Scholarship, New Possibilities.* Bloomington: Indiana University Press, 1999.

Lash, Joseph. *Eleanor and Franklin: The Story of Their Relationship, Based on Eleanor Roosevelt's Private Papers.* New York: W. W. Norton, 1971.

Lasser, Carol, ed. *Educating Men and Women Together: Coeducation in a Changing World.* Urbana: University of Illinois Press in conjunction with Oberlin College, 1987.

Layne, Linda L. Introduction to *Feminist Technology,* edited by Linda L. Layne, Sharra L. Vostral, and Kate Boyer, 1–34. Urbana: University of Illinois, 2010.

Leaming, Barbara. *Katharine Hepburn.* New York: Crown, 1995.

Leidner, Robin. "Stretching the Boundaries of Liberalism: Democratic Innovation in a Feminist Organization." *Signs* 16 (1991): 263–89.

Lerner, Gerda. *The Creation of Female Consciousness.* New York: Oxford University Press, 1994.

Lunardini, Christine A. *From Equal Suffrage to Equal Rights: Alice Paul and the National Woman's Party, 1910–1928.* New York: New York University Press, 1988.

Manekin, Sarah. "Gender, Markets, and the Expansion of Women's Education at the University of Pennsylvania, 1913–1940." *History of Education Quarterly* 50 (August 2010): 298–323.

Mansbridge, Jane. "On the Contested Nature of the Public Good." In *Private Action and the Public Good*, edited by Walter W. Powell and Elisabeth S. Clemens, 3–19. New Haven, Conn.: Yale University Press, 1998.

Mansfield, Stephanie. *The Richest Girl in the World: The Extravagant and Fast Times of Doris Duke*. New York: G. P. Putnam's Sons, 1992.

Marilley, Suzanne. *Woman Suffrage and the Origins of Liberal Feminism in the United States, 1820–1920*. Cambridge, Mass.: Harvard University Press, 1997.

Marks, Lara V. *Sexual Chemistry: A History of the Contraceptive Pill*. New Haven, Conn.: Yale University Press, 2001.

Marsh, Margaret, and Wanda Ronner. *The Fertility Doctor: John Rock and the Reproductive Revolution*. Baltimore, Md.: Johns Hopkins University Press, 2008.

Martin, Patricia Yancey. "Rethinking Feminist Organizations." *Gender and Society* 4 (1990): 182–206.

McCandless, Amy Thompson. *The Past in the Present: Women's Higher Education in the Twentieth-Century American South*. Tuscaloosa: University of Alabama Press, 1999.

———. "The Pollitzer Sisters." In *South Carolina Encyclopedia*, edited by Walter Edgar. Columbia: University of South Carolina Press, 2006.

McCann, Carole. *Birth Control Politics in the United States, 1916–1945*. Ithaca, N.Y.: Cornell University Press, 1994.

McCarthy, Kathleen D. *Lady Bountiful Revisited: Women, Philanthropy, and Power*. New Brunswick, N.J.: Rutgers University Press, 1990.

———. "The Ms. Foundation: A Case Study in Feminist Fundraising." New York: Working Paper, Center for the Study of Philanthropy, City University of New York, 1995.

———. "Parallel Power Structures: Women and the Voluntary Sphere." In *Lady Bountiful Revisited: Women, Philanthropy, and Power*, edited by Kathleen D. McCarthy, 1–31. New Brunswick, N.J.: Rutgers University Press, 1990.

———, ed., *Women, Philanthropy, and Civil Society*. Bloomington: Indiana University Press, 2001.

———. "Women and Political Culture." In *Charity, Philanthropy, and Civility in American History*, edited by Lawrence J. Friedman and Mark D. McGarvie, 179–197. New York: Cambridge University Press, 2003.

———. *Women's Culture: American Philanthropy and Art, 1830–1930*. Chicago, Ill.: University of Chicago Press, 1991.

McCaskill, Kyle Simpson. "Hull House's Hidden Power: The Donors Behind and Beside Jane Addams," 1–30, self-published, www.scribd.com/doc/38906761/hull -house-s-hidden-power-the-donors-behind-and-beside-jane-addams.

McClain, Molly. "The Bishop's School, 1909–2009." *Journal of San Diego History* 54, no. 4 (2008): 235–67.

———. "The Bishop's School: History." https://www.bishops.com/page/about /history/founders.

McKelvey, Blake. "Susan B. Anthony." *Rochester History* 7 (April 1945): 1–24.

McLaughlin, Loretta. *The Pill, John Rock and the Church: The Biography of a Revolution*. Boston: Little, Brown, 1982.

Mead, Rebecca. *How the Vote Was Won: Woman Suffrage in the Western States, 1868–1914*. New York: New York University Press, 2004.

Merkin, Yael. "We Were Much Afraid of Our Voices for a Long Time: Women and Power in Gilded Age New York." PhD diss., Harvard University, in progress.

Meyer, Jimmy Elaine Wilkinson. *Any Friend of the Movement: Networking for Birth Control, 1920–1940*. Columbus: Ohio State University Press, 2004.

Meyerowitz, Joanne, ed. *Not June Cleaver: Women and Gender in Postwar America, 1945–1960*. Philadelphia: Temple University Press, 1994.

Miller, Russell. *Light on the Hill: A History of Tufts College, 1852–1952*. Boston: Beacon Press, 1986.

"Miss Carrie T. Pollitzer, Veteran Teacher, Dies." *Charleston Evening Post*, October 23, 1974.

Mohr, Clarence L. "Coming Together (and Falling Apart): Tulane University and H. Sophie Newcomb Memorial College in the Postwar Decades." *Louisiana History: The Journal of the Louisiana Historical Association* 49 (Winter 2008): 53–92.

Mollner, Carol, and Marie C. Wilson. "History as Prologue: The Women's Funding Movement." In *Women, Philanthropy, and Social Change: Visions for a Just Society*, edited by Elayne Clift, 13–28. Medford, Mass.: Tufts University Press; Hanover: University Press of New England, 2005.

Montgomery, Maureen. *Displaying Women: Spectacles of Leisure in Edith Wharton's New York*. New York: Routledge, 1998.

Moore, Jo Gruidly, and Marianne Philbin. "Women as Donors: Old Stereotypes, New Visions." In *Women, Philanthropy, and Social Change: Visions for a Just Society*, edited by Elayne Clift, 61–73. Medford, Mass.: Tufts University Press; Hanover: University Press of New England, 2005.

Morantz-Sanchez, Regina. *Sympathy and Science: Women Physicians in American Medicine*. New York: Oxford University Press, 1985.

"Mrs. Frank Leslie: New York's Last Bohemian." *New York History*, January 1948.

Murolo, Priscilla. *The Common Ground of Womanhood: Class, Gender, and Working Girls' Clubs, 1884–1928*. Urbana: University of Illinois Press, 1997.

Nagel, Gunther. *Iron Will: The Life and Letters of Jane Stanford*. Palo Alto, Calif.: Stanford University Alumni Association, 1940.

Newman, Louise. "Reflections on Aileen Kraditor's Legacy: Fifty Years of Woman Suffrage Historiography, 1965–2014." *Journal of the Gilded Age and Progressive Era* 14 (2015): 290–316.

Nichols, Carole. *Votes and More for Women: Suffrage and After in Connecticut*. New York, Haworth Press, 1983.

Nickliss, Alexandra M. "Phoebe Apperson Hearst: The Most Powerful Woman in California." PhD diss., University of California, Davis, 1994.

————."Phoebe Apperson Hearst's 'Gospel of Wealth,' 1883–1901." *Pacific Historical Review* 71 (November 2002): 575–605.

Nidiffer, Jana. *Pioneering Deans of Women: More Than Wise and Pious Matrons.* New York: Teachers College, Columbia University, 2000.

Nilan, Roxanne. "Jane Lathrop Stanford and the Domestication of Stanford University, 1893–1905," *San Jose Studies* 5 (1979): 7–30.

————. "The Tenacious and Courageous Jane L. Stanford," *Sandstone and Tile* 9, no.2 (Winter 1985): 3–13.

Noll, Richard. "Styles of Psychiatric Practice, 1906–1925: Clinical Evaluations of the Same Patient by James Jackson Putnam, Adolph Meyer, August Hoch, Emil Kraepelin and Smith Ely Jelliffe," *History of Psychiatry* 10 (1999): 145–89.

Notable American Women: A Biographical Dictionary. 5 vols. Cambridge, Mass.: Belknap Press of Harvard University Press, 1971–2005.

Odendahl, Teresa. *Charity Begins at Home: Generosity and Self-Interest among the Philanthropic Elites.* New York: Basic Books, 1990.

Orleck, Annelise. *Common Sense and a Little Fire: Women and Working-Class Politics in the United States, 1900–1965.* Chapel Hill: University of North Carolina Press, 1995.

Ostrander, Susan. "Moderating Contradictions of Feminist Philanthropy: Women's Community Organizations and the Boston Women's Fund, 1995–2000." *Gender and Society*, February 18, 2004, 29–46.

————. "When Grantees Become Grantors: Accountability, Democracy, and Social Movement Philanthropy." In *Philanthropic Foundations: New Scholarship, New Possibilities*, edited by Ellen Lagemann, 257–70. Bloomington: Indiana University Press, 1999.

————. *Women of the Upper Class.* Philadelphia: Temple University Press, 1984.

Ostrower, Francie. *Why the Wealthy Give: The Culture of Elite Philanthropy.* Princeton, N.J.: Princeton University Press, 1995.

Pak, Susie J. *Gentlemen Bankers: The World of J. P. Morgan.* Cambridge, Mass.: Harvard University Press, 2013.

Pal, Carol. *Republic of Women: Rethinking the Republic of Letters in the Seventeenth Century.* New York: Cambridge University Press, 2012.

Payne, Elizabeth. *Reform, Labor, and Feminism: Margaret Dreier Robins and the Women's Trade Union League.* Urbana: University of Illinois Press, 1988.

Pimlott, Jamie Pamela. *Women and the Democratic Party: The Evolution of EMILY's List.* Amherst, N.Y.: Cambria Press, 2010.

Pinchot, Nancy Pittman. "Amos Pinchot: Rebel Prince," *Pennsylvania History* 66 (Spring 1999): 166–98.

Powell, Walter W., and Elisabeth S. Clemens, eds. *Private Action and the Public Good.* New Haven, Conn.: Yale University Press, 1998.

Quesnell, Quentin. *The Strange Disappearance of Sophia Smith.* Northampton, Mass.: Smith College Library, 1999.

Radke-Moss, Andrea. *Bright Epoch: Women and Coeducation in the American West.* Lincoln: University of Nebraska Press, 2008.

Rauchway, Eric. "A Gentlemen's Club in a Woman's Sphere: How Dorothy Whitney Straight Created the *New Republic*," *Journal of Women's History* 11 (1999): 60–85.

———. *The Refuge of Affections: Family and American Reform Politics, 1900–1920.* New York: Columbia University Press, 2001.

Reed, James. *From Private Vice to Public Virtue: The Birth Control Movement and American Society Since 1830.* New York: Basic Books, 1978.

Remus, Emily. *Consumers' Metropolis: How Monied Women Purchased Pleasure and Power in the New Downtown.* Cambridge, Mass.: Harvard University Press, forthcoming.

Robertson, Nancy Marie. *Christian Sisterhood, Race Relations, and the YWCA, 1906–46.* Urbana: University of Illinois Press, 2007.

Rockwell, Mary Rech. "Elite Women and Class Formation." In *The American Bourgeoisie: Distinction and Identity in the Nineteenth Century*, edited by Sven Beckert and Julia B. Rosenbaum, 153–66. New York: Palgrave Macmillan.

Romney, Susanah Shaw. *New Netherland Connections: Intimate Networks and Atlantic Ties in Seventeenth-Century America.* Williamsburg, Va.: Omohundro Institute of Early American History and Culture, University of North Carolina Press, 2014.

Rose, Marsha Shapiro. "The Other Hand: A Critical Look at Feminist Funding." In *Women, Philanthropy, and Social Change: Visions for a Just Society*, edited by Elayne Clift, 126–36. Medford, Mass.: Tufts University Press; Hanover: University Press of New England, 2005.

———. "Philanthropy in a Different Voice: The Women's Funds." *Nonprofit and Voluntary Sector Quarterly* 23 (1994): 227–42.

Rosenberg, Rosalind. *Changing the Subject: How the Women of Columbia Shaped the Way We Think about Sex and Politics.* New York: Columbia University Press, 2005.

Rosenberger, Jesse. *Rochester: The Making of a University.* Rochester, N.Y.: University of Rochester, 1927.

Rossiter, Margaret W. *Women Scientists in America: Struggles and Strategies to 1940.* Baltimore, Md.: Johns Hopkins University Press, 1982.

Salzman, Neil V. *Reform and Revolution: The Life and Times of Raymond Robins.* Kent, Ohio: Kent State University Press, 1991.

Sander, Kathleen. *The Business of Charity: The Woman's Exchange Movement, 1832–1900.* Urbana: University of Illinois Press, 1998.

———. *Mary Elizabeth Garrett: Society and Philanthropy in the Gilded Age.* Baltimore, Md.: Johns Hopkins University Press, 2008.

Schiebinger, Londa. *Has Feminism Changed Science?* Cambridge, Mass.: Harvard University Press, 1999.

Schlesinger, Marion Cannon. *Snatched from Oblivion: A Cambridge Memoir.* Boston: Little, Brown, 1979.

Schwager, Sally. "Taking Up the Challenge: The Origins of Radcliffe." In *Yards and Gates: Gender in Harvard and Radcliffe History*, edited by Laurel Thatcher Ulrich, 87–105. New York: Palgrave Macmillan, 2004.

Schwarz, Judith. *Radical Feminists of Heterodoxy: Greenwich Village, 1912–1940*. Norwich, Vt.: New Victoria, 1986.

Scott, Anne Firor. *Natural Allies: Women's Associations in American History*. Urbana: University of Illinois Press, 1991.

———. *The Southern Lady: From Pedestal to Politics, 1830–1930*. 1970. Reprint, Charlottesville: University of Virginia Press, 1995.

Sealander, Judith. "Curing Evils at Their Source: The Arrival of Scientific Giving." In *Charity, Philanthropy, and Civility in American History*, edited by Laurence J. Friedman and Mark McGarvie, 217–39. New York: Cambridge University Press, 2003.

———. *Private Wealth and Public Life: Foundation Philanthropy and the Reshaping of American Social Policy from the Progressive Era to the New Deal*. Baltimore, Md.: Johns Hopkins University Press, 1997.

Shapiro, Ann. "A Radcliffe Girl at Harvard: Or Why Members of the Class of 1958 Staged a Revolution in 1993." In *Yards and Gates: Gender in Harvard and Radcliffe History*, edited by Laurel Thatcher Ulrich, 87–105. New York: Palgrave Macmillan, 2004.

Shaw, Wilfred B., ed. "The Department of Obstetrics and Gynecology." In *The University of Michigan: An Encyclopedic Survey*. 2:866–69. Ann Arbor: University of Michigan Press, 1951.

Shaw-Hardy, Sondra, Martha A. Taylor, Buffy Beaudoin-Schwartz, Carmen J. Stevens, Debra Mesch, and Andrea Pactor. *Women and Philanthropy: Boldly Shaping a Better World*. San Francisco, Calif.: Jossey-Bass, 2010.

Simari, Rosalie M. "Philanthropy and Higher Education: Women as Donors." PhD diss., Hofstra University 1995.

Simha, O. Robert. *MIT Campus Planning, 1960–2000*. Boston, Mass.: MIT Press, 2000.

Sklar, Kathryn Kish. "Who Funded Hull House?" In *Lady Bountiful Revisited: Women, Philanthropy, and Power*, edited by Kathleen D. McCarthy, 94–115. New Brunswick, N.J.: Rutgers University Press, 1990.

Sneider, Alison. *Suffragists in an Imperial Age: U.S. Expansion and the Woman Question, 1870–1929*. New York: Oxford University Press, 2008.

Solinger, Rickie. *Pregnancy and Power: A Short History of Reproductive Politics in America*. New York: New York University Press, 2005.

Solomon, Barbara. *In the Company of Educated Women: A History of Women and Higher Education*. New Haven, Conn.: Yale University Press, 1985.

Speroff, Leon. *A Good Man, Gregory Goodwin Pincus: The Man, His Story, the Birth Control Pill*. Portland, Ore.: Arnica, 2009.

Stansell, Christine. *American Moderns: Bohemian New York and the Creation of a New Century*. New York: Henry Holt, 2001.

———. *The Feminist Promise: 1792 to the Present*. New York: Modern Library, 2010.

Stern, Madeline. *Purple Passage: The Life of Mrs. Frank Leslie*. Norman: University of Oklahoma Press, 1953.

Stinson, Byron. "The Frank Leslies." *American History Illustrated* 5 (1970): 12–21.

Stohlman, Martha. *The Story of Sweet Briar College*. Sweet Briar, Va.: Sweet Briar College Alumnae Association, 1956.

Stone, Karen D., Susan F. Rice, and Judith C. Angel. "Women, Money, and Political Clout." In *Women as Donors, Women as Philanthropists*, edited by Abbie J. von Schlegell and Joan M. Fisher. San Francisco, Calif.: Jossey-Bass, 1993.

Storrs, Landon Y. *Civilizing Capitalism: The National Consumers League, Women's Activism, and Labor Standards in the New Deal Era*. Chapel Hill: University of North Carolina Press, 2000.

Strom, Sharon Hartman. *Political Woman: Florence Luscomb and the Legacy of Radical Reform*. Philadelphia, Penn.: Temple University Press, 2001.

Stuart, Amanda. *Consuelo and Alva Vanderbilt: The Story of a Daughter and a Mother in the Gilded Age*. New York: Harper Collins, 2005.

Tax, Meredith. *The Rising of Women: Feminist Solidarity and Class Conflict, 1880–1917*. Urbana: University of Illinois Press, 1980.

Terborg-Penn, Rosalyn. *African American Women in the Struggle for the Vote, 1850–1920*. Bloomington: Indiana University Press, 1998.

Tetrault, Lisa. "The Incorporation of American Feminism: Suffragists and the Postbellum Lyceum." *Journal of American History* 96 (March 2010): 1027–56.

———. "We Shall Be Remembered: Susan B. Anthony and the Politics of Writing History." In *Susan B. Anthony and the Struggle for Equal Rights*, edited by Christine L. Ridansky and Mary M. Huth, 15–56. Rochester, N.Y.: University of Rochester Press, 2012.

Thompson, Anne I., and Andrea R. Kaminski, eds. *Women and Philanthropy: A National Agenda*. Madison: University of Wisconsin, Center for Women and Philanthropy, 1993.

"Though Different, Sisters Had Same Goals." *News and Courier*, October 7, 1984.

Tone, Andrea. *Devices and Desires: A History of Contraceptives in America*. New York: Hill and Wang, 2001.

Tucker, Susan, and Beth Willinger. "Part 1: Beginnings." In *Newcomb College: 1886–2006, Higher Education for Women in New Orleans*, edited by Tucker and Willinger, 1–24. Baton Rouge: Louisiana State University Press, 2012.

———. "Part 3: Lives." In *Newcomb College: 1886–2006, Higher Education for Women in New Orleans*, edited by Tucker and Willinger, 263–86. Baton Rouge: Louisiana State University Press, 2012.

Vaida, Bara, and Jennifer Skalka. "Can Emily's List Get Its Mojo Back?" *National Journal*, June 28, 2008.

Vapnek, Lara. *The Breadwinners: Working Women and Economic Independence*. Urbana: University of Illinois Press, 2009.

von Schlegell, Abbie J., and Joan M. Fisher. *Women as Donors, Women as Philanthropists*. Vol. 2 of *New Directions for Philanthropic Fundraising*. San Francisco: Jossey-Bass, 1994.

Wall, Helena M. "Feminism and the New England Hospital, 1949–1961." *American Quarterly* 32 (Autumn 1980): 435–52.

Wallach, Janet. *The Richest Woman in America: Hetty Green in the Gilded Age*. New York: Nan A. Talese / Doubleday, 2012.

Walsh, Mary Roth. *Doctors Wanted, No Women Need Apply: Sexual Barriers in the Medical Profession, 1835–1975*. New Haven, Conn.: Yale University Press 1977.

Walton, Andrea. "Rethinking Boundaries: The History of Women, Philanthropy, and Higher Education." *History of Higher Education Annual* 20 (2000): 29–57.

————, ed. *Women and Philanthropy in Education*. Bloomington: University of Indiana Press, 2005.

Watkins, Elizabeth Siegel. *On the Pill: A Social History of Oral Contraceptives, 1950–1970*. Baltimore, Md.: Johns Hopkins University Press, 1998.

Waugh, Joan. *Unsentimental Reformer: Josephine Shaw Lowell*, Cambridge, Mass.: Harvard University Press, 1998.

Wedell, Marsha. "Founding Newcomb College." In *Newcomb College: 1886–2006, Higher Education for Women in New Orleans*, edited by Susan Tucker and Beth Willinger. Baton Rouge: Louisiana State University Press, 2012.

Wellman, Judith. "The Seneca Falls Women's Rights Convention: A Study of Social Networks," *Journal of Women's History* 3 (Spring 1991): 9–37.

Whitley, Ann Marshall. *Indiana Fletcher Williams of Sweet Briar*. Sweet Briar, Va.: Sweet Briar College, 1992.

Wiersema, Courtney. "All Consuming Nature: Provisioning in Industrial Chicago, 1833–1893." PhD diss., University of Notre Dame, 2015.

Wilson, Richard Guy. *Harbor Hill: Portrait of a House*. New York: W.W. Norton, 2008.

Wittig, Susan. "Reflections of Sorrow and Hope." *Newcomb News*, January 1981, 2–3, 11–13.

Wolper, Greg. "Woodrow Wilson's New Diplomacy: Vira Whitehouse in Switzerland, 1918." *Prologue* 24 (1992): 226–39.

Woody, Thomas. *A History of Women's Education in the United States*. Vol. 2. New York: Science Press, 1929.

Yohn, Susan M. "Crippled Capitalists: The Inscription of Economic Dependence and the Challenge of Female Entrepreneurship in Nineteenth Century America." *Feminist Economics* 12 (January/April 2006): 85–109.

————. "Let Christian Women Set the Example in Their Own Gifts: The 'Business' of Protestant Women's Organizations." In *Women and Twentieth-Century Protestantism*, edited by Virginia Brereton and Margaret Bendroth, 213–35. Urbana: University of Illinois, 2002.

————. "You Can't Share Babies with Bonds: How Americans Think about Women Making Money." *Iris* 40 (April 2000): 1–20.

Young, Michael. *The Elmhirsts of Dartington: The Creation of a Utopian Community*. London: Routledge & Kegan Paul, 1982.

Zaeske, Susan. *Signatures of Citizenship: Petitioning, Antislavery, and Women's Political Identity*. Chapel Hill: University of North Carolina Press, 2003.

Zahniser, J. D., and Amelia Fry. *Alice Paul: Claiming Power*. New York: Oxford
   University Press, 2014.
Zelizer, Viviana A. "The Social Meaning of Money: 'Special Monies.'" *American
   Journal of Sociology* 95 (September 1989): 342–77.
Zimmerman, Jean. *Love, Fiercely: A Gilded Age Romance*. Boston: Houghton Mifflin
   Harcourt, 2012.
Zumwalt, Rosemary Levy. *Wealth and Rebellion: Elsie Clews Parsons, Anthropologist
   and Folklorist*. Chicago: University of Illinois Press, 1992.
Zunz, Olivier. *Philanthropy in America: A History*. Princeton, N.J.: Princeton
   University Press, 2011.

Index